SECURED LENDING IN EASTERN EUROPE

Comparative Law of Secured Transactions and the EBRD Model Law

SECURED LENDING IN EASTERN EUROPE

Comparative Law of Secured Transactions and the EBRD Model Law

JAN-HENDRIK RÖVER

PhD (Munich), PhD (King's College London),
LLM (LSE), FRSA, Senior Lecturer at the University of Augsburg,
Rechtsanwalt (Munich) and Barrister at Law (Middle Temple)

OXFORD
UNIVERSITY PRESS

OXFORD
UNIVERSITY PRESS

Great Clarendon Street, Oxford OX2 6DP

Oxford University Press is a department of the University of Oxford.
It furthers the University's objective of excellence in research, scholarship,
and education by publishing worldwide in

Oxford New York

Auckland Cape Town Dar es Salaam Hong Kong Karachi
Kuala Lumpur Madrid Melbourne Mexico City Nairobi
New Delhi Shanghai Taipei Toronto

With offices in

Argentina Austria Brazil Chile Czech Republic France Greece
Guatemala Hungary Italy Japan Poland Portugal Singapore
South Korea Switzerland Thailand Turkey Ukraine Vietnam

Oxford is a registered trade mark of Oxford University Press
in the UK and in certain other countries

Published in the United States
by Oxford University Press Inc., New York

British Library Cataloguing in Publication Data

Data available

Library of Congress Cataloging in Publication Data

Röver, Jan-Hendrik.
    Secured lending in Eastern Europe : comparative law of secured transactions and
the EBRD model law / by Jan-Hendrik Röver.
      p. cm.
    ISBN 978–0–19–826013–4
  1. Security (Law)—Europe. 2. Loans—Law and legislation—Europe. 3. Credit—Law
and legislation—Europe. 4. Security (Law)—Europe, Eastern. 5. Loans—Law and
legislation—Europe, Eastern. 6. Credit—Law and legislation—Europe, Eastern.
7. European Bank for Reconstruction and Development. I. Title.
    KJC1886.R68 2007
    346.4707′4–dc22   2007004068

Typeset by RefineCatch Limited, Bungay, Suffolk
Printed in Great Britain
on acid-free paper by
Antony Rowe, Chippenham

ISBN 978–0–19–826013–4

1 3 5 7 9 10 8 6 4 2

FOREWORD

From its inception in the early 1990s the European Bank for Reconstruction and Development recognized the potential importance of secured transactions to the emerging markets of Central and Eastern Europe and our work on legal transition has always given prominence to this area. The evolution of the Bank's work in this field, which constitutes a significant aspect of the EBRD's legal reform work, is documented at <http://www.ebrd.com/country/sector/law/st/>. The first step that the Bank took to encourage reform was the development of the EBRD Model Law on Secured Transactions. That first step was crucial since it provided a basis from which the subsequent legal transition work could build and it is now fascinating to see in this methodical and detailed work how the laws in seven jurisdictions in the region have developed.

EBRD has a special role amongst international financial institutions, because of the unique nature of its region, because of the emphasis placed on promoting the private sector, and because of widespread expectation that countries in the region should catch up rapidly with their western neighbours. When we started our legal transition work secured transactions was hardly a 'hot topic'. We fought to put them high on the reform agenda because of the dramatic effect that an efficient framework for secured transactions can have on the availability of credit. That policy has been vindicated by the development of secured credit markets across the region and the contribution they have made to economic progress.

We emphasized in the introduction to the Model Law that it was *not* intended as detailed legislation for direct incorporation into local legal systems. It *was* intended to form a basis from which national legislation could be elaborated. It is interesting now, twelve years on, to see the influence that it has had. Our work on secured transactions reform has evolved and continues to face new challenges as financial markets grow and change and as our focus moves towards the countries of Central Asia. In 1994 the Model Law was published as a comparative text which drew on a number of advanced legal systems and provided an alternative source to the laws of individual countries. Today a country reforming its secured transactions laws has many other sources to turn to, not least the countries in the region that have already introduced successful reform, and from whose experience much can be learnt. However, the Model Law remains there as a point of reference and as such will doubtless have a role for years to come.

The challenges of reform have inevitably moved on since the Model Law was published. Today's complex project financings and innovative securitization transactions often have to be structured within legal frameworks that are inappropriate. EBRD is determined to remain at the forefront of change in this sector and to continue to assist countries in the region in making their laws and institutions more efficient so that they can benefit fully from modern financing techniques.

Secured Lending in Eastern Europe: Comparative Law of Secured Transactions and the EBRD Model Law does not provide an overview of all of EBRD's work on secured transactions but it shares the same philosophy. It will be of interest to a wide range of readers. For the legal historian it contributes an historical perspective on the rapid development of secured transactions laws during recent years; for the comparative lawyer it provides a study covering seven central and eastern European jurisdictions; for the law reformer it provides detailed analysis which enables the trends of reform to be understood; and for any person interested in secured transactions it constitutes a mine of information.

Working in the EBRD's legal department from 1992 to 1997 alongside John Simpson, Jan-Hendrik Röver played a key role in developing the Model Law. Jan-Hendrik's enthusiasm for secured transactions reform moved with him as he entered the investment banking profession and this excellent book benefits from a comprehensive knowledge of secured transactions reform that Jan-Hendrik has built up since his first days working at the EBRD. This impressive work, for which I congratulate him and which I commend to readers, reflects a thorough understanding of secured lending in the region EBRD serves.

Emanuel Maurice
General Counsel, EBRD
London
November 2006

PREFACE

The legal reforms of secured transactions laws in central and eastern Europe are all but finished. However, after fifteen years of intensive reforms, it is now the appropriate time to review what has been achieved and to consider what is still to be done in the area of secured transactions. This review is of particular significance as central and eastern European secured transactions laws are still largely uncharted territory from the point of view of comparative law.

This is an explanatory and practical, not a learned book. It was written for three classes of readers: first, people involved or interested in the legal reforms taking place in the transition economies of central and eastern Europe (and elsewhere) who want to reflect on the reforms of business laws in general and the adaptation of secured transactions laws to a market economy in particular. The remarks on legal reform were written against the experience of the reforms of the past fifteen years in central and eastern Europe. They focus on the purpose of secured transactions law reform and what is needed, both in the law itself and in the implementation of the law, to enable that purpose to be fulfilled. Second, the book should be of interest to people working in the area of secured transactions law in central and eastern European countries. For them it brings an overview of an area of law of great practical importance, which has developed rapidly and is still developing. Third, it was written for people who want to understand the fundamentals of secured transactions law, which is regarded as an obscure part of the law in many countries. In this respect it may be helpful to bankers, students, and lawyers alike.

This book has three particular features. First, throughout the book the theme will be what characteristics make a secured transactions law useful from a practical point of view. Hence, the purpose of the book is not merely to describe existing rules on security but rather to concentrate on the question of how those rules can be made practical. Second, the book introduces a comparative perspective in order to make the reader aware of significant differences between the secured transactions laws of various states. The basic reference points for the comparative analysis are the EBRD's *Model Law on Secured Transactions* and the EBRD's *Core Principles for a Modern Secured Transactions Law*. In addition, English, German, and US law, which each—among others—influenced the EBRD's work, are used as further reference sources. Inevitably, since this book will focus on seven central and eastern European security laws, these

vii

laws will add another layer of comparative analysis. The focus will be on the laws of Bulgaria, the Czech Republic, Hungary, Poland, Romania, the Russian Federation, and the Slovak Republic. Thus, the principles of security law developed under western laws are contrasted with the principles of the security laws of some of the central and eastern European jurisdictions, as they can now be described after more than fifteen years of legal reforms in central and eastern European countries. The third feature of the book is the focus on the needs of local and international financing. Often security law is described from the perspective of consumers or the financing of goods. However, in particular the experience in central and eastern European countries demonstrates that it is at least equally important to take into account the needs of financial institutions.

The text of this study resulted from the experience of drafting the *EBRD Model Law on Secured Transactions*, of advising various central and eastern European governments on issues of secured transactions law reform and legal reforms generally, and from the practical experience of developing security for international structured financings. This invaluable apprenticeship has led to the conclusion that, ideally, the drafting of new laws should be based on a clear understanding of the basic principles of a particular area of law. The basic principles are analytical and empirical in nature where they are derived from the comparative study of national laws. However, particularly in the area of private law, it is important to supplement these analytical and empirical principles with an evaluation, the basis for which can partly be derived from an economic analysis of the particular field in question. Such analytical and empirical principles, as well as the principles for evaluation, serve as benchmarks for the reform results. They assist in arriving at well-informed and reasoned reforms. Many involved in assisting in the law reform process try to further particular national laws. It seems that this does not necessarily facilitate the process of legal reform because it can easily obscure the underlying issues and may not generate a solution adapted to the local environment.

A work like this is impossible without local partners who check the comparatist's understanding of a foreign law against reality. My special thanks go to members of the international law firm Nörr Stiefenhofer Lutz (Munich), who reviewed the draft texts on central and eastern European secured transactions laws and provided much helpful input. Dr Peter Zier, partner of Nörr Stiefenhofer Lutz and a member of the Advisory Board to the EBRD Secured Transactions Project, kindly coordinated the feedback from the six local offices of Nörr Stiefenhofer Lutz in Prague (Czech Republic), Budapest (Hungary), Warsaw (Poland), Bucharest (Romania), Moscow (Russian Federation), and Bratislava (Slovak Republic), as well as from the partner office of Penkov, Markov, and Partners in Sofia (Bulgaria).

Inevitably this book has benefited further from the support and wisdom of many. John Simpson, who was co-author of *Model Law on Secured Transactions* and kindly commented on parts of this book, has been my guide for many years. The work was first initiated by the former EBRD General Counsel Andre Newburg, whom I would like to thank for his continued encouragement and support. John L Taylor, his successor as General Counsel, has been equally supportive of this work. I owe special thanks to Emanuel Maurice, the current General Counsel, who generously contributed a Foreword to this book. My thanks go also to the members of the international Advisory Board of the EBRD Secured Transactions Project, who made available the benefit of their knowledge and experience.[1] Professor Sir Roy Goode QC OBE FBA has been a constant source of inspiration and I am most grateful to him. Extremely helpful also has been the comparative work and exchange of ideas with Professor Philip Wood. The work carried out at the EBRD by Dr Carsten Dageförde, Jonathan Bates, Dr Thomas A Frick, Dr Frédérique Dahan, Dr Duncan Fairgrieve, and others has provided me with much valuable material. My sincere thanks go also to a number of editors from Oxford University Press who helped this publication to come to light, including Richard Hart (formerly editor at OUP and now publisher of Hart Publishing), Chris Rycroft, Rachel Mullaly, Katarina Wihlborg, Wendy Lynch, Faye Judges, Darcy Ahl, and Alison Floyd.

It is my hope that this text, like the *Model Law on Secured Transactions* and *The EBRD Core Principles for a Modern Secured Transactions Law*, will serve as a starting point from which law-makers can develop individual solutions for their countries, which the practitioner can use to familiarize him or herself with national secured transactions laws and which the student of secured transactions law can use to understand the practical challenges of secured transactions law. I would be more than happy if this book helped to focus attention, in the legal reform process as well as in commercial practice, on the importance of secured transactions law. On a final note I would like to repeat the remark Frédérique Dahan and John Simpson made in a recent article: 'The laws in Central and Eastern Europe are changing and this could lead to a reversal of position with

---

[1] Professor David E Allan, Juan F Armesto, Professor Dr Milan Bakeš, Professor Mark M Boguslavsky with the assistance of Dr Olga V Vorobieva, Professor Ronald CC Cuming, Professor Dr Jan Hendrik Dalhuisen, Professor Aubrey L Diamond QC, Professor Dr Ulrich Drobnig, John Edwards, Professor Christian Gavalda, Marcello Gioscia, Professor Dr Atilla Harmathy, Professor Mary E Hiscock, Dr Jacques Périlleux, Hugh S Pigott, Professor Stanisław Sołtysiński, Ken Tsunematsu, Professor Philip R Wood, John Young, Dr Peter Zier; for a list of the Advisory Board members and their affiliations see EBRD, *Model Law on Secured Transactions* (London, 1994) viii–ix.

their countries having an economic advantage over their Western neighbors in the market for secured credit.'[2]

Jan-Hendrik Röver
January 2007

---

[2] F Dahan and J Simpson, 'The European Bank for Reconstruction and Development's Secured Transactions Project: a model law and ten core principles for a modern secured transactions law in countries of Central and Eastern Europe and elsewhere' in E-M Kieninger (ed), *Security Rights in Movable Property in European Private Law* (Cambridge, 2004) 113.

CONTENTS SUMMARY

CONTENTS

II REFERENCE SYSTEMS OF SECURED TRANSACTIONS LAW

III PRINCIPLES OF SECURED TRANSACTIONS LAWS IN CENTRAL AND EASTERN EUROPE

TABLES OF LEGISLATION, MODEL LAWS, AND LEGISLATIVE GUIDES

Note: The entries in this table that do not have corresponding paragraph references are included to give an overall view of legislation pertaining to the subject area of this book.

D. CENTRAL AND EASTERN EUROPEAN STATUTES

Note: for English translations of central and
eastern European secured transactions laws see
<http://www.ebrd.com/country/sector/law/
st/core/laws>.

E. REGIONAL COLLECTIONS OF CENTRAL AND EASTERN EUROPEAN SECURED TRANSACTIONS LAWS

Breidenbach, Stephan (ed), Handbuch
  Wirtschaft und Recht in Osteuropa
  (Munich, looseleaf)
Breidenbach, Stephan, Campbell,
  Christian, and EBRD (eds),
  Business Transactions in
  Eastern Europe (New York,
  looseleaf)
Brunner, Georg, Schmid, Karin, and
  Westen, Klaus (eds),
  Wirtschaftsrecht der
  osteuropäischen Staaten
  (Baden-Baden, looseleaf)
Pechota, Vratislav and Hazard, John
  N (eds), Russia & The
  Republics: Legal Materials (The
  Parker School Series on East
  European Legal Materials)
  (Huntington/NY, looseleaf)

LIST OF ABBREVIATIONS

GENERAL

ACOJURIS	Agence de Coopération Juridique Internationale (France)
CILC	Center for International Legal Cooperation (Netherlands)
CIS	Commonwealth of Independent States
EBRD	European Bank for Reconstruction and Development (London)
EC Treaty	Treaty of the European Community (as amended by the Treaty of Amsterdam)
ECU	European Currency Unit
GATT	The General Agreement on Tariffs and Trade of 30 October 1947
GtZ	Gesellschaft für technische Zusammenarbeit (Germany)
IBRD	International Bank for Reconstruction and Development (Washington, DC)
IRIS	Institutional Reform and the Informal Sector
NAFTA	North American Free Trade Agreement
OAS	Organization of American States
PFI	Private Finance Initiative
QFC	qualifying floating charge
UCC	Uniform Commercial Code 1998 with 2001 Amendments (US)
UNCITRAL	United Nations Commission on International Trade Law (Vienna)
UNIDROIT	International Institute for the Unification of Private Law (Rome)
USAID	United States Agency for International Development

PUBLICATIONS

AJCL	*American Journal of Comparative Law*
AJIL	*The American Journal of International Law*
BKR	*Zeitschrift für Bank- und Kapitalmarktrecht*
CLJ	*Cambridge Law Journal*
GWLR	*George Washington Law Review*
Harv ILJ	*Harvard International Law Journal*
ICLQ	*International Comparative Law Quarterly*
IPRax	*Praxis des Internationalen Privat- und Verfahrensrechts*
JEEL	*Journal of East European Law* (Columbia University)
OJ	*Official Journal of the European Union*
OJLS	*Oxford Journal of Legal Studies*
Prinzipien	J-H Röver, *Vergleichende Prinzipien dinglicher Sicherheiten. Eine Studie zur Methode der Rechtsvergleichung* (Munich, 1999)
QJ Econ	*Quarterly Journal of Economics*

RabelsZ	*Rabels Zeitschrift für ausländisches und internationales Privatrecht*
Tulane JICL	*Tulane Journal of International & Comparative Law*
Utah LR	*Utah Law Review*
WiRO	*Wirtschaft und Recht in Osteuropa*
YLJ	*Yale Law Journal*
ZEuP	*Zeitschrift für Europäisches Privatrecht*
ZIP	*Zeitschrift für Wirtschaftsrecht (until 1982: Zeitschrift für Wirtschaftsrecht und Insolvenzpraxis)*

PART I

APPROACHING THE SUBJECT

1

CENTRAL AND EASTERN EUROPEAN COUNTRIES AND THE REFORM OF SECURED TRANSACTIONS LAWS

A. Secured Transactions in Central and Eastern Europe

When the Berlin wall fell on 9 November 1989 it was only a matter of several **1.01** years before most central and eastern European countries took the decision to become so-called transition countries and to transform into western-style democracies and market economies. This development became possible due to the withdrawal of the Soviet Union under Mikhael Gorbachev's leadership as the guardian power of other central and eastern European countries. It meant the end to a communist system which had prevailed in Russia for more than seventy years and in most other central and eastern European countries for more than forty years. However, there was no roadmap available for political, economic, and cultural changes of the scale envisaged by the transition countries and their western supporters. One of the tools which was created to foster central and eastern Europe's transition process was the European Bank for Reconstruction and Development (EBRD), established in 1991.

B. EBRD Model Law and Core Principles

In April 1992 at its first Annual General Meeting in Budapest, the EBRD held a **1.02** round table discussion on the reform of economic laws. The round table session

3

was titled 'Economic Law Reform: Creditors' Rights and Secured Transactions in Central and Eastern Europe'. The main finding of this discussion was that central and eastern European countries (twenty-eight of them are so-called 'countries of operations' of the EBRD in 2007)[1] lacked modern laws on secured transactions which were able to provide non-possessory security interests and were also able to cater for the needs of modern financing techniques. Some countries, such as Hungary and Romania, still had laws that pre-dated the communist era but they had not been used in practice during the reign of communism, since centrally planned economies did not rely on debt financing and the respective techniques of securing credit. Financial resources were only necessary for working capital purposes. Investments, particularly in tangible assets but also in services, were made possible by provision in kind and not by financing. William Butler's standard text book on Soviet Law clearly illustrates the Russian approach (and more generally the approach of centrally planned economies) to security interests: they simply did not exist![2] The conclusion from the EBRD round table in 1992 was a call by three eminent central and eastern European lawyers[3] upon the EBRD to develop a model law which could serve as a guide for the necessary reforms of security laws in central and eastern Europe. Within two years the EBRD had developed such a model law (1994), which was followed three years later by the EBRD Core Principles for a Modern Secured Transactions Law (1997). It will be seen later to what extent the Model Law and the Core Principles played their respective roles in reshaping central and eastern European secured transactions laws.

C. Choices in the Process of Reforming Secured Transactions Laws

1.03 The development of the EBRD Model Law and of the later EBRD Core Principles apart, the central and eastern European countries have various choices

---

[1] Albania, Armenia, Azerbaijan, Belarus, Bosnia and Herzegovina, Bulgaria, Croatia, the Czech Republic, Estonia, Georgia, Hungary, Kazakhstan, Kyrgyz Republic, Latvia, Lithuania, FYR Macedonia, Moldova, Mongolia, Poland, Romania, the Russian Federation, Serbia and Montenegro, Slovak Republic, Slovenia, Tajikistan, Turkmenistan, Ukraine, and Uzbekistan. Note that the Parliament of Montenegro declared independence from Serbia on 3 June 2006; it is therefore to be expected that Montenegro will become a Member State of the EBRD. Prior to declaring independence Montenegro already had its own legal system and, in particular, its secured transactions law (the Law on Secured Transactions, adopted on 19 July 2002). Note further that Kosovo also has its own secured transactions law (Regulation No 2001/5 on Pledges, adopted on 7 February 2001) without as yet being an independent state.

[2] WE Butler, *Soviet Law* (2nd edn, London, 1988).

[3] Professor Atilla Harmathy of Hungary, Professor Petar Sarcevic of Croatia, and Professor Stanisław Sołtysiński of Poland.

to make during the reform process. First, of course, they have to put secured transactions laws on their reform agendas. Typically, secured transactions law is not the main focus of political and economic reform programmes; more attention is often given to such areas as constitutional law, labour law, general property law, and competition law. However, as will be shown later, there is a strong practical and economic rationale for having a workable secured transactions law which calls for secured transactions law to be dealt with as a matter of priority. If the EBRD's efforts in the area of secured transactions law reform served only one purpose, it would be to put secured transactions law reform at the top of the list of legal reform issues.

The second issue for central and eastern European countries to decide is which **1.04** general policy decision they should take. In Philip Wood's terms there are debtor and creditor friendly security laws.[4] It is probably more correct to speak about chargor and chargeholder friendly security laws, since the debtor can be a different person from the chargor. However, it is true that a law can put more emphasis on the interests of the person receiving security or it can choose to prefer the person providing security. It is a clear opinion in this book that the first option is preferable since the desired micro- and macroeconomic effects of security can only be generated where security is of real practical use to the securityholder. However, the choice between the two options is a real one and has to be taken—for good or ill.

Third, when it comes to detailed drafting of legal texts, there are various models **1.05** to choose from.[5] The most obvious models are existing national laws which are in practice in other countries. The adoption of such models is often furthered by legal reform programmes financed by individual countries. Hence, it is not surprising that Article 9 of the Uniform Commercial Code (UCC) has served as a model for security law reform in central and eastern Europe.[6] Anglo-American laws (in particular Article 9 of the UCC and English law) have a different understanding of property law than civil law jurisdictions which shows in particular in the distinctions of title and interest on the one hand[7] and of attachment and perfection on the other hand.[8] Even if central and eastern European countries have followed Anglo-American models, they have rarely built their secured transactions laws on the underlying notions of property law found in these laws but rather have tried to fit the models into their civil law traditions. Nevertheless, some countries (Albania, Kosovo, Montenegro, and to

---

[4] PR Wood, *Maps of World Financial Law* (5th edn, London, 2005) 92.
[5] For an approach to legal reform see 3.10–3.20 below.
[6] See 22.24–22.37 below for the main approaches to secured transactions law reform in central and eastern Europe.
[7] See 5.04 and 7.19 below.   [8] See 7.23, 7.41 and ch 14 below.

a limited extent Bulgaria and Romania)[9] have adopted the so-called functional approach to be found in Article 9 of the UCC under which transactions serving the purpose of creating security come within the scope of the secured transactions law.[10]

D. Reforms of Secured Transactions Laws

1.06 Where central and eastern European countries did not want to look at the model of existing national laws but at model legislation and guidelines designed for the needs of their countries they had the possibility of resorting to the EBRD Model Law on Secured Transactions and the EBRD Core Principles for a Modern Secured Transactions Law. As will be explained later, the EBRD tried to combine features from both common and civil law and its two reference guides provide a template for secured transactions law reform with particular emphasis on an economically efficient set of rules.

1.07 When they began their individual law reform processes, the advantage for central and eastern European countries was that they could almost start from scratch and choose the models which were most suited in their opinion. By now most of the countries have reformed their secured transactions laws by introducing new Acts. Many countries introduced registries to record security interests. Thus, many efforts have been made to allow secured credit. Although some of the newly introduced rules may still be deficient, looking back at the state of secured credit in central and eastern Europe in the early 1990s one cannot but admire the energy used to introduce an area of law which only fifteen years ago was virtually non-existent in centrally planned economies.

---

[9] For more detail, see 10.26 and 22.09 below.
[10] For the functional approach see 6.16 and 10.05 below.

2

THE PRACTICAL NEED FOR SECURITY
AND THE ECONOMICS OF SECURITY

A. The Practical Need for Security

Market economies thrive on credit. Credit enables companies and private **2.01** persons to enlarge their scope for financial manoeuvre. With the assistance of credit they are able to finance activities which they are either not able to finance on the basis of their current income or assets or which they are unwilling to finance from their current income or assets. The purchase of real estate for private use is an example of the former situation; the financing of a company acquisition with a large amount of debt to increase the return on own funds (so-called leverage effect) an example of the latter situation. Credit can be used for many purposes, such as financing operating expenses, investment costs, or acquisitions.

There are two main types of credit—loan credit and sale credit. In loan credit **2.02** money is simply provided, typically by a bank. Sale credit is the deferment of the payment under a price-obligation. Sale credit is typically provided by the sellers of goods. Types of credit can be combined, for example in complex project financings there will often be loan credit and sale credit.

Credit can only be extended if there is a sufficient economic base which makes **2.03** it appear likely that the credit will be repaid within the contractual term. A sufficient economic base will, *inter alia*, require two elements: a pool of funds which allows the payment of debt service (ie the repayment of the principal amount as well as the payment of interest) and of financing costs as well as a financial structure which adequately underpins any payment claims. As far as the 'pool of funds' is concerned, credit will typically be given on the basis of three different premises: either the entity receiving credit is expected to generate sufficient profit or cash flow in future to repay the credit, or there is sufficient asset value to support a certain level of credit, or both conditions exist.

2.04   The financial structure of the borrower (which can be a private person, a partnership, or a company) will typically be very simple. There will be a need for sufficient equity, ie own funds, and credit. In recent times financial structures have become more complex with the introduction of the so-called mezzanine layer of financing which ranks between equity and (senior) credit when it comes to payment claims in particular in the insolvency of the debtor.[1] It can take the form, for example, of subordinated debt, ie debt financing which ranks behind the more senior financing, or of convertible bonds. Starting from the three fundamental layers of a financing (equity, senior debt, and mezzanine financing), financial structures can become even more complex with the introduction of multi-layered financings which intersect various layers of junior financing between equity and senior debt and several senior debt tranches. In western-type financings the different layers of financing correspond to different risk profiles which are reflected in different ratings given either by the credit provider or an external rating agency. The different risk profiles typically translate into different terms for the individual financings and in particular into different prices for the respective credit.

2.05   Where there is credit there is in most cases also 'security', although credit can be given both on an unsecured or a secured basis. In many jurisdictions security can also be taken for secured obligations other than credit obligations. However, in practice the main purpose of security is to secure credit obligations. The difference between secured and unsecured credit will typically show in the different terms being offered for both types of credit. Certain types of financing (such as structured financings, for example in the form of acquisition financing or project financing) are not offered on an unsecured basis at all. The differences between unsecured and secured credit exist, however, only if security is regarded as being effective in practice. Unsecured credits are given both for consumer and for business financing. However, secured credits are the norm, particularly if the credit is a large amount and given for the medium to long term. Security can

---

[1] U Ammelung and J-H Röver, 'Mezzaninefinanzierungen in der Praxis. Teil 1: Grundlegende wirtschaftliche, rechtliche und steuerliche Aspekte' (2006) 7–8 *Finanzbetrieb News* 2–6 and 'Teil 2: Instrumente mit fremdkapitalnahen Gestaltungen' (2006) *Finanzbetrieb News* 2–7.

take various forms and ranges from the simple single security interest to complex security arrangements. An example of simple single security interests is land mortgages which secure mortgage loans (both for consumers and businesses), typically with a term of more than ten years. Similarly, so-called 'repo' transactions, where banks transfer title in investment securities in exchange for loan credits, are provided on the basis of title security. More complex arrangements combine proprietary security and security in the form of guarantees of suretyships. The most complex security structures are found with international structured financings, in particular project financings, acquisition financings, and securitizations, which are provided with complex security packages attached to them. In particular international project financings are important for emerging markets where local banking markets are often not able to finance large-scale projects; for their funding commitments, international banks request an optimum security package in return.

In practice, the way in which security is taken varies from jurisdiction to jurisdiction, not least because national security laws show a much greater diversity than contract laws.[2] Equally there are differences between countries in the way companies and private persons are financed. Whereas certain countries (such as Germany) put an emphasis on bank loans for the traditional financing of companies, other countries (for example the United Kingdom) rely to a larger extent on equity markets. As far as private persons are concerned in certain countries much of the consumer spending is financed via credit cards whereas in other countries the use of credit cards is not yet widespread and hence debt financing is based on bank loans. Whereas financings in a national context (for example the financing of local companies by local banks) show a great diversity in approach, certain types of international financings (in particular the financing of cross-border acquisitions and project financing by international banks) demonstrate a convergence in the contractual and security structures used. Such international financings tend to choose to the largest extent possible Anglo-American laws (in particular English law and the law of New York) as the governing law. However, where conflict of laws rules require the application of a law other than the law chosen by the parties, for example where the law of the location of an asset (the so-called *lex situs* rule) applies, international financings integrate local law (and in particular local security interests). The varying customs of contractual and security structures are a matter for detailed treatises dealing with local law. In any event, it is worth keeping in mind that financing and security are a topic with many variations. **2.06**

---

[2] A recent study by the EBRD illustrated this point by demonstrating wide variations in the security arrangements of different countries; H Muent and F Pissarides, 'Impact of collateral practice on lending to small and medium sized enterprises' (Autumn 2000) *Law in Transition* 54–60.

2.07 So far, the practical use of security interests has been discussed in various contexts. An additional element of many security structures is, however, the obligation *not* to provide security to other persons. Such an obligation is called a 'negative pledge' obligation although the security interest not to be provided must in no way only be a pledge (which in many jurisdictions stands for possessory security over movable things). The term 'pledge' is used synonymously for any type of security interest and may sometimes extend to both proprietary security interests and guarantee-type obligations.

2.08 An interesting thought is whether security interests would be superfluous in a world which was governed by a simple 'negative pledge' rule under which nobody was allowed to take security in assets. In such a world national laws would not provide security interests and the negative pledge rule would declare security provided to be null and void. It could seem that such a world would reduce the complexity of security interests which currently exists. This is clearly only a theoretical thought since this scenario would only become realistic where at least the major countries in which credit and security play a significant role (which are pretty much most of the world's countries) would do away with their security laws at the same time. But even if such a totally unlikely event could be assumed it would not seem sensible to suggest such a scenario. The immediate question arising would be how a person providing sale credit would be protected. Surely the retention of title or retention of ownership, which is a typical form of security for the person providing sale credit, is a type of security and necessary to provide some form of safety net to the person selling goods against no or only partial payment. In the no pledge world sale creditors would be left without protection. In such a world loan creditors might take some comfort from the fact that no other security interest would conflict with the enforcement of their claims. However, since they would in many situations not be able to assess fully the amount of credit already provided to a person prior to their financing, they would want to know the economic basis for their financing. This assessment can only be done on the basis of security interests granted to them. Thus it appears that there is a real need for security interests and that a no pledge world—as appealing it may be in its obvious simplicity—is an unworkable scenario.

B. The Economic Rationale for Security

2.09 If both the general mechanics of security law shall be understood and a perspective for legal reform in this area developed one is greatly assisted by reassuring oneself of the economic rationale of security. One of the tools for analysing the economic rationale of security is the economic analysis of law. Richard Posner, one of the proponents of the economic analysis of law,[3] distinguishes a positive and a normative approach to economic analysis.[4] The positive role of economic analysis is to attempt 'to explain legal rules and outcomes as they are', whereas its normative role is 'to change them to make them better'. There are some doubts as to Posner's description of the positive role of economic analysis of law since this tool is designed to explain the economic purpose of legal rules as understood by an economist rather than to 'explain legal rules and outcomes as they are'. However, the importance of a positive role thus defined and the normative role of the economic analysis of law should be recognized. As far as the latter is concerned, economic criteria can provide useful arguments for the evaluation of the effectiveness of legal rules and for their criticism on this basis.

Broadly one can distinguish the micro- and the macroeconomic functions of security.[5] Microeconomics looks at the economic effects of security on individual economic entities, whereas macroeconomics is concerned with the effects on the economy as a whole. **2.10**

1. Microeconomic functions of security

(a) Risk reduction

Security's main economic function is to reduce the creditor's risk of giving credit and thus to enhance its chances of receiving back the credit it has provided. Any provision of credit involves a number of risks: over the life of the credit the value of the money extended can change within an economy because of inflation or deflation; also its value can change in relation to foreign currencies because of fluctuations in exchange rates. Furthermore the prices of credit, ie interest rates, may vary. All of these risks are independent from the payment (in the case of sale credit) or repayment (in the case of loan credit) of a particular credit. Security will do nothing about them because it is only concerned about risks relating to the payment or repayment of credits. Those risks can be two-fold: they comprise the risk of a debtor either not paying or repaying the creditor at the agreed time or of it not paying or repaying at all. The repayment of loan credit has two main components—the principal amount and the price for the credit, ie interest.[6] **2.11**

Every commercial investor (including financial institutions) is interested in **2.12**

---

[3] See R Posner, *Economic Analysis of Law* (5th edn, Boston, 1998).   [4] ibid §2.2.

[5] For an economic analysis of secured transactions, see also G McCormack, *Secured Credit Under English and American Law* (Cambridge, 2004) ch 1; J-H Röver, *Vergleichende Prinzipien dinglicher Sicherheiten. Eine Studie zur Methode der Rechtsvergleichung* (Munich, 1999) (hereinafter Röver, *Prinzipien*) 97–128.

[6] Typically there are also other financing costs (eg arrangement, agency, or prepayment fees).

making a profit from its investment but in many cases the fundamental concern is to obtain protection against loss of the investment. A legal framework for security is a key requirement for creating an investor-friendly climate. An investor which knows that it has legally recognized and effective rights to turn to the assets granted as security in case of non-payment may assess the investment risk quite differently. This may influence its decision whether to invest or not. It may also change the terms on which it is prepared to invest in five ways:

(1) it may lower the interest rate and the other costs (for example fees) on a loan;[7]
(2) it may increase the amount of a loan;
(3) it may extend the period for which the loan is granted;
(4) it will influence the relationship between debt and equity, ie the ratio between credit and investment, which the creditor is prepared to accept with the debtor; and
(5) it may also influence positively other terms of the credit, for example the financial ratios required to comply with and other covenants (such as the limitations on paying dividends to shareholders) or push the repayment towards the end of the repayment period.

2.13 The economic value of security can be formulated in a simple rule which links the economic value to the risk reduction achieved by security: the more the risk of giving credit is reduced, the greater will be the value of security to the lender and the greater will be a security's microeconomic effect. There is a direct relationship between the legal framework, its effectiveness, and the attitude of the investor. If there is a law on secured transactions which is seen to give practical protection and remedies in the case of non-payment of a debt then security can become a major part of the investment decision, both for local and international investors. If the investor is not persuaded that the law gives real protection and remedies then it becomes irrelevant. Since lenders are commercial institutions which have to recover their costs and earn a profit there is no doubt that lending costs (which are greatly driven by costs caused by defaulting creditors) are passed on to borrowers.[8] A costly and inefficient secured transactions system directly increases the lending costs and thus decreases the amount of borrowing in an economy.

2.14 Security interests protect the likelihood of the satisfaction of a debt (but not the satisfaction of the debt itself since they create rights additional to those

---

[7] See eg *World Development Report 2005—A better investment climate for everyone* (Washington, DC, 2005) 121.

[8] See EBRD, *The Impact of the Legal Framework on the Secured Credit Market in Poland* (London, 2005) 2, 3.

under the debt) and thus achieve risk reduction. Such a risk reduction can be achieved in two ways: a positive way and a negative way. Traditionally the value of security is seen in its ability to be enforced by the person taking security and hence in its 'positive function'. In the traditional situations, the assets taken as security have some real value and upon the default of the debtor security will often be enforced. However, some modern forms of financing have developed a different and somewhat surprising attitude to security—they put more emphasis on the 'negative function' of security. For example, if international banks finance a large project whose infrastructure is constructed solely for the purpose of this project—take the example of a pipeline extending several hundred miles—the enforcement of the security interests on the pipeline may not generate much value for the financing banks. Nevertheless they will try to take all the security they can get. The reason behind these security structures (but equally of simple security rights) is to build a shield against third parties: the financing banks understand that they are taking commercial risks in these types of situations and will try to work out any difficulties with the debtor. This could be frustrated if third parties were to enforce against the debtor's assets or even to put the debtor into insolvency. Hence, the financing banks take security mainly to avoid prior security interests of third persons and thus to have the opportunity to restructure the financing. In these situations security interests are not primarily used to be enforced but to avoid the enforcement of security interests by third parties. A third function of security interests, the 'management function', arises if a security interest enables the creditor to appoint a receiver or manager over the assets of the debtor (often a company). This can be interpreted as an attempt to use security interests as a means of enabling a private administration (reorganization) procedure in the interest of increasing the proceeds from the sale of the assets taken as security.

(b) Prevention of risk shifting

Closely related to security's function of risk reduction is its purpose of prevent- **2.15**
ing the debtor from shifting risks to the detriment of creditors. Chris Higson has clearly named the risks facing a creditor once the credit contract has been signed:[9] the debtor 'may issue more debt of equal or greater seniority; it may distribute as dividends or salaries assets the creditors were looking to as security; it may develop a more risky investment strategy, the benefit of which would be reaped by equity but the costs of which might be borne by debt'. Economists see in the conflict between equity and debt-holders an example of the phenomenon of moral hazard. Equity-holders tend to reduce their own risks related to a project by increasing external financing and the riskiness of projects in the

---

[9] C Higson, *Business Finance* (2nd edn, London, 1995) 233.

interest of return. Moral hazard faced by equity-holders contributes to the risk of non-payment of the debt by the debtor. Risk shifting can clearly be prevented by security which has the effect that the debtor (or a third party providing security) is putting its assets at risk in the event of default with the secured debt.

(c) Information about the debtor

2.16 A third purpose of security is to give the creditor information about the debtor's willingness to repay or pay the credit. The economic argument was developed in the context of research into markets with incomplete and asymmetric information (ie one person knows more than the other). In his famous paper, 'The market for "lemons" '[10], George Akerlof demonstrated the phenomenon of adverse selection, which he illustrated using the example of the market for used cars. The seller of a used car knows all its defects whereas the potential purchaser is uninformed about them. When prices are high, good and bad cars (the latter are so-called 'lemons') are on the market. With falling prices more and more better quality cars leave the market whereas bad quality cars remain; thus the probability of purchasing a bad car is increased. That leads to the astonishing effect that with falling prices, demand will not necessarily increase but may decrease. In the extreme there will not be any demand for cars at all.

2.17 In particular Joseph Stiglitz and Andrew Weiss demonstrated the effects of adverse selection in the context of loan credit and security.[11] A bank cannot tell whether a debtor is a serious entrepreneur or just a gambler. When interest rates increase the category of serious entrepreneurs becomes rarer in the pool of applicants for credit. Analogously to the situation described for used cars, the profit of the bank may not increase with the interest rate but decrease. Adverse selection leads to what economists call 'credit rationing'.[12] This can be overcome by security. The serious entrepreneur will be willing to give security whereas the gambler prefers not to provide security which it is most likely to lose. Thus, applicants for credit order themselves into different classes of risk according to their willingness to give security.[13]

---

[10] GA Akerlof, 'The market for "lemons": qualitative uncertainty and the market mechanism' (1970) 84 QJ Econ 488.

[11] J Stiglitz and A Weiss, 'Credit rationing in markets with imperfect information' (1981) 71 *American Economic Review* 393.

[12] See JE Stiglitz, *Economics* (New York, 1993) 553–5.

[13] However, a recent study by the EBRD demonstrated that for lending to small and medium sized enterprises in central and eastern Europe, security may not replace the need for having knowledge about the borrower; H Muent and F Pissarides, 'Impact of collateral practice on lending to small and medium sized enterprises' (Autumn 2000) *Law in Transition* 54. The authors rightly point out that in traditional corporate financings there is usually a continuum along which security is gradually replaced by a better understanding of the borrower as the bank/client relationship develops (ibid 55 n 4).

Although Adam Smith[14] did not use the term 'adverse selection' he was fully **2.18** aware of the underlying phenomenon:

> The legal rate [of interest], it is to be observed, though it ought to be somewhat above, ought not to be much above the lowest market rate. If the legal rate of interest in Great Britain, for example, was fixed so high as eight or ten per cent., the greater part of the money which was to be lent, would be lent to prodigals and projectors, who alone would be willing to give this high interest. Sober people, who will give for the use of money no more than a part of what they are likely to make by the use of it, would not venture into the competition. A great part of the capital of the country would thus be kept out of the hands which were most likely to make a profitable and advantageous use of it, and thrown into those which were most likely to waste and destroy it. Where the legal rate of interest, on the contrary, is fixed but a very little above the lowest market rate, sober people are universally preferred, as borrowers, to prodigals and projectors. The person who lends money gets nearly as much interest from the former as he dares to take from the latter, and his money is much safer in the hands of the one set of people, than in those of the other. A great part of the capital of the country is thus thrown into the hands in which it is most likely to be employed with advantage.

2. Macroeconomic functions of security

(a) Lending and investment

It has been seen that the risk-reducing function of security has six important **2.19** microeconomic side effects: security increases the willingness to lend, lowers the price of credit, increases the amount of credit available, extends the period for which credit is granted, influences the ratio between credit and investment (ie between debt and equity) in an individual project, and influences positively other terms of the credit. These effects will be of great advantage to borrowers but do they matter for the economy as a whole? They do indeed, mainly because of three foremost macroeconomic effects which stem from security: it will make available a lower interest rate for secured credits generally, it will increase the amount of credit available in an economy, and it will ultimately increase total investment and production.

Those qualitative effects were quantified by the economist Heywood Fleisig **2.20** when he compared credit markets in a number of South American economies with the United States' credit market.[15] He estimated, for example, for Bolivia a difference from US interest rates of 34 to 46 per cent attributable to a less risk-reducing legal framework for security. Assuming the same credit costs would

---

[14] A Smith, *An Inquiry into the Nature and Causes of the Wealth of Nations* RH Campbell, AS Skinner, and WB Todd (eds) (Oxford, 1979) vol I, 357.

[15] See his summary: H Fleisig, 'Economic Functions of Security in a Market Economy' in J Norton and M Andenas (eds), *Emerging Financial Markets and Secured Transactions* (London, 1997) 15–38.

prevail in both the United States and in Bolivia, he forecast an increase in the amount of capital available in Bolivia of between US$752 million and US$1,871 million. That would lead to an increase in production of between US$230 million and US$683 million or between 3 and 9 per cent of gross national product! Those numbers should not be taken at face value since it is quite difficult to estimate the production potential of one economy by taking the data from another economy. They demonstrate, however, by order of magnitude the remarkable quantitative dimension of the macroeconomic contribution of security.

(b) Allocation of resources

2.21 In a number of ways security plays a role in the efficient allocation of resources in an economy. Economists attribute an inefficient allocation of resources to transaction costs in particular. The importance of transaction costs was discovered by Ronald Coase.[16] It was, however, Adam Smith who had already given an example of the detrimental effects of transaction costs:[17]

> But where the fees of registration have been made a source of revenue to the sovereign, register offices have commonly been multiplied without end, both for the deeds which ought to be registered, and for those which ought not. In France there are several different sorts of secret registers. This abuse, though not perhaps a necessary, it must be acknowledged, is a very natural effect of such taxes.

2.22 Security with its risk-reducing, non-risk-shifting, and information functions can lower the transaction costs and in particular the information costs of credit contracts. That facilitates the flow of financing and, in turn, an efficient allocation of investment opportunities. Savings, capital, and credit are allocated in an efficient way. It should, however, be noted that unnecessary transaction costs related to security itself can distort its positive effects as can be seen from Adam Smith's above-mentioned example.

3. Critique of the economic functions of security

2.23 A key element of an effective security regime is the satisfaction of the secured creditor in preference to unsecured creditors in an insolvency of the person giving security. It is often claimed that insolvency puts the effectiveness of rights of creditors, and of secured creditors in particular, to the ultimate test. However, it is exactly this preferred satisfaction of the secured creditor which

---

[16] See his collection of essays: RH Coase, *The Firm, the Market, and the Law* (Chicago, 1990). For the impact of transaction costs from a historical perspective, see DC North and RP Thomas, *The Rise of the Western World. A New Economic History* (Cambridge, 1973).
[17] Smith (n 14 above) vol II, 863.

has been criticized in recent times.[18] Critics admit that, as far as the relationship between the person giving security and the person taking security is concerned, security interests lower the risk of losses for the person taking security and thus fulfil one of the microeconomic functions of security. However, as far as the relationship with third persons is concerned, critics point out that the risk of losses is increased for third persons (who are not the beneficiaries of security interests). This means in effect that in the critics' opinion it appears doubtful whether there are efficiency gains from security interests on a macroeconomic level. On this basis they claim that it is equally doubtful to grant secured creditors preferential treatment in insolvency proceedings.

It must be clear that a security interest which does not provide preferential **2.24** treatment in insolvency is not an effective security interest and leaves secured creditors practically in the position of unsecured creditors. Mentioned above are the many situations in which security is seen as either fundamental or at least helpful in mobilizing financing. Hence, there can be no doubt that security mobilizes financing. In some situations such as mortgage financing, but also international structured financings, it is the only way to mobilize financing at all. In some of these situations (think of mortgage lending or project financing) it is not even clear why third persons should be greatly disadvantaged by a party's taking of security. The position that security does not provide macroeconomic efficiency gains must, therefore, be strongly rejected.

It is, however, one thing to reject the idea of taking away preferred satisfaction **2.25** of the secured creditor and quite another to claim that preferred satisfaction must be unfettered. There are limits to the preferential treatment of the secured creditor in insolvency which do not render the security impractical per se. In particular, there are three limitations which have to be considered. (1) Even if the secured creditor can satisfy its secured claims in a preferential way in the insolvency of the person providing security, it may not be the first one to be satisfied out of the insolvency estate. The costs of the insolvency procedure and the claims of a company's employees (for a certain limited period even after the insolvency has been opened) typically and justly rank prior to the secured claims of the secured creditors. (2) The second situation which may call for a limitation of the secured creditor's secured claim is when the security has been received in a doubtful way. This is mainly the case if the security was obtained only shortly before the insolvency was opened and also if security

---

[18] LA Bebchuk and JM Fried, 'The Uneasy Case for the Priority of Secured Claims in Bankruptcy' (1996) 105 YLJ 857–934; H Eidenmüller, 'Vertragliche Vorkehrungen gegen Insolvenzrisiken' in D Hart (ed), *Privatrecht im 'Risikostaat'* (Baden-Baden, 1997) 43, 54ff. See further E-M Kieninger (ed), *Security Rights in Movable Property in European Private Law* (Cambridge, 2004) 8–9.

was granted without the person receiving security providing some real value in exchange. In such situations the security is vulnerable to avoidance by the insolvency administrator. (3) Lastly, in the insolvency of a company it must be the primary goal to ensure the survival of the company as a going concern by restructuring (either the company itself or the company's liabilities) or by selling it in its entirety. The secured creditors can easily defeat the attempt to achieve survival of an insolvent company by enforcing its security over assets which are essential for the operation of the company (such as machinery or real estate). For essential assets of an insolvent company (what is essential must be defined by the insolvency administrator) the enforcement of security interests must, in the author's opinion, be subject to a stay period. In effect, secured creditors may not, for a certain period of time, be able to seek satisfaction for the assets taken as security if those assets are essential for running an enterprise unless the insolvency administrator allows the enforcement of the security interests.

4. Critique of the economic discussion of security

2.26   It may have struck the reader that so far the term 'security' has been used in a very generic sense. The laws of the world, now said to number more than 300,[19] do, however, display a great variety of types of security. Some laws give the creditor wide rights, such as English security law which used to permit the holder of a so-called 'floating charge' given by a company to appoint a receiver once the debtor was in default. The receiver was given the power to manage the company with a view to achieving satisfaction of the creditor.[20] Other laws such as French or German law, never provided the remedy of receivership. If one looks at the great diversity of types of security in national laws one becomes aware of how tentative the use of the word 'security' is. There is no such thing as a generally agreed notion of security rights.

2.27   Economists have rarely taken note of these differences. Much of the writing on the subject comes from American authors who equate security with the types of security found in American law and in particular the security interest in movables under Article 9 of the UCC. When talking about the economic functions of security this must be kept in mind. Not every type of security may fulfil the above-mentioned functions, many may fall well short of them. The economic functions are normative measures for evaluating the economic effectiveness of

---

[19] See PR Wood, 'Where Now in World Financial Law?' (1995) *Butterworths Journal of International Banking and Financial Law* 55; PR Wood, *Law and Practice of International Finance. Comparative Financial Law* (London, 1995) paras 5-1 to 13-2.

[20] Now limited by the Enterprise Act 2002; see 6.07 below. Only in limited situations can a so-called 'administrator' be appointed.

security. They do not necessarily describe the law (or explain the law positively, as Richard Posner would put it).

It should also be pointed out that economists approach the economic analysis **2.28** of security from several directions. Described above, *inter alia*, are findings from the principal agent theory (which pointed out the moral hazard and the adverse selection phenomena), from the analyis of macroeconomic effects of lending and investments as well as transaction costs analysis (the latter is often the main focus of the economic analysis of law). All of these approaches provide useful insights into the economic functions of security. It should, however, be noted that in economic theory these approaches are distinctly different and often discussed in isolation.

3

AN APPROACH TO LAW REFORM

Having discussed the reform of secured transactions laws in central and eastern **3.01** Europe, the practical need for and the economics of security, now the focus will shift to the issues of the legal reform process. The purpose of these remarks is to provide a perspective on the legal reform process in central and eastern Europe and elsewhere.

A. History of Law Reform

The history of the relationship between law reform and the development of **3.02** economic systems is largely a desiderate of the future.[1] It is possible, however, to mention a few important steps.

The direct link between law and economic development is not a new discovery. **3.03** It was the founder of modern economic thinking, Adam Smith,[2] who clearly formulated the need for an adequate legal framework to ensure prosperous economic development. For him the relationship was natural. He taught not only economics but also ethics[3] and law[4] at the University of Edinburgh. In the twentieth century Max Weber and Walter Eucken, in particular, discussed the relationship between law and macroeconomics. Max Weber devoted a

---

[1] See for early developments DC North and RP Thomas, *The Rise of the Western World. A New Economic History* (Cambridge, 1973).

[2] See JK Galbraith, *Economics in Perspective. A Critical History* (Boston, 1987); R Heilbronner, *Worldly Philosophers. The Lives, Times and Ideas of the Great Economic Thinkers* (7th edn, London, 1999).

[3] A Smith, *Theory of Moral Sentiments*, DD Raphael and AL Macfie (eds) (Oxford, 1978).

[4] A Smith, *Lectures on Jurisprudence*, RL Meek, DD Raphael, and PG Stein (eds) (Oxford, 1978).

whole chapter in his monumental work 'Economy and Society'[5] to the sociology of law. He underlined how important the foreseeability of law is for economic activity.[6] Walter Eucken, a member of the Freiburg School of economists and one of the most important economic thinkers for the West German post-war economic system,[7] formulated the relationship even more explicitly: he recognized several legal institutions such as property and liability as constitutive elements of a market economy.[8] These early theories have been confirmed since. Joseph Stiglitz, when he was Chief Economist of the World Bank, pointed out that the economic development of a country is not possible without an adequate law and that, hence, legal reforms must be an integral part of the reform efforts of the World Bank.[9]

3.04   At the end of the nineteenth and the beginning of the twentieth centuries, there were a few important examples of what can be called the 'adoption model of legal reform': reforming countries which adopted foreign laws more or less wholesale. In Japan the 1868 Meiji Restoration began a period of twenty years of institutional modernization. This resulted in the adoption of a number of foreign codes, initially French influenced. At a later stage the French models were replaced by German Acts, notably the German commercial and penal codes. Kemal Atatürk's Turkey also attempted to support economic progress by adopting foreign laws, for example the Swiss Civil Code.

3.05   The use of legal reform as an active and deliberate tool for economic development re-emerged as part of the 'law and development programmes' in the 1960s. The whole concept of development of so-called 'developing' countries had appeared in the 1950s and came to be seen as an important task for the so-called 'developed' countries,[10] many of which were former colonial powers. The law and development programmes went through various phases each of which was characterized by a different emphasis. A first phase lasted from the early 1960s to the mid–1970s. During this phase aid agencies financed many legal technical assistance projects in Africa, Asia, and Latin-America. For example, foreign legal advisers were sent to developing countries and assisted governments with

---

[5] M Weber, *Wirtschaft und Gesellschaft. Grundriß der verstehenden Soziologie* (5th edn, Tübingen, 1972).

[6] ibid 184, 195–8.

[7] DJ Gerber, 'Constitutionalizing the Economy: German Neo-Liberalism, Competition Law and the New Europe' (1994) 42 AJCL 25; A Heinemann, *Die Freiburger Schule und ihre geistigen Wurzeln* (Munich, 1989).

[8] W Eucken, *Grundsätze der Wirtschaftspolitik* (6th edn, Tübingen, 1990).

[9] For his views on the adequate reform methodology, see: J Stiglitz, 'Whither Reform? Ten Years of Transition' in B Pleskovic and JE Stiglitz (eds), *Annual World Bank Conference on Economic Development* (Washington, DC, 2000) 27–56, also published in H-J Chang (ed), *The Rebel Within* (London, 2001) 127–71.

[10] G Feuer and H Cassan, *Droit international du développement* (2nd edn, Paris, 1991).

economic law reforms. It was assumed that legal change would lead to laws in developing countries largely similar to those in western developed countries. This assumption seemed to be rational because many laws in the now developing countries were based upon civilian or common laws inherited from the colonial era. However, progress was slow and results often remained intangible because legal reforms were pursued in countries not committed to market economy and pluralistic political systems. As a consequence, by the mid-1970s, funding for many legal assistance projects had almost ceased.

The 'law and development movement' received a new impetus in the 1970s **3.06** under what a United States Agency for International Development (USAID) study[11] has called the 'New Directions Mandate'. During this second phase donors focused on the specific needs of the poor. The Mandate sought to alleviate poverty and comprised such diverse efforts as improving access to justice and legal literacy as well as activities in the area of human rights. In the 1980s a third phase of the law and development movement was geared towards issues of administration of justice. Various projects attempted to strengthen court procedures, ie the enforcement of rights. Both the activities of the second and the third phase of the movement remained largely invisible.

The break-up of the former communist bloc marked a significant change. Legal **3.07** technical assistance increased dramatically, since wholesale revamping of laws in central and eastern Europe was seen as part and parcel of the transition from state-planned economies to market-oriented (so-called 'transition') economies. Hence, in the 1990s legal reform became an integral part of policy advice, not only of the technical assistance programmes run by many individual countries but also of international organizations. Legal and economic transition in central and eastern Europe coincided with a growing recognition of the private sector as an active player, notably in the area of infrastructure investments; it was acknowledged that private sector activity necessarily requires a predictable legal framework.[12] An illustration of this trend is given by the Charter of the EBRD, which requires the Bank to lend and invest at least 60 per cent of its capital in the private sector.[13]

In the 1990s, legal reform as a tool of economic reform was, however, not **3.08** restricted to countries of the former communist bloc but became a global phenomenon. Legal reform programmes were now offered on three different levels: they were provided by agencies from individual countries (such as

---

[11] USAID, *Weighing in on the Scales of Justice: Strategic Approaches for Donor-Supported Rule of Law Programs* (Washington, DC, 1994).

[12] TW Waelde and JL Gunderson, 'Legislative Reforms in Transition Economies: Western Transplants—A Short-cut to Social Market Economy Status' (1994) 43 ICLQ 345.

[13] Agreement Establishing the Bank for Reconstruction and Development, Art 11(3)(i), (ii).

USAID in the United States, the Agence de Coopération Juridique Internationale (ACOJURIS) in France, the Gesellschaft für technische Zusammenarbeit (GtZ) in Germany, or the Center for International Legal Cooperation (CILC) in The Netherlands), by international financial institutions (the World Bank,[14] the Asian Development Bank, and the European Bank for Reconstruction and Development, in particular, ran comprehensive legal reform programmes in their respective member countries), and the European Union as a supranational organization. The European Union provided assistance via its EU TACIS (for CIS countries) and EU PHARE (for central and eastern European countries outside the CIS) programmes. Whilst most legal reform support had been granted for free by donor countries, the World Bank introduced the concept of legal sector restructuring loans (which were granted, for instance, to the Russian Federation, Kazakhstan, and Georgia) thus enforcing the concept of responsibility on the receiving country.

3.09 In recent years there seems also to have been a shift in the reform tools. It now seems to be recognized that there are no universal solutions to the improvement of legal frameworks; the transplantation of western legal models without regard to local circumstances is seen as counter-productive. The 'adoption model of legal reform' has, therefore, been supplanted by a 'choice model of legal reform' in which the ultimate choices are made by national decision-makers.

B. Methodology of Law Reform

3.10 The perplexing variety of donors and reform approaches leads to the question of which reform methodology should be followed. There is rather little literature on the methodology of law reform.[15] The overview of the history of legal reform has, however, already shown the fundamental approaches. As an initial step, legal reform efforts took a *legislative* approach which concentrated mainly on introducing new laws or making changes to existing laws. This was the starting point of what was called the 'adoption model of legal reform'. In particular the

---

[14] World Bank Legal Department, *The World Bank and Legal Technical Assistance. Initial Lessons, Policy Research Working Paper 1414* (Washington, DC, 1995); AN Vorkink, *The World Bank and Legal Technical Assistance. Current Issues* (Washington, DC, 1997); JH Anderson, DS Bernstein, and CW Gray, *Judicial Systems in Transition Economies. Assessing the Past, Looking to the Future* (Washington, DC, 2005).

[15] See as one of the few examples the often cited article by Waelde and Gunderson (n 12 above) 345; see also EG Jensen and TC Heller (eds), *Beyond Common Knowledge. Empirical Approaches to the Rule of Law* (Stanford, 2003) and J Stiglitz, 'Whither Reform? Ten Years of Transition' in B Pleskovic and JE Stiglitz (eds), *Annual World Bank Conference on Economic Development* (Washington, DC, 2000) 27–56, also published in H-J Chang (ed), *The Rebel Within* (London, 2001) 127–71.

third phase of the law and development movement took a mainly *institutional* approach and discovered that not only did legal texts matter but equally the institutions necessary to enforce them. Both of these approaches can still be found as the basis of many legal reform projects today. However, in the following paragraphs a more comprehensive methodology of legal reform is introduced which takes an *implementation* approach. This comprehensive approach integrates both the legislative and the institutional approaches but puts a more specific focus on the issue of ensuring that the law ultimately works. This requires an understanding of legal reform as an open loop in which the (internal and external) reformers constantly review the relationship between the intentions of a reform (adequately documented, it is hoped, in legal texts) and legal reality, and in which they receive constant feedback from the implementation process.

This implementation approach to legal reform was developed in the course of **3.11** the EBRD's Secured Transactions Project. It comprises in total eight steps, of which four are preparatory and four are implementation steps.[16] It is recognized that the different steps cannot easily be broken down into separate, or even distinguishable, components.[17] However, the distinction at least provides an opportunity to understand the elements of the complex reform process and on this basis to develop individual 'reform plans'.

As far as the *preparation* of legal reform is concerned, the EBRD's Secured **3.12** Transactions Project distinguishes: (1) consensus building; (2) the creation of commitment in the reform country; (3) the drafting of legislative texts; and (4) the adoption of the drafted legislative acts. Consensus building is the foundation of the reform process. A reform country has to be convinced of the need for reform, the goals of the reform, and the issues that have to be addressed. The consensus building stage is primarily concerned about identifying the need for reform. At this stage the reform country must also decide whether it can see value in assistance coming from outside (such as assistance from an international financial institution or a national law reform project). Reform goals and issues should be defined broadly at the consensus building stage. A build-and-build strategy, where a reform project tackles a particular issue only (for example registration of security interests), runs the danger of expending the initial enthusiasm for reform on a side issue without achieving a measured and comprehensive reform. An open question is who has to form part of the consensus building process. At a national level certainly government, parliament, and the judicature (including other legal institutions such as attorneys or notaries) have

---

[16] See J Simpson and J Menze, 'Ten years of secured transactions reform' (Autumn 2000) *Law in Transition* 20, 22–4.

[17] ibid 22.

to be involved. Depending on the build-up of the national civil society, industry and consumer representatives may also have to be involved.

3.13 At the international level a consideration may be whether or not a certain area of law should be harmonized. This is particularly relevant in the area of secured transactions, where the internationally prevailing rule of the conflict of laws regarding property law is the *lex situs* rule. Under this rule a transfer of movable things across borders can lead to a loss of security interests if the country of the assets' new location does not recognize the security interest created earlier.[18] However, any harmonization effort—desirable as it may be—increases the complexity of the legal reform process and, therefore, the practicability of harmonization has to be considered carefully.

3.14 Following the consensus building stage, a governmental institution (such as the Prime Minister's office or the Minister of Justice) has to commit politically to the intended reform. In addition, one or several local representatives with political backing must take on the role of doing the substantive work. The commitment stage is essentially about defining the goals of the reform.

3.15 In the approach championed here, the stage of drafting the law is a local process which has to be driven by local experts. However, it is clearly beneficial if this process stands on a well informed basis. Particularly valuable is the comparative analysis of foreign laws,[19] the reference to reform proposals (such as the EBRD Model Law on Secured Transactions or the EBRD Core Principles for a Modern Secured Transactions Law), or even specific reform proposals prepared in the context of a specific national legal reform programme for an individual reform country. At the drafting stage it is important to identify the issues which have to be covered by the reform. Some general principles should provide a framework for the reform work. Ideally the reform plan will be comprehensive in nature and not adhere to a build-and-build philosophy.

3.16 Once the drafting stage is completed a law has to be passed through the legislative process and administrative acts (regulations and the like) have to be adopted by the respective administrative bodies. The adoption process may lead to undesirable changes to the initial drafts and can create serious problems for the reform.

3.17 The implementation stage of the reform process also comprises four steps: (1) ensuring the practical operation of the law; (2) ensuring acceptance of the law; (3) ensuring application of the law by the courts; and (4) monitoring the

---

[18] See recently E-M Kieninger (ed), *Security Rights in Movable Property in European Private Law* (Cambridge, 2004), who pointed out 'an urgent need for harmonisation in the field of security rights' (29).

[19] See 4.16–4.26 below.

practical reform results. The implementation of a law requires its *practical* operation, ie the practical mechanics have to be in place. This can range from additional drafting of sample documents to the setting up of registration systems and training of people involved in the application of the law. In the case of secured transactions the main task with respect to implementing a modern security law is to implement a workable registration system.

With regard to ensuring acceptance of a new law, as Simpson and Menze **3.18** pointed out, 'rather like a consumer product, a law can fail if the initial public reaction is unfavourable'.[20] Hence, the presentation of a reform to the wider public (in particular the reform's end-users) must be well prepared. The key question is precisely what impact a law reform has on potential users at the moment it becomes effective. Since any reform will inevitably lead to institutional and other changes which may have negative effects in the short term, its overriding goals and positive long-term effects must be communicated clearly. At the same time it must be pointed out that the issue of acceptance is not a single step at the start of the implementation stage only, but must accompany the reform efforts from the very start. However, at the time of introduction of a reform acceptance becomes critical for the future practical role of the reform, which justifies identifying it as a separate step in the overall reform process.

In modern market economies the security that the law provides to the business **3.19** community is based on functioning court systems, since rights are only valuable if they can be enforced. Court decisions apply the general law to specific cases, interpret and develop the written law, and may over time themselves create law.[21] Judges may become involved not only in deciding the substantive issues of a case but may also assist in enforcing the rights established by the courts (for example when they are involved in enforcing security interests). In view of the fundamental importance of courts of law, institutional reforms (an issue which was at the core of the third phase of the law and development movement) play an integral part in a comprehensive legal reform methodology. Proper application by the courts requires that judges (and others responsible for the administration of the court system) receive proper training about the new law itself as well as its practical foundations (such as the economic rationale and the practical working of security in a market economy). In addition, the role of courts can be limited (for example in the procedure for enforcing security, thus reducing the influence of weak local institutions on the reform results).[22]

---

[20] Simpson and Menze (n 16 above) 23.
[21] Either because a legal system recognizes court precedents as a legal source as such or because judgments become law by continued usage of the underlying rule.
[22] Other ways of limiting certain court roles may be for parties to agree on arbitration or—in international transactions—to submit to the jurisdiction of a foreign court.

3.20 Lastly a new law—once introduced—needs constant monitoring. Monitoring allows defects and deficiencies in the law, and also issues with its application, to be identified. A particularly important aspect of the reform process in central and eastern European countries has been that numerous laws have been introduced at great speed, often making it impossible for the laws' users to absorb the full details of each law. The fundamental nature of the central and eastern European reform process makes it necessary to monitor the essential reforms closely. Simpson and Menze made the following proposals for specific monitoring tasks: in their opinion[23] a monitoring exercise should include (1) an assessment of the performance of the law against the objectives that it was originally designed to achieve at the consensus building stage; (2) a systematic review of the practical operation of the law and its perception by its intended users and those involved with its implementation; and (3) a statistical study of the use that is made of security under the law.

---

[23] Simpson and Menze (n 16 above) 24.

4

THE ROLE OF COMPARATIVE LAW AND LAW REFORM

Despite the broad understanding of law reform introduced in Chapter 3, the **4.01** support to reforming countries in drafting legislation remains one of the main elements of legal reform. However, the adoption model of legal reform in which a model act from a country or an institution is mainly translated into a foreign language, is not the one favoured by reforming countries today (although it may still play a covert role with some legal reform projects). Legislative proposals based on a comparative analysis of different laws are more appropriate in today's environment. This warrants some general remarks on comparative law and the so-called principles method of comparative law put forward in this book. First the general roles (or 'dimensions') of comparative law will be considered, then some of the challenges of comparative law according to the so-called movement of 'critical comparative law' and the principles method of comparative law will be discussed, and lastly the position of the principles method within the wider spectrum of comparative methods will be explained.

A. Three Dimensions of Comparative Law

4.02 Three dimensions of comparative law can be distinguished:[1] an analytical, an empirical, and a normative (ie evaluation) dimension.[2] The *analytical* dimension of comparative law is concerned with the understanding of the notions and, where it exists, of the system[3] of domestic and foreign law in force at a certain point in time. For the analytical dimension of comparative law it is important to develop an adequate (and where possible neutral) terminology and to identify a set of relevant legal issues.

4.03 The *empirical* dimension of comparative law comprises all efforts to describe domestic and foreign law in force at a certain point in time. The description of different laws is based on the assumption that there are functionally equivalent institutions in different laws which can be compared with each other. Often such efforts are belittled as being merely 'descriptive comparative law'[4] where they are not related to comparative considerations. It must, however, be underlined that even the mere descriptions of foreign laws may be related to comparative law in two ways. The comparatist who concerns himself with a foreign law will have to undertake analytical work in the sense of the first dimension of comparative law. In addition, the description of foreign laws is a valuable and necessary preparation for a later comparison (which takes place within the empirical dimension of comparative law). Its importance for any conflicts of law issues, which in the end often rely on an application of the national law determined by the conflicts rules, should also not be underestimated.

4.04 Lastly, comparative law has a *normative*, ie evaluative, dimension. It can be used for a critical assessment of domestic and/or foreign law. In this respect comparative law raises the question of which legal model solves a legal issue in the most appropriate way and it provides a rational explanation for this. Comparative law allows the comparatist to distance him or herself from his or her own domestic

---

[1] The English term 'comparative law' is misleading because there can be no comparative *law* but only a comparison of laws. What is called comparative law is, therefore, a certain approach or method but not a body of rules of substantive law.

[2] See Röver, *Prinzipien* 7–8. Also W Fikentscher, *Methoden des Rechts in vergleichender Darstellung, vol III: Mitteleuropäischer Rechtskreis* (Tübingen, 1976) 781, who agrees with this distinction in substance but uses a different terminology; he derived his distinction from the work of the Swiss comparatist Adolf Schnitzer. This distinction concentrates on legal aspects and leaves aside, eg, historic and sociological aspects which may also form part of a comparative analysis.

[3] J Esser, *Grundsatz und Norm in der richterlichen Fortbildung des Privatrechts. Rechtsvergleichende Beiträge zur Rechtsquellen- und Interpretationslehre* (4th edn, Tübingen, 1990), distinguished problem-oriented legal thinking in Anglo-American laws from axiomatic legal thinking in continental European laws. Problem-oriented legal thinking is less concerned with systematic questions (ibid 183–241).

[4] K Zweigert and H Kötz, *An Introduction to Comparative Law* (trans T Weir) (3rd edn, Oxford, 1998) 6.

law and its historically grown solutions. The knowledge of alternative solutions in foreign laws opens the way to a rational critique. However, this leaves open the question of which criteria are supposed to guide such a critique. The criteria come first from the practical experience of the implementation of a foreign law with rules which are different from the local law rules. However, economic criteria also play a role when different laws are contrasted for evaluation purposes. In particular, in the field of secured transactions, the extent to which rules achieve a risk reducing function must be examined.[5]

The three dimensions of comparative law are closely interlinked with each **4.05** other. They are necessary elements in building a comparative perspective on the basis of foreign laws. Only taken together can they enable a rational critique of law or the development of reform proposals on the basis of comparative law. The regulative principles for scientific rationality in this respect are clarity of wording, lack of contradictions, and coherence.[6]

B. Challenges by Critical Comparative Law

The foundations of traditional comparative law which features the three dimen- **4.06** sions just described have been challenged by alternative approaches which can be summarized under the term 'legal post-modernism'.[7] The alternative approaches which target traditional comparative law mainly developed by continental European lawyers are raised foremost in the United States and form part of a broader movement which is often summarized by the term 'critical legal studies'.[8] Since the approach put forward in this study relies on comparative law and the concerns raised by legal post-modernism are serious, this study has to deal with them at least briefly.[9]

---

[5] See 2.11–2.14 above. For economic analysis as an integral part of the process of comparative law, see U Mattei, *Comparative Law and Economics* (Ann Arbor, Mich, 1997); Röver, *Prinzipien* 97–128.

[6] See R Alexy, *Theorie der Grundrechte* (Frankfurt am Main, 1986) 27.

[7] See the excellent summary and analysis by A Peters and H Schwenke, 'Comparative Law Beyond Post-Modernism' (2000) 49 ICLQ 800, who also coined the term 'legal version of post-modernism' for the movement of 'critical comparative law'. The following summary is largely based on Peters' and Schwenke's analysis.

[8] For critical legal studies see M Kelman, *A Guide To Critical Legal Studies* (Cambridge, Mass, 1987); R Unger, *The Critical Legal Studies Movement* (Cambridge, Mass, 1983); H Eidenmüller, 'Rights, Systems of Rights, and Unger's System of Rights: Part 1' (1991) 10 *Law and Philosophy* 1–28; H Eidenmüller, 'Rights, Systems of Rights and Unger's System of Rights: Part 2' (1991) 10 *Law and Philosophy* 119–59.

[9] From the post-modernist literature on comparative law, see in particular N Berman, 'After-shocks: Exoticization, Normalization, and the Hermeneutic Compulsion' (1997) Utah LR 281; V Grosswald Curran, 'Cultural Immersion, Difference and Categories in U.S. Comparative Law' (1998) 46 AJCL, 43; G Frankenberg, 'Critical Comparisons: Re-thinking Comparative Law'

4.07 As Anne Peters and Heiner Schwenke pointed out,[10] legal post-modernism raises five main objections against traditional comparative law which they called: the framework theory; the comparatist's bias argument; the hegemony argument; the contempt of classification; and the contempt of functionalism. First, legal post-modernism claims that legal thought is determined by insurmountable 'frameworks'; hence, there is no common ground that guarantees the possibility of neutral and objective meaning and value. This framework theory is not only at the heart of legal post-modernism but of philosophical post-modernism generally.[11] On the basis of the framework theory, critical comparative law should be concerned mainly with uncovering respective frameworks and, therefore, the focus of comparative law is shifted from the laws to be compared to the history, epistemology, and politics of comparative research itself. The claim that frameworks are irreconcilable must, however, be rejected for several reasons. The framework theory is a form of relativism, which is the position that neither universal knowledge exists (epistemic relativism) nor universally valid norms exist (moral relativism) because insights and values always depend on the standpoint of the epistemic or moral subject.[12] Relativism (here in the form of the claim that cross-cultural discourse is impossible) is, however, untenable since it is self-contradictory. It is obviously a self-contradiction if one asserts that two persons from two cultures can never have commensurable theories and tries to convince at the same time a person from another culture that cultural relativism is true.[13] Another argument against this form of relativism is that cultures are not hermetic, closed entities as the framework theory assumes but interchange in multiple ways. Moreover, there are specific arguments against the framework theory. Its consequence would be that one is never capable of achieving new knowledge or accepting new knowledge which contradicts one's own principles, since everybody is a prisoner of specific frameworks. This assertion runs contrary to the everyday-life experience that an individual can experience something fundamentally and surprisingly new.[14]

(1985) 26 Harv ILJ 411–55, G Frankenberg, 'Stranger than Paradise: Identity & Politics in Comparative Law' (1997) Utah LR 259; J Hill, 'Comparative Law, Law Reform, and Legal Theory' (1989) 9 OJLS 101; D Kennedy, 'New Approaches to Comparative Law: Comparativism and International Governance' (1997) Utah LR 545, P Legrand, *Fragments on Law-as-Culture* (Deventer, 1999); P Legrand, *Le Droit Comparé* Paris (1999) and the review of the last two books by E Örücü in (2000) 49 ICLQ 996–7 as well as Legrand's review of Walter van Gerven *et al* (eds), *Torts* (Oxford, 1998) in (1999) CLJ 439–42; C Rogers, 'Gulliver's Troubled Travels, or the Conundrum of Comparative Law' (1998) 67 GWLR 149.

[10] Peters and Schwenke (n 7 above) 802.

[11] See F Lyotard, *La condition postmoderne: Rapport sur le savoir* Paris (1979).

[12] Peters and Schwenke (n 7 above) 813.   [13] ibid 814.

[14] A method for transcending general frameworks was developed by Wolfgang Fikentscher in the form of synepëics; see W Fikentscher, *Modes of Thought. A Study in the Anthropology of Law and Religion* (Tübingen, 1995) 130–47.

Second, critical comparative law holds that comparatists are unavoidably biased **4.08** due to their own pre-existing understanding.[15] Like the framework theory of which it is a variation, the bias argument must be rejected as self-defeating. In order to raise the bias-reproach, post-modernist critique must be able to occupy a position beyond the frameworks since otherwise it could not recognize the bias. However, transcending the framework is what the critique cannot do according to its own theory. In addition, in order to be consistent the theory would have to conceive itself as biased, which would again be self-defeating.[16]

Third, critical comparative law raises the hegemony argument against trad- **4.09** itional comparative law and claims that because there is no truth there is also no search for truth but only ideology. Legal scholarship generally becomes a mere means for gaining and keeping the exercise of power. This claim meets the arguments which have already been raised against epistemic relativism. It is also self-defeating in an additional way: if there is no truth but only ideology to camouflage aspirations of power then even the post-modernist critique cannot be true but can only consider itself as an ideology to camouflage aspirations of power.[17]

Fourth, a further post-modernist position is to question all types of (scientific) **4.10** categories and classifications. However, the position of inescapable frame-works on which this scepticism of classification is founded has already been refuted.

Lastly, post-modern comparative law holds that the assumption of functional- **4.11** ism on which traditional comparative law is based is directed towards implied or outspoken universalism. Critical comparative law holds that the intellectual process of comparison is inescapably subjective, personal, and contestable. This position is another variation of the framework theory in general and the bias and the hegemony argument more specifically. It is, therefore, subject to the arguments mentioned above.

In summary, the programme of critical comparative law stands on shaky foun- **4.12** dations insofar as it is based on a strict framework theory claiming that cultural frameworks are insurmountable. This does not mean that comparative law should not take a broader approach than just comparing legal rules and should not take a broad approach towards analysing various legal functions.[18] But at the same time it should be noted that the fundamental programme of traditional

---

[15] Or preconception (*Vorverständnis*); see J Esser, *Vorverständnis und Methodenwahl in der Rechtsfindung. Rationalitätsgrundlagen richterlicher Entscheidungsfindung* (Frankfurt am Main, 1972).

[16] Peters and Schwenke (n 7 above) 821.   [17] ibid 824.

[18] For examples of different legal functions, see ibid 828.

comparative law has not been put seriously into question by post-modern comparative law. Comparative law can, therefore, play a role in laying the foundations for legal reform efforts.

C. The Principles Method of Comparative Law

4.13 Comparative law is a method of comparing laws and not a branch of the substantive law itself. However, nowadays comparative law is not only one single method but the comparatist can pursue many different approaches. A real competition of comparative laws has developed. The various methods available are dealt with in paras 4.28–4.34 below. This chapter introduces the principles method of comparative law.[19] The need for the development of the principles method of comparative law arises since the dominating methods of comparative law suffer from inherent limitations. In particular, comparative law in its current form is not well suited to producing practical proposals which can be used in the context of legal reform.

1. The role of principles in comparative law

4.14 Before the principles method itself can be dealt with, it is necessary to step back and examine the role of principles in comparative law. Josef Esser demonstrated in his groundbreaking study, *Principle and norm in the development of private law by judges*,[20] the role of principles as a medium for the development of national laws. From the widespread use of principles as a tool for legal development, he concluded that the foremost task of comparative law would be to find 'universal, not structure-related, fundamental principles' which are common at least to advanced laws.[21] His vision of laws which, in his opinion, would reveal beneath a varied surface an astonishing extent of common ground, was shared by comparatists like Ernst Rabel, Rudolf B Schlesinger, and Konrad Zweigert. Rabel wrote in 1948: ' "General principles", however, do exist in the most effective and comprehensive manner in private law. Legal history and modern laws manifest an abundant wealth of common ideas. Common law and civil law have never been so antagonistic as traditional prejudice presumes and more recently have appreciated each other in many respects.'[22] Rudolf Schlesinger followed

---

[19] For more details, see Röver, *Prinzipien*.

[20] J Esser, *Grundsatz und Norm in der richterlichen Fortbildung des Privatrechts. Rechtsvergleichende Beiträge zur Rechtsquellen- und Interpretationslehre* (4th edn, Tübingen, 1990).

[21] ibid 381.

[22] E Rabel, 'International Tribunals for Private Matters' (1948) *The Arbitration Journal* 209, 212.

this vision by postulating a 'common core of legal systems'.[23] Konrad Zweigert, lastly, went as far as suggesting a '*praesumptio similitudinis*' for comparative law, a presumption of similarity between different laws.[24] Comparative law, it seems, has long been characterized by an optimistic universalism, which was driven by a quest for the common ground of laws.[25]

This universalist view of laws contrasts strongly with the results of many **4.15** detailed comparative studies and the practical experience with legal unification which has progressed slowly outside the inner realm of contract law. For the field of security law, it was demonstrated in another study[26] that unification efforts have so far been based mainly on the concept of recognition of foreign security interests and that only recently under the auspices of UNIDROIT and UNCITRAL have attempts been made to draft conventions based on the concept of core provisions. Both models introduce a mixture of rules dealing with conflict of laws and substantive law; however, where the concept of recognition is used, rules of substantive law are extremely limited. Unification of substantive law proper has only been undertaken on the basis of model provisions, for example the EBRD Model Law on Secured Transactions. This state of affairs cannot be explained by a surprising similarity of laws, as claimed by the universalists, but rather by the many differences between laws in their understanding of property law in general and security law in particular.

2. Analytical and empirical comparative principles

If one wants to make reference to principles in comparative law it seems, there- **4.16** fore, that it is necessary to move away from the ambitious concept of 'universal principles', as looked for by the universalists, and to introduce a more modest concept of principles. In this concept, principles are only seen as analytical and empirical tools.[27] In an earlier study the concept of analytical and empirical comparative principles was introduced which forms the basis for a principles

---

[23] RB Schlesinger, 'The Common Core of Legal Systems. An Emerging Subject of Comparative Study' in KH Nadelmann, AT von Mehren and JN Hazard (eds), *XXth Century Comparative and Conflicts Law. Legal Essays in Honor of Hessel E. Yntema* (Leiden, 1961) 65ff.

[24] K Zweigert and H Kötz, *An Introduction to Comparative Law* (trans T Weir) (3rd edn, Oxford, 1998) 40.

[25] For a general review of the universalist strands in the comparative tradition, see Peters and Schwenk, (n 7 above) 800. The universalist strands in the comparative tradition can be found in the main historical phases of comparative law, ie (i) enlightenment, (ii) historicism, (iii) unificatory enthusiasm, and (iv) functionalism.

[26] See Röver, *Prinzipien* 27–42; cf also 22.01–22.23 below.

[27] eg the principles of unity and multiplicity (10.06–10.07 below) summarize the approach of various legal systems delineating the scope of security interests.

method of comparative law.[28] Such principles should conform to four criteria:[29] they should be functional, positive, general, and potentially universal.

4.17 First, a comparative legal principle must be *functional*. Comparative law is guided, on the one hand, by the general concept of equality according to which similar issues can only be compared with other similar issues.[30] On the other hand, comparative law builds on the expectation that certain solutions in different laws are functionally equivalent to each other. Functionality of a principle follows from it being the solution to a specific legal issue. The interpretation of a comparative principle being the solution to a legal problem is helpful for avoiding it becoming too close to the structures of the examined laws. However, a legal issue and structures of given laws illuminate each other; they stand in a hermeneutic relationship. Therefore, a comparatist will often, for the purpose of defining a legal issue, hark back to the structures of laws subject to review. Ultimately, comparative principles must be derived from legal issues. By concentrating on legal issues a functional comparative principle focuses on specific laws and avoids equating the narrowly focused, more specific rules of different laws. Hence, comparative principles must be neutral with respect to existing laws.

4.18 The response to a legal issue in the form of a comparative principle must follow from the law under consideration. It is in this sense that the comparative principle must be a *positive* one. This distinguishes the principles method of comparative law from the 'universal, not structurally related, fundamental legal ideas' proposed by Josef Esser. Analytical, empirical, comparative principles must be able to be tested against positive law.

4.19 The third criterion of comparative principles is their *generality*. A comparative principle is obviously the more general the less specific the content described by it is. The criterion of generality needs particular explanation since it is decisive for the notion of principles developed here. In order to explain the criterion of generality it is useful to go back to the purpose of the notion of comparative principles. Comparative principles enable comparative law to conduct a broad analysis of foreign laws and thereby also enrich the method of legal reform by facilitating the transfer of comparative work into law texts. It could be argued that both purposes can be equally achieved by a micro-comparison of details, ie

---

[28] See Röver, *Prinzipien* 79–96.   [29] ibid 88–94.

[30] This is the traditional view introduced by John Stuart Mill in his 'A system of logic: ratiocinative and inductive, being a connected view of the principles of evidence and the methods of scientific investigation' (1843) (reprinted as *The Logic of the Moral Sciences* (Chicago, 1994) 76), where under the subheading of the method of agreement he is in search of patterns of invariance. A different view is held by CC Ragin, *The Comparative Method: Moving Beyond Qualitative and Quantitative Strategies* (Berkeley, Cal, 1989); CC Ragin, *Fuzzy-Set Social Science* (Chicago, 2000), who rejects the concept of equality as the basis of comparison.

by way of a rule-by-rule comparison. In addition, one can argue that the distinction between general and specific is difficult to make since it is a matter of degree only. To the argument that micro-comparison is a more adequate approach than macro-comparison it should be said that micro-comparison is surely a possible approach to comparative law. However, particularly with the micro-comparison of areas of law such as security law, it is often the case that the results cannot be translated into clear concepts. Often descriptions of different laws stand alongside each other; several aspects are then chosen for a comparison. The method of types developed by Drobnig (which is discussed in para 4.30 below), the method of legal families ('*Rechtskreise*'), and the macro-comparison, respectively, result in overviews of legal phenomena only. A comparison of laws with the assistance of analytical and empirical principles is an approach which comes close to micro-comparison without losing the advantages in clear description of the method of types. If the principles method is preferred to other methods of comparative law it should be remembered that the various methods are distinguished by their different 'focal lengths'. They are all justified in their own way. Hence, the methods of types and of legal families point out on a general level, and comparative principles on a more specific level, which solution is chosen by a national law.

As far as the distinction between general and specific is concerned, it has to be **4.20** recognized that principles can be created with various degrees of generality. For example, the principle of property right[31] concerns the fundamental characteristics of a security interest, whilst the registration principle (describing the registration requirement of certain types of security interests)[32] is concerned only with the creation of a security interest. Ultimately, the comparatist has a considerable degree of freedom as far as the selection of principles is concerned.

The fourth characteristic of a comparative principle is its *universality*. Universal- **4.21** ity means that a principle may describe a legal approach taken in more than one law, ie it is related to an open class of laws. This characteristic is fundamentally different from the other characteristics. Whilst the characteristics of functionality, positivity, and generality are necessary elements of a comparative principle, the characteristic of universality is a potential one only. A comparative study may show that a comparative principle can only be found in one single law but not in others. The universality of a comparative principle, therefore, turns out to be a working assumption which may have to be discarded at a later point in time. For example, the universality of the principle of abstract contracts in German property law[33] is a working assumption which cannot be confirmed upon further examination.

---

[31] See 10.02–10.03 below.   [32] See 16.77–16.80 below.
[33] ie that the contract creating a property right is legally independent from any underlying legal relationships.

4.22 Integrating the element of universality into the notion of the comparative principle carries the danger that the other principles might lose their distinctiveness. On the other hand the process of creating principles is a new tool for comparative law. When formulating principles it is necessary to try to keep the distinctiveness of a principle as far as possible.[34] The task for the comparatist is ultimately to recognize *relevant* structures. However, the discovery of relevant structures is difficult. It can only succeed if the criteria for their definition are kept flexible. Principles allow the comparatist to design models of approximation.

4.23 The requirements of universality and functionality are at odds with each other. On the one hand the comparative principle is capable of describing properties of several laws. At the same time this description does not contain structures of national laws. Taking legal issues as a starting point for comparative work mediates this tension to a certain extent; however, the tension does not disappear entirely.

4.24 Two general issues of comparative law arise also in the context of the principles method: the selection of laws and the criterion of comparison. As far as the selection of laws is concerned, those laws have to be chosen which promise to show typical characteristics. What has to be considered as 'typical' in the context of a study depends on the purpose of that study. When preparing legal reform it will often be important to highlight some very general principles to start the legal reform process in the drafting stage of a legal reform effort.[35] To deliniate the various possibilities on the basis of comparative law, laws will be chosen which are expected to produce widely differing solutions.

4.25 As far as the criterion of comparison is concerned, the principles method relies on comparative principles which will be demonstrated in the following discussion of security law.[36] In this context the approach found in certain laws will be discussed. These approaches will subsequently be examined under the perspective of the principles method.

4.26 It should be noted that the characterization of a comparative principle developed in this study is close to the concept of a legal type ('*Typus*'). A type in the definition of Leenen is an 'elastic group of requirements' ('*elastisches Merkmalsgefüge*').[37] Such a type is characterized by the variability and graduability of the individual requirements.[38] Further, both comparative principle and legal

---

[34] See the examples of general principles of security law in ch 10 below.
[35] See 3.15 above.   [36] See Part III below.
[37] D Leenen, *Typus und Rechtsfindung* (Berlin, 1971) 34.
[38] K Engisch, *Die Idee der Konkretisierung in Recht und Rechtswissenschaft unserer Zeit* (Heidelberg, 1968) 242.

type are closely related to a 'flexible system' ('*bewegliches System*') as defined by Walter Wilburg.[39]

3. Evaluation of comparative principles

It was explained above that comparative law has three dimensions, an analytical, **4.27** an empirical, and a normative (ie evaluative) dimension. Comparative principles have both an analytical and an empirical function. They assist in understanding the notions and the system of local and foreign law in that they describe foreign law. However, comparative law also has a normative (ie evaluative) dimension which is not yet served by comparative principles. Thus an evaluation of comparative principles forms an integral part of the principles method of comparative law. This evaluation is particularly important in the context of legal reform in which the goal is to find workable solutions, for example for providing security interests. The normative dimension is characterized by the normative measure used. Such a measure can be seen in the economic functions of a legal concept such as security interests.[40] Most importantly, security serves a risk-reducing function. This will provide a measure for evaluating the various legal solutions chosen by different laws.

D. The Principles Method in the Context of Comparative Law

Methods of comparative law fall into several classes. There are methods which **4.28** assist in defining the scope of comparison (see the 'method of legal families' and the 'method of types' below), methods which deal with the criterion of comparison (the functional approach and Schlesinger's factual approach), methods which assume a certain result of the comparison (universalism), and methods which provide criteria for evaluating laws (Mattei's comparative law and economics approach). Lastly, there is a general approach of questioning the activity of comparative law as such (critical comparative law). None of these approaches, used in isolation, is appropriate for the purpose of developing practical proposals for legal reform efforts, as will be shown in the following brief discussion.

The still dominant method of comparative law is the method of legal families **4.29** ('*Rechtskreismethode*') which has been championed in particular by Konrad

---

[39] See K Larenz and C-W Canaris, *Methodenlehre der Rechtswissenschaft* (3rd edn, Berlin, 1995) 209; see also C-W Canaris, 'Bewegliches System und Vertrauensschutz im rechtsgeschäftlichen Verkehr' in F Bydlinski, H Krejci, B Schilcher, and V Steininger (eds), *Das Bewegliche System im geltenden und künftigen Recht* (Vienna, 1986) 103–16.
[40] For more detail, see Röver, *Prinzipien* 97–128.

Zweigert and Hein Kötz[41] as well as René David.[42] The theory of legal families is a way of defining the scope of comparison, and in particular of identifying the laws examined. The method of legal families groups laws into larger blocks where participating laws share a certain 'style'. The comparison can be facilitated, in the opinion of the method of legal families, by chosing 'typical' laws from a legal family. There are three fundamental issues with the method of legal families: first, the distinction between the different legal families is orientated at only a few, very general criteria such as the different sources of law (judge-made law versus codified law). The method of legal families also often concentrates on the differences between laws from the point of view of private law and does not focus on constitutional law, administrative law, criminal law, or procedural law aspects. Third, comparison under the auspices of the method of legal families is prone to circularity, since the results of the comparison often seem to be a mere confirmation of the allocation of a law to a certain legal family. Hence, despite its popularity and its widespread use, the method of legal families cannot claim to be a method of comparative law in the strict sense.

4.30   Another method of defining the scope of comparison in terms of which law to choose is the method of types ('*Typen-Methode*')[43], which was authored by Ulrich Drobnig. According to the method of types each law from which the comparatist can expect stimulation for his particular issue has to be included in a comparison.[44] The method of types also requires basing the comparison on fundamental approaches ('types') to particular issues.[45] Although the method of types partly overlaps with the principles method of comparative law (a principle as understood under the principles method is close to the concept of a legal type)[46] it shows two significant differences. First, the method of types proceeds deductively, ie it starts from legal types which it then compares, whereas the principles method develops legal principles inductively and only then compares the legal results. This seems to be more appropriate with a view to avoiding circular arguments. Second, the method of types is open with respect to its normative measure; in fact it does not even refer to the need for a normative measure explicitly. Clearly the method of types requires that laws have to be compared and criticized under this method, but it remains unclear what this means in practice. On the contrary, the principles method clearly refers

---

[41] K Zweigert and H Kötz, *An Introduction to Comparative Law* (trans T Weir) (3rd edn, Oxford, 1998) 38–40; Röver, *Prinzipien* 11–12.

[42] R David and C Jauffret Spinosi, *Les grands systèmes de droit containporains* (8th edn, Paris, 1982) 21–31.

[43] U Drobnig, 'Methodenfragen der Rechtsvergleichung im Lichte der "International Encyclopedia of Comparative Law" ' in E von Caemmerer, S Mentschikoff, and K Zweigert (eds), *Ius Privatum Gentium. Festschrift für Max Rheinstein zum 70. Geburtstag am 5. Juli 1969* (Tübingen, 1969) 221–33; Röver, *Prinzipien* 12.

[44] Drobnig (n 43 above) 225.   [45] ibid 225.   [46] As was pointed out in 4.26 above.

(at least in the context of secured transctions law) to economic principles as a relevant measure and, therefore, offers—in the sense of the three dimensions of comparative law—a more comprehensive approach.

The main issue tackled by Rudolf Schlesinger's so-called 'factual approach' (sometimes also referred to as the problem oriented method of comparative law)[47] is how to achieve comparability of different laws. The traditional approach of comparative law is to compare functionally equivalent legal concepts, ie the 'functional approach'.[48] The functional approach suffers, however, from its strict link between legal concepts and comparison. This link forces the comparatist to compare larger groups of norms and prevents her from focusing on individual issues.[49] Schlesinger's approach starts earlier than the functional approach, since it requires the comparatist to begin the comparison with legal issues arising in the context of (hypothetical) cases. The principles method also starts the comparison from legal issues, but it is different when it comes to the result of such comparison. Schlesinger's factual approach was prominently used in the context of a comparison of national contract laws[50] and the aim of this study was to find the 'common core' of the rules on formation of contracts. This approach is wrong, since it already assumes from the beginning what it is supposed to prove after the comparison. It is no wonder that the 'common core' approach works in particular in, and is demonstrated using, the example of contract law, since this area of law features great similarities between laws.[51]

4.31

Ugo Mattei combines comparative law and economics, and thus introduces another approach to comparative law.[52] He uses economics as a tool to evaluate legal approaches. This seems, however, to be limited in three ways. First, it

4.32

---

[47] See in particular RB Schlesinger, 'Research on the General Principles of Law Recognized by Civilized Nations. Outline of a New Project' (1957) 51 AJIL 734; RB Schlesinger, 'The Common Core of Legal Systems. An Emerging Subject of Comparative Study' in KH Nadelmann, AT von Mehren, and JN Hazard (eds), *XXth Century Comparative and Conflicts Law. Legal Essays in Honor of Hessel E. Yntema* (Leiden, 1961) 65–79; RB Schlesinger, *Comparative Law. Cases—Texts—Materials* (4th edn, New York, 1980) 37–41; RB Schlesinger, HW Baade, M Damaska, and PE Herzog, *Comparative Law. Cases—Texts—Materials* (5th edn, New York, 1988) 34–9; RB Schlesinger, 'The Past and Future of Comparative Law' (1995) 43 AJCL 477; Röver, *Prinzipien* 94–6.

[48] Röver, *Prinzipien* 14–15 with further references.   [49] ibid 14–15.

[50] RB Schlesinger (ed), *Formation of Contracts. A Study of the Common Core of Legal Systems*, 2 vols (Dobbs Ferry, NY, 1968).

[51] Although the study on 'Security Rights in Movable Property in European Private Law' edited by Eva-Maria Kieninger (Cambridge, 2004), which forms part of the 'Common Core of European Private Law' (or Trento) project, is in principle based on Schlesinger's factual approach (for limitations of the factual approach in the context of secured transactions, see ibid 27–8) it has not assumed the presence of a common core. It remains an 'agnostic legal cartography' (ibid 28, 29).

[52] U Mattei, *Comparative Law and Economics* (Ann Arbor, Mich, 1997).

equates economics with transaction cost analysis. This is too narrow since, for example, macroeconomic factors are neglected.[53] It also appears that Mattei's approach is functional in the sense that it looks mainly at how legal rules work in practice. On the contrary, the approach under the principles method is rules based. Although a functional approach is a useful additional tool in comparative law, it seems that the comparison has to start with the existing rules (whether written or non-written). The principles method does exactly that. Lastly, in the sense of the three dimensions of comparative law, Mattei's approach only covers one dimension of comparative law (namely its evaluative dimension) and, therefore, does not provide a comprehensive framework for comparison.

4.33 Another group of comparative methods stipulates a certain result of the comparison.[54] One can count Schlesinger's factual approach, Josef Esser's principles theory,[55] and Ernst Rabel's approach in this group of comparative methods. Schlesinger's factual approach has already been dealt with. In a similar sense Esser assumed that legal systems contain universal, not structurally linked, fundamental legal principles.[56] Equally, Ernst Rabel referred in his writings to 'general principles' and 'common ideas'.[57] These forms of universalism are particularly prominent examples of a universalist strand in comparative thinking which finds its contemporary examples in universal jurisprudence, the *lex mercatoria* school, and the *ius commune* school.[58] Anne Peters and Heiner Schwenke have traced back universalism even further and identified it in the legal epochs of the enlightenment, of historicism, intra- and transnational unification, and lastly functionalism.[59] A fundamental assumption of universal principles has to be rejected in the context of comparative law since it leads to a 'universalistic fallacy', ie a prejudice for universal principles where comparative law has not yet started its comparison. Contrary to Rabel's general principles, Esser's universal principles, or Schlesinger's common core, legal principles are mere analytical and empirical tools under the principles method used in this study.

4.34 'Critical comparative law', a section of the critical legal studies movement, is mainly criticizing the traditional approach to comparative law but does not

---

[53] For the broader approach of the principles method, see Röver, *Prinzipien* 105–28.

[54] See 4.14–4.15 above.   [55] Röver, *Prinzipien* 81–6.

[56] J Esser, *Grundsatz und Norm in der richterlichen Fortbildung des Privatrechts. Rechtsvergleichende Beiträge zur Rechtsquellen- und Interpretationslehre* (4th edn, Tübingen, 1990) 381.

[57] E Rabel, 'International Tribunals for Private Matters' (1948) *The Arbitration Journal* 209; E Rabel, 'Aufgabe und Notwendigkeit der Rechtsvergleichung' in E Rabel, *Gesammelte Aufsätze, vol III: Arbeiten zur Rechtsvergleichung und zur Rechtsvereinheitlichung 1919–1954. Mit einem Verzeichnis der Schriften Ernst Rabels*, HG Leser (ed) (Tübingen, 1967) 1–21.

[58] Röver, *Prinzipien* 86–7.

[59] A Peters and H Schwenke, 'Comparative Law Beyond Post-Modernism' (2000) 49 ICLQ 803.

itself offer a rational approach to the comparison of laws.[60] As has been shown above, the arguments raised by critical comparative law against traditional comparative law are mainly self-contradictory and, although they raise some valid concerns against the activity of comparative law, cannot replace comparative law as such.

---

[60] See 4.06–4.12 above.

Part II

REFERENCE SYSTEMS OF SECURED TRANSACTIONS LAW

5

SCOPE OF THE ANALYSIS AND FUNDAMENTAL ISSUES OF SECURED TRANSACTIONS LAW

This introduction to central and eastern European secured transactions laws is **5.01** based on a comparative overview. It will contrast central and eastern European laws with four western reference systems of secured transactions law: (1) the law of England and Wales; (2) US law; (3) German law; and (4) the EBRD Model Law on Secured Transactions and the EBRD Core Principles for a Secured Transactions Law. As far as the central and eastern European laws are concerned, the secured transactions laws of the seven Member States of the EBRD will be covered, namely the laws of Bulgaria, the Czech Republic, Hungary, Poland, Romania, the Russian Federation, and the Slovak Republic.

Within these laws the focus will be on security[1] and within this field on *propri-* **5.02** *etary* security.[2] Furthermore, the emphasis will be on *contractual* (or consensual) security interests, ie security which is created by agreement between the parties. Hence, security created by operation of law will not be covered (unless it arises from a security interest initially created by contract). Similarly, security conferred by judicial act in specific circumstances will not be looked at.

Although the scope of the analysis will thus be limited, at the same time not **5.03** only limited rights in property (such as the charge under English law) but also security provided in the form of ownership in an asset (for example retention of ownership arrangements) will be discussed. Thus, a functional approach will be applied to the analysis of security and all legal concepts which serve the purpose of securing an obligation will be examined. Security in immovables, movable things, and rights will also be covered. However, the analysis will concentrate

---

[1] See the discussion of this concept in Röver, *Prinzipien* 130–6.   [2] ibid 137–58.

on the main types of security found in central and eastern European laws and exclude, for example, security in ships, aircraft, and rolling stock, as well as so-called 'financial collateral'.[3] In addition, factoring, financial leasing, repurchase (report), and securitization transactions, although functionally related to security, will not be examined in this study.

5.04 Four issues of terminology will be clarified in this context:

(1) The study will refer to an 'interest' when the word is used in a common law context or a generic sense. Where it is used in a civil law context (and central and eastern European laws generally fall within this group of laws) the study will refer to the term 'right'. Hence, the term 'security right' instead of 'security interest' will be used.

(2) The term 'title' is again used only in a common law context. Where civil laws are concerned the term 'ownership' is preferred.[4]

(3) The notions 'secured transactions' and 'security' will be used in a very broad sense. Unlike the usage under US law, the term 'secured transactions' will not be limited to security in movables (as regulated under Article 9 of the UCC). The term 'security' will also not be limited to traditional security interests as under English law where, for example, retention of title and assignment of receivables are not 'security interests' in a strict sense. The term 'security' will be used although it can sometimes be confused with the similar term 'securities'.

(4) Lastly, 'movable thing' instead of 'movables', 'movable assets' or 'chattels' will be used where tangible movables are involved.

---

[3] The central and eastern European countries which have become members of the EU (ie all central and eastern European reference systems examined in this study save for the Russian Federation; Bulgaria and Romania joined the European Union on 1 January 2007) have implemented in their national laws EU Directive 2002/47/EC on Financial Collateral Arrangements (the so-called 'Financial Collateral Directive'). See further 22.06 below.

[4] eg for the purposes of German law it is more correct to refer to a retention of 'ownership' and not to retention of 'title' because German does not recognize the distinction between title and interest; Röver, *Prinzipien* 142–3.

6

LEGAL MODELS OF SECURED TRANSACTIONS LAW IN WESTERN COUNTRIES

The following provides an overview of western legal reference systems, ie English, **6.01** US, and German secured transactions law.

A. Security Under the Law of England and Wales

English law[1] distinguishes four types of consensual security interests: the pledge, **6.02** the contractual lien, the mortgage, and the equitable charge.[2] The *pledge* is a possessory security interest which can be created in goods as well as in documentary intangibles (ie documents of title and instruments embodying a money obligation). The creditor can take physical possession but it suffices if he holds constructive possession through another person. Surprisingly, constructive possession can even be held through the debtor himself as the creditor's

---

[1] The law of England and Wales forms one legal system and will only be referred to as 'English law' throughout the text for simplicity's sake. It should be noted that the law of the United Kingdom is divided into seven legal systems: the laws of (1) England and Wales, (2) Northern Ireland, (3) the Isle of Man (the latter two are predominantly influenced by English law), (4) Scotland, (5) Alderney and Sark, (6) Guernsey, and (7) Jersey (legal systems 4 to 7 are influenced by continental European law). See PR Wood, *Maps of World Financial Law* (5th edn, London, 2005) 17, 19.

[2] For literature on English secured transactions law, see Bibliography.

trustee-agent.[3] The pledgeholder has an implied power to sell the pledged property in the event of the debtor's default. Since possession is transferred there is no equitable pledge; the pledge is always a legal interest.

6.03 The *contractual lien* is a contractual right of detention for goods having been delivered to the creditor for some other purpose than security (for example storage or repair). It provides only for a right of detention and not for a right of sale.

6.04 The third type of security interest under English law, the *mortgage*, is a transfer of title to the creditor by way of security, upon the express or implied condition that the asset shall be reconveyed to the mortgagor when the sum secured has been paid.[4] A delivery of possession is not incompatible with a mortgage, but this is not a legal requirement of its creation. Hence, the mortgage is a true non-possessory security interest. The mortgage developed historically for land; today, however, security over land is taken either (a) as a charge by way of legal mortgage[5] or (b) as a demise for a term of years absolute. This leaves the mortgage as a security interest in chattels ('chattel mortgage'). The mortgage can be either a legal or an equitable mortgage. It can also be either a fixed or a floating mortgage.[6] Where the security is a written mortgage of goods by an individual, it must in principle conform to the requirements of the Bills of Sale Acts. This security is sometimes called 'security bill of sale'.[7] Mortgages by a company require registration at the Companies' Registry.

6.05 Lastly, the equitable charge is an encumbrance which constitutes the creditor's right to have a designated asset of the chargor appropriated to the discharge of the indebtedness. Like mortgages, equitable charges can be fixed or floating.[8] Since they are mere encumbrances they can only exist in equity (or by statute).[9]

6.06 It has already been mentioned that in the realm of non-possessory security interests, ie equitable charges and mortgages, English law distinguishes between fixed and floating charges and mortgages.[10] Despite this terminology, the

---

[3] R Goode, *Commercial Law* (3rd edn, London, 2004) 585, 649.

[4] ibid 586. Goode uses, however, the word 'ownership' instead of 'title'.

[5] Law of Property Act 1925, s 87(1).

[6] See Goode (n 3 above) 587 n 65, 677 n 7, 685 n 55; the general term 'floating charge' covers not only charges proper but also mortgages.

[7] ibid 586 n 57, 630 n 30.

[8] For floating charges see Goode (n 3 above) 676–89; although Scottish law is generally considered to be a civil law jurisdiction it nevertheless recognizes a floating charge; see GL Gretton, 'Mixed Systems: Scotland' in JJ Norton and M Andenas (eds), *Emerging Financial Markets and Secured Transactions* (London, 1998) 279–92.

[9] Goode (n 3 above) 587.

[10] R Goode, 'Security Interests in Movables under English Law' in K Kreuzer (ed), *Mobiliarsicherheiten—Vielfalt oder Einheit?* (Baden-Baden, 1998) 43, 57.

criterion by which to distinguish between the types of charges is not the way charged property is described by the parties but rather the chargor's power to sell the charged property. However, with respect to floating charges or mortgages, the parties have great freedom in defining the charged property. A floating charge or mortgage can provide for a (partial) crystallization over part of the assets as long as the property which is to be the subject of the partial crystallization is clearly identifiable from the description in the security agreement.[11]

The Enterprise Act 2002, which received Royal Assent on 7 November 2002, **6.07** introduced a number of significant changes to the legal regime of floating charges which ultimately weakened the position of creditors' protection by floating charges or mortgages. In principle, secured creditors lost their right to appoint an administrative receiver in respect of floating charges.[12] Exceptions to this rule are made for so-called 'qualifying floating charges' (QFCs). The transaction in the course of which a qualifying floating charge is created can only (1) be a capital markets arrangement,[13] (2) arise in the context of a private-public partnership project,[14] (3) arise in the context of a utility project,[15] (4) be a project financing with a total debt amount of at least £50 million,[16] (5) arise in the context of a financial markets transaction;[17] or (6) be pursued by a company which is registered as a social landlord.[18] Additional exceptions may be created by the Secretary of State by order.[19] The creditors who, under the new rules, lose the right to appoint an administrative receiver are now able to appoint an administrator; however, this will not require an application to court to obtain a court order, which was necessary previously. The debtor company and its directors were also given a right to appoint an administrator out of court (although only after giving prior notice to a holder of a floating charge who, if he wishes, is generally able to appoint an administrator of his own choice).

Even more fundamental is the second change made to the regime of floating **6.08** charges under the Enterprise Act 2002. Pursuant to section 252 of the Enterprise Act 2002 and section 176A of the Insolvency Act 1986 a fund is made available out of realizations of assets subject to a floating charge, which is to be distributed to unsecured creditors. This seriously limits the value of the floating

---

[11] Goode (n 3 above) 685.
[12] Enterprise Act 2002, s 250 and Insolvency Act 1986, s 72A.
[13] Enterprise Act 2002, s 250 and Insolvency Act 1986, s 72B.
[14] Enterprise Act 2002, s 250 and Insolvency Act 1986, s 72C mostly in the context of the UK Private Finance Initiative (PFI).
[15] Enterprise Act 2002, s 250 and Insolvency Act 1986, s 72D.
[16] Enterprise Act 2002, s 250 and Insolvency Act 1986, s 72E.
[17] Enterprise Act 2002, s 250 and Insolvency Act 1986, s 72F.
[18] Enterprise Act 2002, s 250 and Insolvency Act 1986, s 72G.
[19] Enterprise Act 2002, s 250 and Insolvency Act 1986, s 72H(2)(a).

charge, although it has to be mentioned that the Crown has given up its status as a preferential creditor under the new rules of the Enterprise Act 2002[20] and that the amount of the fund is thought to be roughly equivalent to the average amount generally distributed to the Crown.

6.09 Further changes to English security law have been proposed by the Law Commission in three Consultation Papers.[21] The first Consultation Paper argues in favour of an eventual codification of the law governing security as well as implementation of a new notice-filing system similar to that in existence under the UCC.[22] The proposed filing system would have as its basis a standard form on-line financing statement which, once completed, would appear automatically on the register; this would essentially reduce, if not completely remove, the role of the Companies' Registry in reviewing security filings. The second consultation paper also proposed replacing the current law on registration of mortgages and charges created by companies by a computerized notice-filing system where registration would in principle be done by the secured party (and not the person providing security). However, English commentators on the Law Commission's proposals have highlighted that the proposed reform might face considerable logistical hurdles in England. It should be pointed out that, based on the proposals made under the EBRD Model Law,[23] computer-based registration systems have been introduced successfully, *inter alia*, in Hungary and Slovakia and the concerns of English commentators in the light of these practical experiences, therefore, seem exaggerated. In any event, the English law of security interests can be expected to see significant changes in the near future.

6.10 Real security in the form of pledges, liens, mortgages, and charges provides the chargeholder with a number of rights of enforcement, in particular the right of pursuit, the right of preference, the right of retention or recovery of possession, the right of sale, the right of foreclosure, and the right to ask for an order vesting legal title in the secured creditor.[24] In addition, the holder of a floating charge may have the right to appoint an administrator.[25] However, the debtor has a right to redeem the security, a right which exists in equity (so-called equity of redemption) even after a legal right of redemption has terminated.[26]

---

[20] See Enterprise Act 2002, s 251.
[21] Law Commission, *Registration of Security Interests: Company Charges and Property Other Than Land* (Law Com No 164, 2002); Law Commission, *Company Security Interests* (Law Com No 176, 2004); Law Commission, *Company Security Interests* (Law Com No 296, 2005).
[22] See 6.17 below.   [23] See 7.41–7.42 below.
[24] Goode (n 3 above) 637–42.   [25] ibid 637, 640–1.
[26] There is in principle no equity of redemption in the context of a retention of title; ibid 584 n 47.

A trust is not a separate type of security under English law. However, equitable **6.11** mortgages or equitable charges can be created by either contract or trust.[27] The pledge, the mortgage, the charge, and the lien are mutually exclusive types of security.[28] Hence, a mortgage cannot at the same time be qualified as a charge. However, in practice, terminology is not very strict and in particular the term 'charge' can refer to any type of security interest.

Although there are only four types of consensual security *stricto sensu*, there are **6.12** other legal concepts which, on the basis of a functional analysis, create security for an obligation. For example, the reservation of title or retention of title (sometimes also referred to as 'Romalpa clauses') of a seller under a conditional sale agreement, an import from continental European laws,[29] or the owner under a hire-purchase agreement, does not qualify as security under English law since it is a right *in re sua*[30]. Under a reservation of title the title to goods is not to pass until their full price has been paid. Beyond this simple form of title reservation, the *Romalpa* case[31] demonstrated at least three forms in which a title reservation could be extended: (1) to all sums owing to the seller under prior or subsequent transactions ('all moneys' title retention clause'); (2) to proceeds of authorized sub-sales by the buyer;[32] and (3) to products made from the goods and other materials belonging to the buyer or a third party. A simple reservation of title does not have to be registered for its creation and is not registrable as a mortgage or charge, for example, in the Companies' Register. The extension of retention of title clauses to authorized sub-sales by the buyer, which was held to be valid in the *Romalpa* decision, has not withheld the test of later court decisions.[33] Later decisions have held that this would in effect be the creation of a charge which a company had to register under sections 395 and 396 of the Companies Act 1985. Since, in general, the extended retention of title clauses were not registered, the persons which had apparently received a retention of title were left without the protection of a secured creditor. Similarly a company's extension of a title retention to products and other materials will only be upheld as a charge if it was registered.[34]

---

[27] ibid 584, 587; for trust receipts, see U Drobnig, 'Das trust receipt als Sicherungsmittel im amerikanischen und englischen Recht' (1961) 26 RabelsZ 401. It should be noted that there are no longer trust receipts under US law.

[28] Goode (n 3 above) 617–18.

[29] FH Lawson and B Rudden, *Law of Property* (2nd edn, Oxford, 1982) 203–4; E-M Kieninger, *Mobiliarsicherheiten im Europäischen Binnenmarkt. Zum Einfluß der Warenverkehrsfreiheit auf das nationale und internationale Sachenrecht der Mitgliedstaaten* (Baden-Baden, 1996) 83–92.

[30] Goode (n 3 above) 584.

[31] *Aluminium Industrie Vaassen BV v Romalpa Aluminium Ltd* [1976] 1 WLR 676.

[32] Goode (n 3 above) 608 holds that such an agreement creates a charge on the book debts arising from the sub-sales.

[33] Goode (n 3 above) 608, 720; Kieninger (n 29 above) 86–9.

[34] Goode (n 3 above) 608–9.

6.13 Apart from the reservation of title, the assignment of receivables or book debts by way of security is another form of functional security. Under English law an assignment can be either in the form of a legal assignment[35] or an equitable assignment.

B. Security Under US Law (UCC, Article 9)

6.14 As far as US law[36] is concerned, this study will concentrate on secured transactions in movables.[37] The law of secured transactions in movables has been unified in the United States by way of a model law, Article 9 of the Uniform Commercial Code (UCC).[38] Article 9 of the UCC covers so-called personal property security, ie security in movable things and some types of rights.

6.15 Article 9 of the UCC is often seen by American lawyers as one of the great contributions of American private law in the last century.[39] Although the original text of Article 9 goes back to 1951[40] and was published as the '1952 Official Text', it has constantly been updated and was recently reviewed again (1998 Revisions with 2001 Amendments).[41] What should be clear is that Article 9 is itself not an applicable statute. Secured transactions law like contract law is state law and not federal law in the United States. In order to introduce a greater degree of uniformity between the various state laws in the area of secured transactions, Article 9 was prepared as a model law by the National Conference of Commissioners on Uniform State Laws and the American Law Institute. The first version of Article 9 was drafted foremost by Allison Dunham, Grant Gilmore, and Karl Llewelyn.[42] It was intended for adoption by the states. By now all

---

[35] Law of Property Act 1925, s 136(1).

[36] For literature on the US law of security in movables, see Bibliography.

[37] Security in immovables is left aside because this area of law has not been harmonized in the US.

[38] 'Uniform Commercial Code' is a misnomer from the point of view of a continental European lawyer. First, it is not uniform since the states make specific changes to the UCC and adapt different versions of the code. Second, in general it does not codify commercial law in the continental European understanding. Lastly, it is not an act, but a mere model.

[39] J White, 'Secured Lending in Market Economies: Law and Practice' in J Bates, L Blumenfeld, D Fagelson, V Fedorov, D Labin, J-H Röver, and J Simpson (eds), *International Conference on Secured Commercial Lending in the Commonwealth of Independent States* (London, 1995) 30–2; Permanent Editorial Board for the Uniform Commercial Code, *PEB Study Group Uniform Commercial Code Article 9, Report (December 1, 1992)* (Philadelphia, 1992) 1.

[40] For the origin of UCC, Art 9, see JJ White and RS Summers, *Uniform Commercial Code* (3rd edn, St Paul, Minn, 1988) 2–6.

[41] For the preparatory work, see Permanent Editorial Board for the Uniform Commercial Code (n 39 above) and SL Harris and CW Mooney Jr, 'How Successful Was the Revision of Article 9? Reflections of the Reporters' (1999) 74 *Chicago-Kent Law Review* 1357.

[42] JJ White and RS Summers, *Uniform Commercial Code*, 4th edn, St Paul, Minn, 1995) 715.

fifty states as well as the District of Columbia and the Virgin Islands have adopted Article 9[43] but the versions adopted are not identical in all respects.

There are a few features of Article 9 of the UCC which characterize the general **6.16** thrust of the codification.[44] The single most important characteristic of Article 9 is that it follows the principle of unity for security in movable property.[45] There is only one type of personal security called 'security interest' irrespective of the type of asset that is taken as security.[46] §1-201(37), sentence 1 of the UCC contains the fundamental definition of a security interest: ' "Security interest" means an interest in personal property or fixtures which secures payment or performance of an obligation'.[47] This concept of unity enables American law to simplify greatly the rules of security law. A second, directly related feature, is the exaltation of 'substance over form' which is expressed in §9-109(a) of the UCC.[48] Any transaction with which the parties intend to create a security interest will be covered by the regime of Article 9 of the UCC. This means, in particular, that retention of title clauses, security transfers of title, financial leases, and, in principle, assignments of receivables[49] all fall within the scope of Article 9. Article 9 has, therefore, been called an 'octopus'.[50] Albeit this approach does not extinguish the question of whether or not a transaction is a secured transaction, it greatly limits the danger of a circumvention of Article 9. This is of particular importance in view of the fourth feature of that Article, its reliance on the publicity of security interests.

Third, for the question of whether or not a transaction falls under Article 9 of **6.17**

---

[43] The last state to adopt UCC, Art 9 was Louisiana, which implemented it with effect from 1 January 1990.

[44] See J White, 'Secured Lending in Market Economies: Law and Practice' in J Bates, L Blumenfeld, D Fagelson, V Fedorov, D Labin, J-H Röver and J Simpson (eds), *International Conference on Secured Commercial Lending in the Commonwealth of Independent States* (London, 1995) 30–2.

[45] See ch 10 below.

[46] For variations of this unity principle, see Röver, *Prinzipien*, 185–6.

[47] See the explanation in G Gilmore, *Security Interests in Personal Property* (Boston, 1965) vol I, 333–7.

[48] Hence, UCC, Art 9 is based on the principle of functionality. For more detail, see 10.05 below.

[49] US law used to speak about 'sales of accounts' but in most places the UCC speaks now about 'assignment' (see, eg, UCC, §9-403–§9-406); there was, however, some uncertainty as to what constituted an account under both §9-302(1)(e) and §9-104(f) old version—see White and Summers (3rd edn) (n 40 above) 1000–1 n 1). Exceptionally a sale of accounts was not covered by UCC, Art 9 if it fell under UCC, §9-104(f) old version. UCC, §1-109(a) new version now includes sales of accounts in principle, with the exception, eg, of assignments of claims for wages (see UCC, §9-109(d)(3)–(9) new version).

[50] B Clark, *The Law of Secured Transactions under the Uniform Commercial Code* (Boston, Mass, 1993) (looseleaf) para 1.03.

the UCC, title is not relevant.[51] This concept is expressed by §9-202 of the UCC which is a confirmation of the basic idea of the exaltation of substance over form. That title matters outside the scope of Article 9 can be seen from §2-401(1), second sentence of the UCC. Where the parties have agreed a reservation of title clause, the Code expressly stipulates that title will pass despite the reservation.[52] The fourth characteristic of Article 9 is the prominence it gives to the *publicity* of security interests. The underlying concept is to allow a diligent creditor to find out which security interests have previously been created in an asset. Article 9 establishes a filing system which gives real meaning to the demand of publicity. It establishes a notice-filing system in the sense that the filing refers back to the security agreement between the parties for any details (and therefore does not amount to a full registration). This gives the creditor an excellent tool for risk-evaluation.

6.18 Fifth, the publicity of security interests allows Article 9 of the UCC to determine priorities between different interests in principle according to their time of creation and to have a simple tool for ascertaining the time of creation. Sixth, there is in principle no intervention of a court in enforcement proceedings. The creditor is entitled to self-help repossession and to a private sale of the property taken as security.

6.19 It should be noted that under US law there is no such thing as an English floating charge which can even cover most assets of an enterprise. However, US law recognizes a floating lien, which is a means of taking security in accounts, inventory, and equipment under Article 9 of the UCC, ie collateral which is constantly turning over. There is no special provision on floating liens in Article 9 of the UCC. However, since Article 9 of the UCC recognizes security interests in future ('after-acquired') property, in proceeds, and for future advances under a secured debt it allows the security interest to adapt to changes in the collateral as well as in the secured debt.[53]

6.20 Comparative lawyers see Article 9 of the UCC as an important reference system with a number of features which clearly are conducive to secured financing, and it has become a model for many reforms of secured transactions laws. A few examples must suffice to demonstrate the global influence of Article 9. The US provisions have become a model for the security law in a number of Canadian Provinces. Article 9 was not incorporated literally, but independent Canadian

---

[51] US law of secured transactions, therefore, takes a neutral position between the principles of security in own property and in property held by another person (Röver, *Prinzipien* 168).

[52] See UCC, §2-401(1), second sentence: 'Any retention or reservation by the seller of the title (property) in goods shipped or delivered to the buyer is limited in effect to a reservation of a security interest.'

[53] For details see Clark (n 50 above) ch 10 below.

Acts were prepared. Three different strands of development can be distinguished.[54] Initially the Province of Ontario prepared a Personal Property Security Act which followed Article 9 closely and which came into force in 1967 (a new Act was passed in 1990). The Canadian Bar Association built upon Ontario's work and drafted a model for a Personal Property Security Act, which was agreed in 1970; this model was used in 1973 by Manitoba, in 1980 by Saskatchewan, and in 1986 by Yukon for the drafting of individual Acts. In 1982 the Canadian Bar Association and the Uniform Law Conference passed a second model for a Personal Property Security Act. A third development derives from the Western Canada Personal Property Security Act Committee (latterly the Canadian Conference on Personal Property Security Law), which presented a model based on Article 9, on the basis of which Alberta (1989), British Columbia (1989), Manitoba (1993), New Brunswick (1993), the Northwest Territories (1994), and Saskatchewan (1993) passed personal property security Acts. Only a few Canadian Provinces remain without the influence of Article 9 of the UCC. A Canadian version of English law is applied in Nova Scotia, Newfoundland, and Prince Edward Island, and in Quebec security law has been incorporated in the new Civil Code, which came into force on 1 January 1994 and which is largely independent of Article 9.

Proposals for the reform of security laws based on Article 9 of the UCC were **6.21** made for New Zealand,[55] Australia,[56] and for Latin American countries.[57] It was also used by US development organizations (like USAID and IRIS) for the reform of security laws in central and eastern Europe. After proposals for comprehensive reforms of the secured transactions law of England and Wales had been made, most notably in a study by Audrey Diamond,[58] the Law Commission's new consultation papers[59] now seem to pave the way for

---

[54] For further details, see RCC Cuming and RJ Wood, *Saskatchewan and Manitoba Personal Property Security Acts Handbook* (Toronto, 1994) iv, 1–3.

[55] NZ Law Commission, *Report No. 8: A Personal Property Securities Act for New Zealand* (Wellington, 1989); a Draft Personal Property Securities Act is presented in this report.

[56] Australian Law Reform Commission, *Report on Personal Property Securities* (Sydney, 1993).

[57] AM Garro, 'Security Interests in Personal Property in Latin America: A Comparison with Article 9 and a Model for Reform (1987) 9 *Houston Journal of International Law* 157; AM Garro, The Reform and Harmonization of Personal Property Security Law in Latin America (1990) 59 *Revista Jurídica Universidad de Puerto Rico* 1–155 (with a draft text of a model law for secured transactions which borrows from UCC, Art 9). See now the Organization of American States' (OAS) Model Inter-American Law on Secured Transactions, which was adopted in 2002; for the text see <http://www.oas.org/DIL/CIDIP-VI-securedtransactions_Eng>.

[58] AL Diamond, *A Review of Security Interests in Property* (London, 1989); see also the earlier proposal by R Goode and LCB Gower, 'Is Article 9 of the Uniform Commercial Code Exportable? An English Reaction' in JS Ziegel and WF Foster (eds), *Aspects of Comparative Commercial Law: Sales, Consumer Credit, and Secured Transactions* (Montreal, 1969) 298–349.

[59] Law Commission, *Registration of Security Interests: Company Charges and Property Other Than Land* (Law Com No 164, 2002); Law Commission, *Company Security Interests* (Law Com No 176, 2004); Law Commission, *Company Security Interests* (Law Com No 296, 2005).

a computerized notice-filing system along the lines of the Article 9 filing system.

C. Security Under German Law

6.22 German security law[60] is characterized by the principle of multiplicity.[61] In principle, there are different types of security rights for each type of asset. In addition, there are limited security rights as well as types of security based on the notion of ownership. The security rights of practical relevance are:

- the pledge of rights arising from a bank account ('*Pfandrecht am Kontoguthaben*') or shares ('*Pfandrecht an Gesellschaftsanteilen*');
- the security transfer of ownership in movable things ('*Sicherungsübereignung*') and the retention of ownership ('*Eigentumsvorbehalt*');
- the security assignment of receivables ('*Sicherungsabtretung von Forderungen*'); and
- the non-ancillary[62] land mortgage by way of security ('*Sicherungsgrundschuld*').

1. Pledge

6.23 The first group of security rights in movables, ie movable things and rights, are security rights proper. German law provides for the possessory pledge ('*Pfandrecht*') in movable things (§§1204–1258 of the Civil Code), a pledge in receivables[63] (§§1273, 1279–1290), and a pledge in other rights (§§1273–1278, 1291–1296). Other rights include rights arising from negotiable instruments.[64] Of practical importance are only the pledge of rights in a bank account and the pledge of shares. The pledge in movable things has become obsolete in commercial practice.

2. Retention of ownership, security transfer of ownership, and security assignment of receivables

6.24 The second group of security in movables is based on the notion of owner-ship (or holding as far as rights are concerned). The law itself provides for the retention of ownership where goods are sold (§455 of the Civil

---

[60] For literature on German security law, see Bibliography.

[61] See 10.06–10.07 below.

[62] Under German law this is referred to as 'non-accessory'. However, in this study the term 'ancillary' will be used, which should be more familiar to English-speaking readers.

[63] 'Choses in action' in English law terminology.

[64] Not in the narrow sense of English law (where a transfer of the document transfers the obligations to pay) but in the wider sense of 'securities'.

Code).[65] The retention of ownership is a transfer of ownership under the condition precedent (§158(1) of the Civil Code) that the sales price is paid. This simple form of retention of ownership ('*einfacher Eigentumsvorbehalt*') was developed further by practice, legal doctrine, and ultimately customary law which, in particular, added the retention of ownership extended to other debts ('*erweiterter Eigentumsvorbehalt*') and a retention of ownership extended to future property ('*verlängerter Eigentumsvorbehalt*'). A retention of ownership extended to other debts extends the secured debt. Whereas under a simple form of retention of ownership only the obligation to pay the sales price triggers the transfer of ownership under the condition precedent, the extended retention of ownership clause extends the trigger to additional debts. In effect the same collateral provides security for several debts. The retention of ownership extended to future property provides that in a case where the purchased good is sold prior to payment of the purchase price, the purchase price obligation under the second sale is assigned to the initial seller ('*Vorausabtretung*'). The retention of ownership extended to future property is thus, in the terminology of English law, a limited tracing by way of agreement. Retention of ownership clauses extended to other debts and retention of ownership clauses extended to future property can be combined ('*Klauselkombination*').

Curiously the retention of ownership creates for the person purchasing the goods a so-called expectancy right ('*Anwartschaftsrecht*'). Whilst the purchaser does not hold full ownership in the goods purchased, the expectancy right is a right *in rem* which can be transferred separately to third parties. Third parties can even acquire this expectancy right in good faith (by way of analogy to §§929–935 of the Civil Code). The expectancy right cannot be found in the provisions of the Civil Code. It is rather a development of customary law. **6.25**

The second type of security in movables based on the notion of ownership is the security transfer of ownership ('*Sicherungsübertragung*'). It was created by practice, legal doctrine, and customary law because the limitations of the pledge (which is strictly possessory where movable things are concerned, and where there is a need to notify third parties where choses in action are concerned) and the retention of ownership (its purpose is to secure payment obligations in sales transactions) proved to be impractical. The security transfer exists in three different forms: the security transfer of ownership in movable things ('*Sicherungsübereignung*'); the security assignment of receivables ('*Sicherungsabtretung*' or '*Sicherungszession*'); and the security transfer of other **6.26**

---

[65] Note that under German law a sales contract creates only rights *in personam* between the parties. The transfer of ownership has to be effected by a separate contract in combination with the required publicity, in many cases a transfer of possession to the new owner.

rights ('*Sicherungsübertragung sonstiger Rechte*'). All these forms of security transfers are *in rem* a full transfer of a right to a new owner or holder. These transfers follow the respective rules of a transfer of the type of asset in question.[66] However, whilst the new owner or holder of the asset is not limited in his actions *in rem* in any way, he is limited by way of a separate security agreement ('*Sicherungsabrede*') between the parties. According to this agreement the new owner or holder of the asset may sell it only for security purposes, ie to recover the secured debt in case of a default. The security transfer is a form of trust ('*Treuhand*') under German law which is associated, unlike its English equivalent, with no rights *in rem* but creates only obligations between the parties. The contract creating obligations between the parties must be distinguished clearly from the contract which forms part of the creation process of proprietary security. Similar to the situation with retention of ownership clauses, the security transfer can take three forms: it can be a simple security transfer, a security transfer extended to other debts, or a security transfer extended to future property.

3. Non-ancillary land mortgage by way of security

6.27   Security rights in immovables, ie immovable things, are limited to limited security rights proper. The security transfer of ownership in immovables, although legally possible, is of no importance in practice for two reasons. The obligation to transfer ownership in real estate has to be notarized pursuant to §313 of the Civil Code which is costly. In addition, the transfer of ownership in real estate is subject to a real estate purchase tax ('*Grunderwerbssteuer*').[67]

6.28   The security right used most often in practice is the non-ancillary land mortgage by way of security ('*Sicherungsgrundschuld*') (§§1191, 1113–1190 of the Civil Code). This security right can, in principle, exist without a secured debt—this is why it is called 'non-ancillary'. Hence, even if a secured debt has been satisfied the non-ancillary land mortgage continues to exist. It can, therefore, be used, for example, for several borrowings. However, in practice the non-ancillary land mortgage by way of security is accompanied by a security agreement creating a link between the security right and the secured debt and defining the parties' rights and obligations. This non-ancillary land mortgage is another example of a trust ('*Treuhand*') under German law. The Civil Code provides for the non-ancillary land mortgage (§1191 with a reference to the provisions on the

---

[66] Security transfer of ownership: Civil Code, §929, first sentence and §930 or §929, first sentence and §931; security assignment: §398; security transfer of other rights: §413 in connection with the relevant provisions.

[67] See also R Serick, *Eigentumsvorbehalt und Sicherungsübertragung. Neue Rechtsentwicklungen* (2nd edn, Heidelberg, 1993) 24–5.

ancillary land mortgage, §§1113–1190) but does not refer to the security agreement. It therefore provides only for the simple non-ancillary land mortgage ('*einfache Grundschuld*').

Another security right in real estate is the ancillary land mortgage ('*Hypothek*', §§1113–1190 of the Civil Code). The Civil Code provides numerous provisions on the ancillary land mortgage and thereby indicates that—at the time of its initial drafting just before 1900—it viewed this security right as the most important for real estate.[68] Practice has, however, developed differently and made the non-ancillary land mortgage by way of security the most important security right in real estate. Lastly, the non-ancillary land mortgage can not only secure a single debt but also the payment of recurring payments (non-ancillary annuity land mortgage, '*Renten[grund-]schuld*') (§§1199-1203). Again, this type of security right is not often found in practice. **6.29**

---

[68] The legislator also provided that the ancillary land mortgage is the security right which has to be used in a procedural context. If a claim is enforced against real estate, the creditor can ask the land register to register an enforcement mortgage ('*Zwangshypothek*', Civil Procedure Code, §§866–868 and Civil Code, §§1184–1185). Also an enforcing creditor can ask to register an injunctive mortgage ('*Arresthypothek*', Civil Procedure Code, §932, Civil Code, §§1184–1185).

7

CHARGES UNDER THE EBRD MODEL LAW ON SECURED TRANSACTIONS[1]

A. The EBRD

The European Bank for Reconstruction and Development (EBRD) is an inter-   **7.01**
national organization formed to assist central and eastern European countries in
their transition from centrally administered to market-oriented economies.[2] Of

---

[1] For literature on the EBRD Model Law on Secured Transactions, see Bibliography.

[2] See Agreement Establishing the European Bank for Reconstruction and Development, Art 1, signed in Paris on 29 May 1990; the English text of the Agreement is printed in IFI Shihata, *The European Bank for Reconstruction and Development. A Comparative Analysis of the Constituent Agreement* (London, Dordrecht, and Boston, 1990) 109–63. The French, German, and Russian

the original authorized capital stock of 10 billion ECU, 3 billion ECU[3] were paid in by the members and a further 7 billion ECU were committed as callable shares.[4] In addition, the EBRD was given the power to borrow in national and international capital markets.[5] The capital stock originally authorized was increased by another 10 billion ECU by a decision of the EBRD's Board of Governors in April 1996[6] and an additional €2 billion have been paid in since the initial capital payments were made. The Bank's capital resources are to be used to foster private sector development by loans or guarantees to, and equity investments in, enterprises and the financing of public sector infrastructure projects.[7] Its charter puts special emphasis on the EBRD's private sector activities because it requires the EBRD to lend and invest at least 60 per cent of its capital in the private sector.[8] In this respect the EBRD is, however, able to invest in projects which are state sector projects initially and become private sector projects subsequently by way of privatization of the project company.[9] Special funds provided to the EBRD by its members are used, *inter alia*, for a Nuclear Safety Account[10] and so-called technical assistance projects. Projects assisting central and eastern European countries in their legal reforms, such as the EBRD's Secured Transactions Project, are technical assistance projects.[11]

B. History of the Model Law on Secured Transactions

7.02   The EBRD must operate, like other investors in central and eastern Europe, in a still-evolving legal environment. At the time of the EBRD's inception in 1990 the legal foundations of democratic institutions and a market economy existed only to a minor extent in the formerly communist countries of central and eastern Europe. It was not only contract law, property law, and the law of commercial transactions that had been neglected for a long time: also company

---

texts are equally authentic (see Agreement Establishing the European Bank for Reconstruction and Development, Art 63(3), second sentence).

   [3] The adoption of the Agreement Establishing the European Bank for Reconstruction and Development predates the abolition of the ECU. The EBRD's capital is now denominated in euros.

   [4] For details see Agreement Establishing the European Bank for Reconstruction and Development, Arts 4–6.

   [5] ibid Art 20(1) No 1.

   [6] Resolution of the Board of Governors No 59 of 15 April 1996.

   [7] Agreement Establishing the European Bank for Reconstruction and Development, Arts 2 and 11.

   [8] ibid Art 11(3)(i), (ii).

   [9] The whole project is qualified as a private sector project; see ibid Art 11(3)(iii).

   [10] A Newburg, 'The Nuclear Safety Account' (Autumn 1995) *Law in Transition* 7–8.

   [11] See generally A Newburg, 'Some Reflections on the Role of Law in the Transition Process' (August 1995) 58 and 59 *International Practitioner's Notebook* 22–4.

law, competition law, financial and insolvency law did not meet the requirements of a modern market economy, if they existed at all. As already pointed out
in Chapter 1, the lack of practical and practised laws on secured transactions in
central and eastern European countries at the time of the fall of the Berlin wall
was particularly noteworthy.

From September 1992, the European Bank worked on a regional technical **7.03**
assistance programme aimed at the preparation of a Model Law on Secured
Transactions,[12] the drafting of Core Principles for a Modern Secured Transactions
Law, and later on the implementation of modern security laws in the EBRD's
countries of operations. The purpose of the Model Law is to support central and
eastern European countries in the reforms of their secured transactions laws.
A round table discussion on 'Economic Law Reform: Creditor's Rights and
Secured Transactions in Central and Eastern Europe' at the first Annual General
Meeting of the European Bank, held in April 1992 in Budapest, stated that
there was a lack of adequate security rights across the region and that, therefore,
the central and eastern European secured transactions laws had to be reformed.[13]
In particular Attila Harmathy from Hungary, Petar Sarcevic from Croatia, and
Stanisaw Sotysiński from Poland drew the conclusion that the need for modern secured transactions laws might best be addressed by developing a model
law. Soon it was decided that this brief should be taken up by the EBRD and
the Secured Transactions Project was set up.[14]

From the very beginning the EBRD involved lawyers from central and eastern **7.04**
Europe in the project. Soon after the Annual General Meeting, an international
Advisory Board was formed. This Board comprised twenty leading academics
and practitioners of secured transactions law, both from reform countries and
established market economies.[15] This Advisory Board has greatly influenced the
project by commenting on drafts of the Model Law and by taking part in a
public discussion in April 1993 at the second EBRD Meeting of the Board of
Governors, in London. The text of the Model Law was drafted by a two-man
team with experience in both continental European and Anglo-American laws.[16]

---

[12] For the genesis of the Model Law, see also J Simpson and J-H Röver, 'Introduction' in
European Bank for Reconstruction and Development, *Model Law on Secured Transactions*
(London, 1994) v; Editorial, 'Secured Transactions Project' (Winter 1992/93) *Law in Transition* 4;
Editorial, 'The EBRD's Secured Transactions Project' (Autumn 1993) *Law in Transition* 6.

[13] Editorial, 'A Regional Approach to Secured Transactions' (Autumn 1992) *Law in
Transition* 3.

[14] For other international efforts in the area of secured transactions law, see ch 22 below.

[15] For a list of the Advisory Board members see the Preface above.

[16] The members of the drafting team were John L Simpson and Jan-Hendrik M Röver.

An initial discussion paper,[17] and first[18] and second working drafts[19] were submitted. In April 1994, the final draft[20] was presented at the EBRD's third Meeting of the Board of Governors, in St Petersburg,[21] after consultations with the members of the Advisory Board and a large number of other interested parties.

C. The Notion and Functions of the Model Law

1. Awareness of the importance of secured transactions

7.05 The principal aim of the Model Law is to raise awareness of the need for proprietary security in a market economy and, hence, the importance of secured transactions. It does this by summarizing principles of modern secured transactions laws. With its aim of raising the awareness about the importance of secured transactions it can already be used to good effect at the first stage of the legal reform process[22] when the need for reform must be identified.

2. Guide to secured transactions legislation

7.06 The Model Law is also a guide to secured transactions legislation and thereby seeks to be of assistance to national legislators. In this respect the Model Law only provides a basic framework for national legislators. The Model aims at providing the essential elements without being overly complex, whilst leaving scope for the later introduction of refinements as an economy and a law develop. It cannot be compared with comprehensive national secured transactions legislation under French law or Article 9 of the UCC. The Model is composed of only thirty-five articles, albeit with many sub-articles. The limitation to a basic

---

[17] J Simpson and J-H Röver, 'Law on Secured Transactions—Discussion Paper', 10 December 1992.

[18] See U Drobnig, 'First working draft of the Model Law on Security Rights for Eastern Europe' (Autumn 1993) *Law in Transition* 7–9.

[19] See J Simpson and J-H Röver, 'Second working draft of the Model Law' (Autumn 1993) *Law in Transition* 10–11.

[20] For the text see Appendix 1 and <http://www.ebrd.com/country/sector/law/st/>.

[21] cf Editorial, 'Presentation of the Model Law on Secured Transactions in St Petersburg' (Summer 1994) *Law in Transition* 12–14; J Simpson and J-H Röver, 'Model Law on Secured Transactions completed' (Winter/Spring 1994) *Law in Transition* 1–2; EBRD, *Model Law on Secured Transactions. Speeches given at the Presentation of the Model Law during the Third Annual Meeting of the EBRD on 16 April 1994 in St Petersburg* (London, 1994) which contains the following articles: J Simpson and J-H Röver, 'Preface' (iii); U Drobnig, 'The Comparative Approach of the EBRD's Model Law' (1–2); A Harmathy, 'The Hungarian Experience with the Model Law' (3–4); MM Boguslawskij, 'The Model Law from the Russian Perspective' (5–9); J Edwards, 'The International Practitioner's View on the Model Law' (10–13).

[22] For the stages of the legal reform process, see 3.12–3.20 above.

framework was prompted by two main reasons. (1) The Model Law's limitations as to its contents allow it to be flexible and to respect national legal traditions. Because of the dependence of secured transactions law on private law and civil procedure law, the Model Law does not offer a detailed text for turnkey incorporation into national law.[23] Every provision and every principle to be found in the Model Law inevitably requires careful adaptation and refinement in the light of the laws and practice of each country. (2) The content of the Model Law is not only limited because of the dependence of secured transactions law on related areas of law; the limitations also reflect respect for national legislation. Attila Harmathy pointed out that there is no comprehensive model for national secured transactions laws because it is the task of the national legislator to develop provisions and to harmonize them with the law of a country.[24]

3. Need for implementation

Model laws themselves are not applicable laws; they serve as templates which have to be implemented into national law or texts of public international law. A model law is a legislative proposal which is often prepared by international organizations[25] and sometimes drafted by private groups.[26] Occasionally model laws are used to unify areas of law within a country. For example the US Uniform Commercial Code (UCC) is not a federal law applicable in the United States. It is a model law prepared by the National Conference of Commissioners on Uniform State Laws and the American Law Institute, which has been implemented as state law.[27]   **7.07**

Model laws vary as to the degree of implementation. Certain model laws, such as the US UCC, are implemented with very few changes, if any. However, other model laws only serve the purpose of legislative guides and do not require or even expect unadapted implementation. The EBRD Model Law falls into the second class of model laws.   **7.08**

---

[23] J Simpson and J-H Röver, 'Introduction' in EBRD, *Model Law on Secured Transactions* (London, 1994) v.

[24] A Harmathy, 'Das Recht der Mobiliarsicherheiten—Kontinuität und Entwicklung in Ungarn' in KF Kreuzer (ed), *Mobiliarsicherheiten. Vielfalt oder Einheit?* (Baden-Baden, 1999) 75–90.

[25] eg UNCITRAL Model Law on International Commercial Arbitration; UNCITRAL Model Law on International Credit Transfers; the UNIDROIT Principles of International Commercial Contracts *also* fulfil the function of a model for national legislation (see Preamble, last sentence).

[26] See Draft International Antitrust Code prepared by the International Antitrust Code Working Group; W Fikentscher and A Heinemann, 'Der "Draft International Antitrust Code"—Initiative für ein Weltkartellrecht im Rahmen des GATT' (1994) *Wirtschaft und Wettbewerb* 97.

[27] See 6.15 above.

4. Model laws as an instrument for the harmonization of law

7.09 Model laws often intend to harmonize areas of law. Then their aim is to be adopted by a number of countries (or states within one country as in the case of the UCC) more or less wholesale. Examples are the UNCITRAL Model Law on International Commercial Arbitration, which has by now been adopted by about a hundred countries, or the UNCITRAL Model Law on International Credit Transfers. The US UCC offers an example for an intra-state model law intending to harmonize an area of law within one country.

7.10 The EBRD model provisions, however, do not have the ambition of harmonizing central and eastern European security laws. Their primary function is not harmonization of law nor are they intended as a complete law for turnkey incorporation into local law. This is the result of a number of factors. The area of secured transactions does not lend itself to international unification. It is very much dependent on many areas of national law such as contract, property, civil procedure, and insolvency law. Not surprisingly the variety of solutions in the area of secured transactions is enormous, as the study prepared by Ulrich Drobnig for UNCITRAL demonstrated as early as the 1970s.[28] In addition, an international consensus about the fundamentals of secured transactions is only just about to emerge. Recently the study 'Security Rights in Movable Security in European Private Law'[29] provided an overview mainly of western European secured transactions laws which may eventually serve as preparation for unification between European laws. This is in stark contrast, for example, to the field of international sales of goods law, where after fifty years of successive attempts the Vienna Convention on the International Sale of Goods finally provided a successful instrument. The failure of UNCITRAL to draft a model law for security in movables in the 1970s served as a healthy warning not to be too ambitious. However, UNCITRAL is now pursuing the project of drafting a legislative guide for secured transactions.[30]

7.11 Although the content of the Model Law is necessarily limited, it appears to be the ideal vehicle for the support of secured transactions law reform. First, it is not based on a single national law, but derived from comparative work. A guiding principle was to produce a text that is compatible with the civil law concepts of many central and eastern European laws, while drawing on the common law solutions that were developed to accommodate modern financing techniques. The comparative approach was ensured by the involvement of an international Advisory Board and drafting by a team with mixed nationalities

---

[28] U Drobnig, 'Legal principles governing security interests (document A/CN.9/131 and annex)' (1977) VIII *UNCITRAL Yearbook* 171–221.

[29] Edited by E-M Kieninger (Cambridge, 2004).   [30] See 22.11 below.

and backgrounds. Second, the Model Law gives drafting examples which can stimulate national legislators. It would have been possible just to give general advice; but the advice has to be applied and it is often only from the practical drafting of a law that the nature and extent of the legal issues are properly understood. It therefore seemed more efficient, and of more help to those seeking to develop their own laws, to draw up a guide in the form of a model law. Third, the Model Law gives central and eastern European countries a common starting point for their secured transactions law reforms. The more successful the principles underlying the Model Law are in practice, the more secured transactions laws in central and eastern Europe will be harmonized, which would be remarkable progress in an area of law still characterized by a great deal of diversity and a lack of attempts to harmonize.

D. Use of the Model Law[31] and the History of other EBRD Involvement

The fundamental objective of the Model Law has been to encourage the countries of central and eastern Europe to improve their legal frameworks and their practical application for secured lending for the benefit of creditors and borrowers, thereby assisting these countries in the transition process. It was always understood (and is indeed part of the legal reform methodology underlying the EBRD Secured Transactions Project) that the drafting of legislation is only one of the steps in putting into place a complex system in which many parts interact with each other. Institutions and rules for the registration and publication of charges, for their enforcement, and for their recognition in insolvency proceedings have to be established and put into practice. The EBRD's role in this process, in which the Model Law has served as a valuable reference point, consists of initiating discussions about a workable secured transactions environment and in defining achievable objectives, proposing revisions to existing laws or draft laws, exchanging views with policy and law-makers on the rationale for such revisions, and providing training to all those who have to apply a secured transactions system. **7.12**

When the EBRD presented its Model Law on Secured Transactions in 1994 there were many questions about the practical value of this effort. The *Financial* **7.13**

---

[31] For more details, see J Simpson, 'Ten years of secured transactions reform' (2001) *Butterworths Journal of International Banking and Financial Law* 5; J Simpson and J-H Röver, 'The EBRD's Secured Transactions Project: a progress report' (Spring 1996) *Law in Transition* 20–4; C Dageförde, 'Five years of the Secured Transactions Project—a survey' (Spring 1997) *Law in Transition* 12–13.

Times Eastern European Business Law put it most bluntly: 'A Model Law with nowhere to go?'.[32] More than ten years later there are tangible results from the EBRD's work and it is now also possible to put the criticism into perspective. The model law project has indeed been of benefit in that it has helped to stimulate practical legal reform in many of the EBRD's countries of operations. Particularly prominent has been the example of Hungary. Work on a new Hungarian draft security law was furthered by the Model Law and there was an exchange of information during the drafting of this law. This cooperation was facilitated by Attila Harmathy, being both a member of the EBRD's Advisory Board to the Secured Transactions Project and the chairman of the Hungarian Security Law Reform Commission. The draft law was passed by the Hungarian Parliament in April 1996 and the EBRD subsequently assisted in setting up a registration system.[33] Although the new Hungarian security law has been drafted quite independently from the Model Law, there are a number of parallels between the principles underlying both texts.[34]

7.14 In 1996 the Moldovan Parliament passed a Security Act incorporating many principles of the Model Law.[35] As of 1 January 2003, in Slovakia new provisions on security rights became effective which build upon the Model Law.[36] As in Hungary, the registered security is recorded electronically with the Chamber of Notaries. Consultation and cooperation with national officials in connection with the preparation of new secured transactions legislation has also taken place in a number of other countries, including Azerbaijan, Bulgaria, Georgia, Kyrgyzstan, Latvia, Poland,[37] Romania, and the Russian Federation. In November 1994 the Model Law, along with Article 9 of the US UCC and the pledge provisions of Part 1 of the new Russian Civil Code, served as a framework for discussion of secured commercial lending in the CIS at a conference in Moscow.[38] The conference was co-sponsored by several Russian institutions, among them the High Arbitration Court of the Russian Federation, as well as

---

[32] May 1994, 2–5.

[33] For early reports, see I Gárdos, 'New Hungarian legislation on security interests: an improvement in the Hungarian secured lending environment' (Summer 1996) *Law in Transition* 1–6; J Bókai and O Erdős Szeibert, 'Die Mobiliarhypothek und deren Register' in Bundesnotarkammer (ed), *Festschrift für Helmut Schippel zum 65. Geburtstag* (Munich, 1996) 843–68; J Simpson, 'New System for the registration of charges in Hungary' (Summer 1996) *Law in Transition* 7–10.

[34] Described in more detail at 9.09–9.14 below.

[35] Act No 601 'Lege cu privire la gaj' in *Monitorul Oficial al Republicii Moldova* Nos 61–62 of 20 September 1996, 28–33.

[36] Allen & Overy and EBRD, *Guide for Taking Charges in the Slovak Republic* (Bratislava, 2003) and 9.32–9.34 below.

[37] See in particular EBRD, *The Impact of the Legal Framework on the Secured Credit Market* (London, 2005).

[38] See J Bates, L Blumenfeld, D Fagelson, V Fedorov, D Labin, J-H Röver and J Simpson (eds), *International Conference on Secured Commercial Lending in the Commonwealth of Independent States. Conference Proceedings* (London, 1995).

USAID and the EBRD, and stimulated the drafting of a new Russian Mortgage Act on the draft of which the EBRD commented extensively.[39]

More general approaches to secured transactions were presented by the EBRD **7.15** in its 'Core Principles for a Modern Secured Transactions Law'[40] and with the 'Guiding Principles for the Development of a Charges Registry'.[41] Later the EBRD moved to factual studies of the laws and benchmarking on a regional basis, in particular with its regional survey for secured transactions (currently as of 2005)[42] and the EBRD survey on enforcement of pledges (2003).[43]

E. Underlying Philosophy of the Model Law

The underlying philosophy of the Model Law will be explained before the **7.16** content of the Model Law is discussed more specifically. The main purpose of the Model Law is *economic*, in that it attempts to provide a framework for secured credits with a view to facilitating the provision of credits in central and eastern European countries. The authors of the Model Law have dealt with some economic aspects in the preface to the text of the Model Law.[44] However, what is specifically needed from an economic point of view was only spelt out in more detail later, namely in the EBRD Core Principles for a Modern Secured Transactions Law which will be introduced below.[45] A particular feature of the Model Law is its emphasis on facilitating secured lending including complex modern financing transactions. In view of modern financing, a particular emphasis was put on making it easy to take security even for complex debt structures as well as taking security over complex assets. Another concept of the Model included with a view to facilitating modern financing was the introduction of a security agent (charge manager), in order to translate the English law practice of a security trustee into the context of continental European laws.

The second feature of the Model Law is the attempt to merge features of **7.17** common and civil law. In order to illustrate this thesis it is useful to indicate some of the main differences between common and civil law (if this generalization may be permitted at this point) in the field of security. The following

---

[39] See J Simpson and J-H Röver, *Comments on the Draft Federal Act on Mortgage (Pledge of Real Estate) of the Russian Federation* (London, 1996).
[40] See ch 8 below.   [41] See ch 16 below.
[42] <http://www.ebrd.com/country/sector/law/st/>.   [43] ibid.
[44] See J Simpson and J-H Röver, 'Preface' in EBRD, *Model Law on Secured Transactions* (London 1994) v.
[45] See ch 8 below.

remarks are intended to serve only as an introduction to the complex comparison between different secured transactions laws.

7.18 (1) Generally speaking, common law is characterized by its permissive attitude towards the regime of property rights, whereas most civil laws take a more restrictive approach. For example, German property law is governed by the two principles of the limited number ('*numerus clausus*') of property rights (in principle only the property rights recognized by law can be used by the parties) and the principle of strict form (ie the property rights are only provided in the form specified in the respective laws). In particular, the principle of strict form triggers discussions about the lawfulness of certain security rights. Whereas English law also only recognizes a limited number of property rights (without explicitly following the principle of *numerus clausus* of property rights), it is certainly more permissive with respect to the specific content of the agreement between the parties (which is regarded as a contract governed by the principle of freedom of contract). The Model Law has firmly opted for the permissive approach found under common law jurisdictions.

7.19 (2) On a conceptual level, common law and civil law are different in their understanding of ownership. Whereas ownership under most civil law jurisdictions is a single, undivided notion, common law jurisdictions tend to distinguish between interest and title.[46] Although the English language text (other than, for example, the German translation) speaks about 'title', it means 'ownership' in the continental European sense.

7.20 (3) A particular feature of the US secured transactions law under Article 9 of the UCC is its functionalism,[47] which can be contrasted to the formal approach taken by most other jurisdictions (except for the jurisdictions which have followed closely the US model, for example most of the Canandian provinces). Whereas functionalism is a well-known approach in comparative law, it is rare to find it as a rule of substantive law. The Model Law has opted for the formal approach.

7.21 (4) A common law feature specific to English law is the 'floating charge', in particular as a security interest covering almost all the assets of a company. Some civil law jurisdictions like French law have introduced enterprise security as well, but none has gone as far as English law as far as (a) the broad scope of the interest and (b) the right to appoint an administrator are concerned.[48] The Model Law has to some extent followed the example set by English law by introducing a broad scope to its enterprise charge and allowing the appointment

---

[46] For details, see Röver, *Prinzipien* 142–3.   [47] See 6.16 above.
[48] For changes to the law of floating charges, see 6.07–6.08 above.

of a charge administrator. It has, however, shunned the introduction of the English law concept of 'crystallization', which from the point of view of many civil law jurisdictions would turn the enterprise security into a personal rather than a proprietary security right.

(5) In many civil law jurisdictions the description of the secured debt and the **7.22** secured asset in principle have to be *specific*. It is only possible to a limited extent to make a general description of the secured debt and the secured asset and it is, hence, rather difficult to provide security for future debts and in future assets. Common law with its concept of a pool of assets, and English law in particular with the concept of a floating charge, are generally more permissive as far as the general description of secured assets (but also of the secured debt) is concerned. The Model Law has firmly followed the common law approach but at the implementation stage it is important to adapt the Model Law's approach to the requirements of the local law.

(6) Specific to common law jurisdictions is the distinction between the two **7.23** steps of 'attachment' and 'perfection' in the creation of a security interest, whereas civil law jurisdictions almost without exception recognize only a one-step creation of a property right.[49] The drafters of the Model Law felt no need to establish the common law approach of a two-step creation of security interests and have instead opted for the one-step creation known under civil law.

(7) Civil law jurisdictions traditionally either rely on full-scale registration of **7.24** security with courts or—where they use ownership devices for the purpose of providing security—no registration at all. English law provides for registration in the Companies' Register at Companies House, which is an administrative institutition and not a law court; it also created registers for security interests by companies only. US law, under Article 9 of the UCC, introduced a notice filing system which provides the public only with a general idea of the arrangements between the parties.[50] The Model Law has taken a route which is similar to the Article 9 notice filing approach. Although the Model Law refers to 'registration', the amount of information to be registered is limited and the purpose of registration is to publicize the charge.

(8) An issue closely related to registration is the possibility of acquiring a **7.25** security interest in good faith if it has been registered although in fact it has not been created pursuant to the law. Whereas civil law jurisdictions relying on registration often provide for good faith acquisition as well, the possibility of good faith acquisition on the basis of registration is more limited in common

---

[49] See ch 14 below. However, eg Bulgaria and Romania, two civil law jurisdictions, have now adopted the two-step creation approach for security rights.

[50] See 6.17 above and ch 16 below.

law jurisdictions.[51] The Model Law does not provide for good faith acquisition of charges.

7.26 (9) The concept of a 'trust' under which several persons can hold an asset at different levels (ie as trustee and beneficiary) and the assets are immune from the trustee's creditors if they are kept segregated,[52] is well established in common law jurisdictions but creates difficulties in civil law jurisdictions. The latter are more used to creating obligations between the parties (the German '*Treuhand*') or by using agency concepts. The Model Law has not referred to trust concepts since they did not seem adaptable to continental European laws.[53]

7.27 (10) Traditionally, the enforcement of security rights in civil law jurisdictions was put in the hands of the courts and their agents, whereas common law has long recognized the possibility of self-help enforcement mechanisms. However, in recent years civil law jurisdictions have found ways to introduce self-help mechanisms into the enforcement process of security rights. The Model Law equally has put strong emphasis on self-help enforcement.

F. Organization of the EBRD Model Law

7.28 The Model Law is divided into five large Parts. Part 1[54] contains general provisions which determine who can give a charge and who can receive a charge, as well as general rules concerning the secured debt and the charged property.

7.29 Part 2[55] deals with rules on the creation of charges and introduces the general distinction between registered charges, which have to be registered in a charges' register; possessory charges, for which registration is not required but where the chargeholder takes, and must retain, possession of the charged property; and unpaid vendors' charges, which protect suppliers of goods who seek a retention of ownership. Part 2 also contains rules about the defences of a chargor against a charge (such as payment of the secured debt) and the rights and obligations of chargor and chargeholder, and introduces the concept of a charge manager who is designed to stand in the place of the chargeholder for most dealings concerning the charge.

7.30 Part 3[56] provides for the cases where third parties are involved, in particular

---

[51] See 16.77–16.80 below.
[52] See PR Wood, *Maps of World Financial Law* (5th edn, London, 2005).
[53] See, however, the trust concept in particular in the law of Liechtenstein (Law on Trust ('*Gesetz über das Treuunternehmen*') of 10 April 1928).
[54] Model Law on Secured Transactions, Arts 1–5.   [55] ibid Arts 6–16.
[56] ibid Arts 17–21.

the priorities between different chargeholders, the transfer of a secured debt (and a charge), the licence of the chargor to deal in charged property, and the acquisition by third parties of things or rights which are subject to a charge.

Part 4[57] sets out a system of enforcement proceedings. The Model Law allows **7.31** the person taking security to enforce the charge immediately after a failure to pay the secured debt. There is no requirement for a separate court order to enable the chargeholder to enforce his charge and the Model Law allows considerable flexibility to the person enforcing a charge, whilst including necessary protections against abuse. The enforcement rules have to be adapted to local procedural rules. In particular, the Model Law has to fit in with local insolvency laws; it was thought, however, that the scope of the Model Law should be limited to secured transactions law proper and, therefore, Article 31 of the Model Law on Secured Transactions contains only a few general principles to be taken into account by local insolvency legislation. Part 4 of the Model Law is completed by a definition of the different events which cause a charge to terminate.

Lastly, Part 5[58] sets out rules for registration in a separate charges' register. **7.32** Again these need to be supplemented according to the needs of each country. In this context it is of particular importance that registration does not involve cumbersome procedures but remains a simple, low cost administrative act.

G. Key Concepts of the EBRD Model Law

A few typical provisions can demonstrate the general approach and style of **7.33** the text.[59]

1. Single security right

The Model Law is based on the concept of a single security right for all types **7.34** of things and rights.[60] The concept of a single security interest is even broader than the concept of the security interest under Article 9 of the UCC, since it covers real estate as well as in principle all types of rights. The Model does not, however, go as far as the so-called functional approach of Article 9, which covers 'any transaction which is intended to create a security interest'.[61] Hence, security devices such as transfer of ownership to movable things, assignment of

---

[57] ibid Arts 22–32.   [58] ibid Arts 33–35.
[59] See also; J-H Röver, 'Security in central and eastern Europe and the EBRD's Model Law on Secured Transactions' (Autumn 1994) *Law in Transition* 10–14.
[60] Model Law on Secured Transactions, Art 1.1; principle of unity; for a comparative overview see Röver, *Prinzipien* 170–87.
[61] UCC, §9-102(1)(a); see 6.16 above and Röver, *Prinzipien* 174–5.

receivables by way of security, or financial leases remain possible and retain their legal nature. Only the retention of ownership is replaced by the concept of the unpaid vendor's charge.

7.35 The single security right is called a 'charge'. This label may seem unfortunate because it may lead to the misunderstanding that the security right under the Model Law is based on the notion of the English security interest 'charge'. The term 'charge' is, however, only a linguistic borrowing from the English language. The security established by the Model Law is subject to the rules of the Model Law and has little in common with the English charge. The word 'security', on the other hand, was not used for the right created by the Model Law because it can be, and often is, confused with 'securities' in the sense of 'negotiable instruments'.

7.36 Calling the charge a 'single security right' provides a comfortable label. It does not, however, say in which sense the right is a unitary one. One has to distinguish several aspects in order to understand the concept of a single security right. First, the Model is applicable to all types of property. Article 5.2 of the Model Law on Secured Transactions emphasizes this wide scope of application. Second, the general provisions of the Model Law in Articles 1 to 5 apply to all charges. Third, the provisions on the involvement of third parties in Articles 17 to 21 of the Model Law on Secured Transactions apply equally to all charges. The same can be said about the provisions on enforcement in Articles 22 to 32 of the Model Law on Secured Transactions and the insolvency principles of the Model Law.[62] The Model Law does not, however, create a single right as far as the creation of the charge is concerned. In this respect it distinguishes three different ways of creating a charge, namely the registered charge,[63] the possessory charge,[64] and the unpaid vendor's charge.[65]

7.37 Hence, the concept of a single security right is to create in principle a single charge, regardless of the nature of the property, the character of the debt, or the attributes of the person giving or receiving the charge.

2. Right in property[66]

7.38 The charge is a limited right in property[67] and not a mere contractual obligation. The liability of the chargor under the charge is limited to a right to

---

[62] Model Law on Secured Transactions, Art 31.
[63] ibid Arts 6.1.1, 6.2.8, 8.   [64] ibid Arts 6.1.3, 6.4, 10.
[65] ibid Arts 6.1.2, 6.3, 9.
[66] ibid Arts 1.1, 21.1, 21.2, 26.1, 31.3; for the charge as a property right see also J Simpson and J-H Röver, *EBRD Model Law on Secured Transactions. A Response to Comments by John A. Spanogle* (Washington, DC, 1995) 4–5; for a comparative overview see Röver, *Prinzipien* 137–58.
[67] See wording in Model Law on Secured Transactions, Art 1.1: 'encumbered'.

sell the charged property in enforcement proceedings in order to satisfy a secured debt.[68] Proprietary qualities of the charge are also demonstrated by the fact that charged property can, in principle, not be acquired by third parties free from the charge,[69] albeit there are exceptions to this rule.[70] The Model Law also indicates that the charge must give priority in the insolvency of the chargor over unsecured creditors.[71] However, this is formulated as a principle only. Issues of insolvency law were generally left to national law.

3. Securing business credits

An important limitation of the scope of the Model Law must be highlighted **7.39** which also emphasizes its nature as a mere model. The Model Law is limited to securing business credits.[72] A natural person can only give security in relation to business transactions and not for consumer transactions. The reason for this restriction is that the EBRD did not want to enter the difficult and highly political field of consumer protection. It was also thought that adequate rules on consumer protection should form part of appropriate consumer protection legislation rather than being included in the secured transactions law. The EBRD also saw the more immediate need for improvement of the business environment. However, the Model Law can be extended to cover consumer transactions also. This will require the addition of adequate rules on consumer protection. The basic elements for secured transactions in a business context and in a consumer context are the same. It is, therefore, possible to build from the Model Law a more comprehensive system encompassing consumer transactions.

4. Flexible definition of secured debt and charged property

There is a great flexibility in the way in which the parties can define the debt **7.40** which is secured and the things and rights which are given as security.[73] The secured debt can be a single debt or more debts, the charged property can be one or more things or rights.[74] In both cases they can be described specifically or generally.[75] They can be present or future and they can change during the life of the charge, as long as they are identified at the outset.[76] The Model Law even allows the charged property to be described as all the assets of an enterprise and thereby introduces the concept of an enterprise charge.[77] These principles allow a similar flexibility in describing and identifying secured debt and

---

[68] ibid Art 26.1.   [69] ibid Art 21.1.   [70] ibid Art 21.2.
[71] ibid Art 31.3.   [72] ibid Art 2, first sentence.
[73] ibid Arts 4.1, 5.1; 4.3.2, 7.3.2; 5.5, 7.3.4, 8.4.4; 4.3.4, 4.4, 5.8, 6.8; 5.6.
[74] ibid Arts 4.1, 5.1.   [75] ibid Arts 4.3.2, 7.3.2; 5.5, 7.3.4, 8.4.4.
[76] ibid Arts 4.3.4, 4.4, 5.8, 6.8.   [77] ibid Art 5.6.

charged property to that found under US floating liens[78] or English floating charges.[79]

5. Public registration of charges

7.41   The Model Law works on the principle that charges should be a matter of public knowledge. Since Roman law, there has been scepticism about the idea that a person may create secret rights in its assets. A person who gives assets as security but does not indicate this to his potential creditors creates an impression of 'false wealth'. The Model achieves publicity by relying on registration of charges in a separate charges' register. It does not put its emphasis on possession as a means of achieving publicity because efficient business finance requires chargors to be left in possession of charged assets to work with them. The Model Law's registered charge provides a legal framework to achieve this objective. Unlike common laws,[80] which regard registration as a requirement for perfection of a security interest which has attached previously, the consequences which flow from the registered charge depend on a registration.

7.42   This system obviously requires the existence of a registry for charges. Much of the time spent on the EBRD's Secured Transactions Project has been used in working on the implementation aspects of adequate national registration systems. The information required to be registered should be minimal. The Model Law itself aims at making the procedure as simple and as cost-efficient as possible for the parties, whilst still providing sufficient information on the register for third parties to be adequately informed. The EBRD promoted electronically-based registers rather than paper-based registration.[81]

7.43   However, the Model Law recognizes possessory charges which do not require any registration but only the taking of possession.[82] Another exception from the registration requirement is the unpaid vendor's charge.[83] The unpaid vendor's charge replaces reservation of ownership arrangements by a charge in favour of the unpaid vendor of goods—ownership passes to the purchaser and simultaneously a charge is given in favour of the vendor. Its purpose is to avoid registration for short-term credits in the context of the sales of goods.

---

[78] B Clark, *The Law of Secured Transactions under the Uniform Commercial Code* (Boston, Mass, 1993) (looseleaf) ch 10.

[79] R Goode, *Commercial Law* (3rd edn, London, 2004) 676–89.

[80] In particular UCC, Art 9 and the provisions of English law governing company charges.

[81] For more details, see EBRD, *Publicity of Security Rights. Guiding Principles for the Development of a Charges Registry* (London, 2004) and ch 16 below.

[82] Model Law on Secured Transactions, Arts 6.1.3, 6.4, 10.

[83] ibid Arts 6.1.2, 6.3, 9.

6. Use of charged property

The basic rule is that a third party acquires charged property subject to any **7.44**
existing charges.[84] However, the chargor can transfer title to charged property
free from the charge without the consent of the chargeholder in cases in which
he holds a legal licence to do so.[85] The three cases of such a legal licence are sales
in the ordinary course of trading activities, transfers in the ordinary course of
business, and certain assets subject to an enterprise charge. In addition, chargor
and chargeholder can agree an additional contractual licence.[86] In the cases of a
legal or a contractual licence the chargor is, within the limits of the respective
licence, free to deal in the charged property.

7. Broad rights of enforcement

Part 4 of the Model Law regulates the end of the life of a charge, which can **7.45**
occur by virtue of enforcement or other events of termination.[87] Enforcement
aspects are essential for the proper working of security. The Model Law therefore contains detailed rules on enforcement. It must, however, be seen on a
jurisdiction-by-jurisdiction basis how these rules can be adapted to an individual law and can be tied in with the existing court procedures. The central aim
of the enforcement mechanism is to provide, as much as possible, for a cost-
efficient and speedy self-help regime for the chargeholder without the need to
rely on recourse to a court.

The beginning of this process depends on the charge becoming immediately **7.46**
enforceable,[88] which by definition requires that there is a failure to satisfy (ie in
most cases pay) the secured debt.[89] There is no requirement for a separate court
order to enable the person taking security to enforce his charge but he must
deliver an enforcement notice to the chargor in order to inform the chargor
about the beginning of enforcement proceedings. The remainder of Part 4 of the
Model Law sets out rules for the procedures which apply when a chargeholder
seeks to enforce his charge.

Articles 23 and 24 of the Model Law on Secured Transactions govern the **7.47**
next steps in the quest of the chargeholder for satisfaction of the secured
debt. Article 23 sets out measures for the protection of the charged property.
These measures relate, for example, to taking possession of movable things[90]
and the maintenance of charged property's value.[91] The chargeholder is also
empowered to apply to the court for orders in relation to protecting the charged
property.[92]

---

[84] ibid Art 21.1. [85] ibid Art 19. [86] ibid Art 20. [87] ibid Arts 22–30.
[88] ibid Art 22.2. [89] ibid Art 22.1. [90] ibid Art 23.1. [91] ibid Art 23.4.
[92] ibid Art 23.5.

7.48 Once protection is assured, the chargeholder may rely on the measures for realizing the charged property.[93] The Model Law adopts the principle that enforcement should in the first instance be a matter of self-help by giving the holder of the charge the right to sell the charged property. The person holding the charge is being given broad, but clearly defined, rights to sell the charged property in whichever way he considers most appropriate. The means of transfer by way of sale is, therefore, flexible[94] whilst the chargeholder is obliged to endeavour to realize a fair price.[95] Purchasers of charged property from either a chargeholder or an enterprise administrator are protected by Article 26 and acquire ownership to charged property under this provision.

7.49 Any interested party may apply for court protection[96] and claim damages for loss suffered as a result of wrongful or abusive enforcement.[97] Persons who may be entitled to the proceeds of sale are further protected by the requirement that distribution be made through a depositary of the proceeds.

8. Enterprise charge[98]

7.50 The Model Law opens the way to taking a charge over all the assets of an enterprise. The enterprise charge under the Model Law has three distinct features. The Model Law allows: (1) the description of the charged property as all the business assets of an enterprise,[99] (2) the pool of assets to make constant changes to its composition,[100] and (3) in enforcement proceedings the choice of an alternative method of enforcing the charge by appointing an 'enterprise administrator' to continue the enterprise and to realize the charge by selling the enterprise as a going concern.[101] In addition, a special rule for priorities exists for enterprise charges (under Article 17.5). The enterprise charge will typically be taken by financial institutions and will often conflict with the security taken by suppliers of goods, which are secured by a retention of ownership clause or equivalent security.[102] Under the Model Law the supplier will take priority under an unpaid vendor's charge pursuant to Article 17.3.

7.51 The main purpose of this procedure is to prevent liquidation and to keep the enterprise alive as a going concern. Thus, it allows for an enterprise in financial

---

[93] Model Law on Secured Transactions, Art 24.   [94] ibid Art 24.4.
[95] ibid Art 24.3.1.   [96] ibid Art 29.   [97] ibid Art 30.
[98] ibid Arts 5.6, 8.4.5, 22.7, 25.   [99] ibid Art 5.6.
[100] There is a legal licence for the transfer of charged property in Model Law on Secured Transactions, Art 19.3; it covers property which needs to be registered not only in the charges' register. For the different aspects of a security right which is dynamic in nature in respect to the charged property, see 12.55 below.
[101] This additional remedy is called 'enterprise charge administration', Model Law on Secured Transactions, Art 25.
[102] eg an unpaid vendor's charge under Model Law on Secured Transactions, Art 9, or a purchase money security interest under UCC, Art 9.

distress to be rehabilitated whilst potentially increasing the amount recovered by creditors. Under the provisions relating to enterprise administration, the enterprise administrator is in a position of carrying on the business of the enterprise and finally selling it as a going concern. Such a remedy would necessarily have to be applied in a manner consistent with the applicable insolvency law.

The concept of the enterprise charge clearly draws on the concept of the English **7.52** floating charge over the assets of an enterprise which has, however, recently experienced limitations under English law.[103]

9. Minimum restrictions

Traditionally, property law in civil law countries consists predominantly of **7.53** mandatory provisions.[104] In many respects this is also true for the Model Law. Nevertheless, the parties to the charge are given maximum flexibility to arrange their relationship as best suits their needs. Mandatory requirements and restrictions on what the parties can agree have been kept to a minimum. The flexibility resulting from this policy is best seen in the wide freedom of the parties to determine, ie define and identify, the secured debt and the charged property.[105]

H. Critique of the Model Law

Critical comments on the Model Law on Secured Transactions have focused on **7.54** three issues:[106]

(1) whether or not the inclusion of immovable property and thereby the creation of a charge encompassing all types of property was adequate;
(2) whether or not the unpaid vendor's charge concept creates a regime which is too favourable to credit sellers; and
(3) whether or not the enforcement provisions are too protective and therefore too much in favour of the chargor.[107]

---

[103] See 6.07–6.08 above.   [104] See 7.18 above.   [105] See 7.40 above.

[106] See JA Spanogle, *EBRD Model Law on Secured Transactions* (Washington, DC, 1994); J Simpson and J-H Röver, *EBRD Model Law on Secured Transactions. A Response to Comments by John A. Spanogle* (Washington, DC, 1995); JA Spanogle, 'A Functional Analysis of the EBRD Model Law on Secured Transactions' (1997) III NAFTA: *Law & Business Review of the Americas* 82–95, also published in JJ Norton and M Andenas (eds), *Emerging Financial Markets and Secured Transactions* (London, 1998) 157–73; K Kreuzer, 'The Model Law on Secured Transactions of the EBRD from a German Point of View' in JJ Norton and M Andenas (eds), *Emerging Financial Markets and Secured Transactions* (as above) 175–95.

[107] For additional analysis, see Bibliography.

1. Inclusion of immovable property

7.55 The Model Law has indeed, from its earliest stages of development, been designed to include immovable property; the Hungarian, the Moldovan, and the Slovak secured transactions laws have embraced this approach.[108] This inclusion is not an essential element, but a rigid exclusion of immovable property would have been against the underlying philosophy of establishing a facilitative legal framework for all types of assets. At the same time it has always been acknowledged that security laws often make a distinction between security in land and security in movables. This may also be a convenient approach for many countries in central and eastern Europe, particularly where the concept of a separate land mortgage is practised and where a working land registry is in place. However, the Model Law is intended to represent a starting position and there is no reason why, in substance, the legal nature of a charge as a property right should not be the same for both movable and immovable property. All security rights can be reduced to the same conceptual foundations.[109]

7.56 In many jurisdictions ownership of land will be shown in a separate register. In that case, under the Model Law, registration of a charge also in the separate register would be required under Article 11 of the Model Law on Secured Transactions. If the charge over land is not registered in the charges' register but only in the land register, the value to potential creditors of a search at the charges' register is reduced. The position of other types of property with ownership registered in a separate register (for example ships or aircraft) is similar. It may be possible to introduce registration systems with automatic computerized linkage between different registers. As long as this link is not introduced the inconvenience of dual registration has to be weighed against the advantage of easily accessible information.

2. A tale of two creditors: lender and credit seller

7.57 Early consultations during the drafting process of the Model Law indicated a strong desire to include the credit seller in the scope of the Model and this led to the inclusion of the concept of an unpaid vendor's charge. Retention of ownership has become an accepted practice in much of Europe and it was felt that if the Model avoided the issue, uncertainty would arise for lenders as to whether ownership of property had passed to a borrower, or had been retained by the supplier, as well as on questions of priority. The unpaid vendor's charge

---

[108] English law is also based on the notion that the security interests are generic interests which can be used for various types of assets.

[109] See FH Lawson and B Rudden, *The Law of Property* (2nd edn, Oxford, 1982) vi, 77, 78, 146, 225–6; see also the English Law of Property Act 1925 whose title is: 'An Act to Assimilate the Law of Real and Personal Estate'.

transforms the security of the unpaid vendor for a limited period of six months into substantially the same right as that of the registered chargeholder. In addition, the Model envisages a very simple means of converting an unpaid vendor's charge into a registered charge.[110]

The relative priorities of lender and credit seller are essentially an economic question. In any market economy the supply of goods on credit and the lending of money are both important components to supporting economic activity. If a supplier has no security over the goods he has supplied he is less likely to agree to credit. If the supplier is given security then a lender is less likely to grant credit on the basis of security over the same goods. Two parties cannot both be expected to grant credit on the basis of the same security unless they are persuaded that it is adequate to cover both of them. Somewhere a balance has to be struck and the Model seeks to do this in the context of jurisdictions where secured lending is new and many businesses may rely on the credit that is given to them by their suppliers. The attraction of inventory financing has to be set against the dangers of businesses raising money against the security of assets that they have not paid for and the lender taking priority over the unsuspecting supplier. **7.58**

The idea of requiring registration for all unpaid vendor's charges (and thereby adhering to the principle of publicity) was rejected since it would favour the major sophisticated supplier and the lender over the small supplier, who would find registration more of a burden, both administratively and psychologically. The absence of registration makes it more difficult for potential lenders to determine with any certainty whether a charge exists over recently acquired assets. No system of registration can produce perfect transparency which reveals all limitations on a person's right to the property he appears to own. In practice, lenders may have to assume that any property of a borrower that has been acquired within the preceding six months is subject to a charge unless the borrower demonstrates that the vendor has been paid or that no charge has been created. **7.59**

The system provided in the Model does not preclude lending secured on inventory. However, the lender who relies on security over the inventory has to ensure that the same inventory has not been supplied by a vendor in reliance on an unpaid vendor's charge. This is similar to the position in many jurisdictions where retention of ownership or title provisions are commonly included in sale contracts. There are many ways in which the lender can protect himself by contract (such as by ensuring that the vendor is paid, by ensuring that no vendor's charge is created in the first place, or by supplementing his security). **7.60**

---

[110] Model Law on Secured Transactions, Art 8.2.

7.61 Although it seems that the unpaid vendor's charge is both an elegant and appropriate concept, in practice law reformers in central and eastern Europe have not warmed to it. None of the transition countries has adopted this concept. Most simply allow retention of ownership arrangements.

3. Enforcement provisions of the Model Law

7.62 It has always been recognized that the enforcement provisions will have to be adapted to existing civil procedure laws of a country even more than other parts of the Model Law. They can, therefore, only give a first idea of what a workable enforcement system for secured transactions might look like. It is, however, important to realize that the Model Law does not try to promote single-sidedly the interests of the chargeholder. It seeks to strike a balance between interests of both chargor and chargeholder. As the chargor faces the danger of losing his rights in the charged property he must have a way of challenging improper acts of the chargeholder. Also the interests of other parties with rights in the charged property cannot be ignored. Where protections lead to a loss of efficiency in the security regime this is counter-balanced by a gain in social peace.

I. Conclusion

7.63 The Model Law has demonstrated that it can serve as a basis from which national law can be developed. It is an example of law reform assistance which does not rest on a ready-made solution taken from a specific national law. The EBRD's Secured Transactions Project also recognized that legal reform is not only the drafting of legislation but rather a complex process in which drafting is only one step. Therefore, the Model Law enables an application of what was earlier called the 'choice model of legal reform'. Both the method of using a model law for the purpose of law reform and the principles of secured transactions law underlying the Model Law[111] (if not its actual text) may stimulate future reform work. As already indicated in the Preface, it may well be that this exercise of developing modern legislation for secured transactions in central and eastern Europe will even provide useful lessons for other parts of the world.

---

[111] Which were summarized in the EBRD 'Core Principles for a Modern Secured Transactions Law'; see next chapter.

8

THE EBRD CORE PRINCIPLES
FOR A MODERN SECURED
TRANSACTIONS LAW

A. Purpose of the Core Principles

In 1997 the Model Law was complemented by the European Bank's 'General **8.01** Principles of a Modern Secured Transactions Law'[1] which were redrafted and renamed as 'Core Principles for a Secured Transactions Law'.[2] Looking at the methodology of law reform developed for the purpose of the EBRD Secured

---

[1] See J-H Röver and J Simpson, *General Principles of a Modern Secured Transactions Law* (London, 1997), also published in (1997) III *NAFTA: Law & Business Review of the Americas* 73–81 and in JJ Norton and M Andenas (eds), *Emerging Financial Markets and Secured Transactions* (London, 1998) 143–55.

[2] For the text see Appendix 2 and <http://www.ebrd.com/country/sector/law/st/>; see also F Dahan and J Simpson, 'The European Bank for Reconstruction and Development's Secured Transactions Project: a model law and ten core principles for a modern secured transactions law in countries of Central and Eastern Europe (and elsewhere)' in E-M Kieninger (ed), *Security Rights in Movable Property in European Private Law* (Cambridge, 2004) 98, 101.

Transactions Project,[3] the Model Law provides a template for the drafting stage. However, before drafting can even begin there must a consensus on the need for reform and the basic reform goals which are formulated during the commitment stage. It is these elements of the reform process which the Core Principles seek to address.

8.02 The relationship between the Core Principles and the Model Law is close, since the Core Principles formulate more generally what was implemented in a specific draft for the purposes of the Model Law. The close relationship between Core Principles and Model Law is not surprising given the history of the Model Law. The way in which the Model Law was drafted was to postulate a set of general principles (which were derived primarily by comparing different laws and by defining the economic rationale of secured transactions law). To be sure, the Model Law is only one option of implementing the Core Principles; there are certainly other ways of implementing them in an adequate way. However, in clearly spelling out how the Core Principles could be implemented the Model Law assists in further understanding the full scope of the Principles.

8.03 To a large extent the Core Principles form analytical and empirical, comparative principles in the sense of the 'principles method' of comparative law.[4] Hence, the Core Principles correspond to the principles method of comparative law in that they formulate relevant principles in the sense of this method. It should be noted, however, that they are limited to a set of principles dealing with the Model Law only, whereas the comparative principles under the principles method of comparative law are used for comparing different laws. The Core Principles not only contain analytical and empirical, comparative principles, they also contain certain principles which can be used for the *evaluation* of analytical and empirical principles. It is this twofold nature which should be borne in mind when analysing the Core Principles.

B. Purpose of Security and Objectives of Reform

8.04 The first Principle is 'that security should reduce the risk of giving credit, leading to an increased availability of credit on improved terms'. This goes back to the economic rationale of security which was discussed earlier. The Model Law builds on the microeconomic functions of security and aims at creating the macroeconomic effects already discussed. The fundamental assumption for achieving the economic goals of security is that security reduces the risk of

---

[3] See 3.10–3.20 above.   [4] See 4.13–4.27 above.

providing credit from the perspective of the credit provider. This principle is clearly a tool to evaluate security laws.

C. Effectiveness of Security Law—Ensuring that Security Achieves its Purpose

1. Quality of the security right and manner of creation[5]

The next group of principles is concerned with the effectiveness of secured **8.05** transactions law. These principles do not deal with specific aspects of a security right but again provide tools for the evaluation of the law. The first principle to be mentioned in this context is the second Principle which appears to consist in fact of three principles, ie 'the law should enable (i) the quick, cheap and simple creation (ii) of a *proprietary* security right [emphasis added] (iii) without depriving the person giving the security of the use of his assets'.[6] The second Principle, hence, introduces the concept that the security right provided should be proprietary. This fundamental nature of the security right is confirmed, for example, by Principle 3, which provides for satisfaction from security in priority to third persons, and by Principle 5, which deals with the effectiveness of security against third persons in the insolvency of the person providing security. Particularly relevant in the context of the effectiveness of secured transactions law is the focus on the effectiveness of the creation process. Not only do the Core Principles require a reduction of transaction costs but they also remind law-makers to allow 'quick and simple' creation.

2. Costs of creating, maintaining, and exercising the security right

The first Core Principle will only be effective if transaction costs do not effect- **8.06** ively prohibit the use of security. Hence, under the sixth Principle 'the costs of taking, maintaining and enforcing security should be low'. The transaction costs for the creation of security were already mentioned in the second Principle. However, whereas the second Principle focuses generally on creation, the sixth Principle highlights again the transaction costs, for all aspects of secured transactions law. The explanatory text of the Core Principles points out correctly that high transaction costs will immediately be reflected in the price of credit and are, therefore, bound to lead to a reduction of activity in the credit market.

---

[5] The concept of 'certainty of the security right' which was to be found in the General Principles was not included in the Core Principles.
[6] For the second Principle see 8.11 below.

3. Means of recovery of the debt from the secured assets

8.07 The first principle can only be implemented if there are effective means of enforcing a security right. Hence, the fourth Principle asks that 'enforcement procedures should enable prompt realisation at market value of the assets given as security'. Not only must the creation of a security right be swift; the enforcement must also be a prompt process. As far as the proceeds of enforcement are concerned, the Core Principles point out that the assets should be sold at market value.

D. Encouraging the Use of Security in the Widest Possible Range of Circumstances

1. Contractual flexibility

8.08 Whereas the last two groups of Core Principles were tools for evaluating security legislation, the third group of Core Principles can be interpreted as analytical and empirical principles. They are direct reflections of provisions in the Model Law. For example, under Principle 10, 'as far as possible the parties should be able to adapt security to the needs of their particular transaction'. The Core Principles see the operation of security law mainly as a task for the parties. This view is clearly influenced by the general view taken under the Model Law that it provides rules only for commercial transactions and not consumer transactions.

2. Types of assets, types of debts, and types of person

8.09 According to Principle 7 'security should be available (a) over all types of assets, (b) to secure all types of debts, and (c) between all types of person'. In the earlier version of the Core Principles (which were then still referred to as the 'General Principles') this point was spelt out further. The General Principles stated as far as assets are concerned that (1) security can be given over all types of assets, (2) it can be given over assets which are acquired subsequently, and (3) it may be given over a changing pool of assets. As far as the secured debt is concerned, they specified that (1) security can be given for any present or future debt or debts and (2) it can be given for a changing pool of debt. As far as the person providing security is concerned, the General Principles stated that security may be given to any person to whom the secured debt is owed. All these specific rules remain correct. However, Core Principle 7 now summarizes all the specific points in one simple principle.

3. Publicity

Pursuant to Principle 8 'there should be an effective means of publicising **8.10** the existence of security rights'. The commentary to the principle recognizes possession, notification, or registration as means of publicizing a security right. Obviously, where possible, publication of security should be by way of registration (either by full registration or by notice filing),[7] thus not preventing the person providing security from using the charged assets, particularly where movable things are concerned.

4. The person giving security may hold and use the secured assets

The second Principle provides also that 'the law should not deprive the person **8.11** giving the security of the use of his assets'. This is an analytical and empirical principle (like the other principles of the third group) whose main application is that security over movable assets should in principle not be possessory. It was one of the cardinal deficiencies of traditional civil law security laws that they provided mainly for possessory security in movable things and this principle states firmly that this defect should be overcome.

5. Priorities

Under Principle 9 'the law should establish rules governing competing rights of **8.12** persons holding security and other persons claiming rights in the assets given as security'. Clearly a law relying on limited property rights should deal with the issue of competing rights by providing simple priority rules. Where ownership-based security is concerned, good faith acquisition may play a role in determining the rights of competing securityholders.

6. Enforcement

Pursuant to Principle 3 'if the secured debt is not paid, the holder of security **8.13** should be able to have the charged assets realised and to have the proceeds applied towards satisfaction of his claim prior to other creditors'.[8] Priority against third persons is a key element of a proprietary right and therefore highlighted in the Core Principles.

---

[7] For this distinction, see ch 16 below.
[8] It would probably be useful to add 'general' creditors since there may be—at least in insolvency proceedings which are covered by the broad wording of this Principle—specific creditors with prior rights.

7. Insolvency

8.14 Under Principle 5 'the security right should continue to be effective and enforceable after the bankruptcy or insolvency of the person who has given it'. Again this is a key element of a proprietary right. However, the explanatory text of the Core Principles recognizes that this principle may find exceptions in practice, in particular with a view to a moratorium with respect to the realization of security in the interest of keeping a company or other enterprise as a going concern.

9

CENTRAL AND EASTERN EUROPEAN SECURED TRANSACTIONS LAWS

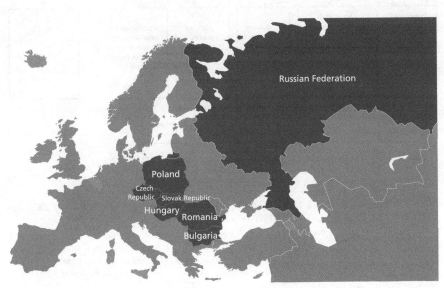

Figure 9.1. Map of central and eastern European reference countries

A. Bulgarian Law

9.01 Bulgarian law[1] provides in Article 133 of the Law on Obligations and Contracts that in principle the debtor's 'entire property' shall serve as a basis for the satisfaction of the creditors's rights. However, Articles 138 to 148 of the Law introduce the guarantee as a means of securing obligations by a personal right. In its 1950 Law on Obligations and Contracts, Bulgarian law sets out a number of traditional security rights.[2] They are the traditional security rights of the civil law tradition, namely the possessory pledge of movables;[3] the pledge of receivables, which requires the notification of the debtor of the pledged receivables for its enforceability against the debtor;[4] and the mortgage in immovables which must be recorded with the recording office administered by the regional courts.[5] The possessory pledge of movable things and the pledge of receivables are similar to the pledges found under many other civil law jurisdictions (including German law) and meet the same practical limitations in modern business

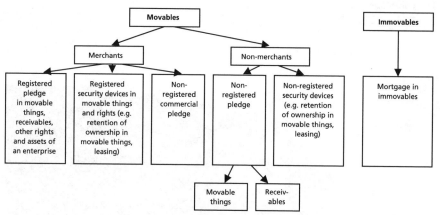

Figure 9.2. Main proprietary security rights under Bulgarian law

---

[1] See J Simpson and J-H Röver, *Comments on the Current State and Reform of Bulgarian Collateral Law* (Washington, DC, 1995).

[2] Law on Obligations and Contracts, Art 149 refers to security in the form of a pledge or a mortgage. Security rights are regulated in the context of the Law of 'Obligations' since they secure debts. However, Bulgarian law conceptualizes security rights—like other legal systems—as proprietary rights, ie rights which are created in defined assets and which are satisfied preferentially in enforcement and the debtor's insolvency.

[3] See ibid, Art 156. Possession is a requirement for the 'validity' of the pledge contract and not—as in most other civil law jurisdictions—a requirement for the creation of the security right as such.

[4] ibid, Art 162.

[5] ibid, Art 166. The records are paper-based and contain notarial deeds. Searching has to be done against the name of the parties and is cumbersome in practice. The Law on Cadastre and Property Register provided a land register in electronic form; however, this has not yet been implemented.

life. For all practical purposes they can be regarded as almost obsolete security rights.

The traditional trio of security rights is complemented by a 'non-possessory, **9.02** registered pledge' which is governed by the Law on Registered Pledges, adopted on 22 September 1996 and in force since 1 April 1997.[6] The registered pledge can be created in movable things, receivables and other rights (mainly securities, shares in partnerships,[7] and limited liability companies, as well as dematerialized shares in joint stock companies),[8] and the assets of an enterprise.[9] In principle such a pledge can be created only if the pledgor is a merchant.[10] A registered pledge is valid and enforceable against third persons only if it is registered in a register for pledges.[11]

There is also a 'commercial pledge' (governed by the Law on Commerce, the **9.03** Law on Registered Pledges and the Law on Obligations and Contracts), which secures rights arising from 'commercial transactions', ie transactions involving merchants on both sides of the agreement. However, commercial pledges in movable things mostly require dispossession similar to the simple possessory pledge and are left outside the scope of this study.

With regard to other security devices in movable things and rights (quasi- **9.04** security beyond the traditional limited security rights) such as retention of ownership in movable things, leasing, security assignment of receivables, and security transfer of ownership, Bulgarian law opts for an Article 9 UCC-like approach where these security devices are provided by a merchant.[12] These quasi-security transactions, which are defined in Article 12(2) of the Law on Registered Pledges, may be pursued by the parties but their priority against third

---

[6] An amendment was made on 24 April 2006.

[7] There are two types of partnership under Bulgarian law, a general partnership and a limited partnership. Pursuant to Law on Commerce, Art 76 a general partnership is a partnership formed by two or more persons for the purpose of pursuing commercial transactions under a trade name. The partners shall be liable jointly and severally and their liability shall be unlimited. Pursuant to ibid Art 99 a limited partnership is a partnership formed by two or more persons for the purpose of pursuing commercial transactions under a trade name; however, one or more of the partners shall be liable jointly and severally for the partnership's obligations and their liability is unlimited, whereas the other partners' liability shall be limited to the amount of their contribution. Both limited and general partnerships are legal entities under Bulgarian law.

[8] A pledge of shares is created in different ways depending on the type of share. Ordinary shares are pledged by endorsement and transfer of possession.

[9] Law on Registered Pledges, Art 4.

[10] Or another person referred to in Law on Commerce, Art 2 (see Law on Registered Pledges, Art 3). This is similar to the limitation of scope under the EBRD Model Law.

[11] Law on Registered Pledges, Art 12(1).

[12] ibid Art 3. The EBRD Model Law has a similar limitation of scope for so-called unpaid vendor charges, which are essentially retention of ownership clauses, creating a charge.

persons[13] depends on their registration in the pledges register.[14] Hence, as far as registration is concerned, they are treated like a registered pledge. However, whereas security devices under Article 9 of the UCC legally create only a security interest—notwithstanding the true legal nature of the transaction intended by the parties—the security devices under Bulgarian law retain their own legal nature upon their perfection. Security devices are not subject to the same rules as pledges generally and there is no concept of a single set of rules for all transactions that are intended to create a security right (irrespective of form). Hence, Bulgarian law only implements the substance principle of Article 9 of the UCC (also referred to as the 'principle of functionality') to a limited extent.

9.05 Security devices created by non-merchants (or other persons referred to in Article 2 of the Law on Commerce) are not subject to registration.

B. Czech Law

9.06 Czech law on secured transactions is governed mainly by sections 152 to 174 of the Civil Code of the Czech Republic,[15] which entered into force on 1 January 2002. Czech secured transactions law is characterized by the same duality as some other continental European secured transactions laws (such as German law): on the one hand there are the traditional security rights provided under the

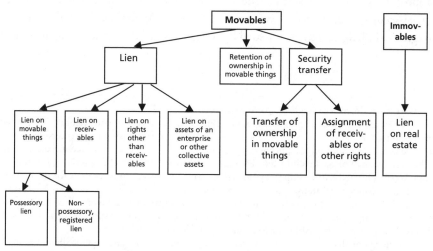

Figure 9.3. Main proprietary security rights under Czech law

---

[13] In US secured transactions law the effectiveness of security interests against third persons is referred to as 'perfection'.

[14] Law on Registered Pledges, Art 12(2).   [15] Act No 40/1964, as amended.

Czech Civil Code and on the other hand non-possessory security rights developed by practice and case law. The traditional security rights are the lien on real estate,[16] the lien on movable things,[17] the lien on receivables,[18] and the lien on rights other than receivables.[19] The lien on real estate is created upon registration in the real estate register ('cadastre') whereas the lien on movable things is created in principle upon the transfer of possession to the lienholder. However, the parties may agree that a transfer of possession to movable things is not required; such a lien is created only if it is registered in the Collateral Register,[20] which was established in computerized form in 2002. The lien on receivables requires the notification of the receivable's debtor to be effective towards him.[21] Liens can also be created in rights other than receivables, in particular shares of partnerships and companies,[22] securities (including mortgage bonds), and intellectual property rights.[23] A particular form of security right is the lien on the assets of an enterprise or other collective assets which is provided explicitly by the Civil Code[24] and which has to be registered in the Collateral Register.[25] The introduction of the non-possessory, registered lien in movable things and the lien on the assets of an enterprise was the main thrust of the Czech Civil Code's amendment in 2002.

Given the practical limitations of security in movables (both movable things and rights) which are provided by the requirement of a transfer of possession for security in movable things prior to the reform of the Civil Code in 2002 and the requirement of a notification of a debtor for a lien in receivables (which still exists), Czech law developed a number of security rights in legal practice and case law which do not require possession or notification. In particular, Czech law adopted the security transfer of ownership in movable things[26] and the **9.07**

---

[16] Civil Code, s 157 and Commercial Code, s 299. Czech law provides only an ancillary lien on real estate, ie a security right which is directly dependent in its existence on the secured debt (see Civil Code, s 152: 'to secure a receivable'). The non-ancillary land mortgage known to German law has not been adopted by Czech law.

[17] Civil Code, s 157.   [18] ibid s 159.

[19] ibid s 154. This was introduced in the Civil Code by the 2002 reform but surprisingly not provided under the previous version of the Civil Code.

[20] ibid s 158(1).

[21] Alternatively the lienholder can provide proof to the receivable's debtor that the lien was established (ibid, s 159(2), second case).

[22] For discussion in Czech pre-reform legal literature about the possibility of liens in shares, see TO Schorling, *Das Recht der Kreditsicherheiten in der Tschechischen Republik* (Berlin, 2000) 99–102.

[23] Civil Code, s 154. See for a lien in trademarks Trademark Law, s 17 which requires registration in the trademark register, and Schorling (n 22 above) 102 (whose comments refer to Act No 137/1995, the previous version of the Trademark Law).

[24] Civil Code, s 153(1).   [25] ibid s 158(1).

[26] Based on Civil Code, s 553 which provides in para 1 that the performance of an obligation can be secured by the assignment of a right (eg ownership) held by the debtor. There is controversy in Czech legal literature whether s 553 really amounts to the transfer of ownership (similar

security assignment of receivables or other rights[27] similar to the security devices to be found under German law.[28] Both security rights require no publicity towards third parties for their creation and are, hence, secret security devices. It should be noted that the provision of section 553 of the Civil Code does not limit the security transfer of ownership to movable things. However, there is no practical need for a security transfer of ownership in immovables, since the lien on real estate allows the person giving security to keep possession of the secured asset.[29] Although the non-possessory, registered lien in movable things has made the need for a security transfer of ownership in movable things less necessary, in practice it is still a widely used security device. The Civil Code changes with respect to liens did not address questions of the general description of the secured debt or assets or the issues of future assets. That may also explain why the concept of security transfer is still commonly used.

9.08 The concept of security transfer is complemented by the retention of ownership in movable things as a means of securing sales credits. In view of the rather sketchy regulatory treatment of secured transactions in Czech codified law (even after the 2002 reform) the current state of Czech secured transactions law is best characterized by the title of an article on Czech secured transactions law: 'a case of pre-reform'.[30] Work on additional reforms of the Czech Republic's secured transactions law is still ongoing.

C. Hungarian Law

9.09 Hungary reformed its secured transactions law as one of the first transition countries. Work on a new Hungarian draft secured transactions law was furthered by the EBRD Model Law and there was an exchange of information during the drafting of this law. This cooperation was facilitated by Attila Harmathy, being both a member of the EBRD's Advisory Board to the Secured Transactions Project and the chairman of the Hungarian Security Law Reform Commission. Hungary started work on modifying its laws on charges in 1992 and this led to an amendment to the Civil Code in April 1996. In December

---

to the situation under German law) or whether it simply permits an agreement to prohibit the transfer of ownership. If one holds the opinion that it amounts to a transfer of ownership, it is unclear how ownership is retransferred to the initial owner upon satisfaction of the secured debt. For more detail, see Schorling (n 22 above) 76–7.

[27] Civil Code, ss 554, 524–530.

[28] See generally Schorling (n 19 above) 76–86, 103–9; TO Schorling, 'Secured transactions in the Czech Republic—a case of pre-reform (Autumn 2000) *Law in Transition* 66–9.

[29] Schorling (n 22 above) 83.

[30] TO Schorling 'Secured transactions in the Czech Republic—a case of pre-reform (Autumn 2000) *Law in Transition* 66–9.

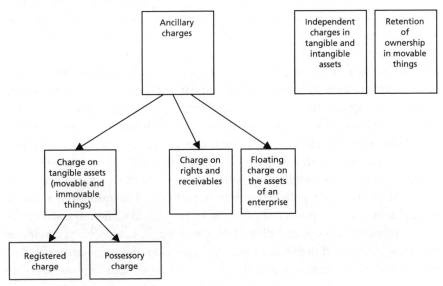

Figure 9.4. **Main proprietary security rights under Hungarian law**

2000 further amendments to the Civil Code were made in Law CXXXVII on the Modification of the Legislation on Charges, which became effective on 1 September 2001 and again amended the Hungarian Civil Code.[31]

Although the new Hungarian secured transactions law has been drafted quite **9.10** independently from the EBRD Model Law, there are a number of parallels between the principles underlying both texts. Foremost, both texts are based on the concept of a single security right for all types of assets.[32] As far as the creation of charges is concerned, the Hungarian Civil Code distinguishes mainly between (1) registered charges over tangibles (movable and immovable)[33] of which charges over movable things have to be registered in a charges' registry administered by the Hungarian Chamber of Notaries,[34] whereas charges of immovables have to be registered in the land registry;[35] (2) possessory charges over movable things;[36] (3) floating charges over the assets of an enterprise;[37] and (4) charges over rights and receivables which do not require registration.[38] The EBRD assisted in setting up an electronic registration system for movable things[39] and the charges' registry which became operative on 1 May 1997.

---

[31] A minor revision was made in 2004 which transposed the EC Financial Collateral Directive into Hungarian law.

[32] See Hungarian Civil Code, s 251(1).   [33] ibid ss 261–264.   [34] ibid ss 262(2).

[35] ibid s 262(1).   [36] ibid ss 261(1), 265.   [37] ibid s 266.

[38] ibid ss 267–268.

[39] For comments made at the time when the register was set up, see I Gárdos, 'New Hungarian legislation on security interests: an improvement in the Hungarian secured lending environment' (Summer 1996) *Law in Transition* 1–6; J Bokaí and O Erdôs Szeibert, 'Die Mobiliarhypothek

9.11 Hungarian law allows great flexibility regarding the ways in which the parties can describe and identify the secured debt and the charged property. Furthermore, it introduces public registration as the rule for the creation of charges (with the exception of possessory charges and charges in rights and receivables).[40] In addition, enforcement does not necessarily require a court decision but can be initiated on the basis of a notarized document.[41] The law even introduces an enterprise charge (referred to as 'floating charge' in the English translation) and allows the charging of all the assets of an enterprise;[42] differently from the EBRD Model Law it does not, however, provide for the remedy of a sale of an enterprise as a going concern by an enterprise administrator. It should be noted that the enterprise charge is a concept which was already known to Hungarian law in the 1920s. Attila Harmathy pointed out that Act XXI of 1928 introduced a special lien on 'industrial enterprises', which could be established without specifying the secured property in detail, and allowed dispossessing the debtor.[43] The enterprise charge cannot be used in practice since the initial plan of incorporating detailed rules on the enforcement of enterprise charges has never been implemented.

9.12 As far as the relationship between charge and secured debt is concerned, Hungarian law distinguishes in principle two main types of security rights, the charge which is dependent in its creation and existence on a secured debt (so-called 'ancillary charge') and the independent charge, which is independent from a secured debt. The feature of an independent charge is not to be found in the EBRD Model Law. Rather it is reminiscent of the non-ancillary land mortgage under German law. Differing from the non-ancillary land mortgage under German law, the independent charge is clearly not limited to real estate but can be created for all types of assets, including the assets of an enterprise. Like the enterprise charge the concept of an independent charge has not found much application in practice.

9.13 Another security right is the '*óvadék*', a charge over financial collateral, ie money, claims under a bank account, security, or other financial instruments. The charge provisions are applied in a subsidiary manner to the provisions on '*óvadék*' and this security right can, therefore, be regarded as a sub-type of the charge. Hungarian law also recognizes the retention of ownership in movable things as a

---

und deren Register' in Bundesnotarkammer (ed), *Festschrift für Helmut Schippel zum 65. Geburtstag* (Munich, 1996) 843–68; J Simpson, 'New System for the registration of charges in Hungary' (Summer 1996) *Law in Transition* 7–10.

[40] Civil Code, s 262.

[41] ibid s 262(2). Private sales are regulated by Government Decree No 12/2003 (I 30) on the Sale of Charged Property through Non-judicial Enforcement.

[42] Civil Code, s 265.

[43] A Harmathy, 'The EBRD Model Law and the Hungarian Law' in JJ Norton and M Andenas (eds), *Emerging Financial Markets and Secured Transactions* (London, 1998) 197, 208.

means of securing sales credits. In addition, the security transfer of ownership and the security assignment of rights and receivables are available under Hungarian law, although they undermine the publicity principle set forth for secured transactions in the Hungarian Civil Code's provisions on charges. Neither security transfers of ownership nor security assignments are recognized by way of statute but were created by practice in the 1990s. However, the Hungarian Supreme Court decided that claims assigned by way of security are part of the insolvency estate of the debtor and the assignee is not entitled to collect the claims assigned by way of security after the commencement of insolvency proceedings. It was argued that the assignee is to be treated as an unsecured creditor since the Insolvency Act recognizes only a chargeholder as a secured creditor. The security transfer of ownership was re-characterized as a charge by the Supreme Court and is therefore subject to the respective form requirements. Therefore security transfers of ownership and security assignments are unattractive under Hungarian law.

Hungary is currently in the process of recodifying its Civil Code.[44] It seems that **9.14** the reform will not change the fundamentals of Hungarian secured transactions law. However, it is intended to facilitate further secured lending, making it more efficient and lowering its cost, thus increasing the competitiveness of the Hungarian economy by improving its legal framework. The reform is expected to reduce the sub-types of the charge and, for example, to eliminate the enterprise charge. It seems also that the independent charge could be excluded from the new Hungarian Civil Code since it was not found to be of practical use. Furthermore, the reform is expected to improve the system of registration of charges and, in particular, to lower registration and notarization costs.

D. Polish Law

Polish law, like Bulgarian law, features a two-tiered secured transactions law: **9.15** alongside a group of largely unreformed, traditional security rights stands a modern legislation providing for a registered security right in movable things and rights. This registered security right is provided by special legislation[45]

---

[44] Ministry of Justice and Law Enforcement, 'Background Paper for the International Seminar on the Law of Proprietary Security Rights in the Proposal for a new Hungarian Civil Code' (Budapest, 2006); Ministry of Justice and Law Enforcement, 'Discussion Paper on functional equivalents to security for the International Seminar on the Law of Proprietary Security Rights in the Proposal for a new Hungarian Civil Code' (Budapest, 2006); Ministry of Justice and Law Enforcement, 'Discussion Paper on the charges register for the International Seminar on the Law of Proprietary Security Rights in the Proposal for a new Hungarian Civil Code' (Budapest, 2006).

[45] Law on Registered Pledges and the Pledge Registry, adopted on 6 December 1996 and entered into force on 1 January 1998. See WA Rich, 'Poland's new collateral law' (Summer 1997) *Law in Transition* 1–6.

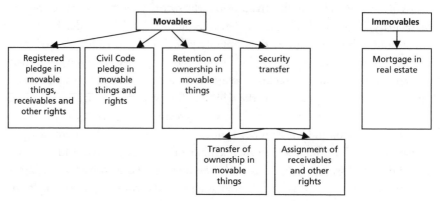

Figure 9.5. Main proprietary security rights under Polish law

prepared with the help of technical assistance organizations USAID and IRIS.[46] The EBRD commented on drafts of the legislation but was not directly involved in the development of the new security right under the Law of Registered Pledges and the Pledge Registry which entered into force on 1 January 1998. The registered 'pledge'[47] is created only if it is registered in a computerized and centralized pledge registry. Pledgeholders of a registered pledge can only be certain qualified persons, mainly financial institutions.[48] The registered pledge cannot be used to encumber all the assets of an enterprise. Only 'a collection of movable things or rights constituting an economic entity'[49] may be encumbered and thus real estate assets of an enterprise cannot be covered by the registered pledge. There are also pledges created by tax offices against a debtor. However, they are not registered in the pledge register but a separate Central Register of Treasury Pledges.

9.16   The Civil Code provides traditional security rights in movable things and rights. The pledge in movable things can be created only by transfer of possession in the pledged asset to the pledgeholder[50] and the pledge in receivables requires notice to the debtor of the pledged receivable for its creation.[51] The land

---

[46] The American lawyer in charge of the Polish secured transactions law reform project was Ronald Dwight from the IRIS Center at the University of Maryland, US. 'IRIS' stands for 'Institutional Reform and the Informal Sector'.

[47] The translation of the security right as 'pledge' is misleading for the English reader since it suggests a possessory security right, whereas the security provided under the Polish Law on Registered Pledges and the Pledge Registry is clearly a non-possessory right.

[48] Law on Registered Pledge and the Pledge Registry, Art 1. In particular, pledgeholders can be state and municipal entities, domestic banks, foreign banks, international financial organizations, and other lending institutions.

[49] ibid, Art 7.   [50] Civil Code, Art 307(1).

[51] ibid Art 329(2). The Civil Code provides no clear instructions as to the creation of pledges in rights other than receivables. Pursuant to Art 329(1), the rules applicable to the transfer of such rights apply.

mortgage in real estate is governed by a separate 1982 Law on Land Registries and Mortgage, which shows many similarities with the German provisions on ancillary land mortgages.

The possibility of retaining ownership in a movable asset is also important for the securing of sales credits.[52] In practice, the security transfer of ownership in movable assets and the security assignment of receivables (and other rights) are recognized security devices, although they are not specifically provided for under the Civil Code. The recognition of these security devices is based on the principle of freedom of contract. In addition, the concept of a security transfer of ownership is expressly regulated in the Banking Law as a form of security for a bank providing loans. Pursuant to Article 101(1) of the Banking Law a debtor or a third party may transfer ownership in movable things or securities to a bank by way of security in order to secure the bank's claim. Security transfers and security assignments are mainly used by creditors to whom registered pledges are not available, due to this security type's limited scope (for example non-bank foreign companies that do not carry on business in Poland cannot use registered pledges). The reason is that security transfers and security assignments can, unlike the registered pledge, be taken by any type of creditor without limitation. The security transfer and the security assignment are often used as so-called 'interim security' (until registered pledges and mortgages are registered). **9.17**

A recent assessment of the Polish secured transaction law by the EBRD,[53] conducted jointly with the National Bank of Poland, found serious issues with the current law in practice. In particular the registration of pledges and mortgages and the enforcement process were seen not to be efficient means of 'reducing the risk of lending' which is the main purpose of security.[54] The use of registered pledges under Polish law is in steady decline. The number of pledge registrations declined from almost 350,000 in 1999 to around 74,000 in 2004.[55] Consequently, it is to be expected that Polish security law will undergo further reform. **9.18**

E. Romanian Law

Romanian law introduced a registered security right in movable things, receivables, and other rights in its Law Concerning Certain Measures for the Acceleration of the Economic Process, which was adopted on 27 May 1999 and **9.19**

---

[52] ibid Arts 589–90.
[53] EBRD, *The Impact of the Legal Framework on the Secured Credit Market in Poland* (London, 2005).
[54] See 2.11–2.14 above.   [55] EBRD (n 53 above) 9.

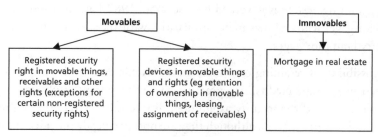

Figure 9.6. Main proprietary security rights under Romanian law

subsequently amended.[56] The Law came into force on 26 June 1999 and from December 2000 the security register ('Electronic Archive of Security Rights in Personal Property') became operational. It allows the creation of possessory and non-possessory security rights, subject to registration in an electronic registry. A security right is validly established with the execution of the written agreement regarding the creation of the respective security right, whilst registration is performed for publicity reasons. Registration with the security register serves a twofold purpose: first, it makes the security right effective towards third parties and second, it establishes priorities between different creditors holding security rights in the same asset. The security right is, therefore, closely modelled on Article 9 of the UCC but the Law does not fully share the functional approach of US secured transactions law for movables.[57] Although the Law applies not only to the outright creation of security rights but also includes, in particular, assignments of receivables, conditional sales, leasing, and rental contracts, it does not go as far as re-characterizing security devices as security rights.[58] Article 2 of the Law Concerning Certain Measures for the Acceleration of the Economic Process is a compromise, in that it applies the provisions of the Law to other agreements which in themselves are not regarded as security, in particular the provisions on priority, publicity, and enforcement. The Law further establishes an exclusive regime for all transactions having the purpose of creating security in movable things and rights. The security right in movables is created in two steps: the formation of a security agreement will already attach the security right between the parties (and defines priorities against other security rights). Once the security right is registered (or one of the exceptions from the registration requirement applies), it is perfected, ie effective against third parties. This two-step approach is closely modelled on the example of Article 9 of the UCC.

---

[56] Also referred to as 'Legal Treatment of Security Interests in Personal Property' (Law No 99/1999, Title VI) published in the *Official Gazette* Part I, 27 May 1999.

[57] Among central and eastern European law, the secured transactions laws of Albania, Kosovo, and Montenegro feature a functional approach; see 10.20–10.26 and 22.09 below.

[58] Law Concerning Certain Measures for the Acceleration of the Economic Process, Art 2.

Article 30 of the Law Concerning Certain Measures for the Acceleration of the **9.20** Economic Process provides for exceptions from the registration requirement, in particular for security rights securing debts with a low value.

Mortgages in real estate, which are created in accordance with the rules of the **9.21** Romanian Civil Code, are outside the scope of the Law Concerning Certain Measures for the Acceleration of the Economic Process.

F. Russian Law

Russia was one of the first east European jurisdictions to introduce comprehen- **9.22** sive secured transactions legislation.[59] The Pledge Law was enacted as early as 29 May 1992 and attracted great attention in many Commonwealth of Independent States (CIS) countries. In several of the CIS countries it has served as a model for the introduction of their own secured transactions laws.[60] Strangely this early Law was not replaced when the Russian Federation imple- mented a new Civil Code in 1994,[61] 1995,[62] and 2001[63] respectively[64] contain- ing a section on secured transactions (Articles 334 to 358 of the Civil Code) but

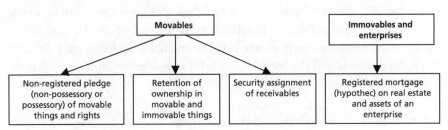

Figure 9.7. **Main proprietary security rights under Russian law**

---

[59] For an introduction, see A Makovsky, 'The Law of Secured Lending in Russia and the CIS' in J Bates, L Blumenfeld, D Fagelson, D Labin, J-H Röver, and J Simpson (eds), *International Conference on Secured Commercial Lending in the Commonwealth of Independent States. Conference Proceedings* (London, 1995) 13–18 (English version), 105–10 (Russian version).

[60] Kyrgyzstan (Law on Pledge adopted on 4 April 1997); Tajikistan (Law on Mortgage adopted on 20 June 1994 and subsequently amended in 1995 and 1998). Turkmenistan (Law on Pledge, adopted on 1 October 1993); and Uzbekistan (Law on Pledge, adopted on 1 May 1998). The secured transactions laws of Azerbaijan (Law on Mortgage, adopted on 3 July 1998) and Kazakhstan (mainly regulated by Civil Code, Arts 292–326 of 27 December 1994) have, however, chosen a separate route and provided for registered pledges.

[61] Part I (General Provisions).

[62] Part II (Specific Contracts, Law of Torts, Law of Unjust Enrichment).

[63] Part III (Succession Law and Private International Law).

[64] Work on the Russian Civil Code was led by Professor Alexander Makovsky, Deputy Chair- man of the Research Centre for Private Law under the President of the Russian Federation, Moscow.

was left intact.[65] Hence, today both the Pledge Law 1992 and the Civil Code are applied in parallel, the earlier, however, only to the extent that it does not contradict the Civil Code. The provisions of the Civil Code governing charges and the Pledge Act are inconsistent in part.

9.23 Russian secured transactions law in principle provides mainly four proprietary security rights:[66]

(1) a registered pledge (called a 'mortgage' or 'hypothec') on real estate[67] or the assets of an enterprise[68]—aircraft, space objects, river vessels,[69] and sea ships[70] are also classified as immovable property and governed by the same rules as immovables;

(2) a non-registered pledge on all assets other than real estate and the assets of an enterprise mortgaged under an enterprise mortgage,[71] and some specific assets governed by the same rules as immovables;

(3) retention of ownership in movable and immovable things;[72] and

(4) security assignments, which is a common way of taking security over receivables.[73]

9.24 The registered pledge over immovables and assets treated like immovables is covered by the Civil Code and more specifically the Law 'On Mortgage (Real Estate Pledge)', dated 22 July 1998.[74] This Law also covers enterprises, which are treated like immovables by Russian law. At the end of 2004 a number of legislative amendments were enacted which entered into force on 1 January 2005 and strengthened the legal framework for real estate mortgages. Federal

---

[65] Although it has been amended several times since 1992, the latest instance being 26 July 2006.

[66] See also the list of security rights in Civil Code, Art 329, which is not exhaustive and refers mainly to personal security such as guarantees and suretyships.

[67] A distinction is made between a mortgage on land (see Civil Code, Art 334(2), Pledge Law, Art 41, and the Law on Mortgage) and a mortgage in buildings (referred to in Civil Code, Art 334(2), Pledge Law, Arts 42–5, and the Law on Mortgage). The mortgage on land also covers buildings located on the respective land, unless the mortgage agreement stipulates otherwise (Law on Mortgage, Art 64(1)). However, a mortgage of a building is possible only if both the building and the land (or the lease right to land) are mortgaged (Law on Mortgage, Art 69(2)).

[68] Russian law understands the enterprise as a conglomerate or pool of assets, which can be encumbered as such. In this study it is referred to as a 'pledge of the assets of an enterprise', since the pool of assets consists of the individual assets.

[69] See Pledge Law, Art 40.

[70] Ship mortgages pursuant to the Merchant Shipping Code, Federal Law No 81-FZ of 30 April 1999 are not included in this study.

[71] Also excluded from the scope of this study are pledges on agricultural products, raw materials, and food pursuant to Federal Law No 100-FZ of 14 July 1997.

[72] Civil Code, Art 491.   [73] ibid Arts 382ff.

[74] Hereinafter referred to as 'Law on Mortgage'. For comments on a draft version of this law, see J Simpson and J-H Röver, *Comments on the Draft Federal Act on Mortgage (Pledge of Real Estate) of the Russian Federation* (London, 1996).

Law No 213-FZ of 30 December 2004 amended the Civil Code and abolished the requirement for notarial certification of mortgage agreements. The same Law further amended the Civil Code in providing that unfinished constructions constitute immovable property. The practical consequences of this legislative change are that unfinished constructions can be mortgaged and that the finished building is mortgaged automatically upon construction. Federal Law No 216-FZ of 30 December 2004 amended the Law on Mortgage to the effect that a land plot acquired in a transaction financed by a third party lender is mortgaged to the latter by operation of law upon registration of the borrower's ownership to the land plot. The same applies to the acquisition of lease rights in land plots financed by third parties. Lastly, a new Construction Participation Law[75] was enacted to facilitate the creation of a mortgage in real estate where various investors provide loans for a joint development, entitling each lender to become the owner of a part of the construction upon completion. If all lenders register a Joint Construction Agreement at the Federal Registration Service ('*federalinaja shlushba registrazii*', an administrative state registration body) a mortgage in real estate is created automatically by operation of law.

In principle a non-registered pledge can cover all assets other than real estate, assets of an enterprise mortgaged under an enterprise mortgage, and some specific assets governed by the same rules as immovables. There are, however, two practical limitations: **9.25**

- It should be noted that under Russian law rouble amounts (either in cash or as book entries in bank accounts) may not be pledged. However, it is widely acknowledged that money denominated in foreign currency (euros, US dollars, etc), either in the form of cash or as rights in bank accounts, can be pledged.[76]

- Although both Article 336(1) of the Civil Code and Article 4(2) of the Pledge Law provide explicitly for the pledge of receivables, it is not widely used in practice because the law does not contain detailed provisions on this type of security.

It is interesting to note that Article 488(5) of the Civil Code provides that goods or real estate purchased on a credit basis are pledged (if movable property is concerned) or mortgaged (if real estate is involved) to the seller by operation of law unless the parties agree otherwise. It is remarkable that this applies even to a purchase of real estate or shares in Russian companies, although a real estate mortgage usually has to be registered. However, in practice, parties to a contract will typically opt out of Article 488(5) of the Civil Code. **9.26**

---

[75] Federal Law No 214-FZ of 30 December 2004, in force since 1 April 2005.
[76] For more detail, see 12.33–12.35 below.

9.27 Contractual retention of ownership for movable things, and also for immovable things, is recognized under Russian law. Security assignments exist but it is still questionable under Russian law whether future receivables under an already existing contract can be assigned. In practice, therefore, the parties will assign receivables—where possible—under foreign law.

9.28 A security device sometimes found in practice is the transfer of ownership in movable things for a nominal consideration combined with the obligation to retransfer ownership to the previous owner at the same nominal price upon satisfaction of the secured debt. It is, however, doubtful whether such a purchase and repurchase ('repo') transaction is valid under Russian law. Russian courts often regard it as a circumvention of the provisions on pledges, which are considered to be mandatory. From this point of view repo transactions are considered invalid, a position confirmed by the Highest Arbitrazh Court.[77] The court qualified a share repurchase agreement as a sham transaction and declared it null and void because it considered the share purchase to be intended to secure loan repayment obligations of the seller, and that the parties were trying to avoid issues connected with the creation and enforcement of pledges. The court ruled that this repo transaction constituted a pledge, in substance. As a result, each party to the repurchase agreement was obliged to give as restitution to the other party, on the basis of claims for unjust enrichment, all shares or money it had received on the basis of the invalid agreement.

9.29 In practice, Russian secured transactions law is characterized by an avoidance of proprietary security. Even for complex transactions, Russian banks prefer a guarantee (an independent obligation which can only be issued for consideration by banks). Other creditors use suretyships (which can be issued by corporate entities or private individuals), letters of credit, contractual penalties, and other forms of security; retention of ownership in movable things as a form of proprietary security is also common. Guarantees will be combined with a power to collect money from the debtor's accounts (typically held by the debtor with the lending or agent bank). Mortgage lending is still emerging in Russia, since for many years long-term loans did not exist in Russia although they were possible legally. This is now changing, with increasing support from the Russian government being given to lending banks.[78]

9.30 Russian secured transactions law is clearly in need of reform. This has also been recognized by the Russian government, which has asked several ministries and

---

[77] See Ordinance of the Presidium of the Highest Arbitrazh Court of the Russian Federation dated 6 October 1998, case No 6202/97.

[78] eg by long-term refinancings through the Agency for Housing Mortgage Lending.

the Central Bank of the Russian Federation to prepare, by 2008, legislative proposals dealing, *inter alia*, with the following issues:[79]

- the introduction of escrow accounts to be held with banks (including foreign ones);
- detailed provisions on the pledge of rights in bank accounts;
- the abolition of the requirement to sell pledged property at public auctions and the introduction of a simple procedure for the transfer of ownership in pledged property from the pledgor to the pledgeholder;
- the strengthening of the enforcement of mortgages in real estate in out-of-court proceedings, in particular on the basis of agreements certified by a public notary; and
- the separation of pledged property from a bankrupt's estate if the pledgor becomes insolvent.

The proposals seem to call for specific changes to Russian secured transactions **9.31** law but not for its comprehensive reform which would, however, be desirable. It remains to be seen whether or not piecemeal reform will lead to a wider use of proprietary security, in particular in complex financings.

G. Slovak Law

In 2002 Slovakia amended its Civil Code and introduced rules on a modern **9.32** registered unitary security right (charge) in movable things, rights, land, and even enterprises.[80] The Slovak reform was substantially supported by the

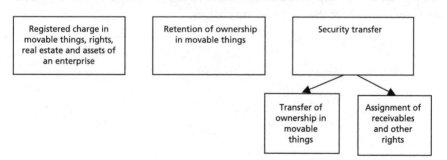

Figure 9.8. Main proprietary security rights under Slovak law

---

[79] 'Development Strategies for the Banking Sector of the Russian Federation for the Period until 2008', approved by Joint Declaration No 983p-P13 and No 01-01/1617 of the Government of the Russian Federation and the Central Bank of the Russian Federation respectively of 5 April 2005.

[80] The amending law was adopted on 19 August 2002 and entered into force on 1 January 2003. An introductory guide in Slovak and English is provided by Allen & Overy and EBRD, *Guide for Taking Charges in the Slovak Republic* (Bratislava, 2003).

EBRD. The responsible law-maker on the Slovakian side was Professor Lucia Zitnanska (who later became Minister of Justice). The new security right is created only if it is registered at the Central Registry of Charges.[81] Possessory charges can be created without registration under §151e(5) of the Civil Code but need registration for priority purposes. Like Hungarian law, Slovak law established an electronic security register which is held and administered by notaries and not by courts.

9.33 Slovak pre-reform secured transactions law featured possessory pledges and pledges in receivables and other rights. The respective provisions of the Civil Code were deleted at the time of introduction of the new rules and these security rights will only continue to exist if they were created before 1 January 2003.[82] The new rules have, however, kept the concept of a possessory pledge provided that the parties agree on a charge creation by transfer of possession.[83]

9.34 The only major proprietary security outside the new security rules is the retention of ownership in movable things as a way of securing sales credit. Slovak law has not adopted the concept of the unpaid vendor's charge to be found under the EBRD Model Law, which transforms retention of ownership arrangements into a charge.[84] Non-public security transfers of ownership in movable things[85] and security assignments of receivables[86] are also known under Slovak law. However, they seem to be in decline in practice due to the attractive legislative regime for charges. In addition, there is uncertainty as to how an asset which has been transferred to the person taking security is retransferred to the person giving security once the secured debt has been satisfied, in particular whether the retransfer occurs automatically or whether it must be effected by the parties. Ownership-based security is, however, still possible despite the comprehensive nature of the new rules on charges.

---

[81] Civil Code, §151e(1); M Števček, 'Non-Possessory Charges' ('*Nepossesórne záložné právo—de lege ferenda*') (2000) 6 *Bulletin slovenskej advokacie* 51.
[82] Allen & Overy and EBRD (n 80 above) 31.   [83] Civil Code, §151e(5).
[84] ibid §601.   [85] Civil Code, §553.   [86] ibid §554.

Part III

PRINCIPLES OF SECURED TRANSACTIONS LAWS IN CENTRAL AND EASTERN EUROPE

10

GENERAL PRINCIPLES OF SECURED TRANSACTIONS LAW

A. Analytical Framework

There are a number of general comparative principles which summarize in general terms the characteristics of a secured transactions law.[1] It is possible to distinguish in particular the principle of property right,[2] the principles of security in own property (ie ownership-based security) and in property held by another person (ie limited property rights),[3] the principles of form and functionality,[4] and the principles of unity and multiplicity.[5] **10.01**

---

[1] For more details, see Röver, *Prinzipien.*   [2] ibid 137–58.   [3] ibid 159–69.
[4] ibid 170–8.   [5] ibid 179–87.

1. Principle of property right

10.02 The western reference systems described above feature a class of security which can be distinguished from personal rights by its specific proprietary legal effects. The principle of property right has two elements: (1) the security interest is created in particular assets of the person giving security (which may include a changing pool of assets) and (2) the security interest has effects not only between the parties to the security agreement but also against third parties. Against the background of the principle of property right it can be shown that proprietary security interests provide security in three different ways: (a) they prevent non-satisfaction of the secured debt by giving additional remedies to the securityholder; (b) they also allow the securityholder to receive satisfaction from secured property where the secured debt is not satisfied; (c) lastly, security interests designate certain assets for the satisfaction of the securityholder in priority to other creditors; the securityholder may use this allocation positively or negatively. It is used positively if the securityholder enforces the security interest and it is used negatively if he excludes other creditors from enforcing their rights in certain assets. In the latter case security rights serve as mere protective rights.[6]

10.03 The western reference systems show three different types of proprietary effect: (1) German law and the Model Law in particular implemented a one-step proprietary effect: proprietary rights are created once all legal requirements are fulfilled both as between the parties and against third parties. (2) US law features a two-step proprietary effect: the security interest attaches in a first step between the parties and has effects against third parties only when perfection requirements are met. (3) English law starts from the premise of a two-step proprietary effect. However, it also distinguishes between legal and equitable rights, ie two different levels of proprietary effect. In addition, it recognizes a floating charge which provides a true property right only once a crystallization event has transformed the floating charge into a fixed charge.

2. Principles of security in own property and in property held by another person

10.04 Many legal systems recognize two types of security, security in own property (ie ownership-based security where ownership is transferred to the securityholder, for example retention of title under English law and retention of ownership

---

[6] For this aspect of security interests, see 2.14 above and PR Wood, *Project Finance, Subordinated Debt and State Loans* (London, 1995) para 5-1; see also a similar distinction with respect to the functions of events of default in project finance loan agreements by J-H Röver, 'Projektfinanzierung' in UR Siebel (ed), *Projekte und Projektfinanzierung* (Munich, 2001) 223–4.

under German law) and in property held by another person (ie where security is created in the form of a limited property right, for example charges under English law and pledges under German law).[7] The Model Law introduces with the charge a security right in property held by another person only. The security interest in movables under US law leaves behind the distinction between security in own property and in property held by another person. The security interest provides the securityholder with an entitlement (an interest), ie the power to enforce the security interest. Even if the parties intended to create a title-based form of security, Article 9 of the Uniform Commercial Code (UCC) will transform their agreement into a security interest in the form of a limited interest in property.

3. Principles of form and functionality

The scope of security interests can be determined by reference to the principles **10.05** of form and functionality. According to the 'form principle', the parties choose which security interest shall govern their legal relationship. Parties have a certain freedom of choice between different types of security. This is the approach of English and German law and to a limited extent the Model Law. The 'functionality principle' is quite different; here the scope of a security interest is determined on the basis of whether or not the parties' agreement fulfils a security function. Thus security interests in a narrow sense, but also security devices such as retention of title, are governed by the rules of secured transactions law and security devices are requalified as security interests. This principle is applied under Article 9 of the UCC and under the rules of the security acts of those Canadian provinces which have implemented Article 9.

4. Principles of unity and multiplicity

Under the 'principle of unity', which can be found under Article 9 of the UCC **10.06** for security in movables and under the Model Law for all types of property, the law provides only one type of security or very few types of security. However, with the principle of unity may come certain distinctions concerning different types of creation, different types of collateral, etc. The principle of unity can be supported by the principle of functionality. Since it is one of the purposes of the principle of functionality to define the scope of security law widely, the risk that security devices might not fall under the rules of secured transactions law is avoided.

Pursuant to the 'principle of multiplicity', several or even many types of security **10.07**

---

[7] It should be noted that the notion of ownership is different in common law and civil law jurisdictions; as far as terminology is concerned, the term 'title' is used in the context of common law and the term 'ownership' in the context of civil law; see 5.04 above.

interests exist in parallel. The security interests may not be legislated but may be provided by case law or customary law. This can be found in English and German law.[8] The form principle, which tends to lead to a dissipation of security interests, is advantageous for a multiplicity of security interests. Differentiation of security interests is often oriented to the two fundamental elements of a security interest, the secured debt and the charged property. There are laws which, like German law, develop security rights with different types of dependency between security right and secured debt. In addition, different types of security can be created for immovable and movable things, receivables, other rights, etc which can each follow their own distinct rules. Other criteria for differentiating are the contents of an interest (security in own property or security in property held by another person) or the type of possession in the charged property (possessory and non-possessory security). The distinction between the principle of unity and the principle of multiplicity is, hence, linked closely to the distinction between the principles of form and functionality.[9] Both the principle of unity and the principle of multiplicity can find their limitations. English law is an important model for this, where the different types of security interests (in a narrow sense) have in principle the same rules as far as priority, enforcement, and insolvency are concerned.

B. Eastern European Secured Transactions Laws

1. Principle of property right

10.08 Central and eastern European jurisdictions have endorsed the principle of property right, which is remarkable given the fact that fifteen years ago proprietary security was almost non-existent in these countries. A few examples serve to illustrate the emergence of proprietary security in central and eastern Europe. There is Bulgarian law, where pledges, mortgages, and security devices such as the retention of ownership in movable things, are created in particular assets and can be held against third parties as rights with priority in satisfaction from the secured assets. Inclusion of the Bulgarian provisions on secured transactions in the 'Law on Obligations and Contracts' is no reason to doubt their proprietary nature. Similarly, the lien under Czech law is a property right that encumbers specific assets[10] and is opposable against third parties. In enforcement and

---

[8] Jurisdictions such as French law provide an even larger number of security interests than these reference systems.

[9] Often no distinction is made between the two groups of concepts; see eg K Milger, *Mobiliarsicherheiten im deutschen und US-amerikanischen Recht—eine rechtsvergleichende Untersuchung* (Göttingen, 1982) 47–8.

[10] See only Civil Code, s 153(1).

insolvency of the person giving the lien, the secured creditor receives satisfaction from the particular asset which has been encumbered in priority to other creditors. The same holds true for retentions of ownership and security transfers. For Hungarian law the principle of property right is most clearly expressed for the independent charge in section 269(1) of the Civil Code which provides that the chargeholder 'may seek satisfaction solely from the charged asset encumbered with the charge'. However, the same principle applies also to simple charges (ie charges dependent on the secured debt) and retention of ownership arrangements. The provisions on charges are currently found in the law of obligations (Part IV of the Civil Code) under the heading 'ancillary obligations securing the performance of the contract'. It is intended to underline the proprietary nature of charges by moving the provisions on charges to the provisions on property law of a reformed Civil Code. Pursuant to Polish law a Civil Code pledge is created in particular assets.[11] An interesting provision is Article 333 of the Civil Code pursuant to which both the pledgor and the pledgeholder can demand performance under the secured debt if a pledge on rights has been agreed. This is surprising since prior to enforcement it should be clear that only the pledgor can demand performance under the secured debt. (See, however, §1281 of the German Civil Code which provides for the debtor's performance jointly to the pledgor and the pledgeholder.)

The security right in movables under Romanian law is a right in personal property which is demonstrated in particular by Article 9(1) of the Law Concerning Certain Measures for the Acceleration of the Economic Process. This provision states explicitly that the security right is a 'right *in rem*'. This qualification triggers two essential aspects. First, the secured party enjoys a right to follow the secured asset irrespective of the person in whose hands it is. Second, the secured party has the right to be satisfied from the secured asset in preference to other (unsecured) creditors or creditors who have a security right with a lower ranking.[12] The mortgage under Romanian law is a right in real estate which secures payment or performance of an obligation.[13] Therefore, the mortgageholder will have a right to follow the immovable assets irrespective of the person in possession of the asset[14] and the right to be satisfied from the secured immovable property in preference to other unsecured creditors and creditors having a right in the same real estate with a lower ranking. **10.09**

Russian law does not explicitly qualify security rights as property rights. Sometimes it is even claimed that a pledge (both the non-registered and the **10.10**

---

[11] Civil Code, Art 306.
[12] See also Law Concerning Certain Measures for the Acceleration of the Economic Process, Art 9(2).
[13] Civil Code, Arts 1746ff.   [14] ibid Art 1790.

registered pledge) does not constitute a property right. However, the principle of property right for security rights under Russian law is confirmed by Article 334(1) of the Civil Code which provides a right of priority for the pledgeholder in preference to other [unsecured] creditors; by Article 1 of the Pledge Law, again providing priority to the pledge; and Article 1(1) of the Law on Mortgage, which provides priority to the mortgageholder. In addition, Article 23 of the Pledge Law and Article 1(1) of the Law on Mortgage provide that the secured debt is to be satisfied from the pledged property.

10.11 For Slovak law the property principle is expressed in §151a of the Civil Code which provides that the secured claim is satisfied from the asset subject to the charge.[15] The same applies to retentions of ownership in movable things and security transfers.

2. Principles of security in own property and in property held by another person

10.12 The duality between ownership-based security and security based on limited property rights, which is so characteristic of many secured transactions laws, is also emerging in central and eastern European countries, with the retention of ownership being a widely recognized way of securing purchase price obligations, and security transfers of ownership and security assignments being a tried and trusted way to avoid impracticable national provisions on pledges. This is already exemplified by Bulgarian law, which provides both security in own property (ie retention of ownership in movable things) and security in property held by another person (mortgages and pledges). Article 12(2) of the Law on Registered Pledges refers explicitly to retentions of ownership in movable things, however, it requires the registration of such an arrangement for it to be perfected if the pledgor is a merchant; security devices given by a non-merchant require no registration for their perfection. Czech law also features both security in own property and in property held by another person. Retention of ownership and security transfers are both security in own property whereas with the lien Czech law provides limited security rights in property held by another person. Hungarian law puts the emphasis on security in property held by another person. The charge is a security right in assets owned by the chargor. At the same time Hungarian law recognizes retention of ownership and thus security in own property.

10.13 The emphasis under Polish law is on security in property held by another person. The pledge is a limited property right in an asset granted by the pledgor. However, Polish law also recognizes retention of ownership arrangements and security

---

[15] F Faldyna, J Hušek, and Z Des, *Securing and Discharging Debts* (*Zajištění a zánik zavazků*) (Prague, 1995) 11.

transfers of ownership with respect to movable things. Romanian law is also focused on security rights in the form of limited property rights (security rights in movables and mortgages in real estate). It provides for retentions of ownership or security transfers of ownership; however, they are covered by the same registration regime as other types of security. Russian secured transactions law recognizes both security in property held by another person in the form of non-registered pledges and registered mortgages (which are limited property rights) and security in own property in the form of retention of ownership arrangements[16] and security assignments.[17] The unitary security right of the charge is a limited property right and Slovak law is thus based on the principle of security in property held by another person. However, since Slovak law recognizes retention of ownership arrangements it also allows security in own property.

3. Principles of form and functionality

The central and eastern European laws mostly follow the principle of form. **10.14** Bulgarian law is primarily based on the principle of form and can only be regarded as having incorporated the principle of functionality to a limited extent. Although Article 12(2) of the Law on Registered Pledges provides for a number of 'functional' security rights, such as retention of ownership in movable things and leasing arrangements, to be registered in the pledge register it does not go as far as Article 9 of the UCC and re-characterizes these agreements as security rights. Czech law follows strictly the principle of form. Functional security is not transformed into security rights but keeps the legal form intended by the parties. Hungarian law also follows the principle of form. The 'charge' is a limited security right and must be created as such. Similarly, retention of ownership arrangements keep their legal nature. However, pursuant to decisions of the Hungarian Supreme Court a security transfer of ownership can be re-characterized as a charge. It should also be noted that the Hungarian Supreme Court decided that claims assigned under a security assignment cannot be collected by the assignee after the commencement of insolvency proceedings, thus strongly limiting the effect of security assignments. The substance principle has, therefore, found application under Hungarian law as a way to limit the development of new types of security. Polish law adheres to the principle of form and thus security rights are created in exactly the legal form chosen by the parties. This applies to Civil Code pledges, registered pledges, real estate mortgages, retentions of ownership, and security transfers alike.

The Romanian secured transactions law for movables falls short of the principle **10.15** of functionality. Pursuant to Article 2 of the Law Concerning Certain Measures

---

[16] Civil Code, Art 491.   [17] ibid Arts 382ff.

for the Acceleration of the Economic Process, assignments of receivables,[18] conditional sales, and leasing agreements are covered by the same rules as outright security rights. Privileges and rights of retention (if they are not created in the context of conditional sales) are, however, excluded from the application of the general rules on security rights for movables.[19] And what is more important, security devices are not re-characterized as security interests but keep their distinct legal character. Similarly, real estate mortgages follow the traditional principle of form. They are intended as limited property rights and create just these. Under Russian secured transactions law the principle of functionality is equally unknown; it is fully built upon the principle of form. However, Russian courts may have reference to the substance of a transaction and declare transactions invalid which attempt to avoid the statutory pledge provisions. Lastly, Slovak law is based on the principle of form. Both the charge and the retention of ownership are recognized by law as what the parties intend them to be: a limited property right and an ownership arrangement, respectively.[20]

4. Principles of unity and multiplicity

10.16 Modernized central and eastern European laws gravitate towards the principle of unity, whereas old style secured transactions laws are more often built upon the principle of multiplicity. Bulgarian law follows the principle of a limited multiplicity since it provides a number of different security rights but the number of security rights is rather limited, thus avoiding unnecessary complexity—whereas Czech law comes close to the principle of unity by providing only three different types of security, the lien, the retention of ownership, and the security transfer. Hungarian law is built on a single security right—the charge—and thus is based on the principle of unity. It even goes so far as to provide the same security right for both movable and immovable assets. The charge is complemented in practice only by the retention of ownership in movable things. Hungarian secured transactions law thus implements almost fully the principle of unity. Written Polish law comes equally close to the principle of unity since the security rights provided under Polish law are just the mortgage in real estate, the registered and unregistered pledge, and the retention of ownership in movable assets. However, the decline of the registered pledge in practice has led to the development of security transfer of ownership and security assignment of receivables. In practice Polish law is, therefore, gravitating towards the principle of multiplicity.

---

[18] But not the assignment of intellectual property rights or inheritance rights; see Law Concerning Certain Measures for the Acceleration of the Economic Process, Art 8.

[19] ibid Art 8.

[20] It should be noted that the laws of Albania, Kosovo, and Montenegro have implemented the functional approach; see 22.09 below.

As in the other reform jurisdictions in central and eastern Europe, the introduction of the new security law for movables in Romania meant that the law moved towards the unity principle. There are effectively only the registered security right in movables, registered security devices, and the mortgage in real estate. Russian law incorporates the principle of unity. It recognizes only four types of proprietary security, namely non-registered pledges for movable assets (movable things and rights), registered mortgages for real estate and assets treated like real estate (like the mortgage on the assets of an enterprise), retentions of ownership in movable and immovable things, and security assignments of receivables. Lastly, Slovak law provides for the unitary security right of the charge and is thus based on the principle of unity which is diluted only mildly by the recognition of the retention of ownership. **10.17**

C. Comparative remarks and evaluation

1. Principle of property right

The principle of property right is of fundamental importance to any security law which intends to achieve the macro- and microeconomic functions of security. Only Czech law still relies—as far as statutory law is concerned—on its pre-transformation security rights, whereas the other central and eastern European legal systems have introduced new security rights with proprietary effect, sometimes to complement existing security regimes, sometimes to replace them. **10.18**

Of the central and eastern European laws examined in this study only Bulgarian and Romanian law opted for the proprietary effect of their security rights in movables to be established in two steps. Following the US model of Article 9 of the UCC, they require an attachment and a perfection of security rights. It should be noted that where the proprietary effect is created in two steps, the attachment step offers only limited protection to the securityholder. It appears that the principle of one-step proprietary effect serves the risk-reducing function of security better. However, the proprietary effect of a particular security interest can always—even under the principle of one-step proprietary effect—be affected by the proprietary effect of another security right (a situation arising when different security rights conflict with each other). **10.19**

Interests like the floating charge under English law which initially has no full proprietary effect seem even more doubtful, since fixed charges take priority until the floating charge crystallizes.[21] Such security cannot provide effective risk **10.20**

---

[21] The effects of the floating charge have recently been weakened by the Enterprise Act 2002, in particular, by the introduction of a fund for unsecured creditors; see 6.08 above.

reduction to the securityholder and is, therefore, in practice often accompanied by fixed charges on important assets. There are several laws in central and eastern Europe (namely Hungarian and Russian laws) which implemented concepts similar to a floating charge over the assets of an enterprise; however, they understand these rights to have full proprietary effect. It should be added that the English floating charge traditionally had the added benefit of the remedy of a company administrator who could be appointed upon crystallization of the charge. However, the central and eastern European laws which adopted concepts similar to the floating charge over the assets of an enterprise have not implemented this remedy. It has now also been limited in its application under English law.[22]

2. Principles of security in own property and in property held by another person

10.21 Both security in own property (ie ownership-based security) and in property held by another person (ie security in the form of limited property rights) seem to be adequate with a view to the risk reducing and the information functions of security. Hence the dualism of, for example, retentions of ownerships and pledges found under many central and eastern European security laws is a workable approach to provide for economically effective security in practice.

10.22 It should, however, be noted that security in property held by another person allows the person giving security to create several security interests in the same charged property. With security in own property the person giving or retaining security loses its entitlement in the charged property once it has granted a security interest;[23] additional ownership transfers or retentions are in principle not possible.

10.23 Although both security in own property and in property held by another person can equally fulfil the economic functions of security, ownership-based security may create complications, in particular where a law has developed security in own property in order to overcome structural weaknesses in existing security interests. This can be shown using the example of German law, where security for loan credit and security for sale credit conflict if both the loan creditor and the sale creditor have taken a security assignment of the same (future) receivables. Ownership-based security of loan and sale creditor can thus

---

[22] See 6.07 above.

[23] This, however, is not the case with respect to assignments under English law—according to which several assignments are ranked pursuant to their priority and are not mutually exclusive.

conflict[24] with different laws having different preferences as to whether the loan creditor or the sale creditor shall prevail. Only law systems which avoid these conflicts (like English or US law) are able to maximize the economic benefits of security law.

3. Principles of form and functionality

The functional approach to security interests over movable property was born in the 1950s in the United States as part of a major overhaul of the great variety of laws and concepts in all of the American states that were used to secure claims using movable property, which resulted in Article 9 of the UCC.[25] The diversity was problematic since 'a creditor faced a myriad of different rules on when a security device was enforceable, on how a security interest was to be enforced and the relative priority of the holder of a security interest . . . To replace these different security devices the drafters of Article 9 began by drafting separate chapters focusing on financing for specific classes of collateral. After several drafts they discovered so many common provisions in these chapters that they decided to amalgamate them into a single uniform framework'.[26]   **10.24**

The functional approach is achieved by the following key features: **10.25**

(1) substance rather than form determines whether Article 9 of the UCC applies; a security interest is created if the transaction functionally falls within the definition of security interest—for instance, a seller on credit who provided in the agreement that he would retain title over the goods until full payment was made for the goods, would in law retain only a security interest over the goods;

(2) the regime supersedes what the parties may have expressed in their agreement;

(3) unique terminology that applies to all transactions whose function is the same, a sort of umbrella imposed by law—a security interest, which is an interest in personal (movable) property or fixtures which secures payment or performance of an obligation, secured party, security agreement, and collateral;

(4) a unique set of rules, from creation to registration, priority and enforcement, which applies to all secured transactions.

---

[24] The conflict arises because the bank will typically take a generally defined security assignment of all receivables, whereas the sale creditors will have an assignment of the receivables arising from the future sale of the goods in which the bank has retained ownership. Typically, the conflict of two assignments is dealt with under English law by priority rules.

[25] See 6.14–6.19 above.

[26] P Winship, 'Selected Security Interests in the United States' in JJ Norton and M Andenas (eds), *Emerging Financial Markets and Secured Transactions* (London, 1998) 267–78.

10.26 There is a spectrum of options for dealing with the functional approach, with each option having different costs and benefits:

(1) *Adopt a functional approach in full.* This involves total re-characterization of security devices, such as lease and retention of title arrangements, as a security right and the provision of a complete set of rules (as regards, for example, creation, registration, and enforcement) to apply to all security rights. Substantial legislation is required to introduce this idea and make sure it is fully implemented. This is the approach taken under the secured transactions laws of Albania, Kosovo, and Montenegro.[27]

(2) *Adopt a formal approach but provide for certain common provisions for security rights and defined quasi-security transactions.* This retains the formal classification of each transaction but specifically requires their registration in the security register and may also harmonize enforcement and other rules. Substantial legislation is needed but not as extensive as for option (1) above. This approach is to be found in Bulgaria and Romania.[28]

(3) *Retain a formal approach.* The secured transactions reform only covers traditional security rights and does not touch the other instruments already in existence in the Civil Code or specific laws (for example leasing law). It will be necessary to address some priority issues between creditors with different, conflicting rights over the same assets, or to ensure that the system does not contain any loophole (especially in terms of publicity to third parties), but this does not need to be done immediately and can be dealt with subsequently when it can be seen how the secured credit market has evolved, and what practical problems have arisen. This is the approach to be found in most central and eastern European countries.

10.27 One reason for introducing the functional approach is to avoid any circumvention of secured transactions law (in particular the publicity provisions). However, circumvention is only a problem if it leads to conflicting or confusing results. If the basic secured transactions law contains sound provisions for priority and enforcement, the person taking security will normally gravitate naturally towards a security right and away from alternative devices. The only problem that may need covering is publicity of other devices, but to achieve that, adopting a functional approach is not necessary.

10.28 For central and eastern European countries functionality has multiple drawbacks:

(1) It introduces a sophisticated concept which is inappropriate for central and eastern European transition markets, especially when the market usually does not suffer from a myriad of security devices with conflicting priority

---

[27] See 22.09 below.   [28] See 9.04, 9.19 above and 22.09 below.

rules, but rather from a *lack* of security devices. A functional system may produce a 'simple' result by having all security interests aligned, but the way it achieves that (especially transaction requalification) and the legislative and practice changes needed to implement it are certainly not simple.

(2) Western European countries do not have a functional approach. Retention of title or ownership and financial leasing, for example, are generally used in Europe. Financial leasing has increased dramatically in central and eastern Europe and seems to be working satisfactorily. A central and eastern European country needs to reflect carefully before adopting a diametrically different approach to that of its neighbours.

(3) An issue in transition countries is improving the implementation of the law by the courts and the judiciary. Rapid economic development continually adds to the need for improvement. Training on the new features of a secured transactions law (covering issues such as generally described collateral and creditor-led enforcement) is needed, without adding the complexity of a functional approach.

Application of the functionality principle can prevent the circumvention of a **10.29** secured transactions system. In this sense it implements the principle of risk reduction since it provides a creditor with the comfort that he cannot be caught out by interests which are functionally equivalent to security but are not subject to the rules of secured transactions law. This is particularly dangerous for a creditor where such interests are not (at least potentially) known to him due to a lack of publicity. The functionality principle is, therefore, certainly an attractive legislative model. However, as demonstrated above, the same results can be achieved by combining the principle of form with additional provisions, for example on registration for security devices.

The principle of form (and the intermediate option of combining a formal **10.30** approach with common provisions for security rights and security devices) also has its economic legitimacy, and it seems particularly suited to the needs of central and eastern European countries. The economic efficacy of the principle of form can ultimately be evaluated only in the context of the principles of unity and multiplicity. Most central and eastern European laws feature only a few security rights, for instance Hungarian and Slovak secured transactions law (which feature three main types of security rights only) clearly being the most transparent and simple to apply. Central and eastern European laws are, therefore, not yet prone to the issues of conflicts which can paralyse a secured transactions law.

4. Principles of unity and multiplicity

The principle of unity limits the possibilities of collisions between different **10.31** types of security interests. Proprietary security leads to collisions if several security interests are created in the same secured property. However, the provision of different types of security interest in itself does not yet lead to collisions. The existence of mortgages in immovable property and of non-possessory security rights in movable things is not problematic since it does not create any relevant collision between different types of security interests. The allocation of security interests in movable things attached to real estate either to the law of movable property or real estate law is a matter of scope of these areas of law. It has to be noted as well that an avoidance of conflicts is not achieved completely by the principle of unity, since within the principle of unity distinctions with respect to the various types of secured property are often made even if only one type of security right exists (this is exemplified by Hungarian law). In any event, the person taking security finds an optimal implementation of the risk reduction principle with the principle of unity—as long as the 'internal differentiations' of the principle of unity are kept to a minimum.

10.32 The principle of multiplicity reduces the economic efficacy of security. The differentiation of many types of security is often the result of historic vagaries, which slowly undermine the system of security law. It is difficult to guarantee the coordination of different types of security. However, English law demonstrates that despite an application of the principle of multiplicity at the surface, with a unitary solution to the issues of priority, enforcement, and insolvency, a coordination between different types of security can be achieved. Here the principle of multiplicity in its effects is getting so close to the principle of unity that a loss of economic efficacy is avoided.

10.33 As already pointed out, central and eastern European security laws tend towards the principle of unity (with Hungarian and Slovak law achieving this with three major types of security rights). They have, therefore, taken a structurally beneficial decision in the process of building up their secured transactions laws.

11

SECURED DEBT

A. Analytical Framework

The legal life of the debt (or the 'claim', as it is referred to by some secured **11.01** transactions laws) secured by a security right is not a matter for security law but for contract law.[1] Security law must, however, determine three general points with respect to the debt secured by the security right:

(1) The first issue is the content of the secured debt, in particular:
   (a) the understanding, in terms of a given law, of what constitutes a debt;
   (b) whether only monetary or also non-monetary obligations can be secured;
   (c) whether only unconditional or also conditional debts can be secured;
   (d) whether only present or also future debts can be secured;
   (e) whether only debts governed by local law or also debts governed by foreign law can be secured;
   (f) whether the secured debt must be valid and enforceable; and
   (g) whether or not an advance is necessary.

---

[1] The term 'contract law' should be construed widely.

(2) The second issue is the extent to which the secured debt is secured. With respect to the secured debt we have to distinguish two components, the principal amount on one hand and the additional amounts on the other hand. The principal amount is, for example, the amount of a loan extended to a debtor. In this example additional amounts will be interest, damages, or enforcement costs, ie sums closely related to the secured principal amount, and other related sums. Albeit both principal amount and additional amounts taken together may form the secured debt (depending on the provisions of the respective law or the parties' agreement) it is helpful to distinguish between the two categories.

(3) A security right is created for the purpose of 'securing a debt'. The last issue is, hence, the relationship between:

   (a) the secured debt and the security right; and

   (b) possibly the relationship between the security right and contracts defining the relationship between the security right and the secured debt (such as the security agreement under German law).

Typically there will be a link between the security right and the debt secured by it (which is most obvious in the fact that a security interest can only be enforced once the secured debt has not been satisfied).

11.02 The flexibility demonstrated by the individual laws shows to what extent they allow dynamic security with respect to the secured debt. Although the secured debt is one of the most important building blocks of the security right it is rarely treated systematically in legislation on secured transactions.

B. Eastern European Secured Transactions Laws

1. Bulgarian law

11.03 Bulgarian law is relatively quiet when it comes to the debt secured by a security right. As far as the content of the secured debt is concerned it is possible to secure both monetary and non-monetary obligations.[2] In addition, one can learn from Article 5(1) of the Law on Registered Pledges that unconditional and conditional debts can be secured; the same provision also makes it clear that both present and future debts can be secured. There are no such clarifications in the Law on Obligations and Contracts for the non-registered pledge of movable things, for claims, or for the mortgage of immovables. Neither the Law on

---

[2] This is confirmed indirectly for non-registered pledge of movable things by Law of Obligations and Contracts, Art 160 which provides special enforcement rules for the situation where 'the secured claim is monetary or liquidated damages in cash'.

Registered Pledges nor the Law on Obligations and Contracts requires an actual advance for the security right to attach or to become perfected.

For the extent of the secured debt, Article 5(1) of the Law on Registered Pledges **11.04** confirms that one or more debts can be secured.[3] The Law of Obligations does not state explicitly that several debts can be secured. Neither Law contains provisions on the definition of the secured debt. Current practice is that the secured debt must be defined specifically under the Law of Obligations, whereas the Law on Registered Pledges was clearly drafted with the idea of allowing both specific and general definition of the secured debt. There is no stipulation of a maximum amount. Additional amounts can be agreed between the parties as part of the secured debt. Article 5(2) of the Law on Registered Pledges stipulates that the following amounts become additional amounts by operation of law, interest on a debt and liquidated damages emanating from the secured debt. Under the Law on Obligations and Contracts the debt secured by a mortgage extends to interest for the two years preceding the year of serving a writ of execution (ie commencing enforcement proceedings), the current year, and for all the following years until the date of sale of the property.[4] In addition, the mortgage of real estate secures the creditor's expenses incurred for its creation and renewal, and court and enforcement expenses.[5]

The Law on Obligations and Contracts confirms for the relationship between **11.05** secured debt and security right, that the non-registered pledge of movable things and claims, as well as the mortgage of immovables, are transferred upon a transfer of the secured debt and that the pledge terminates upon termination of the secured debt.[6] The non-registered pledge and the mortgage are, therefore, rights which are tied closely to the secured debt. The registered pledge in movables, rights, and the assets of an enterprise 'secures the secured debt' and, therefore, is also tied to the secured debt.[7]

However, with security devices such as the retention of ownership and security **11.06** transfers of ownership, in principle secured debt and retained or transferred ownership in the secured asset are independent from each other unless the parties provide otherwise (which they will, for example, by stipulating a condition subsequent under a retention of ownership arrangement which transfers ownership upon payment of the second debt).

---

[3] If the secured debt is interest bearing, this relates to the secured debt's principal amount.
[4] Law of Obligations and Contracts, Art 174, second sentence.
[5] ibid Art 174, third sentence. [6] ibid Art 150.
[7] Law on Registered Pledges, Art 5(2).

2. Czech law

11.07 As far as the content of the secured receivable is concerned, one can find explicit confirmation for the lien in that both monetary and non-monetary claims can be secured.[8] Both unconditional and conditional receivables can be secured,[9] as well as present and future receivables.[10] Czech law also covers the case where a receivable is limited to a certain time period and confirms that such a debt can equally be secured.[11] Advances under the secured claim must not be made for the lien to be created. The same rules apply for the content of receivables secured by retentions of ownership and security transfers (although the former will predominantly secure a sales price claim).

11.08 The extent of the secured receivable is primarily defined by the parties. There is no confirmation in the Czech Civil Code that one or more receivables can be secured by a lien. However, for non-monetary claims it is stipulated that they are secured up to a maximum amount which is the claim's 'market price' at the time of the lien's creation,[12] a rather impractical concept. Additional amounts are covered if they are defined as a secured claim by the parties. 'Appurtenances of receivables' are covered by operation of law.[13] There are no provisions on the extent of the secured claims for retentions of ownership and security transfers, and thus this issue relies on the parties' agreement. The parties can agree in particular that a retention of ownership or a security transfer secures not only one but several claims.

11.09 The relationship between secured claim and lien is equally sparsely documented. One can learn from section 152 of the Civil Code that the lien is 'used to secure a claim' (the typical wording used to indicate that the creation of the lien requires a secured claim) and from section 170 of the Civil Code that the termination of the secured claim will lead to the termination of the lien as well. As far as retentions of ownership and security transfers are concerned, they are in principle independent from the claim secured by them. However, the parties will provide in their agreement when ownership passes for a retention of ownership (it is conditional on the payment of the secured claim) and when it is retransferred for a security transfer.

3. Hungarian law

11.10 Under Hungarian law one has to distinguish two regimes as far as charges are concerned: ancillary and independent charges. The following remarks about the secured claim are in principle relevant only to the ancillary charge. Under

---

[8] Civil Code, s 155(1), first sentence, (2), (5).   [9] ibid s 155(3).
[10] ibid s 155(3).   [11] ibid s 155(4).   [12] ibid s 155(2).
[13] ibid s 155(1), second sentence.

Hungarian law both monetary and non-monetary claims can be secured.[14] However, non-monetary claims must be 'determinable in money' thus mirroring the respective wording of Article 4.2 of the Model Law on Secured Transactions.[15] Further, Hungarian law allows the securing of both unconditional and conditional claims[16] as well as present and future claims.[17] As far as the enforceability of secured claims is concerned, Hungarian law provides that a charge securing an unenforceable claim is null and void.[18]

When it comes to the extent of the secured claim, Hungarian law does not **11.11** spell out that one or more claims can be secured but refers to 'a claim' only. However, it was the intention of the Hungarian legislator[19] that several claims can also be secured by a charge. Hungarian law clearly provides for a charge which is flexible with respect to the secured claim and allows for constant changes in the secured claim. A maximum amount of the secured claim must in principle not be stipulated unless the charge is a so-called 'registered framework charge' which secures claims arising from a legal relationship (for example claims in damages provided by law) or an executory title. Additional amounts can be secured by way of agreement between the parties.[20] However, the second sentence of section 251(3) of the Civil Code provides that interest, cost of enforcement of the claim, and the charge, as well as necessary expenditures incurred on the charged asset, are covered by operation of law. In order to avoid disputes about the extent of the cover, the parties will consider clarifying the secured claims in their agreement even if they are secured by operation of law.

The relationship between secured claim and charge is, in principle, close. The **11.12** charge requires the existence of a secured claim,[21] the charge extends only as far as the secured claim,[22] and the transfer of the secured claim leads automatically to a transfer of the charge.[23] The charge also terminates with the secured claim[24] but several cases must be distinguished:

- The charge clearly terminates if the secured claim cannot be enforced due to a statute of limitation.[25]

---

[14] Civil Code, s 251(1), first sentence.   [15] ibid s 251(1), first sentence.
[16] ibid s 251(2).   [17] ibid s 251(2).   [18] ibid s 251(1), second sentence.
[19] The Official Commentary of the Civil Code refers to 'claims', see also Civil Code, ss 251(1), second sentence, and 263.
[20] Implied in Civil Code, s 254(1).
[21] ibid s 251(1) 'to secure her/his claim'. In systematic terms, it is not quite correct that Hungarian law has included this provision in the chapter on 'common rules' since there is a form of charge, the independent charge, which does not secure a claim.
[22] ibid s 251(3), first sentence.   [23] ibid ss 251(4), first sentence, and 259(3).
[24] ibid s 259(3). However, the charge will continue to exist if the law provides otherwise.
[25] ibid s 264(1).

- Where the secured claim is satisfied from the charged asset, the charge terminates but the secured claim remains in existence if the owner of the charged asset and the debtor of the secured claim are different persons.[26] The claim is transferred by operation of law to the owner of the charged asset[27] and thus provides the owner with a recourse claim.
- If a third party satisfies the chargeholder the charge is transferred to him.[28] It is unclear what happens to the secured claim but it must be assumed that it is transferred as well.

11.13 As already pointed out, Hungarian law also provides an independent charge where the relationship between secured claim and charge is more complex. In principle the independent charge does not secure a 'personal claim against the chargor'.[29] However, there is typically a link between the charge and a secured claim created by a separate agreement between the parties.

11.14 A retention of ownership will predominantly secure a sale price obligation. There are no provisions on the extent of the secured claim for retention of ownership and therefore this issue has to be dealt with by agreement between the parties. They can agree in particular that a retention of ownership secures not only one but several claims. The retention of ownership is in principle independent from the claim secured by it. However, the parties' agreement will stipulate that ownership passes upon satisfaction of the secured claim and thus provide a close link between secured claim and retention of ownership.

4. Polish law

11.15 Under Polish law five regimes for secured transactions need to be distinguished: the Civil Code pledge in movable things and receivables, the registered pledge, the retention of ownership, security transfers, and the real estate mortgage. As far as the retention of ownership is concerned, the secured debt will mainly be a sales price obligation which the parties define in a sales agreement. For the registered pledge the law provides that only certain types of claims can be secured. The creditor of a claim must be a public institution, a bank or international financial institution, a company, or another entity conducting economic activity in Poland.[30] No such limitations are made under the Civil Code for non-registered pledges and mortgages in real estate. The registered pledge can only secure monetary claims, which can be denominated either in local or

---

[26] Civil Code, s 259(1).
[27] ibid s 259(1). The transfer may be partial only, since the law provides that it occurs only to the 'extent of the satisfaction'.
[28] ibid s 259(2).   [29] ibid s 269(1).
[30] Law on Registered Pledges and the Pledge Registry, Art 1.

foreign currency.[31] Similarly the Civil Code pledge can only secure 'receivables'[32] and the mortgage in real estate can secure only monetary claims.[33] The Civil Code leaves open whether claims denominated in foreign currency can be secured by a Civil Code pledge. Both registered pledges and Civil Code pledges can secure unconditional and conditional claims,[34] as well as present and future claims.[35] Pursuant to Polish case law and doctrine the same applies for simple real estate mortgages although this is not specifically provided under the Law on Land Registries and Mortgage.[36] However, Article 102(2) of the Law on Land Registries and Mortgage provides for a special type of real estate mortgage, the maximum amount mortgage, by which future as well as conditional claims can be secured. Retentions of ownership do not secure conditional and future claims which do not relate to the claim for payment of the purchase price.

The secured claim may be one or several claims under Polish law, although the **11.16** latter is not expressed clearly by the provisions on the respective security rights. In particular claims secured by registered pledges must be defined clearly. Pursuant to Article 3(2) No 4 of the Law on Registered Pledges and the Pledge Registry the pledge agreement must specify the secured claim, its amount, and the legal relationship giving rise to the claim. A maximum amount must, in principle, not be stated by the parties for a Civil Code pledge or a registered pledge. However, they may opt for registered pledges to define a liability limit under the pledge.[37] Registered pledges securing future or conditional claims secure only up to the amount specified in the pledge agreement.[38] The mortgage in real estate can secure monetary claims which must have a defined amount.[39] The maximum amount mortgage, a special form of the Polish mortgage in real estate, requires only a maximum amount for the secured claim; however, the secured claim may fluctuate in its amount.[40] The pledge is not extended to additional amounts by operation of law for registered pledges under the Law of Registered Pledges except for compensation obtained by the pledgor for the loss, destruction, damage, or devaluation of the pledged property.[41] However, under the Civil Code non-registered pledges extend to claims connected with the secured claim, in particular claims for interest, damages for the non-performance or improper performance of a claim, expenses made on the secured

---

[31] ibid Art 5.   [32] Civil Code, Art 306, §1.
[33] Law on Land Registries and Mortgage, Art 68.
[34] Civil Code, Art 306, §2 for non-registered pledges, Law on Registered Pledges and the Pledge Registry, Art 6 for registered pledges.
[35] Civil Code, Art 306, §2, Law on Registered Pledges and the Pledge Registry, Art 6.
[36] Note, however, the reference to future debts in Law on Land Registry and Mortgages, Art 102(2) for a special type of mortgage, the maximum amount mortgage.
[37] Law on Registered Pledges and the Pledge Registry, Art 3(2).
[38] ibid Art 6.   [39] Law on Land Registry and Mortgages, Art 68.
[40] ibid Art 102(1).   [41] Law on Registered Pledges and the Pledge Registry, Art 10.

asset, and enforcement costs.[42] The mortgage extends by operation of law to interest claims (which are not time-barred) and procedural costs which a court orders to be paid to the mortgage holder.[43] There are no provisions on the extent of the secured claims for retentions of ownership and thus this issue relies on the parties' agreement. The parties can agree in particular that a retention of ownership secures not only one but several claims. Similarly the parties will have to make arrangements for a claim secured by a security transfer.

11.17 The relationship between secured claim and pledge is close for non-registered pledges, which can only be created if a receivable exists[44] and are transferred if a secured claim is transferred.[45] Registered pledges also require the existence of a claim for their creation[46] and are transferred with the transfer of the secured claim.[47] A termination of the secured claim will result in the termination of the registered pledge unless the pledge agreement provides differently.[48] There is no good faith acquisition if a registered pledge is transferred but the secured claim does not exist. A mortgage in real estate is only created if a secured debt exists[49] and terminates when the secured debt is satisfied in full.[50]

5. Romanian law

11.18 Article 10(1) of the Law Concerning Certain Measures for the Acceleration of the Economic Process is the main provision of the Romanian law on security in movables dealing with secured debt. It provides that any type of obligation,[51] ie both monetary and non-monetary obligations (including the obligation to omit doing something) can be secured. Both unconditional and conditional debts, as well as present and future debts,[52] can be covered. Furthermore, the Law confirms that both severable and non-severable debts can be secured. In

---

[42] Civil Code, Art 314.

[43] Law on Land Registry and Mortgages, Art 69. In the case of a maximum amount mortgage ('deposit mortgage') these claims must be within the maximum amount defined for the secured debt; ibid Art 104.

[44] Civil Code, Art 306, §1: 'in order to secure a receivable'.

[45] ibid Art 323, §1, first sentence. If the parties choose to exclude the pledge from the transfer it will terminate (Art 323, §1, second sentence).

[46] Law on Registered Pledges and the Pledge Registry, Art 1 ('to the claims').

[47] ibid Art 17(1); however, the law requires to transfer a secured claim only to a qualified party whose claims can be secured pursuant to ibid Art 1. Where this requirement is not met the pledge will terminate, ibid Art 17(2).

[48] ibid Art 18(1); the parties can provide otherwise.

[49] Law on Land Registry and Mortgages, Art 65(1) ('securing a defined debt').

[50] ibid Art 84.

[51] Also confirmed in Law Concerning Certain Measures for the Acceleration of the Economic Process, Art 9(1) ('any obligation').

[52] ibid Art 10(1). That future debts can be secured is also confirmed in Art 16(3) for the special case of future advances and Art 20(1).

addition, pursuant to the Law, monetary debts can be denominated in local or foreign currency. The broad scope of the Law is limited by the requirements that the basis for the secured debt must be an agreement, thus excluding, for example, obligations arising by operation of law (such as tort law), and that the secured debt must be a 'civil or commercial obligation'.[53] As far as the identification of the debt is concerned, the Law contains the explicit confirmation that the debt has to be determined or determinable.[54] However, an advance, as under US law, is not necessary.

With respect to the extent of the secured debt, there is no clarification that both **11.19** one and more debts can be secured. However, the secured debt must be determined in the security agreement or be 'likely' to be determined.[55] In any event, the security agreement must provide a maximum amount for the secured debt.[56] An interesting concept is contained in Article 23(3) of the Law Concerning Certain Measures for the Acceleration of the Economic Process: if the creditor enforces a security right both over the secured property and its products (to which the security right extends by operation of law)[57] the debt is secured only up to the maximum amount which is defined by the market value of the secured property upon enforcement. Certain 'additional amounts' are included by operation of law,[58] namely accrued and unpaid interest, expenses incurred in taking possession and selling the secured property during enforcement, reasonable expenses in obtaining and maintaining possession of the secured property, and expenses on maintenance of the secured property.

The relationship between secured debt and security right is only sparsely **11.20** documented in the Law Concerning Certain Measures for the Acceleration of the Economic Process. Clearly the creation of the security interest requires the existence of a debt[59] and the termination of the secured debt will lead in principle to the termination of the security right also.[60] However, the Law does not provide for an automatic transfer of the security right with the assignment of the secured debt. Rather, it requires the direct transfer of the security right.[61]

Romanian law on security in movables provides all the ingredients for security **11.21** which is dynamic with respect to the secured debt. Most importantly it allows

---

[53] ibid Art 1.
[54] ibid Art 10(1). Strangely the law provides that the debt must only be 'likely' to be determined in order to be sufficiently determinable.
[55] ibid Art 10(1).
[56] ibid Arts 15, 26(1), first sentence. The debtor has in such a case the right to request a statement regarding the value of the secured debt, ibid Art 26(1), second sentence.
[57] ibid Arts 7, 12, and 24.
[58] ibid Art 10(2), second and third sentences. The parties can agree otherwise.
[59] ibid Art 9(1) ('to secure the fulfillment of any obligation').   [60] ibid Art 27(1).
[61] ibid Art 43.

the taking of security for all types of debts. Although it is not clearly regulated whether or not security can be taken over several debts, there are indications in the first sentence of Article 26(1) of the Law Concerning Certain Measures for the Acceleration of the Economic Process that the Law allows dynamic security rights with respect to the secured debt, since it refers explicitly to variable 'credit lines'.

11.22   The Romanian Civil Code provides that real estate mortgages may either be created by agreement or by operation of law.[62] The contractual mortgage is created by agreement between the parties pursuant to the provisions of the Civil Code.[63] The mortgage created by operation of law involves the transfer of a right in land and its effects are provided by law.[64] The contractual mortgage is subject to the specificity principle, ie the mortgage agreement must properly define the mortgaged property and the secured amount. Mortgages are ancillary rights in that they cannot exist without the secured debt. Hence, once the secured debt terminates, the mortgage terminates automatically as well.

6. Russian law

(a) Type of secured debt

11.23   Russian law distinguishes between the registered pledge (referred to as a mortgage or hypothec) on real estate or the assets of an enterprise, a non-registered pledge on all other assets, a retention of ownership in movable and immovable things, and security assignments of receivables.

- There is no limitation under the Civil Code or the Pledge Law to monetary obligations as secured debt and, hence, all types of obligations with a monetary value can be secured by a pledge. Pursuant to Article 4(3) of the Pledge Law both present and future debts can be secured, the latter, however, only if their amount is specified.
- The Law on Mortgage specifies that a mortgage can secure, in particular, debts arising from loan agreements, sale contracts, leases, or other contracts, as well as claims in damages.[65] It is necessary that the debts are accounted for in the financial accounts of both the creditor and the debtor.[66] The concept of private registers and book-keeping is prevalent under Russian law.[67] It is

---

[62] Civil Code, Art 1748.   [63] ibid Art 1749(2).   [64] ibid Art 1749(1).
[65] Law on Mortgage, Art 2.   [66] ibid Art 2.
[67] Similarly, shares in a joint stock company are recorded in a register held by the company (for companies having fewer than 50 shareholders) or by an external licensed registrar (for companies having 50 shareholders or more and for joint stock companies which have fewer than 50 shareholders but decide to transfer the maintenance of their shareholders' register to an independent registrar). Details of the shares in a limited liability company must be provided in its charter (in per cent and absolute rouble terms), which is registered by the state in the Uniform State Register for Legal Entities.

obvious that the private registration and book-keeping concept is (1) cumbersome for private individuals and (2) a source of endless disputes in practice. For example, law firms are not willing to give their opinions as to the ownership of shares in joint stock companies recorded in a shareholders' register maintained by the company. According to the last sentence of Article 9(4) of the Law on Mortgage, an obligation, the amount of which will be determined in future, may be secured by a mortgage. For undetermined debts, the mortgage agreement must indicate the procedure used to determine the amount. Based on Article 9(4) it appears that under the Law on Mortgage future and/or conditional debts can be secured. However, this is not entirely certain under Russian mortgage law.

• With respect to retention of ownership in movable or non-movable things it will predominantly secure a sale price obligation, whereas a security assignment of receivables can secure all types of obligations.

(b) Extent of the secured debt

As far as the extent of the secured debt is concerned, for pledges both **11.24** Article 339(1) of the Civil Code and Article 54(3) of the Pledge Law (the latter for the pledge of rights which are not monetary claims) require the specification of the secured debt in the pledge agreement for non-registered pledges. Under the Law on Mortgages the debt secured by a mortgage must be defined in the mortgage agreement;[68] a maximum amount of the secured claim can be defined and the mortgage is then limited to this maximum amount.[69] For enterprise mortgages the amount of the secured debt must be no less than half of the enterprise's value[70] and the secured debt must in principle fall due one year or later after the signing of the mortgage agreement.[71] These provisions alone are sufficient to render enterprise mortgages impractical (although the enterprise's value is determined in principle by an estimate made by the parties,[72] a provision which should help to mitigate the valuation issue in practice).

There are no provisions on the extent of the secured debt for retention of **11.25** ownership and the security assignment of receivables. Apparently, the Civil Code's intention is that a retention of ownership shall secure the debt fully, ie including the principal amount, interest, and claims in damages (if any). However, for the avoidance of doubt the extent of the secured debt should be dealt with by agreement between the parties. They can agree, in particular, that a retention of ownership or a security assignment of receivables secure not only one but several claims.

---

[68] Law on Mortgage, Art 9(4).   [69] ibid Art 3(3).   [70] ibid Art 71(1).
[71] ibid Art 71(2).   [72] ibid Art 9(3).

11.26 The debt secured by a non-registered pledge extends by operation of law to the following additional amounts (the list is not exhaustive but indicates only the most important claims in practice):[73]

- interest on the principal amount of the secured debt;
- contractual penalties (if any);
- enforcement costs;
- damages for losses caused by a delay in satisfaction of the secured debt;
- claims for necessary expenses for maintenance of pledged property; and
- claims for the valuation costs of pledged property.[74]

11.27 Similarly, under the Law on Mortgage the mortgage extends, for example, to interest claims, claims in damages, and enforcement costs.[75] Necessary expenses incurred on the real estate by the mortgage holder are also secured.[76] No provisions exist for contractual retentions of ownership and security assignments; however, the parties may freely agree on them in a contract.

(c) Relationship between secured debt and security

11.28 The relationship between the secured debt and a non-registered pledge is strictly ancillary.[77] Pursuant to Articles 334 ('obligation secured by the pledge') and 337 ('pledge shall secure the claim') of the Civil Code and Articles 1 ('for the fulfilment of an obligation') and 4 of the Pledge Law the pledge requires the existence of a secured debt. Furthermore, it only exists to the extent of the secured debt's amount.[78] Upon transfer of the secured debt the pledge follows automatically.[79] The situation is complex with respect to the consequences of a termination of the secured debt for the pledge. In principle, a termination of the secured debt also results in the termination of the pledge.[80] However, if a third party has satisfied the pledgeholder, both the secured debt and the non-registered pledge are transferred to the third party.[81]

11.29 The assignment of a mortgage leads automatically to the secured debt's transfer unless otherwise agreed.[82] Consequently, the mortgage cannot be qualified as an ancillary right from a Russian law point of view.

11.30 The retention of ownership and a security assignment of receivables are in principle independent in their creation and existence from the debt secured by them. However, the parties' agreement for a retention of ownership will

---

[73] Civil Code, Art 337 and Pledge Law, Art 23.
[74] Not mentioned in Pledge Law, Art 23.   [75] Law on Mortgage, Art 3(1).
[76] ibid Art 4.   [77] See generally Pledge Law, Art 4(4).
[78] Civil Code, Art 337 ('claim in the amount at the moment of its satisfaction'), Pledge Law, Art 23 ('full amount as determined at the moment of the debt's satisfaction').
[79] Pledge Law, Art 20.   [80] ibid Arts 31, 34.   [81] ibid Art 27.
[82] Civil Code, Art 355.

stipulate that ownership passes upon satisfaction of the secured debt and thus provide a link between secured debt and retention of ownership.

7. Slovak law

The charge under Slovak law can secure both monetary and non-monetary **11.31** claims provided that their value (in particular for non-monetary claims) is determined or determinable.[83] Both unconditional and conditional claims, as well as present and future claims, can be secured.[84]

Slovak law stipulates only that 'a claim' can be secured.[85] However, this does not **11.32** exclude the possibility of securing several claims by a charge. In particular, Slovak law allows the securing of a fluctuating claim.[86] It requires the specification of the secured claim or claims in the charge agreement.[87] The statement of a maximum amount of the secured claim is required for claims the value of which is not specified in the charge agreement[88]—this is particularly relevant for secured claims with a varying amount.[89] The charge covers additional amounts by operation of law: interest owed on the secured claim and other 'appurtenances', by which the Civil Code means default interest and the enforcement costs.[90] Contractual penalties and other financial sanctions for violating a credit or other agreement are generally not covered by the charge unless otherwise agreed.[91]

The relationship between secured claim and charge is ancillary in several **11.33** respects.[92] First, the law requires the existence of a secured claim.[93] Second, the transfer of a claim automatically effects the transfer of the charge.[94] Third, defences against the secured debt can be held against the charge.[95] Lastly, the termination of the secured claim leads to the termination of the charge.[96]

---

[83] Civil Code, §151c(1).

[84] ibid §151c(2); J Svoboda, *Commentary to the Slovak Civil Code* (*Občiansky zákonník Komentár*) EPP 1–2/1999, 99.

[85] eg ibid §151a.

[86] Allen & Overy and EBRD, *Guide for Taking Charges in the Slovak Republic* (Bratislava, 2003) 12–13.

[87] Civil Code, §151b(2).   [88] ibid §151b(3).

[89] Allen & Overy and EBRD (n 86 above) 12.   [90] ibid 13.

[91] J Búreš and L Drápal, *Pledge Law in Court Practice* (*Zástavní právo v soudní praxi*) (Prague, 1997) 7.

[92] E Giese, P Dušek, J Koubová, and L Dietschová, *Securing Claims in the Czech Republic* (*Zajištění závazků v České republice*) (Prague, 1999) 20. Note that it is good practice in Slovak law to refer also to Czech case law and legal writing. The provisions of the civil codes of the Czech and Slovak Republics show great similarities and Czech law can, therefore, provide guidance for questions of Slovak law (and vice versa).

[93] Civil Code, §151a ('to secure a claim').   [94] ibid §151c(3).

[95] An exception is made for a secured claim which has expired under a statute of limitations, ibid §151ma(2).

[96] ibid §151md(1).

C. Comparative Remarks and Evaluation

1. Analytical principles

11.34 There are three fundamental approaches connected with secured debt: (1) whether a secured transactions law allows the securing of all types of debts (principle of the parties' maximum freedom) or whether there are limitations (limitation principle); (2) whether the secured debt is ancillary (sometimes also referred to as 'accessory') to the security right or independent in some form; and (3) whether the secured debt can be flexible (dynamic) under the security right or whether there is an understanding of secured debts as being rather static.

(a) Types of debt

11.35 Hungarian and Slovak law in particular, but also Bulgarian and Romanian law, can be considered as providing the parties with maximum freedom in terms of the type of debt which can be secured. However, there is still uncertainty under some of the laws regarding whether or not future or conditional debts can be secured.

(b) Relationship between security right and secured debt

11.36 Three analytical principles can be identified with respect to the relationship between security right and secured debt:

(1) the principle of close dependence (English law, US law, accessory rights under German law);

(2) the principle of independence (non-accessory rights under German law); and

(3) the principle of choice between dependence and independence (Model Law).

11.37 Whereas under the principle of dependence the security right reacts to changes in the secured debt during the various phases of the security right's legal life, the security right is relatively free from the secured debt under the principle of independence. Even if the security right is dependent on the secured debt, this is more in the nature of a 'framework right'[97] whose exact content is only defined

---

[97] '*Rahmenberechtigung*'; this is the expression used by E Becker-Eberhard, *Die Forderungsgebundenheit der Sicherungsrechte* (Bielefeld, 1993) 6, 13, 37; the concept of a 'framework right' was famously introduced by Wolfgang Fikentscher (see W Fikentscher and A Heinemann, *Schuldrecht* (10th edn, Berlin, 2006) paras 1572–83) to explain the nature of the 'right to an enterprise' ('*Recht am eingerichteten und ausgeübten Gewerbebetrieb*'), a special tort based on German Civil Code, §823(1). However, in the context of the 'right to an enterprise', 'framework right' means that a balancing of interests ('*Güterabwägung*') is necessary to confirm the right in an individual case. Becker-Eberhard uses the word to highlight the referential relationship between one right (the security right) and another (the secured debt).

by its interaction with the secured debt. The purpose of dependence is twofold. First, it serves as a legislative simplification[98] because the effects of any changes in the secured debt are clearly defined by reference to dependence and do not have to be taken care of by the parties. Second, it is one way of achieving protection of the debtor.

The most important aspect of dependence between security right and secured **11.38** debt is the need for a (at least future) secured debt at the time of creation of the security right. However, as far as the existence of a secured debt as a requirement for the creation of the security right is concerned, two different approaches have to be distinguished:

(1) many legal systems deem the mere existence of a secured debt, even if it is future, to be sufficient (German law, Model Law);
(2) several legal systems go further and require an actual indebtedness, advance, or giving of value (English law, US law).

Further consequences of the dependence between secured debt and security can **11.39** be that changes in the extent of the secured debt have an effect on the extent of the security (in particular under English law and accessory land mortgages under German law) or a transfer of a dependant right occurs together with a leading right. Where there is dependence between secured debt and security it may be possible to hold defences (ie issues affecting the creation, existence, or enforceability of a right, for example the satisfaction of a debt) against the secured debt and also against the security. If and to the extent that the secured debt (as described and identified by the parties) terminates, the security will normally terminate too. English law features the interesting option of an inchoate security interest, which enables the parties to 'warehouse' the security interest during periods in which there is no actual secured debt. Dependence may also be evident from the rules on enforcement, in that the enforceability of the security is tied to a default under the secured debt.

It is interesting to note the existence of security rights which are based on the **11.40** principle of independence, such as the non-ancillary land mortgages under German and Swiss law[99] or the independent charge under Hungarian law. These independent rights are rare exceptions to the rule that in most legal systems security rights are closely dependent on the debt they secure. However, even in the case of independent rights the parties will typically create a link between both mortgage and secured debt at least by way of an agreement, thus limiting the independence of the security right.

---

[98] See D Medicus, 'Die Akzessorietät im Privatrecht' (1971) *Juristische Schulung* 497, 498 for German ancillary ('accessory') rights.
[99] '*Grundschuld*' and '*Schuldbrief*', respectively.

11.41   The EBRD Model Law introduces a concept of choice between dependence and independence. In principle, the Model Law charge is dependent on the secured debt but the freedom to choose the degree of dependency is left to the parties, since they are free to define the secured debt in whatever way is suited to their needs. This is a particular interpretation of the concept of the security right as a framework right.[100]

11.42   Against this background it becomes clear that the understanding of the security right in central and eastern European reference systems is that the security right is ancillary to the secured debt, for example with respect to its creation, its extent, and its termination. The concept of an independent charge can only be found under Hungarian law and has not been applied much in practice. However, the ancillary rights found under central and eastern European laws are often combined with considerable freedom for the parties to define the secured debt, similar to the freedom of choice found under the EBRD Model Law.

(c)   Static or dynamic secured debt

11.43   A security right can be static or dynamic in relation to the secured debt. Where the parties decide to secure a changing pool of present and future debts with a constantly changing composition and a fluctuating amount, the security right will be highly dynamic in nature. An example of this type is security taken for all moneys becoming due and payable under a supply agreement. The dynamic nature of the security will be most obvious from the fluctuating amount of the outstanding debt. Such fluctuations will not only occur with supply agreements but also with current accounts combined with an overdraft facility. They are also related to revolving credits, ie credits which are renewed automatically when an outstanding amount has been repaid.

11.44   There are four building blocks which are required in order to provide a security right which is truly dynamic in relation to the secured debt and, therefore, covers a changing pool of debts. (1) The parties must be able to secure not only a single but also several debts; (2) they must be able to secure future debts (US and English law refer to 'future advances'); (3) they must be able to describe the secured debt generally; (4) lastly, security for future debts must obtain the same priority as security for present debts created at the same time.

11.45   Central and eastern European laws have, to varying degrees, introduced the concept of a security right which is flexible with respect to the secured debt. There remain at times uncertainties as to the exact degree of flexibility of a security right. However, central and eastern European laws in their initial reforms of secured transactions laws have already done away with most of the

---

[100]   See 11.37 above.

limitations which, for a long time, limited the usefulness of many secured transactions laws.

2. Normative evaluation

The EBRD constantly highlighted the fundamental importance of proper   **11.46** regulation of all aspects of the secured debt. This is underlined by Article 4 of the Model Law and Principle 7(b) of the Core Principles for a Secured Transactions Law (which states that 'all types of debts' shall be able to be secured). By allocating a specific provision for the secured debt in the 'general provisions' of the Model Law, the EBRD demonstrated the importance given to the treatment of the secured debt.

It is of particular importance that a secured transactions law should provide for   **11.47** the securing of future debts, ie debts which are created or become owed by the debtor after the creation of the security right. The possibility of securing future debts is necessary for a number of types of debts, for example current accounts and revolving credits. The securing of future debts is also essential for many modern financing techniques, for example cash flow-based financings, such as project financings,[101] or acquisition financings which make assumptions on future cash flow[102] and try to secure access to such cash flow by taking security over future receivables. Security for future debts is thus an essential feature of a modern secured transactions law. This is sometimes criticized because it is said to endanger unsecured debts, may exclude security with a lower priority, and may be preferential.[103] The first two objections can be met, *inter alia*, by introducing the requirement of a maximum amount for the secured debt. The problem that security over future debts may be preferential can be dealt with in the rules of voidable preferences of insolvency law.

On a more general level, modern financing also relies on the ability of the   **11.48** security right to be dynamic with respect to the secured debt. It should be noted that the need for the security right to be flexible is not only limited to the secured property, where it is often identified, but extends to the secured debt.

---

[101] J-H Röver, 'Projektfinanzierung' in UR Siebel (ed), *Handbuch Projekte und Projektfinanzierung* (Munich, 2001) 153–241.

[102] For the assessment of risks, see PL Bernstein, *Against the Gods. The Remarkable Story of Risk* (New York, 1996).

[103] These objections are referred to in PR Wood, *Comparative Law of Security and Guarantees* (London, 1995) para 19-249.

12

CHARGED PROPERTY

A. Analytical Framework

Proprietary security is security in defined assets and provides satisfaction limited **12.01** to these assets only.[1] Similar to the situation of the secured debt, security law must determine three general points with respect to the issue of the secured property (also referred to as 'charged' property in this study):[2]

(1) The type of secured property which can be taken as security—in particular (a) the definition of the property, (b) whether unconditional or also conditional property can be charged, (c) whether present or also future property can be charged, and (d) whether the property can be located inside or also outside the jurisdiction whose law is applicable.

(2) The extent to which secured property is taken as security—with respect to

---

[1] See discussion of the principle of property right in 10.02–10.03 above.
[2] UCC, Art 9 uses the term 'collateral' (see definition in UCC, §9-102(1)(12)) UCC. Under English law 'collateral' also means the assets subject to the security interest. In non-technical language the term 'collateral' is often used for the security interest itself. The Model Law refers to 'charged property' instead of 'collateral'.

this issue one has to distinguish two components: the principal charged property and any additional charged property. The principal charged property can be one asset or several assets. It can be limited by a maximum value of the charged property which may be determined by the parties to the security agreement or may be subject to a limit set by law. The security can be static or dynamic in nature. The additional charged property can be created either by agreement between the parties (often with respect to proceeds of sale and products) or by operation of law. Albeit both principal and additional charged property taken together will form the charged property, it is helpful to distinguish between the two categories as shall be seen.

(3) The relationship between the charged property and the security right—the fact that the security right is often closely dependent on the debt it secures—has already been discussed. Similarly the issue of the relationship between the security right and the secured property has to be addressed. This relationship is the necessary consequence of the security interest having a proprietary nature, ie creating a link between a person and defined assets. Similar to the dependency between secured debt and security right, the relationship between security right and secured property has various aspects: (a) The secured property may have to exist in order for the security interest to be created, (b) any changes in the secured property may influence the extent of the security interest, (c) any transfer of title to or ownership in the secured property may affect the secured property, (d) any defence against rights to the secured property may also be held against the security interests, (e) changes in the secured property may terminate the security interest, and lastly (f) the nature of the secured property may influence the security interest in enforcement proceedings.

12.02 The flexibility demonstrated by the individual laws shows to what extent they allow dynamic security with respect to the secured property. Although the secured property is one of the most important building blocks of the security right it is—like the secured debt—rarely treated systematically in legislation on secured transactions.

B. Eastern European Secured Transactions Laws

1. Bulgarian law

12.03 The types of property which can be taken as security under the Law on Obligations and Contracts are movable things (under a possessory pledge),[3]

---

[3] Law on Obligations and Contracts, Art 156.

receivables (under a pledge of receivables),[4] and immovables (under a mort-gage).[5] A special situation arises with a debt already secured by a security right. In this respect, Article 171 of the Law on Obligations and Contracts confirms that claims secured by a mortgage can be taken as security and mortgaged. Equally Article 7 of the Law on Registered Pledges confirms that a debt secured by a registered pledge can be pledged. The non-possessory, registered pledge pursuant to the Law on Registered Pledges can be created in movable things, receivables and other rights (mainly securities, shares in partnerships, limited liability companies, and joint stock companies),[6] and the assets of an enterprise[7] but in principle only by merchants.[8] The Bulgarian Law on Obligations and Contracts does not refer to future property and it is therefore doubtful whether future property can be taken as security. However, the Law on Registered Pledges explicitly provides for security in future and even in conditional property.[9]

The Law on Registered Pledges clearly provides for a pledge in one or more **12.04** assets.[10] However, under the Law on Obligations and Contracts there is no such clear provision.[11] The issue whether pledged property can be defined both specifically and generally is not clarified in Bulgarian legislation. However, the Law on Registered Pledges which allows security both in one and several assets indicates that a general definition of the pledged property must be possible. This is confirmed by the fact that the Law on Registered Pledges provides for a pledge in the assets of an enterprise and thus a group of assets which can be described only generally.

There is, in principle, no extension of the secured property by operation of law. **12.05** However, where accounts receivables are pledged, the pledge extends to interest on the account receivable.[12] If secured property is destroyed or damaged the pledgeholder has only a contractual claim of preferential satisfaction from any insurance or compensation payments;[13] even this (preferential) claim is lost if the pledgeholder is informed about a payment and does not object within a

---

[4] ibid Art 162.   [5] ibid Art 166.

[6] Only dematerialized shares as far as joint stock companies are concerned.

[7] Law on Registered Pledges, Art 4.

[8] ibid Art 2. This is similar to the limitation of scope under the EBRD Model Law.

[9] Law on Registered Pledges, Art 5(1). See also ibid Art 4(2), second sentence, for future crops.

[10] See ibid Art 4(2): definition of pledged property in 'generic terms'.

[11] See eg Law on Obligations and Contracts, Art 156: 'the pledged movable thing', but Art 162: 'transferable claims'.

[12] Law on Registered Pledges, Art 4(3).

[13] Law on Obligations and Contracts, Article 154, first sentence. See Law on Registered Pledges, Art 10, No 1 for registered pledges. The registered pledge extends also to the equivalent amount of a compensation payment if the actual payment cannot be identified; see Law on Registered Pledges, Art 10, No 3.

three-month period from the time of notification.[14] A mortgage extends to income from the mortgaged property.[15] Lastly, the registered pledge extends to proceeds of sale[16] or the equivalent amount in money if the proceeds cannot be identified.[17]

12.06 The relationship between security right and secured property under Bulgarian law is close (and can be called 'ancillary'). The creation of a charge under Bulgarian law requires the existence of the secured property. This is most evident in the case of the possessory pledge where the pledge is created only if possession in the secured asset is transferred to the pledgeholder. However, registered pledges can be created in future property and, therefore, require the existence of the pledged property at the latest at the time of enforcement. The situation of a sale of pledged property is interesting. Under the Law on Obligations and Contracts the property will remain encumbered by the pledge or mortgage. However, pursuant to section 155 of the Law on Obligations and Contracts the purchaser of the pledged property assumes the rights of the pledgeholder or mortgageholder upon payment of the secured debt. This is confirmed in section 178 of the Law on Obligations and Contracts for mortgages.[18] Under the Law on Registered Pledges the pledge terminates if the pledged property to which the pledge has attached is transferred in the ordinary course of the pledgor's (who is in principle a merchant) business *and* the acquired rights are 'incompatible with the security rights'.[19] This means that the attached pledge will continue if a sale is outside the pledgor's ordinary course of business. Where the pledge has been perfected the pledge will continue.[20] The pledge in movables terminates under the Law on Obligations and Contracts if the pledged asset is returned to the pledgor.[21] Where pledged movable things are processed or become part of other movable things, the pledge does not terminate but continues in the newly created movable thing.[22] In enforcement it is clear that the pledgeholder can ask only for satisfaction from the pledged assets under the pledge.[23]

---

[14] Law on Obligations and Contracts, Art 154, second sentence.   [15] ibid Art 172(2).

[16] Law on Registered Pledges, Art 10, No 2.   [17] ibid Art 10, No 3.

[18] Strangely, Law on Obligations and Contracts, Art 178 does not refer to the 'debtor', thereby suggesting that the purchaser has only preferential rights as against third persons. This is not a satisfactory situation since the purchaser, after payment of the secured debt, must in particular have a right of recourse against the debtor.

[19] Law on Registered Pledges, Art 7; the latter will always be the case if the purchaser acquires ownership in the pledged property.

[20] ibid Art 13(1).

[21] Law on Obligations and Contracts, Art 159 expresses this in a complicated way. According to this provision the creditor 'shall be entitled to preferential satisfaction . . . only if he has not returned the pledged asset to the debtor'.

[22] Law on Registered Pledges, Art 4(4).

[23] eg Law on Obligations and Contracts, Art 159 for pledges on movable things: 'satisfaction from the pledged property's proceeds from enforcement', and ibid Arts 173, 175 for mortgages: 'preferential satisfaction from the sale proceeds of the mortgaged property'.

2. Czech law

The types of property which can be taken as security under the traditional **12.07**
security rights provided under the Czech Civil Code are real estate (in the form
of the lien on real estate),[24] movable things (in the form of the lien on movable
things),[25] receivables (in the form of the lien on receivables),[26] and rights
other than receivables (shares, securities, or intellectual property rights).[27]
Security can also be taken on the assets of an enterprise or other collective assets
(in the form of the lien on the assets of an enterprise, other collective assets, or
sets of things).[28] Furthermore, security can be taken on a debt which is itself
subject to a lien.[29] However, Czech law also adopted the security devices of the
security transfer of ownership in movable things and the security assignment of
receivables to be found for example under German law.[30] Movable things can
also be taken as security under the retention of ownership in movable things as a
means of securing sales credits. Czech law does not clearly allow encumbering
future property either in the context of liens or for retentions of ownership or
security transfers. However, since the Civil Code allows a lien on the assets of an
enterprise, it clearly does not prohibit the creation of security in future assets.

Czech law allows more than one asset to be encumbered. Section 153(1) of **12.08**
the Civil Code provides that 'an enterprise, another collective asset, or a set
of things' can be encumbered by a lien. Sections 156(2) and 161(2) of the Civil
Code confirm, in addition, that 'collective assets, collections of things or movable things can be encumbered'. For retentions of ownership or security transfers
the parties can agree that not only one asset but several assets should be secured.

The secured property of a lien extends to appurtenances as well as to unseparated **12.09**
fruits (such as apples on a tree) of a thing by operation of law.[31]

The relationship between lien and secured asset is ancillary. The creation of a **12.10**
lien under Czech law requires the existence of the secured property. The lien
terminates with the secured asset ceasing to exist.[32] Enforcement from the lien is
limited to the sales proceeds from the secured asset.[33] The same rules apply to
retentions of ownership and security transfers.

---

[24] Civil Code, s 157. Czech law provides only an ancillary lien on real estate, ie a security right
which is directly dependent in its existence on the secured debt (see ibid s 152: 'to secure a
receivable'). The non-ancillary land mortgage recognized by German law has not been adopted by
Czech law. See 11.09 above.

[25] Civil Code, s 157.   [26] ibid s 159.   [27] ibid s 154.   [28] ibid s 153(1).

[29] ibid ss 173–4. The law refers to a 'sublien' in such cases.

[30] TO Schorling, *Das Recht der Kreditsicherheiten in der Tschechischen Republik* (Berlin, 2000);
TO Schorling, 'Secured transactions in the Czech Republic—a case of pre-reform' (Autumn
2000) *Law in Transition* 66–9.

[31] Civil Code, s 153(2).   [32] ibid s 170(1).   [33] ibid s 165(1), first sentence.

12.11 The sketchy nature of Czech codified security law makes it difficult for the parties to create flexible security rights in fully valid form. Particularly cumbersome is the missing clarification with respect to future ('after-acquired') property.

3. Hungarian law

12.12 The Hungarian Civil Code provides charges over real estate, registered charges over other types of property, and possessory charges in movable things, ie charges under the Hungarian Civil Code can, in principle, be taken over all types of property. Future property can be charged with respect to rights and receivables[34] and naturally where an enterprise charge is created.[35] However, there is no reference to future property in the sections on possessory or registered charges. The fact that charges can be created in the assets of an enterprise allows the conclusion that future property is capable of being charged. Retentions of ownership are created in movable things only.

12.13 The secured asset of a charge may be not only one but also more assets.[36] For a retention of ownership, the parties can agree that not only one asset but several assets are taken as collateral.

12.14 There are in principle no extensions of the property secured by a charge by operation of law. However, the parties to the security agreement may agree, for example, to extend the security to proceeds of the charged asset.[37] In a case where a charged asset is sold to prevent damage to it, the purchase price substitutes the charged asset by operation of law.[38]

12.15 The relationship between a charge (both an ancillary and an independent charge—terms which relate to the relationship between charge and secured debt) and a charged asset can be described as ancillary. The creation of a charge under Hungarian law requires the existence of charged property. This is most evident in the case of the possessory charge where the charge is created only if possession is transferred to the chargeholder.[39] A transfer of ownership in the charged property or the creation of any other rights does not in principle affect the charge.[40] However, the sale of a charged asset encumbered with a registered charge[41] terminates the charge if the asset is sold in trade or in the ordinary

---

[34] Civil Code, s 267(1), second sentence.
[35] ibid s 266(1) which provides that the 'whole of an enterprise' can be charged.
[36] ibid s 253(1). See also ibid s 267(1), third sentence: rights and receivables can be defined by general description.
[37] ibid s 252(2). Where the charge is a possessory one the charge holder is obliged to collect natural fruits, ibid s 265(4), first sentence.
[38] ibid s 260(4).   [39] ibid s 265(1).   [40] ibid s 256(1), first sentence.
[41] The provisions on registered charges apply also to floating (enterprise) charges, see ibid s 266(6) and to independent charges, see s 269(5).

course of business and the purchase is made in good faith.[42] The registered charge is also terminated if the charged asset is a good of everyday life and purchased against payment by a buyer in good faith[43] from a person who is not the owner of the charged asset. A possessory charge can equally be acquired in good faith provided that the transfer is 'in the context of trade relationships'.[44] The charge terminates in particular if the chargeholder acquires ownership in the charged asset[45] or the charged asset is destroyed.[46] A possessory charge terminates if the charged asset is returned by the chargeholder to its owner[47] or the chargeholder loses possession to the charged asset without recovering it within one year.[48] The enforcement of the charge is limited to the property charged.[49]

As far as retentions of ownership are concerned, they are in principle dependent **12.16** on the asset secured by them. The parties will provide in their agreement when ownership passes under a retention of ownership clause (it is conditional on the payment of the secured claim). The retention of ownership terminates if: (1) the condition precedent is realized or (2) the asset is destroyed.

Under Hungarian law the parties are clearly in a position to create charges **12.17** which are flexible with respect to the secured property. Not only can they take security in either one or several assets, but they can also create security in future property and the composition of the secured property may change constantly.

4. Polish law

The types of property which can be secured under the Polish Law on Registered **12.18** Pledges and the Pledge Registry are movable things and transferable property rights;[50] similarly under the Civil Code movable things[51] and transferable rights[52] can be encumbered by a pledge. The retention of ownership is limited to movable things. Article 65(1) of the Law on Land Registry and Mortgages defines the assets which can be mortgaged. These are mainly the land and the building standing on the respective land plot as well as certain rights in real estate (in particular ownership rights in flats). There is no clarification in the law regarding whether or not conditional or future property can be pledged by Civil Code or registered pledges. However, as far as a security assignment of future receivables is concerned, case law, legal doctrine, and legal practice agree that

---

[42] ibid s 262(6), first sentence.   [43] ibid s 262(6), second sentence.
[44] ibid s 265(1), second sentence.   [45] ibid s 259(4).   [46] ibid s 260(1).
[47] ibid s 265(6), first sentence.   [48] ibid s 265(6), second sentence.
[49] See ibid ss 251(1) ('satisfaction from the charged asset') and 255(1) ('satisfaction from the charged assets').
[50] See Law on Registered Pledges and the Pledge Registry, Art 7(1).
[51] Civil Code, Art 306, §1 ('movable').   [52] ibid Art 327.

such an assignment is effective and that the provisions of the Civil Code apply by way of analogy. It is, however, required that the assignment contract defines precisely the assigned receivables and the legal relationship giving rise to the receivables. There is only an 'expectation to acquire receivables in future' if no legal relationship exists from which receivables could arise. It is unclear under Polish law whether such an expectation to acquire a receivable in future can be assigned. Since receivables (like other assets) cannot be transferred earlier than they arise, the assignment contract over future receivables will effectively have two components: an obligation to transfer receivables once they arise and the actual assignment. The transfer of the receivables to the assignee will occur automatically without the need to execute additional agreements. Instead of agreeing a security assignment of future receivables, the parties may agree a mere obligation of the assignor to assign the receivables in future, once they arise. This would require the parties to enter into a second contract which assigns the receivables. The obligation to assign future receivables requires only a general description of the assigned receivables as to the type or origin and the maturity date (and possibly other general characteristics).

12.19 The new Law on Registered Pledges and the Pledge Registry provides clearly the possibility to encumber one or more assets.[53] This is not clearly expressed under the Civil Code, which refers throughout only to a pledge in 'a movable'[54] or a right.[55] However, as far as retentions of ownership are concerned, the parties can agree that not only one asset but several assets are secured. If ownership is transferred in a movable thing which is identified generally (ie as to its type) or to a group of assets, the debtor or the third party are required to single out and mark the asset or the group of assets. Further, they have to keep a record of any changes concerning the asset or the group of assets to which ownership has been transferred[56] unless the agreement provides otherwise.

12.20 Under the Law on Registered Pledges and the Pledge Registry the security right extends by operation of law to any movable things into which it is altered, for example in a manufacturing process, or to which the secured asset is added.[57] In addition, the pledge extends by operation of law to compensation obtained for loss, destruction, and damage as well as devaluation of the secured asset.[58] In addition, a Civil Code pledge extends to proceeds of sale (but there is a need to

---

[53] Law on Registered Pledges and the Pledge Registry, Art 7 which provides for pledges over (1) things identified as to type and (2) a collection of things or rights constituting 'an economic entity'.

[54] See eg Civil Code, Art 306, §1.

[55] Terminology is variable. Sometimes the Civil Code refers to 'rights' (see title of ch 2 and Art 327) but also to 'a receivable debt' (see eg Art 331).

[56] Banking Law, Art 101(2).

[57] Law on Registered Pledges and the Pledge Registry, Art 8.   [58] ibid Art 10.

place the sales proceeds in court deposit).[59] In this respect, a special rule applies to pledges on receivables: if the secured asset (in this case the receivable) is satisfied, the pledge extends to the proceeds from the satisfaction.[60] Under the Civil Code the pledge extends in principle to fruits of the pledged asset whose transfer to the pledgeholder reduces the amount of the secured debt.[61] The mortgage in real estate extends by operation of law to accessories (such as land machines) on the land or parts of the land (for example fruits) as long as they have not been sold in the ordinary course of business and removed from the mortgaged land plot.[62] The sales contract needs to carry an officially confirmed date (the so-called '*data certa*'). The mortgage extends also to claims under rent agreements covering the mortgaged real estate[63] and insurance claims under an insurance policy insuring the real estate.[64] In addition, claims in damages for diminished value of the mortgaged property are covered by the mortgage, provided that the mortgagor was not responsible for the value reduction.[65] Under retention of ownership arrangements the parties have to determine which assets are covered by the retention. There is no automatic extension of the retention agreement to other assets.

Both under the Law on Registered Pledges and the Pledge Registry and the Civil **12.21** Code the relationship between the pledge and the secured asset is close. As for the creation of the security right under the Law on Registered Pledges and the Pledge Registry it requires the existence of a secured asset.[66] This is confirmed by the requirement to specify the collateral pursuant to Article 3(2) of the Law. Strangely the Law on Registered Pledges and the Pledge Registry does not provide explicitly for security in future property. Mortgages in real estate clearly require immovable property for their creation.[67] A transfer of ownership in the secured asset by way of sale may terminate the registered pledge but only if (1) the purchaser of the secured asset has no actual knowledge of the pledge agreement or would not, in the case of diligent enquiries, have acquired such knowledge at the time when possession or ownership in the pledged property are transferred to the purchaser *or* (2) the collateral is sold in the ordinary course of the pledgor's business, the purchaser takes the pledged asset for value, and the purchaser is not acting in bad faith at the time of the pledged property's acquisition.[68] The reference to 'bad faith' in the second situation indicates that the burden of proof for the issue of 'bad faith' is with the purchaser. However, the

---

[59] Civil Code, Art 321, §2.   [60] ibid Art 332.   [61] ibid Art 319.
[62] Law on Land Registry and Mortgages, Arts 84–87.   [63] ibid Art 88.
[64] ibid Art 89.   [65] ibid Art 93.
[66] See Law on Registered Pledges and the Pledge Registry, Arts 2(2) ('movable things encumbered') and 7(2) ('may encumber').
[67] Law on Land Registry and Mortgages, Art 65.
[68] Law on Registered Pledges and the Pledge Registry, Art 13.

pledgor may covenant not to sell or encumber the pledged assets. In such a case a sale or encumbrance will only be valid if the purchaser acted in good faith with respect to this negative covenant.[69] Under the Civil Code the non-registered pledge does not terminate if the pledged asset is sold.[70] It also does not terminate if the pledgeholder acquires ownership of the pledged asset, in particular if a third party holds a pledge (or another encumbrance) in the secured asset.[71] Under the Civil Code it is not possible to covenant that the secured asset is not transferred or encumbered.[72] If real estate encumbered by a mortgage is sold, the mortgage will not terminate. Termination of the security right will occur if a movable thing which has been taken as security becomes a component part of an immovable.[73] The pledge will also terminate if the pledged asset is sold pursuant to Article 13 of the Law on Registered Pledges and the Pledge Registry. The Law does not contain a provision on the destruction of secured property but this must be a case in which the security right terminates by its very nature. The Civil Code pledge terminates if possession in the pledged asset is returned to the pledgor.[74] Enforcement of the pledge will be made against the collateral,[75] enforcement of a real estate mortgage against the encumbered immovable property.[76]

12.22   As far as retentions of ownership are concerned, they are in principle dependent on the asset secured by them. The parties will provide in their agreement when ownership passes under a retention of ownership clause (it is conditional on the payment of the secured claim). The retention of ownership terminates if: (1) the condition precedent is realized, (2) the asset is destroyed, or (3) ownership is acquired from the purchaser in good faith. In the latter case, possession of the movable asset must be transferred and the purchaser must act in good faith with respect to the existence of the ownership of the transferor.[77]

12.23   Polish law allows the creation of security rights (in particular under the Law on Registered Pledges and the Pledge Registry) which are flexible with respect to the charged property. Not only can they take security in either one or several

---

[69] Law on Registered Pledges and the Pledge Registry, Art 14(1), (2).

[70] Civil Code, Art 306, §1 ('regardless of whose property is has become'). Art 325, §2 confirms that the pledge does not terminate if the pledged asset is acquired by the pledgeholder (but only if the secured debt is encumbered with [another] right of a third party).

[71] ibid Art 325, §2. In other words, the pledge terminates if no such right exists.

[72] ibid Art 311.

[73] Law on Registered Pledges and the Pledge Registry, Art 9(1). In such a case the pledgeholder has the right to demand the creation of a mortgage over the real estate, ibid Art 9(2).

[74] Civil Code, Art 325, §1.

[75] Law on Registered Pledges and the Pledge Registry, Arts 20 ('against the collateral') and 21 ('from the pledged property').

[76] Law on Land Registry and Mortgages, Art 65(1) ('satisfaction from the real estate').

[77] Civil Code, Art 169, §1.

assets, but they can also create security in future property and the composition of the charged property may change constantly.

5. Romanian law

The types of property which can be secured under the Law Concerning Certain **12.24** Measures for the Acceleration of the Economic Process are goods, in the sense of movables (movable things and rights).[78] Article 6 of the Law lists many types of movable property and clarifies, in particular, that an accessory to real estate (which is not permanently connected to the real estate) can be charged by a security right under the Law.[79] Pursuant to Article 18 of the Law future property can be taken as security.[80] In such a case the security right becomes effective as soon as the chargor obtains ownership of the asset.

The security right can cover one or more assets.[81] Both Article 10(3) and **12.25** Article 16(1) of the Law Concerning Certain Measures for the Acceleration of the Economic Process confirm that the secured property can be described, for the purposes of the security right, specifically or generally. However, if the security right relates to a certain amount of money held in a bank account, such account shall be identified properly. The definition of the secured property must be made at the date of the security agreement.

The secured property extends by operation of law to products obtained from the **12.26** realization of secured property pursuant to Articles 7 (second alternative) and 12 of the Law Concerning Certain Measures for the Acceleration of the Economic Process.[82] In addition, an asset which replaces the secured property is covered by the security right.[83] Fruits and products of the secured property are not automatically covered by the attached security right. However, the parties can agree in the security agreement that the attached security right extends to additional secured property and they must then specify the requirements for this extension and the manner in which the fruits and products are credited against the secured debt.[84] If the securityholder is in possession of the secured property and the security right is perfected, he collects fruits for the benefit of the person giving security.[85] The fruits will then be applied first to expenses for the maintenance of

---

[78] See Law Concerning Certain Measures for the Acceleration of the Economic Process, Arts 1 and 7, first alternative. Movables ancillary to real estate can also be subject to security rights, ibid Art 6(2).

[79] See ibid Art 6(2); a security right does not terminate if a moveable thing is connected with real estate as an ancillary, ibid Art 24(2).

[80] This is confirmed by ibid Art 16(1), first sentence, which refers to a description of 'future property'.

[81] ibid Art 10(3).

[82] This is confirmed by ibid Art 23(2) for enforcement proceedings.

[83] ibid Art 24(1), first alternative.   [84] ibid Art 16(2).   [85] ibid Art 39(2).

the secured property, second to interest on the secured debt, and third to the principal of the secured debt.[86]

12.27   The creation of the security right depends clearly on the secured property being owned by the chargor.[87] This is underlined by Article 18(1) of the Law Concerning Certain Measures for the Acceleration of the Economic Process pursuant to which a security right can be created in future movable property but will become 'effective' only once the chargor has received ownership in the charged asset. A transfer of ownership in an asset which has been encumbered by a security right will not terminate an attached security right provided that the purchase price exceeds the equivalent amount in Romanian Lei of €1,000.[88] The same applies for perfected security interests.[89] However, as far as products are concerned, an attached security right will terminate over such products if a securityholder only seeks enforcement with respect to the products.[90] The security right does not terminate if the secured property is incorporated in a new asset[91] or if it becomes accessory to real estate.[92] The Law does not contain a provision on the destruction of secured property but this must be a case in which the security right terminates by its very nature. The enforcement of the security right can only be made against the secured asset.[93]

12.28   Romanian law on security in movables provides all the ingredients for security which is dynamic with respect to the secured property (static security is equally possible). In particular the fact that more than one asset, as well as all the assets owned by the person giving the security right, can be taken as secured property, that the secured property can be described generally, and can be future property allow a dynamic security right, whose secured property can adapt over time.

12.29   With respect to real estate mortgages, under the Romanian Civil Code only immovable assets may be mortgaged. Mortgages may only be created by the actual owner of an immovable asset, and future property cannot be mortgaged.[94] The mortgage in real estate extends by operation of law to accessories (for example constructions). If the real estate encumbered by a mortgage is sold, the

---

[86]   Law Concerning Certain Measures for the Acceleration of the Economic Process, Art 39(2).

[87]   See ibid Art 1 ('security rights securing the fulfilment of a civil or commercial obligation').

[88]   Pursuant to Law Concerning Certain Measures for the Acceleration of the Economic Process, Arts 23(1) and 38(1) the security right maintains its existence even if the secured asset has, eg, been sold. However, this does not prevent the person giving security from disposing of the secured property, eg by way of sale, ibid Art 21(1). Art 21(3) confirms that such dispositions are legally valid.

[89]   ibid Art 38(1).

[90]   ibid Art 23(1). In practice the securityholder will therefore never limit enforcement to the products.

[91]   ibid Art 24(1), second alternative ('an asset which incorporates the value of the secured property').

[92]   ibid Art 24(2).   [93]   See ibid Arts 11(1), 23(2), 63(1).   [94]   Civil Code, Art 1775.

mortgage will not terminate. In cases where the real estate is destroyed or else its value decreases, the mortgage extends to the rights of the mortgagor arising from such destruction or devaluation, in particular insurance claims.

6. Russian law

(a) Type of secured property

Property which may be pledged or mortgaged can be any property, including **12.30** movable and immovable things.[95] Rights and even assets of an enterprise as a whole can be mortgaged.[96] In particular the following assets can be subject to a real estate mortgage:

- land;
- buildings used by enterprises;
- privately used buildings and flats; and
- buildings under construction.

The enterprise mortgage is a useful tool for covering the assets of an enterprise as **12.31** a going concern; however, the enterprise mortgage under Russian law does not provide the remedy of appointing a receiver or manager over the enterprise. Under Russian law there is no need to create an enterprise mortgage alongside security rights over particularly valuable or important assets of an enterprise, as is the practice under English law, where fixed and floating charges (or mortgages) are both created in the same assets. Since there is no concept of crystallization under Russian law for enterprise mortgages, a stand-alone enterprise mortgage is sufficient protection.

However, there are a number of exceptions to the general rule that any property **12.32** may be pledged. The following cannot be mortgaged:

- property which is withdrawn from circulation (so-called '*res extra commercium*');
- personal claims (for example alimony claims, claims in damages for loss of life or injuries);
- rights whose transfer is prohibited by law;[97]
- real estate which is owned by the state or public local entities; and[98]

---

[95] For details on real estate assets, see Law on Mortgage, Arts 5, 62–64. The mortgage of land does not necessarily extend to buildings on the respective land; it extends to these only if this is provided in the mortgage agreement, ibid Art 64(1). However, a mortgage of a building is possible only if both the building and the land are mortgaged, ibid Art 69(2).

[96] For mortgages of the assets of an enterprise, see ibid Art 69(1).

[97] Civil Code, Art 336. The last case is also reflected in Pledge Law, Art 6(1) according to which only property which can be 'alienated' can be charged.

[98] Law on Mortgage, Art 63(1).

- property which is already pledged, unless the pledgeholder agrees to a subsequent pledge.

12.33 A particular situation exists with respect to bank accounts. Although Russian law allows a non-registered pledge in any property which can be sold at a public auction, pursuant to a decision by the Russian Supreme Arbitration Court in 1996, amounts in bank accounts cannot be sold at auction and thus cannot be pledged.[99] Further, in 1998 there was an additional judgment that money in a bank account is not a tangible asset and therefore cannot be pledged.[100] The decisions did not differentiate between rouble amounts and foreign currency; however, since then the understanding has developed in such a way that foreign currency amounts can be sold at auction and pledged. Although these decisions are not strictly binding on lower courts, it is clear that in practice pledges of rouble amounts in a bank account currently cannot be taken under Russian law. Legislative reform of this issue is planned.[101]

12.34 There are several ways in practice to provide some security for lenders with respect to rouble amounts in bank accounts. One way is to limit contractually (by an 'account withdrawal agreement') the debtor's powers to withdraw money from an account and to grant the lender (in most cases a bank) the right to withdraw money from the debtor's bank account. The debtor thereby agrees that the lender shall have the right to debit from the debtor's account maintained with a bank any and all amounts due to the bank, for example pursuant to a loan agreement, without the debtor's prior consent. Note, however, that the withdrawal right may be terminated early by the debtor at any time. Under Russian law, account holders cannot be validly restricted from closing an account, which limits the reliability of this security tool. However, the unauthorized closing of a bank account by a borrower may be qualified as an

---

[99] Judgment of the Highest Arbitrazh Court No 7965/95 of 2 July 1996.

[100] Information letter of the Highest Arbitrazh Court No 26 of 15 January 1998. This was similar to the situation under English law as long as the rule from the famous case *Re Charge Card Services Ltd* was applied ([1986] 3 All ER 289; confirmed by the Court of Appeal in *Morris v Agrochemicals Ltd; Re BCCI (No 8)* [1996] Ch 245, also published in [1996] 2 BCLC 254). In this decision it was held by Millett J that a charge over a credit balance by a bank is conceptually impossible, for the debtor cannot become his own creditor and sue himself. R Goode (*Commercial Law* (London, 1982) 721) had previously put forward this view. It has also been argued in favour of this position that a debt is not property as between the creditor and the debtor, but only as between the creditor and a third party (R Goode, *Commercial Law* (2nd edn, London, 1995) 660). This position was, however, controversial in English law. The decision in *Re Charge Card Services Ltd* was reversed by the House of Lords (*Morris v Rayners Enterprises Inc /Morris v Agrichemicals Ltd; Re BCCI (No 8)* [1998] AC 214, [1997] 4 All ER 568). Lord Hoffmann, delivering the decision of the House of Lords, established that it is perfectly possible for a bank to take an equitable charge over money deposited with it.

[101] See 9.30 above.

event of default under the loan agreement, entitling the lender to request early repayment of the loan and the payment of default interest.

Another way of dealing with the unavailability of pledges over rouble bank accounts under Russian law is to open offshore bank accounts for foreign currency into which payments are made. However, it should be noted that from a Russian law perspective the law applicable to the pledge over the offshore bank account will be the law of the pledgor's country of incorporation (if it is a company) unless agreed otherwise in the pledge agreement. Under Russian law, the applicable law is not the law applicable in the place of the account's location.[102] However, under English law, for instance, a debt is in principle situated in the country where the debtor resides[103] and this will be the place of the account. Hence it is important to look to the law applicable to the creation of pledges in accounts and consider whether it allows for effective security in accounts.

12.35

Secured property of non-registered pledges and mortgages may also be future property;[104] however, there is no clear statement under Russian law as to whether property transferred to the pledgor or mortgagor under a condition precedent ('conditional property') can be pledged or mortgaged. It should be noted that whether or not future rights under already existing contracts can be pledged is still disputed under Russian law.

12.36

Retentions of ownership are created in both movable things and immovable property and security assignments in receivables only.

12.37

(b) Extent of secured property

A non-registered pledge may comprise one or more assets. Russian law provides for pledges of goods in circulation (such as inventories, raw materials, or products) or processing.[105] The value of the pledged property must not become less than the value defined in the pledge contract.[106] The parties may, however, opt out of this provision in their pledge contract. A breach of an opting out provision entitles the pledgeholder to request early performance of the secured debt by the debtor and to claim damages for losses arising from early termination.

12.38

For a retention of ownership and for security assignments of receivables, the parties can agree that not only one asset but several assets are taken as collateral.

12.39

---

[102] Civil Code, Art 1211.

[103] Dicey, Morris, and Collins, *Conflict of Laws* (14th edn, London 2006) para 22-026.

[104] Civil Code, Art 340(6), Pledge Law, Art 6(3). See also Civil Code, Art 340(2) for enterprise mortgages or mortgages of a 'property complex as a whole' ('acquired during the period of the mortgage').

[105] Civil Code, Art 357, Pledge Law, Art 46(1).

[106] Pledge Law, Art 46(1), first sentence.

12.40   Russian law has special provisions on the value of pledged property. Pursuant to Article 10(1) of the Pledge Law the value of the pledged property must be defined by the parties; otherwise the pledge contract is invalid. This provision applies to mortgages on real estate or enterprises as well. A value definition should be particularly important for pledges of goods in circulation or processing. It should also be relevant for pledges of rights because pursuant to Article 54(3) of the Pledge Law the parties must determine the value of a right which cannot be determined in money terms in the pledge contract. The value provisions of Russian law protect the pledgor from pledging assets with a value substantially exceeding the amount of the secured debt, but this concept has no practical consequences. There are no published court decisions which declare a pledge contract null and void because the value of the pledged property substantially exceeds the amount of the secured debt. Thus, the value requirement is rather superfluous since it is of no practical importance whether the parties correctly define the value of the asset. The only relevant issue in practice is, in any event, the amount of sales proceeds received from the enforcement of the pledge.

12.41   A non-registered pledge extends by operation of law to accessories and inseparable fruits of the principal secured property.[107] Insurance claims are additional secured property of a pledge by operation of law.[108] No automatic extensions are provided for mortgages, retentions of ownership and security assignments. However, a mortgage of a land plot automatically leads to the creation of a mortgage of buildings and constructions located on it.

(c) Relationship between security and secured property

12.42   Article 334(1) of the Civil Code and Article 1 of the Pledge Law confirm that the non-registered pledge is closely related to the secured property; the same applies to the mortgage. Interestingly, Russian law provides for the case of substitution of the secured property with the pledgeholder's consent.[109] On the one hand, Russian law prohibits the pledgor from selling (or more generally alienating) the pledged property without the pledgeholder's prior consent, unless a law or the pledge contract provides otherwise.[110] On the other hand, if movable things are pledged (with the exception of goods in circulation or processing) the purchaser may be unaware (bona fide) of the fact that they are subject to a pledge. In this event the purchaser is deemed to be a good faith acquirer with respect to the property. However, the purchaser acquires the

---

[107] Civil Code, Art 340(1), Pledge Law, Art 6(2). The pledge contract or law can provide differently.
[108] Civil Code, Art 334(1) unless the 'loss or the damage has taken place for reasons for which the pledgeholder is responsible'.
[109] Pledge Law, Art 8.   [110] Civil Code, Art 346(2), first sentence.

ownership subject to a pledge because Russian law stipulates that the pledge shall continue to exist if the pledged property is purchased[111] unless the pledged property is goods in circulation or processing.[112]

A bona fide purchase of mortgaged real property, pledged registered shares in, or **12.43** pledged debt instruments (bonds) issued by Russian companies is legally impossible because these pledges or mortgages must be registered by the state (as far as mortgages are concerned) or with the shareholders or bondholders register of the company. Mortgaged real estate can only be sold to a third party if the mortgagor agrees or if provided in the mortgage agreement.[113] If a mortgage deed has been issued, the right to transfer has to be provided in the deed and the requirements contained in the deed must be complied with.[114] Should the transfer rules for mortgaged property not be complied with, the mortgageholder can claim to have the transfer declared invalid or demand satisfaction of the secured debt and enforcement of the mortgage even if the secured debt is not yet due.[115] If the third party to which mortgaged property has been transferred in violation of the transfer rules knew or should have known about the mortgage, it may become liable for the secured debt.[116] Property subject to an enterprise mortgage can be sold if this does not reduce the total value of the enterprise's assets.[117] The pledge terminates if the pledged property has been destroyed.[118]

As far as retentions of ownership are concerned, they are in principle dependent **12.44** on the asset secured by them. The parties will provide in their agreement the event upon which ownership of the secured asset is transferred; usually, the transfer of ownership of the retained property is conditional on the payment of the secured debt. The retention of ownership terminates if (1) the condition precedent is fulfilled or (2) the asset is destroyed. It also terminates if ownership is acquired from the purchaser in good faith. In the latter case possession of the movable asset must be transferred and the purchaser must act in good faith with respect to the existence of the transferor's ownership.[119]

(d) Dynamic security

There is only limited scope for a dynamic pledge with respect to secured pro- **12.45** perty under Russian law. Admittedly, Russian law provides for an enterprise mortgage and allows security in future property as well as a pledge for goods in circulation and processing. However, the details of a dynamic pledge are still unclear under Russian law.

---

[111] Pledge Law, Art 32. The pledgor has an unlimited right to dispose of the pledged asset unless the parties agree otherwise, ibid Art 20, first sentence. This provision clearly contradicts Civil Code, Art 346 and shall not apply.
[112] Pledge Law, Art 46(2).   [113] Law on Mortgage, Art 37(1).   [114] ibid Art 37(2).
[115] ibid Art 39, first sentence.   [116] ibid Art 39, second sentence.
[117] ibid Art 72(1).   [118] Pledge Law, Art 34.   [119] Civil Code, Art 302.

7. Slovak law

12.46 Slovak law has been developed using the EBRD Model Law as an example, and most of the Model Law's concepts can be found in Slovak security law. As far as charged property is concerned, a charge under Slovak law can cover a thing, a right,[120] an intangible asset, and residential or non-residential premises provided they are transferable.[121] Things can either be tangible movable assets or immovable assets. Hence, Slovak law follows the Model Law's unitary approach. Furthermore, Slovak law also encompasses the concept of an enterprise charge, ie a charge over the assets of an enterprise or part of an enterprise.[122] A prohibition on creating charges has no proprietary effect[123] (but may be valid as an obligation between the parties). Given the example of the Model Law it is not surprising that Slovak law clearly allows charges in both present and future property.[124] A charge can also be created if the ownership acquisition to the charged property is subject to a condition subsequent.[125]

12.47 The principal charged property can be either one or more assets.[126] Slovak law clearly embraces the concepts of a static and a dynamic charge, since the possibility of charging several assets, the possibility of describing the charged property generally in the charge agreement[127] and the charge register, and the possibility of charging future assets allow a charge which is constantly changing with respect to the charged property.[128] The charge extends to certain assets as additional charged property by operation of law, namely insurance rights[129] and interest and other appurtenances where the charge is created over a claim.[130] Furthermore, fruits, additions, and attachments are included in the principal

---

[120] J Bičovský, J Fiala and M Holub, *Commentary on the Civil Code (Občiansky zákonník—poznámkové vydanie s judikatúrou, I. diel, 6 doplnené vydanie)* (Bratislava, 1998) 204.

[121] Civil Code, §151d(1) first sentence; Allen & Overy and EBRD, *Guide for Taking Charges in the Slovak Republic* (Bratislava, 2003) 8–9; J Fiala, J Hurdík, and A Sedláková, *Pledge Law and Easements (Zástavní právo a věcná břemena)* (Brno, 1992) 23.

[122] Civil Code, §151d(1); Allen & Overy and EBRD (n 121 above) 11; E Giese, P Dušek, J Koubová, and L. Dietschová, *Securing Claims in the Czech Republic (Zajištění závazků v České republice)* (Prague, 1999) 31; A Rozehnal, *Credits Secured by Charges (Úvěry zajištěné zástavním právem)* (Prague, 1997) 81.

[123] Civil Code, §151d(6).

[124] ibid §151d(4); Allen & Overy and EBRD (n 121 above) 10.

[125] Civil Code, §151d(4).

[126] ibid §§151d(1), second sentence, (5), 151f(1); Allen & Overy and EBRD (n 121 above) 11.

[127] Civil Code, §151b(4).   [128] See Allen & Overy and EBRD (n 121 above) 11.

[129] Civil Code, §151mc(3); Allen & Overy and EBRD (n 121 above) 11–12, 26. However, the chargor is under no obligation to insure the charged property, Civil Code, §151mc(1).

[130] ibid §151mb(1).

charged property.[131] However, a charge does not extend to proceeds of sale of the charged property.[132]

The charge under Slovak law is ancillary to the existence and the ownership of **12.48** the charged property. A transfer of ownership of the charged property leads in principle to a transfer to the new owner which includes the encumbrance.[133] However, the charge agreement may stipulate that ownership of the charged property can be transferred free from the charge.[134] In addition, if ownership in the charged property is transferred, the charge does not terminate but is 'not effective against the purchaser of the charged property' provided that (1) the chargor transfers in the normal course of business and within its business activities or (2) the purchaser acts in good faith with respect to the non-existence of a charge taking into account all circumstances.[135] As such, a good faith acquisition will be difficult if the charge is registered in the charges register, since the purchaser will then have to prove that he acted in good faith.[136] The charge terminates if the charged property ceases to exist.[137]

C. Comparative Remarks and Evaluation

1. Analytical principles

The fundamental issues faced in connection with the secured property are **12.49** (a) whether a secured transactions law allows the securing of all types of property (principle of the parties' maximum freedom) or whether there are limitations (limitation principle); and (b) whether the secured property can be flexible (dynamic) under the security right or whether it is seen as being static.

(a) Types of charged property

Most central and eastern European secured transactions laws are permissive **12.50** with respect to secured property. However, Russian law in particular features limitations concerning rouble amounts in bank accounts.

Future property, ie property which becomes owned by the person giving the **12.51** security right after creation of the security right, is of special relevance. There are two situations in which property can be said to be future. First, existing things or rights may exist at the time of the creation of the security right but not yet be

---

[131] ibid §151d(2); Allen & Overy and EBRD (n 121 above) 11; J Fiala, J Hurdík, and A Sedláková, (n 121 above) 25.

[132] Civil Code, §151h deals with the sale of charged property but does not refer to an extension of the charge to proceeds of sale.

[133] ibid §151h(1).   [134] ibid §151h(1).   [135] ibid §151h(3), first sentence.

[136] ibid §151h(3), second sentence.   [137] ibid §151md(1)b.

owned by the person giving the security right at that time. For example, the person giving the security right may intend to acquire a car in two weeks' time but is currently not its owner.[138] Second, things and rights may also be future because they do not yet exist at the time of creation of the security right.[139] For example, financing may be provided for a building which has yet to be built. From a legal point of view both situations can be treated in the same way.

12.52 At first sight it seems problematic to allow future property to be covered by security rights, since a property right can, in principle, only be established in property which is owned by the person creating rights in the property. There is, however, a great practical need for security rights over future property. This can be illustrated by an example:

> A lender proposes to finance the business of a car manufacturer. The manufacturer intends to enter into a series of long-term supply contracts to various wholesale sellers of cars. The rights to payment for the cars under the proposed contracts will be extremely valuable to the manufacturer and similarly to the lender, from the perspective of security. Those future rights should be able to be included in the secured property.

12.53 How can one overcome the conceptual difficulty that property rights can in principle only be created in property which is owned by the person creating rights in the property? Under German law security rights (pledge, accessory land mortgage, non-accessory land mortgage, and retention of ownership) in principle cannot be created in future property. At the time of creation of the security right, the person giving security must own the charged property. A security transfer of ownership in movable assets can be done for future assets; it is created by way of 'anticipated agreement' ('*antizipierte Übereignung*'). There is a serious disadvantage to this approach: the security right will only take effect from the date on which all requirements for the creation of the right are complied with. In particular the transfer of ownership (ie the security right) is only effected from the time of the property becoming owned by the person giving security. In addition, where the security right is a security transfer of ownership, the future property is first acquired by the person giving security and only a 'logical second' later by the person receiving security. This is of practical importance when the person giving security has gone into insolvency before acquiring the future right. Common law jurisdictions are more favourable towards the creation of security in future property. Under Article 9 of the UCC it is possible to create security interests over so-called after-acquired property,

---

[138] Note that the right to receive goods or services in the future is present property for it is already held by the person giving the security.

[139] For rights it can be distinguished further whether or not the basis from which the right will arise already exists; see R Serick, *Eigentumsvorbehalt und Sicherungsübertragung. Neue Rechtsentwicklungen* (2nd edn, Heidelberg, 1993) 87 n 31.

ie assets which become owned in future. Similarly there are no objections to security over future property with immediate priority under English law. However, the recognition of security in future property works under English law only in equity and not at common law; it therefore creates equitable rights only (which are inchoate). This has certainly influenced the solution which was found for the Model Law. There the parties can include future property in the charged property (Article 5.8 of the Model Law), ie property which the person giving the charge does not own at the time of creation of the charge. The charge attaches automatically once the chargor becomes the owner of a thing or right taken as security (Article 5.9) but takes priority from the time of its creation (Article 6.9).

The accumulation of charged property under a future property clause (English **12.54** and US law as well as the Model Law) can continue endlessly. However, this accumulation of property finds its end at the time of opening of insolvency proceedings.[140] The accumulation may also be voidable prior to insolvency because it is qualified under insolvency law as a preference or a fraudulent conveyance.[141] That the scope of the respective insolvency provisions must be carefully limited is illustrated by a famous US case. In its *Benedict v Ratner*[142] decision, the US Supreme Court struck down as a fraudulent conveyance an assignment of present and future debts ('accounts receivable' in the US terminology) under which the debtor was allowed to collect the debts, use the proceeds as it saw fit, not notify the debtors of the assignment, and generally not account to the lender. The court held that such 'unfettered dominion' by the debtor over the collateral and its proceeds worked a fraud on other creditors and was voidable in bankruptcy.[143] The UCC at last avoided the unfortunate effects of *Benedict v Ratner* by means of §9-205, which provides that 'a security interest is not invalid or fraudulent against creditors by reason of liberty in the debtor to use, commingle or dispose of all or part of the collateral . . . or to collect or compromise accounts or chattel paper'.

(b) Static and dynamic charged property

A security right can be static or dynamic not only with respect to the secured **12.55** debt but also with respect to the secured property. Seven building blocks are

---

[140] The common law rule against perpetuities under English law (which is specific to this legal system) is no limitation to the accumulation in practice.

[141] JH Dalhuisen, 'Security in Movable and Intangible Property. Finance Sales, Future Interests and Trusts' in AS Hartkamp, MW Hesselink, EH Hondius, CE du Perron, and JBM Vranken (eds), *Towards a European Civil Code* (Nijmegen, 1994) 361, 380.

[142] 268 US 353 (Brandeis J).

[143] See also B Clark, *The Law of Secured Transactions under the Uniform Commercial Code* (Boston, Mass, 1993) (looseleaf) para 10.01(4); G Gilmore, *Security Interests in Personal Property* (Toronto, 1965) vol 1, ch 8.

required in order to provide a security right which is fully dynamic in relation to secured property and, therefore, covers a changing pool of assets: (1) The parties must be able to secure not only a single but also several assets; (2) they must be able to secure future property (US law refers to 'after-acquired property'); (3) they must be able to describe the secured property generally; (4) security over future property must obtain the same priority as security over present property taken at the same time; (5) the person giving security must in principle have the power to use and to dispose of secured property; (6) flexibility can be enhanced even further by a rule of internal law which provides that a security right is created whether or not secured property is inside or outside the jurisdiction of creation;[144] (7) lastly, there should be no general provisions on fraudulent conveyances in insolvency which prevent a dynamic security right.

12.56 The fixed charge (or fixed mortgage) of English law is the best example of a security interest which is static in nature. However, the term 'fixed charge' implies that such a charge cannot be taken over circulating assets, and although this was a correct interpretation of the law until 1978, the situation changed with *Siebe Gorman & Co Ltd v Barclays Bank Ltd*.[145] Since then the determining factor for a fixed charge has been that the creditor manages the funds in the hand of the chargor prior to crystallization.[146] Thus, in English law the term 'fixed charge' primarily refers not to the asset concerned but to the nature of the charge. The floating charge (or floating mortgage) is defined by the debtor's management power over its funds. In addition, the English floating charge requires an event of crystallization for the transformation of the floating right into a fixed charge, ie a right in an identified asset. Despite the need for a crystallization event, the floating charge creates an immediate security interest from the point of view of English law.[147]

12.57 Western reference systems deal with the different building blocks of a dynamic security right in different ways. The floating charge or floating mortgage of English law (which can cover the assets of a company)[148] is defined by building block (5), the chargor's management power (and not by the type of description of the charged property as one might assume based on the term

---

[144] See eg Model Law on Secured Transactions, Art 5.7.

[145] [1979] 2 Lloyd's Rep 142; R Goode, *Commercial Law* (3rd edn, London, 2004) 680.

[146] For more detail, see R Goode, *Legal Problems of Credit and Security* (2nd edn, London, 1988) 52–5.

[147] R Goode (n 145 above) 679.

[148] See *Re Panama, New Zealand and Australian Royal Mail Co* (1870) 5 Chancery Appeal Cases 318. The English floating charge is characterized by its potentially subordinated priority; a so-called fixed charge can always supersede a floating charge. It should also be noted that suppliers will be able to claim secured goods under retention of title clauses. Both aspects moderate the chargeholder's position under a floating charge.

used). English law also allows for building blocks (1) to (3). However, it does not implement building block (4), since fixed charges can take priority over any prior floating charge and the floating charge does not translate into a fixed charge until a so-called crystallization event occurs. A similar approach is chosen for the Quebec floating hypothec, under which the effects of the hypothec are suspended until a crystallization event occurs.[149] Floating interests which require a crystallization event are not proprietary rights (rights *in rem*) before this event occurs.[150] In practice this often leads to a combination of fixed and floating security rights over the same secured property because only the fixed security right gives adequate priority.

The security interests under Article 9 of the UCC (the floating lien) and the **12.58** EBRD Model Law encompass most of the building blocks of a dynamic security interest. They are able (1) to cover several assets, (2) to secure future property and (3) to describe charged property generally; and (4) they also provide to the person giving security the power to use and dispose of the charged property. They (a) extend the security in compensation for the previous concession automatically to proceeds;[151] (b) they also feature simple registration or notice filing systems and can (c) also cover future debts (ie offer a dynamic security interest also with respect to the secured debt). (d) Both Article 9 of the UCC and the Model Law have refrained from the concept of crystallization found under English law. Under the Model Law a charge covering a pool of assets is valid security from the time of agreement and registration.[152] This concept is accompanied by provisions covering the question of the time of creation of the charge. The main idea is that a charge is only enforceable from the time at which the person giving the charge becomes the owner of the secured property. Similarly, under Article 9 of the UCC, the 'first-to-file-or-perfect' rule also has to be applied with respect to future property.

Although German law is not completely hostile towards dynamic security rights **12.59** with respect to rights and movable things, it allows them mainly in the form of security transfers of ownership extended to future property and retentions of ownership extended to future property. It does not implement all of the building blocks of a dynamic security interest. Security over several assets is

---

[149] See Civil Code of Quebec, Art 2715(1).

[150] U Drobnig, *Empfehlen sich gesetzliche Maßnahmen zur Reform der Mobiliarsicherheiten? Gutachten F für den 51. Deutschen Juristentag* (Munich, 1976) F 83ff; M Wenckstern, 'Die englische Floating Charge im deutschen Internationalen Privatrecht' (1992) 56 *RabelsZ* 624, 650; Röver, *Prinzipien* 149–50.

[151] In this respect it should be noted that the definition of 'proceeds' under UCC, Art 9 extends beyond mere proceeds of sale and includes eg insurance claims for loss or damage to the collateral (UCC, §9-102(a)(64)).

[152] Where registration is required.

conceptually limited by the principle of specificity, ie the concept that a proprietary legal relationship is always with one individual asset only (for example ownership of each book in a library is conceptually transferred separately).

12.60 Many of the central and eastern European secured transactions laws recognize security in future property. However, this remains an area where, for some laws, further legislative clarifications seem desirable.

2. Normative evaluation

12.61 As for secured debt, the EBRD puts great emphasis on the importance of proper regulation of all aspects of secured property. This can be seem from Article 5 of the Model Law and Principle 7(a) of the Core Principles for a Secured Transactions Law (security should be able to be taken 'over all types of assets'). By allocating a specific provision to deal with secured property in the 'general provisions' of the Model Law, the EBRD demonstrated the importance given to the treatment of secured property.

12.62 A security interest should be dynamic in nature in relation to charged property. It is particularly important to allow the parties to create security in a changing pool of present and future property which changes its composition during the lifetime of the security and the final components of which are not yet known at the time of the security right's creation. A shortfall in any of the building blocks of a dynamic security interest seriously limits the risk-reducing function of a security right. An examination of the dynamic security interests shows a similarity in approach between Article 9 of the UCC (floating lien) and the class charge under the Model Law. Both seemed to deal adequately with the requirements of a modern dynamic security interest. Under English law the floating charge or floating mortgage is too weak, since it requires an additional fixed charge to provide full proprietary protection. The solution under German law seems equally inadequate, being restricted, *inter alia*, by the principle of specificity.

13

PERSON GIVING AND PERSON TAKING SECURITY

A. Analytical Framework

The persons who can grant and take security are typically the natural and legal **13.01** persons recognized by national law generally. This is, thus, an issue for the general law of persons of a national law, which is beyond the scope of this study. However, there are a few specifics of security law with respect to persons which should be highlighted. They relate to (1) certain restrictions as to the persons who can grant or take security and (2) persons who can act on behalf of the securityholder.

B. Eastern European Secured Transactions Laws

Bulgarian law limits the use of registered pledges to merchants and other types **13.02** of persons defined in Article 2 of the Law on Commerce.[1] It also requires registration of security devices (such as retention of ownership in movable things, leasing, security assignments of receivables, and security transfers of ownership in movable things) only by merchants and the persons defined in Article 2 of the Law on Commerce.

---

[1] Law on Registered Pledges, Art 3.

167

13.03   An enterprise charge under Hungarian law can be created conceptually only by partnerships and companies, not by individuals.[2]

13.04   There are two specific features of Polish law with respect to the persons involved in creating a security right. First, registered pledges can be created by qualified pledgeholders only.[3] These are mainly financial institutions, such as domestic banks, foreign banks, international financial organizations, and other lending institutions. In addition, the state and municipal entities qualify as pledge-holders. The reference to 'entities conducting economic activity in Poland' is broad but without real practical relevance. Second, Polish law provides for an 'administrator of a pledge',[4] for registered pledges a concept similar to the charge manager under the EBRD Model Law. The pledge administrator can be appointed if (1) more than one lender has provided a loan to the borrower, (2) the lenders' loans can be qualified as a 'syndicated loan' and (3) at least one of the lenders is a qualified pledgeholder under Article 1 of the Law on Registered Pledges. The pledge administrator allows the creation of a registered pledge for all pledgeholders (even if not all of them are qualified pledgeholders, although this will be a merely theoretical situation); he can exercise the pledge-holders' rights and the pledgor's claims can be made against him. It should be noted that the notion of a 'syndicated loan' is rather vague, since banks may either split a loan amount between them from the beginning or may decide to 'syndicate' part or the whole of the loan subsequent to the payment of the loan to the borrower. Polish law is designed to cover both situations.

13.05   For Romanian law, Article 4 of the Law Concerning Certain Measures for the Acceleration of the Economic Process defines the parties to a contractual security right. The 'debtor' is the person who owes the secured debt. However, as under Article 9 of the UCC, the term 'debtor' also covers the owner of the secured property if the person granting security and the person owing the secured debt are different. This terminology is somewhat misleading since the legal relationships under the secured debt and the security right can easily be confused. The 'creditor' is, pursuant to Article 4 of the Law Concerning Certain Measures for the Acceleration of the Economic Process, the securityholder (who is always identical with the person to whom the secured debt is owed). It seems to be preferable to refer to him as the 'securityholder' to distinguish clearly between security right and secured debt.

13.06   Article 19 of the Law Concerning Certain Measures for the Acceleration of the Economic Process underlines that natural and legal persons can be either

---

[2] Civil Code, s 266(1). The EBRD Model Law's enterprise charge is, however, limited to companies, as is the English law's floating charge or mortgage over the assets of a company.
[3] Law on Registered Pledges and the Pledge Registry, Art 1.   [4] ibid Art 4.

Romanian or foreign, and both can become party to a security agreement. The same is true with respect to the parties of the secured debt.

Under Russian law, Article 335(1) of the Civil Code provides that the pledgor **13.07** can either be the debtor of the secured debt or a third person. The pledgor must either be the owner of the pledged asset[5] or its holder (the latter if a right is pledged).[6]

There are no limitations under Slovak law as to who can grant a charge and who **13.08** can receive a charge to secure debts due to him.[7] In particular there is no discrimination between local and foreign creditors. The chargeholder may appoint another person to be registered as chargeholder and to act vis-à-vis third parties in all respects as if he were the chargeholder.[8]

C. Comparative Remarks and Evaluation

1. Analytical principles

Two approaches can be found with respect to the persons giving and taking **13.09** security: the approach which allows all legal entities known to a national law as well as foreign entities to create security, and the approach that only certain entities can create security (principle of limited personal scope). Bulgarian and Polish law have introduced secured transactions legislation with a limited personal scope, whereas the other central and eastern European reference systems have opted for an open approach. The EBRD Model Law seems to encompass the concept of a limited personal scope of secured transactions law since charges may be created by the chargor only as part of its 'business activity'.[9] However, this limitation of scope was only meant to be a way of avoiding issues of consumer protection law and not as a policy statement.[10] This is confirmed by Article 7(c) of the Core Principles for a Secured Transactions Law which makes clear that security should be able to be created 'between all types of person'.

The Model Law's concept of a charge manager,[11] which draws on the English **13.10** law concept of a security trustee, who holds the security in trust for all chargeholders, can be found in Polish (pledge administrator) and Slovak law (but without the common law connotations of the trust concept). The charge

---

[5] Civil Code, Art 335(2) and Pledge Law, Art 19.   [6] Civil Code, Art 335(3).
[7] Allen & Overy and EBRD, *Guide for Taking Charges in the Slovak Republic* (Bratislava, 2003) 8.
[8] This is explicitly provided in the context of the registration provisions; see Notary Code, §73d(1)f.
[9] Model Law on Secured Transactions, Art 2.   [10] See 7.39 above.
[11] Model Law on Secured Transactions, Arts 3.2, 16.

manager under the Model Law is more than a mere representative of the chargeholder; in practical terms he stands in the place of the chargeholder for the purposes of all dealings with third parties in relation to the operation of the charge. If he were a mere representative or agent, a third party dealing with him would have to check each time that he was validly appointed and empowered.

2. Normative evaluation

13.11 Any limitation in the personal scope of a secured transactions law clearly excludes classes of persons from the beneficial risk-reducing effect of security. The limitations should, hence, be avoided.

13.12 In order to facilitate modern financing techniques, in particular the concept of a charge manager as found under the Model Law should be considered. In commercial practice there are circumstances where the security right secures a debt or a series of debts owed to a number of different creditors. An example is an issue of secured bonds. A company may give security for bonds it issues and the benefit of that security will be available to all bondholders, including persons who subsequently acquire the bonds. Another example is when a loan is made by a syndicate of banks, as is often the case for large loans in the international markets. The loan is made by, say, twenty banks and any security right given to secure the loan should benefit all those banks and any other bank which might subsequently acquire the rights of any of them under the loan.

13.13 In these cases there can be tens, if not hundreds, of securityholders. The debtor will sometimes not even know who his creditors are, especially when they are constantly changing as in the case of a bond. Thus there is a practical problem. How can the debtor or any third party deal with the securityholder? If he has to deal individually with each securityholder the management of the security can become complicated and inefficient. If at enforcement each securityholder has to be party to any proceedings, or worse has to initiate separate proceedings, the system quickly becomes unworkable. In most laws contractual relationships will try to achieve the same results as found with a security trustee under English law. However, it seems preferable to introduce a concept like the charge manager, who in practical terms stands in the place of the chargeholder for the purposes of all dealings with third parties in relation to the operation of the security right.

<h1 style="text-align:center">14</h1>

<h1 style="text-align:center">CREATION OF SECURITY</h1>

A. Analytical Framework

1. Two-step or one-step approach

There are two different approaches to the creation of a security interest: the one-step approach and the two-step approach.[1] The United States, England, and other common law countries follow a two-step approach where security interests are created between the parties (this is referred to as an 'attachment') and, upon completion of additional requirements, also against third parties (this is referred to as 'perfection'). Most civil law countries, however, follow the one-step approach where security rights are created at the same time between the parties and against third parties. Under the two-step approach there are two phases in the creation of a security interest. **14.01**

2. Requirements for the creation of security

In general terms the creation or perfection of a security right may require the following: **14.02**

---

[1] See also 10.03 above, dealing with the types of proprietary effect.

(1) An agreement between the parties about the creation of a security right—such an agreement must be validly formed and may require a certain content. Typically, the rules of general contract law apply to the formation of such an agreement.

(2) Publicity, as for other *in rem* rights—this may be in the form of taking possession, in the form of registration or filing in a security register,[2] giving notice to a third party, but may also not be required at all. The perfection requirement would typically have to be met, if a two-step approach is taken towards the creation of security rights, to achieve the effectiveness of the security right against third parties.

(3) Compliance with additional creation requirements—such as form requirements for the agreement between the parties, licence by a public body, or additional registration or filing in a register other than the security register.

(4) Power to dispose of the property—typically the person giving security will have to be the owner/holder or titleholder of the secured property and needs the power to dispose of the secured property (which may be lost, for example in insolvency proceedings).

(5) Existence of a secured debt—since the purpose of security rights is to secure a debt, there is typically a requirement that a secured debt must exist for the creation of the security right. However, there are important exceptions, for example with respect to future debts.

(6) Defences against the security right—it is important to consider defences which can be raised against the security right. Defences are a category not often considered systematically under national laws. However, it is clear that a security right should no longer be enforceable if the parties agree to terminate the security right. Events like this must be able to be held against the rights arising under a security right. Typically there are two legal relationships which may affect the security right: the legal relationship between the person giving security and the securityholder (ie the legal relationship upon which the security right is based) and the legal relationship between the debtor and the securityholder (ie the secured debt).

B. Eastern European Secured Transactions Laws

1. Bulgarian law

14.03 Bulgarian secured transactions law provides (a) a registered pledge for movable things and rights if a merchant (or another person referred to in Article 2 of the Law on Commerce) is the pledgor (b) registered for security devices such as

---

[2] For the distinction between registration and filing, see 16.02 below.

retention of ownership clauses again if the person giving the security is a merchant or another qualified person, (c) traditional pledges in movable things and receivables, (d) mortgages in immovable property, and also (e) non-registered security devices, such as a retention of ownership if the pledgor is not a merchant (or another qualified person).

The non-possessory,[3] registered pledge can be created in movable things, **14.04** receivables, other rights, and assets of an enterprise[4] and requires the following for its creation between the parties (ie for its attachment):

(1) the pledgor must in principle be a merchant (or another qualified person);[5]
(2) a pledge agreement,[6] which must in principle be made in writing[7] except in the case of a pledge in the assets of an enterprise where, in addition, the signatures under the agreement must be notarized;[8]
(3) the person giving the pledge must have the right to do so (ie be the owner or holder of the pledged asset)[9] although the registered pledge can also be created in future property[10]—there is no good faith acquisition of a pledge from a pledgor who is not in fact the owner or holder of the pledged asset;
(4) the secured debt must exist,[11] although a future debt can also be secured;[12]
(5) there must be no defences against the pledge or the secured debt—these defences are not referred to explicitly in the Law on Registered Pledges.

The pledge must be registered at the pledges registry.[13] However, this is a 'per- **14.05** fection' requirement, ie a requirement for the effectiveness of the registered pledge against third parties but not a requirement for the pledge's creation between the parties.[14] Like English and US secured transactions law, Bulgarian law provides a two-step creation process for a security right. Hence, the security agreement is sufficient for the attachment of the security right, ie its creation between the parties. The registration is valid for a period of five years from the time of registration, but can be renewed prior to its expiry.[15]

There are additional perfection requirements for special types of pledges. **14.06** The pledge of an account receivable requires notice to the account debtor of

---

[3] See explicitly Law on Registered Pledges, Art 1(1).   [4] ibid Art 4(1).
[5] ibid Art 3(1). For exceptions see ibid Art 3(2) and (3).   [6] ibid Art 2.
[7] ibid Art 2.
[8] ibid Art 21(1). The requirement of notarized signatures exists also for registered pledges of shares, ibid Art 19(1).
[9] This requirement is not mentioned in the Law on Registered Pledges but must evidently be complied with since the registered pledge is a property right which can only be established by the owner or holder of the asset in which it is created. This is confirmed by Law on Obligations and Contracts, Art 167(3) which contains this requirement for mortgages.
[10] Law on Registered Pledges, Arts 5(1) and 4(2), second sentence.   [11] See ibid Art 5.
[12] ibid Art 5(12).   [13] ibid Art 12(1).   [14] See explicitly ibid Art 12(1).
[15] ibid Art 30(2).

the pledged account receivable to be effective against the account debtor.[16] Special registration and form requirements apply to pledges of dematerialized securities, shares in limited liability and joint stock companies, and the assets of an enterprise.[17] The taking of possession is, however, not a perfection requirement under the Law of Registered Pledges.

14.07 The Law on Registered Pledges extends the registration requirement to certain security devices for movable things and rights[18] if the person providing the security device is a merchant or another qualified person. There are four such security devices which are covered by the registration requirement:

(1) the pledge of accounts receivable (which consequently cannot be subject to a pledge of receivables under the Law on Obligations and Contracts)— Bulgarian law contains no legal definition of 'accounts receivable' (although the concept seems to be derived from Article 9 of the UCC[19] under which accounts receivables are the right to payment of a monetary obligation arising under certain circumstances, Bulgarian law has its own concept of receivables—in particular it is not limited to monetary obligations);

(2) the retention of ownership in movable things;

(3) the leasing of movable things; and

(4) the transfer of property, ie security transfer of ownership in movable things or the security assignment of receivables.

14.08 Pledges in movable things and in receivables as well as registered mortgages in immovable property are dealt with in the Law on Obligations and Contracts. The possessory, non-registered pledge in movable things requires:

(1) a pledge contract;[20]

(2) the transfer of possession to the pledged asset;[21]

(3) that the pledgor is the owner of the pledged movable thing;[22]

(4) that the secured debt exists;[23] and

(5) that there are no defences against the pledge or the secured debt.[24] The Law rightly emphasizes that a pledge securing a third person's obligation is subject to all the defences which the debtor of the secured claim may have. In addition, any of the pledgor's defences arising under the pledge can be raised.

---

[16] Law on Registered Pledges, Art 17(1) and (2).   [17] ibid Arts 18–21.

[18] ibid Art 12(2).   [19] See in particular the definition of 'account' in UCC, §9-102.

[20] Law on Obligations and Contracts, Art 156(1).   [21] ibid Art 156(1).

[22] This is not mentioned in the Law on Obligations and Contracts but must evidently be required since the possessory pledge is—like the registered pledge—a property right. This is confirmed by Law on Obligations and Contracts, Art 167(3) which contains this requirement for mortgages.

[23] ibid Art 149 ('a claim may be secured').

[24] See ibid Art 151 for defences against the secured debt.

The way in which the law deals with the form of the pledge contract is interest-   **14.09**
ing. It requires the contract to be in written form but does not make this a
creation requirement.[25] Rather a pledge securing a claim exceeding 5 levs[26]
cannot be enforced 'against third parties' if the pledge contract is not in writing
and is neither dated nor contains an identification of the pledged property and
the secured claim. Non-compliance with the written form requirement can,
therefore, be raised as a defence by a third person against the enforcement of the
pledge if the pledgeholder claims effects against the third person.

The non-registered pledge of receivables has creation requirements similar to   **14.10**
those for the pledge of movable things. The transfer of possession is replaced by
the requirement of giving notice to the debtor of the pledged receivable.[27] In
addition, the pledgor is under an obligation to transfer to the pledgeholder
documents evidencing the pledged receivable (such as a bond instrument).[28]
This is not a creation requirement but an obligation of the pledgor.

Bulgarian law also provides the retention of ownership in movable things as   **14.11**
a way of securing sales credit. The creation requirements for a retention of
ownership in movable assets are as follows:

(1) an agreement about the transfer of ownership in a movable thing;
(2) that the agreement is made under the condition precedent of the payment
    of the purchase price for the asset (thus linking the security arrangement
    with a secured debt);
(3) the transferor must be the true owner of the asset;[29]
(4) pursuant to Article 12(2) of the Law on Registered Pledges retentions of
    ownership must be registered at the pledges register to be effective against
    third parties if the person giving security is a merchant (or another qualified
    person)—if he is not, the retention of ownership must not be registered;
(5) there should not be defences against the retention agreement (defences
    against the secured debt are not relevant for the retention of ownership).

The creation requirements for a security transfer of ownership are as follows: **14.12**

(1) an agreement on such a transfer of ownership between the parties;
(2) in principle the transfer of ownership requires a transfer of possession,
    however, the parties may agree otherwise and will do so in practice;

---

[25] ibid Art 156(2). However, a pledge of a claim secured by a mortgage must be made in
writing with notarized signatures and this seems to be a creation requirement.
[26] The Law on Obligations and Contracts referred to 5,000 levs initially. However, from 5 July
1999 the Bulgarian lev was re-denominated and 1,000 old leva ('BGL') were exchanged for 1 new
lev ('BGN'); see Lev Re-Denomination Law, Art 1.
[27] Law on Obligations and Contracts Art 162.   [28] ibid Art 163.
[29] Good faith acquisition is possible should the transferor not be the owner of the asset.

(3) pursuant to Article 12(2) of the Law on Registered Pledges security transfers must be registered at the pledges register to be effective against third parties if the person giving security is a merchant (or another qualified person)—if he is not, the security transfer must not be registered; and

(4) the transferor must be the true owner of the transferred asset.

14.13 There is no requirement for a secured debt for the security transfer to be valid and enforceable. Defences against the transfer of ownership can be raised but not defences against the secured claim.

14.14 Mortgages of immovable property require that:

(1) the mortgage contract has been formed[30] with specific content[31]—if either creditor, owner or debtor, the mortgaged property, the secured debt, or the secured amount are uncertain from either the mortgage contract or the application for recording to the recording office at the regional court, the mortgage is invalid;[32]

(2) the contract is in writing with notarized signatures;[33]

(3) the contract is recorded with the recording office at the respective regional court[34] (the Law on Land Registries provided for a land register in electronic form, however this has not yet been implemented—once registration has been implemented, in practice it will be valid for only ten years but may be renewed if the parties want to extend the term of the mortgage);[35]

(4) the mortgagor is the owner of the property when the mortgage contract is concluded;[36]

(5) the secured debt exists;[37] and

(6) there must be no defences against the mortgage or the secured debt.[38]

2. Czech law

14.15 Czech secured transactions law is characterized by the same duality as other continental European secured transactions law: on the one hand there are the traditional security rights provided under the Czech Civil Code, ie the lien on real estate,[39] the lien on movable things,[40] the lien on receivables,[41] and the lien

---

[30] Law on Obligations and Contracts, Art 166.   [31] ibid Art 167(2).
[32] ibid Art 170.   [33] ibid Art 171.   [34] ibid Art 166.   [35] ibid Art 172.
[36] ibid Art 167(3).   [37] ibid Arts 149 ('a claim may be secured') and 173.
[38] See ibid Art 151 for defences against the secured debt.
[39] Civil Code, s 157. Czech law provides only an ancillary lien on real estate, ie a security right which is directly dependent in its existence on the secured debt (see ibid s 152: 'to secure a receivable'). The non-ancillary land mortgage known to German law has not been adopted by Czech law.
[40] ibid s 157.
[41] ibid s 159. Surprisingly there is no security right in rights other than receivables provided under the Civil Code.

on rights other than receivables.[42] The non-possessory, registered lien on movable things and the lien in the assets of an enterprise have been incorporated into the framework of the traditional lien provided by the Civil Code. On the other hand, Czech law adopted the security transfer of ownership in movables and the security assignment of receivables and other rights to be found for example under German law.[43] The forms of security transfers are complemented by the retention of ownership in movable things as a means of securing sales credits.

The traditional security rights (called 'liens'), including the non-possessory, **14.16** registered lien on movable things, provided under the Civil Code require a contract,[44] which identifies the encumbered property and the secured debt.[45] This must be in written form[46] or in a notarial deed if a lien in movable things is created without transfer of possession[47]—for liens on immovables not registered in the cadastre, collective assets, collections of things, or movable things for which possession is not transferred to the person taking security, the pledge agreement must be in the form of a notarial deed;[48]

The contract must be made public, either: **14.17**

(1) by registration in the Real Estate Register where immovables are concerned;[49]
(2) by transfer of possession where a movable thing is concerned;[50]
(3) by registration in the Collateral Register where the parties agree that transfer of possession to a movable thing is not required;[51] or
(4) by giving written notice to the debtor of the encumbered receivable where a receivable is concerned.[52]

As far as rights other than receivables are concerned particular provisions on the publicity of security rights in such rights must be consulted.

The person must be the rightful owner of the property. However, where the **14.18** encumbered asset is a movable thing an acquirer will acquire the possessory lien

---

[42] ibid s 154.
[43] TO Schorling, *Das Recht der Kreditsicherheiten in der Tschechischen Republik* (Berlin, 2000); TO Schorling, 'Secured transactions in the Czech Republic—a case of pre-reform' (Autumn, 2000) *Law in Transition* 66–9.
[44] Civil Code, s 156(1), first case.   [45] ibid s 156(2).   [46] ibid s 156(1).
[47] ibid ss 156(3), 158(2).   [48] ibid s 156(2).
[49] ibid s 157(1). Liens in immovables not yet registered at the cadastre (Real Estate Register) must be registered in the Collateral Registry maintained by the Czech Chamber of Notaries, ibid s 158(1).
[50] ibid s 157(2), (3). Either possession must be transferred to the person taking security or a custodian.
[51] ibid s 158(1).
[52] ibid s 159(2). Note that notification is a requirement for the effectiveness of the lien in receivables in relation to the debtor of the encumbered receivable. The Civil Code does not make it a requirement of the creation of the lien.

even from a person who is not the owner of the encumbered asset if (a) possession in the encumbered asset is transferred and (b) the person acquiring the lien acts in good faith with respect to the ownership of the encumbered asset.[53] The Civil Code states that this is not possible where the encumbered asset is, for example, an immovable, a collective asset, a collection of things, a receivable, or a share.[54] The discussion of whether section 151d of the Civil Code (which contained the section 161(1) rule of the Civil Code before the revision of the Civil Code which became effective in 2002) can also be applied to the good faith acquisition of liens in real estate, although its wording required a 'transfer of possession',[55] and therefore became obsolete. The Civil Code does not provide for good faith acquisition of a non-possessory, registered lien in movable things if the person providing the lien is not the owner of the secured asset. Lastly, it should be noted that Czech law provides no clarification as to whether or not a future asset can be taken as collateral for a lien.

14.19   There must be a secured claim.[56] However, the Civil Code allows the creation of a lien for future claims.[57] Defences against (a) the secured debt and (b) the lien can both be raised against the lien even if this is not explicitly provided in the Civil Code.[58]

14.20   The Civil Code explicitly provides for a lien on the assets of an enterprise or other collective assets.[59] The creation of such a lien requires that the lien agreement is made in a notarized deed[60] and that the lien is registered in the Collateral Register.[61]

14.21   The security transfer of ownership in movable things[62] requires the following:

(1) There must be an agreement on such a transfer of ownership between the parties. In this respect it should be noted that only the debtor of the secured debt can transfer ownership in an asset and not a third party; this follows directly from section 553 of the Civil Code.

(2) In principle, the transfer of ownership requires under section 133 of the Civil Code the transfer of possession. However, pursuant to section 133(1)

---

[53] Civil Code, s 161(1).   [54] ibid s 161(2).

[55] For details of this controversy, see Schorling, *Das Recht der Kreditsicherheiten* (n 43 above) 51–2.

[56] Civil Code, s 152 ('to secure a receivable').   [57] ibid s 155(3).

[58] Schorling, 'Secured Transactions' (n 43 above) 67. Only Civil Code, s 170 provides a reference to defences; in particular s 170(2) provides that the lien is not affected if the secured debt is statute barred.

[59] ibid s 153(1).   [60] ibid s 158(2).   [61] ibid s 158(1).

[62] The security transfer of ownership pursuant to Civil Code, s 553 is not necessarily limited to a transfer of ownership in movable things; however, there is no practical need for a security transfer of ownership in immovables, since the lien on real estate allows the person giving security to keep possession of the secured asset; see also Schorling, *Das Recht der Kreditsicherheiten* (n 43 above) 83.

the parties may agree otherwise. In the context of a security transfer of ownership the parties will typically agree that ownership shall be transferred without a transfer of possession.[63] In view of the clear provision in section 133(1), not even the establishment of constructive possession (ie the parties agree that the transferor holds possession to the transferred asset on behalf of the new owner) is required.

(3) The transferor must be the true owner of the transferred asset. The Civil Code does not provide for good faith acquisition of ownership in a movable thing if possession to the asset is not transferred to the new owner. It is unclear whether or not future property can be subject to a transfer of ownership in a movable thing.

(4) For the security transfer to be valid and enforceable, there is also a requirement for a secured debt.[64]

There is no requirement to register or to make the security transfer public in any other way. Defences against the transfer of ownership can be raised as well as defences against the secured claim, since the transfer requires the existence of a secured claim for its creation. **14.22**

In addition to the agreement on the transfer of ownership, the parties have to enter into a separate security agreement which must be made in writing.[65] Under this agreement they will agree mainly on the claim secured by the security transfer, the manner in which the transferor will recover its ownership in the transferred asset upon payment of the secured debt, and the manner in which the new owner can satisfy itself from the asset should the secured debt not be paid. **14.23**

In contrast to the security transfer of ownership in movable things, a security transfer of receivables or other rights can be made either by the debtor of the secured debt or a third party.[66] It can certainly be made for present debts. However, there is disagreement as to whether or not a security transfer of future debts is possible under Czech law.[67] **14.24**

The retention of ownership in movable things has the following requirements: **14.25**

(1) an agreement about the transfer of ownership in a movable thing;

(2) that the agreement is made under the condition precedent of the payment of the purchase price for the asset (thus linking the security arrangement with a secured claim); and

---

[63] Schorling (n 41 above) 81–2.
[64] Civil Code, s 533(1) which provides that the performance of an obligation can be secured by the assignment of a right (eg ownership) held by the debtor.
[65] ibid s 533(2).
[66] ibid s 554; Schorling, *Das Recht der Kreditsicherheiten* (n 43 above) 103.
[67] Schorling, *Das Recht der Kreditsicherheiten* (n 43 above) 104–7.

(3) the transferor must be the true owner of the asset (it is unclear whether or not future property can be subject to a retention of ownership in a movable thing).

14.26 There is no registration requirement for a retention of ownership. The existence of a secured receivable is not a requirement for the creation of the retention of ownership—however, the secured receivable is referred to in the condition precedent for the transfer of ownership and it is possible to secure future receivables under retention of ownership arrangements.

Consequently, only defences against the retention of ownership and not against the receivables secured by the retention of ownership can be raised against the retention of ownership.

3. Hungarian law

14.27 As far as the creation of charges under Hungarian law is concerned, it is advisable first to distinguish broadly between the charge, which is dependent in its creation and existence on a secured claim (simple or ancillary charge) and the independent charge, which is independent from a secured claim, and second, between the registered charge, the possessory charge, the charge on rights and receivables, and the enterprise charge.

14.28 For the registered ancillary charge, which can be created in real estate and movable things,[68] the following creation requirements exist:

(1) a charge agreement[69]—the minimum content requirements are set out in the provisions on the registration procedure;[70] it is particularly important that the charged assets are described sufficiently and that the secured debt is defined by a maximum amount;[71]

(2) the charge agreement must be in the form of a public notary's deed[72] or, in the case of real estate, in written form;[73]

(3) registration of a charge over real estate in the real property registry[74] or registration of a charge in movable things in the charges register held by the National Chamber of Public Notaries;[75]

(4) the chargor's ownership of the charged asset—there is no good faith acquisition of a charged asset from a chargor who in fact is not its owner or holder (it should be noted that a charge can be created in future property);

---

[68] The registered charge is open to tangibles only (see chapter title before Civil Code, s 261). The broad definition of charged assets in ibid s 252(1) covers any 'tangible thing', and thus movables as well as immovables.

[69] ibid s 254(1).   [70] ibid s 262(3), (4) and Law Decree No 11/1960, s 47(5), (6).

[71] Law Decree no 11/1960, s 47(6).   [72] Civil Code, s 262(2).

[73] ibid s 254(2).   [74] ibid s 262(1) second sentence.   [75] ibid s 262(2).

(5) the existence of a secured claim[76]—however, it is possible to create a charge in future claims;[77]

(6) there must be no defences against:

    (a) the charge, or

    (b) the secured claim,

    for example a provision on a transfer of the ownership of the charged asset where the chargor does not perform its obligations renders the charge agreement 'null and void'.[78] Similarly, the charge is null and void if the secured claim is unenforceable.[79]

A possessory charge, which can be created in movable assets only,[80] has the same **14.29** creation requirements as the registered charge save for registration, which is replaced by transfer of possession in the charged asset.[81] The charge agreement must only be in written form.[82] Possession can be transferred either to the chargholder[83] or a third person.[84] A possessory charge can be acquired from a chargor who is not the owner of the charged asset provided that the chargholder acts in good faith with respect to the chargor's ownership and the acquisition is part of 'trade relationships'.[85]

The charge on rights and receivables also has the same creation requirements as **14.30** the registered charge. However, the registration requirement is replaced by the requirement to notify the debtor of the charged right or receivable.[86] Notification is not a creation requirement but rather a requirement for the enforceability of the charge ('for the enforcement of the charge'). A charge on rights or receivables cannot be acquired in good faith from a chargor who is not the holder of the right or receivable.

The floating or enterprise charge is a special concept of Hungarian law. This type **14.31** of security right already had a place in Hungarian security law but the EBRD Model Law's concept of an enterprise charge helped to develop this concept further during the Hungarian reform process. This type of charge covers the assets of an enterprise or part of the assets of an enterprise which can operate on a stand-alone basis. It has not found acceptance in practice, in particular because detailed provisions on the enforcement of a floating charge were never enacted.

---

[76] ibid s 251(3).   [77] ibid s 251(2).

[78] ibid s 255(2). This is similar to the prohibition of an automatic transfer clause ('*Verfall-klausel*') under German pledge law (German Civil Code, §1229).

[79] Civil Code, s 251(1), second sentence.

[80] ibid s 262(1), first sentence, provides that real estate can be charged by a registered charge only.

[81] ibid s 265(1).   [82] ibid s 254(2).   [83] ibid s 265(1), first sentence.

[84] ibid s 265(1), second sentence. The person is called the 'charge holder' in an unofficial English translation of the Civil Code provided by the EBRD on its website <http://www.ebrd.com>.

[85] ibid s 265(1), third sentence.   [86] ibid s 267(2), first sentence.

14.32   An enterprise charge can be created by partnerships and companies, but not by individuals, and requires:

(1) a charge agreement,[87] which must be in the form of a public notary's deed,[88] and must be registered in the charges register;[89]

(2) that the chargor (ie the entity giving the charge) is the owner or the holder of the charged assets; no charge can be created in good faith in assets which are in fact not owned or held by the chargor (the enterprise charge can be created in present and future property and will in fact almost always include future property);

(3) as for other ancillary charges of Hungarian law, the existence of a secured claim is required (it is possible to create the enterprise charge in present and future claims); and

(4) that there are no defences against (a) the charge or (b) the secured claim.

14.33   Apart from the ancillary charges, Hungarian law also recognizes the so-called 'independent charge' where the charge does not require the existence of a secured claim for its creation.[90] Although the charge is referred to as an 'independent' charge, there is typically a link between the charge and a secured claim created by a separate agreement between the parties. The independent charge is clearly not limited to real estate but can be created for all types of assets, including the assets of an enterprise. The creation requirements are the same as for ancillary charges, and an independent charge can be in the form of a registered charge, a possessory charge, a charge in rights and receivables, or an enterprise (floating) charge.[91]

14.34   Lastly, the retention of ownership has the following creation requirements:

(1) an agreement about the transfer of ownership in a movable thing;

(2) that the transfer agreement is made under the condition precedent of the payment of the purchase price for the asset (thus linking the security arrangement with a secured claim); and

(3) that the transferor is the true owner of the asset.

14.35   The existence of a secured receivable is not a requirement for the creation of the retention of ownership—it is possible to secure future receivables under retention of ownership arrangements. Consequently, only defences against the retention of ownership and not against the receivables secured by the retention of ownership can be raised against the retention of ownership. There is no registration requirement for a retention of ownership.

---

[87] Civil Code, ss 254(1) and 266(1), first sentence.   [88] ibid s 266(1), first sentence.
[89] ibid s 266(1), first sentence.   [90] ibid s 269(1).
[91] This follows from ibid s 269(4).

4. Polish law

Like for example Bulgarian law, Polish secured transactions law features a two-tier structure. Alongside largely unreformed, traditional security rights there is modern legislation providing for a registered security right in movables and rights. Mortgages in real estate, retention of ownership in movable things, the security transfer of ownership in movable things, and security assignment of receivables complement this system of secured transactions. **14.36**

Registered pledges which can be created in any movable thing or transferable right[92] are created if the following requirements are met: **14.37**

(1) A pledge agreement[93] must be drawn up, specifying:
   (a) the date of the pledge agreement;
   (b) the details of the pledgor, the pledge, and the debtor of the secured claim; and
   (c) the pledged assets and the secured claim (including its amount and the legal relationship giving rise to the claim).[94]
(2) The agreement must be made in writing.[95]
(3) The pledge must be entered in the pledge register;[96] an application for registration of the pledge can only be made within one month from the signing of the pledge agreement.[97]
(4) The pledgor must have the right to dispose of the pledged property.[98] However, the pledge can be acquired in good faith,[99] pursuant to the general rules which require a transfer of possession;[100] this transfer of possession occurs constructively if a pledge is registered in the pledge register.[101] In addition, registration constitutes public knowledge and can be the basis for a good faith acquisition of a non-existent pledge by a third party.[102] However, a good faith acquisition based on registration is not possible if the registration was not made in accordance with the application and pledgor or pledgeholder requested the respective correction of the registry.[103] With respect to the pledgor's right to dispose, it should be noted that there is no clarification in the law regarding whether or not conditional or future property can be pledged by registered pledges.

---

[92] Law on Registered Pledges and the Pledge Registry, Art 7. An exception is made in this provision for sea ships.

[93] ibid Art 2.   [94] ibid Art 3(2).   [95] ibid Art 3(1).

[96] ibid Art 2(1). In addition, the registered pledge on a registered motor vehicle must be noted in the vehicle registration document, ibid Art 12. However, this notation is not a requirement for the pledge's creation, ibid Art 38.

[97] ibid Art 3(3).   [98] ibid Article 2(1).   [99] ibid Article 2(3), first sentence.

[100] Civil Code, Art 169, §1.

[101] Law on Registered Pledges and the Pledge Registry, Art 2(3), second sentence.

[102] ibid Art 38.   [103] ibid Art 38(2).

(5) There must be a specific claim which shall be secured.[104] The claim can be denominated in both local and foreign currency.[105] The claim may also be future.[106]

(6) There should be no defences against
  (a) the registered pledge, or
  (b) the secured debt.
  Such defences are not referred to explicitly in the Law on Registered Pledges and the Pledge Registry.[107]

14.38 A transfer of possession in movable things is explicitly *not* a creation requirement for registered pledges.[108]

14.39 A Civil Code pledge of movable things requires the following:

(1) a pledge contract,[109] to which no form requirement is attached;[110]
(2) the transfer of possession in the pledged asset to the pledgeholder or a third party;[111]
(3) the pledgor's right to pledge the asset (ie the pledgor must be the asset's owner), however, the general rules on good faith acquisition of ownership apply[112]—there is no clarification in the law regarding whether or not conditional or future property can be pledged;
(4) the existence of a secured debt.[113]

14.40 The Civil Code confirms that the pledgor may raise the debtor's defences against the secured debt if debtor and pledgor are different persons.[114] In addition, defences can be raised against the pledge itself (for example that the pledge contract was not formed validly).

14.41 A Civil Code pledge in rights has the same requirements as the Civil Code pledge of movable things[115] but the contract must be made in writing with an authenticated date[116] and, where receivables are involved, in principle notice

---

[104] Law on Registered Pledges and the Pledge Registry, Arts 1, 18(1). The latter provision provides that in principle the pledge terminates with the secured claim; however, the pledge agreement can provide otherwise.

[105] ibid Art 5.   [106] ibid Art 6.

[107] See, however, Civil Code, Art 315 for defences against the debt secured by a Civil Code pledge.

[108] Law on Registered Pledges and the Pledge Registry, Art 2(2).

[109] Civil Code, Art 307, §1.

[110] Whereas the pledge agreement for a pledge in a right must be made in writing; ibid Art 329, §1, second sentence.

[111] ibid Art 307, §1.   [112] ibid Art 309.

[113] ibid Art 306, §1 ('in order to secure a receivable debt').

[114] ibid Art 315. However, the time limitation of a secured debt may not be raised as a defence against the pledge, ibid Art 317, first sentence.

[115] ibid Art 329, §1, first sentence.   [116] ibid Art 329, §1, second sentence.

must be given in writing to the debtor of the receivable taken as security.[117] For pledges in rights, the Civil Code requires in addition compliance with the requirements provided for the transfer of the respective right.[118]

The mortgage of real estate follows the rules of the Law on Land Registry and   **14.42**
Mortgages. A mortgage is created if the following requirements are met:

(1) There is a mortgage agreement.[119] The maximum amount mortgage is a special type of mortgage which secures a secured debt up to a specified maximum amount.[120] It requires that the maximum amount is defined in the mortgage agreement. This is similar to the German maximum amount ancillary land mortgage ('*Höchstbetragshypothek*').[121]

(2) The mortgage is registered in the real estate register.[122]

(3) The mortgagor is the owner of the real estate. If someone is registered as the owner of real estate it may be assumed that he is the owner; there is good faith acquisition if in fact the mortgagor is not the owner of the real estate.[123]

(4) There is a secured debt.[124] However, the mortgage cannot be acquired in good faith if the secured debt does not exist. As far as maximum amount mortgages are concerned, future as well as conditional claims can be secured by them.[125] Although the Law on Land Registries and Mortgages is quiet on this point, the same applies to simple mortgages in real estate.

Mortgages can be subject to two types of defences: defences against the mort-   **14.43**
gage agreement and defences against the secured debt. The law clarifies that the mortgagor can raise the defences of the debtor of the secured debt (a necessary clarification where both are different persons).[126] However, it should be noted that the time limitation of a secured claim (with the exception of the right to claim interest) is not a defence against the mortgage.[127] Lastly, a prohibition to mortgage property cannot be held against the mortgage.[128]

The retention of ownership has the following general creation requirements: **14.44**

---

[117] Civil Code, Art 329, §1, first sentence. This requirement is a creation requirement. There is an exception from this requirement if documents certifying the right are transferred or endorsed, ibid Art 329, §2.

[118] ibid Art 329 §1 (German Civil Code, §1274(1), first sentence, for pledges in rights under German law is similar).

[119] For its contents, see Law on Land Registry and Mortgages, Art 65(1).

[120] ibid Art 102(1).   [121] German Civil Code, §1190.

[122] Law on Land Registry and Mortgages, Art 67.   [123] ibid Art 5.

[124] ibid Art 65(1).   [125] ibid Art 102(2).   [126] ibid Art 73.

[127] ibid Art 77. This does not apply to interest claims which may not be time-barred, ibid Arts 69, 77.

[128] ibid Art 72 (the provision refers to the '*obligation*' to sell or encumber the real estate' (emphasis added)).

(1) An agreement must be drawn up concerning the transfer of ownership in a movable thing, typically in a sales contract.

(2) The agreement must be made under the condition subsequent of the payment of the purchase price for the asset (thus linking the security arrangement with a secured debt). Article 589 of the Civil Code stipulates: 'If the seller retains the ownership of a movable thing sold until payment of the purchase price, it shall be deemed, in case of doubt, that the transfer of ownership in the thing takes place subject to a condition subsequent.'

(3) The retention of ownership must be confirmed in writing if possession of the movable thing is transferred to the buyer.[129] In addition, the retention of ownership is effective against the buyer's creditors only if the agreement has an officially confirmed date ('*data certa*').

(4) The transferor must be the true owner of the asset. Good faith acquisition is possible should the transferor not be the owner of the asset.

14.45 There is no registration requirement for a retention of ownership. There should not be defences against the retention agreement (defences against the secured debt are not relevant for the retention agreement).

14.46 The requirements for a security transfer of ownership are as follows:

(1) There must be an agreement on such a transfer of ownership between the parties.

(2) If ownership is transferred in an asset which is identified generally (ie as to its type) or to a group of assets, the debtor or the third party are required to single out and mark the asset or the group of assets. Further, they have to keep a record of any changes concerning the asset or the group of assets to which ownership has been transferred[130] unless the agreement provides otherwise.

(3) In principle, the transfer of ownership requires a transfer of possession. However, the parties may agree otherwise and will do so in practice.

(4) The transferor must be the true owner of the transferred asset. The Civil Code does not provide for good faith acquisition of ownership of a movable thing if possession of the asset is not transferred to the new owner.[131] It is unclear whether or not future property can be subject to a transfer of ownership in a movable thing.

14.47 There is no requirement for a secured debt for the security transfer to be valid and enforceable. Defences against the transfer of ownership can be raised but not defences against the secured claim. There is no requirement to register a security transfer.

---

[129] Civil Code, Art 590.   [130] Banking Law, Art 101(2).
[131] Civil Code, Art 169, §1.

Lastly, the security assignment of receivables requires an agreement on a security **14.48** assignment between the parties. In the case of a security assignment of future receivables, the assignment contract must define precisely the assigned receivables and the legal relationship giving rise to the receivables. The assignor must be the true holder of the transferred receivables.

There is no requirement for a secured debt for the security assignment to be **14.49** valid and enforceable. Defences against the security assignment can be raised, but not defences against the secured debt, since the assignment does not require the existence of a secured debt for its creation. There is no requirement to register or to make the security assignment public in any other way (for example by giving notice to the debtor of the assigned receivable).

5. Romanian law

The registered security right in movable assets,[132] receivables, and other rights **14.50** follows the example of Article 9 of the UCC in that its rules apply not only to the outright creation of security rights but also include in particular assignments of receivables, conditional sales, leasing and rental contracts.[133] However, the security devices covered by the Law Concerning Certain Measures for the Acceleration of the Economic Process are not re-characterized as security rights but keep their intended legal nature.

The Law Concerning Certain Measures for the Acceleration of the Economic **14.51** Process also follows US law in its two-step creation process for security rights. The requirements with respect to the creation of the security right between the parties (so-called 'attachment')[134] are as follows:

(1) There must be a security agreement[135] containing, in particular, a specific or general description of the secured property,[136] in authentic form or in a deed under private signature and with the signature of the person giving the security right.[137]
(2) The chargor must have the right to grant security in the secured property;[138]

---

[132] Including movables which are 'ancillary' to real estate; Law Concerning Certain Measures for the Acceleration of the Economic Process, Art 6, Nos 2, 3. Where a movable is documented by a document of title, the security right must be created in this document of title, ibid Art 25.

[133] ibid Art 2.

[134] An attachment also defines priorities against other attached security rights and therefore has third-party effect.

[135] Law Concerning Certain Measures for the Acceleration of the Economic Process, Arts 13(1), 14(1).

[136] ibid Art 16(1).   [137] ibid Art 14(2).

[138] This is not provided explicitly under the Law Concerning Certain Measures for the Acceleration of the Economic Process but follows from the nature of the security right as a right *in rem*.

a contractual provision in the security agreement prohibiting the sale of secured property does not affect the validity of the transfer of the secured property.[139] No pledge can be created in good faith in assets which are in fact not owned or held by the chargor. The security right can be created in present and future property.

(3) There must be a secured debt,[140] which must be determined or be 'likely' to be determined.[141] It is possible to create the security right in present and future debts.

(4) There shall be no defences against:

    (a) the security right, or

    (b) the secured debt.

14.52 For the creation of a security right as against third parties (and the establishment of the corresponding ranking)[142] the additional registration of the security right in the security register (the 'Electronic Archive of Security Rights in Personal Property') is required.[143] A transfer of possession in movable assets is not required.[144] There are a number of exceptions to the registration requirement, namely for security rights securing an obligation with a value of less than €300,[145] for security rights in money bills or coins, physical securities and other legal documents,[146] undocumented securities which are transferred by respective amendments in the 'records kept for the market',[147] and ships and aircraft for which separate registries exist.[148]

14.53 Pursuant to Article 11(2) of the Law Concerning Certain Measures for the Acceleration of the Economic Process it is not possible to limit a person's power to transfer accounts receivables by agreement or to require the consent of the account debtor (and it is not even possible to create a respective obligation). Hence, accounts receivables can be encumbered by a registered security right even if the parties to the agreement creating the accounts receivables intended to limit the power to transfer the receivables.

14.54 A mortgage in real estate is created pursuant to the rules of the Civil Code and Law No 7/1996 on the Cadastre and Real Estate Publicity:

---

[139] Law Concerning Certain Measures for the Acceleration of the Economic Process, Art 21(3).
[140] ibid Art 9(1).   [141] ibid Art 10(1).   [142] ibid Art 28.   [143] ibid Art 29(1).
[144] ibid Art 9(3).
[145] ibid Article 30(1), first bullet point: the security right can be created either by registration or by taking possession.
[146] ibid Art 30(1), second bullet point: taking possession of the physical document is the only method of 'perfection'.
[147] ibid Art 30(1), third bullet point.
[148] ibid Article 30(1), fourth bullet point.

(1) by a mortgage agreement which must define both the mortgaged real estate and the amount of the secured debt—should any of these elements not be defined the agreement will be null and void;[149]

(2) the mortgage agreement must be made in notarized form;

(3) the person issuing the mortgage must be the owner of the real estate;

(4) a mortgage is valid between the parties to the mortgage agreement without any registration. However, the registration of the mortgage in the land register is necessary in order to make the mortgage effective against third parties.

(5) there must be a secured debt; and

(6) there shall be no defences against (a) the security right, or (b) the secured debt.

6. Russian law

There are four main types of proprietary security under Russian law: the **14.55** registered pledge (called a mortgage or hypothec) on real estate or the assets of an enterprise, the non-registered pledge on all other assets, the retention of ownership in movable and immovable things, and security assignments of receivables.

(a) Pledge

The creation of the non-registered pledge requires the following: **14.56**

(1) An agreement (pledge contract) between the parties.[150]

(2) The agreement must be made in writing or in notarial form, respectively.

(3) The pledgor must have the right to pledge the pledged property.[151] The pledged property may be future;[152] no pledge can be created in good faith in assets which are in fact not owned or held by the pledgor; a negative pledge provision between two parties in a pledge agreement[153] prevents the creation of a subsequent pledge; the negative pledge provision has, hence, proprietary effect.

(4) There must be a secured obligation. It is possible to create an enterprise charge in present and future debts (the latter only if the amount of the secured debt is specified).[154]

(5) There shall be no defences against (a) the pledge or (b) the secured debt.

---

[149] Civil Code, Art 1772.

[150] Civil Code, Arts 334(3), first sentence 339(1), Pledge Law, Arts 3, 10(1), 55, and Law on Mortgage, Art 1(1).

[151] For mortgages, see Law on Mortgage, Arts 6, 7.

[152] Civil Code, Art 340(6), Pledge Law, Art 6(3).   [153] Civil Code, Art 342(2).

[154] Pledge Law, Art 4(3).

There are defences against the pledge in particular if the parties are limited in their ability to create a pledge or the property is not eligible to be pledged. It should also be noted that, pursuant to Article 10(1) of the Pledge Law, the value of the pledged property must be defined by the parties, otherwise the pledge contract is invalid. However, in practice there appear to be no consequences if the value provision is not complied with.

14.57 The pledge agreement must contain details of the secured debt, its amount, the terms of its discharge, the pledged property, and its value as well as other substantive terms.[155] Furthermore, the agreement must also indicate who is in possession of the pledged property.[156] This requirement is reminiscent of the outdated concept of the possessory pledge.

14.58 In principle the agreement must be in writing.[157] However, a pledge which secures a debt arising out of a contract certified in notarial form must be certified by a notary.[158] If the form requirements are not complied with, the pledge is void pursuant to Article 12 of the Pledge Law.

14.59 Possession is in principle not a requirement for the creation of a pledge under Russian law. However, Russian law allows both possessory and non-possessory pledges. Article 338(1) of the Civil Code provides that the possessory pledge (where possession in the pledged property is transferred to the pledgeholder) shall be the rule ('unless otherwise stipulated'),[159] and thereby clearly follows an outdated concept of security law. Unless otherwise provided by the pledge contract, the pledge is created if (a) the pledge contract is executed by the parties and (b) the property is actually handed over to the pledgeholder (for possessory pledges this is a creation requirement).[160] The main legal consequence of a possessory pledge is that it creates different rights and obligations between the parties as compared with a non-possessory pledge.[161]

14.60 There are two main rights and obligations related to possession of the pledged property. Possession determines which party (the pledgor or the pledgeholder) (a) shall insure the pledged property against loss and damage (in any case at

---

[155] Note that Pledge Law, Art 10(1) only required reference to the secured debt and the charged property, whereas Civil Code, Art 339(1) extended the requirements.

[156] Civil Code, Art 339(1), second sentence. Note that only Pledge Law, Art 10(1) requires the inclusion of the other terms of the security agreement and only Civil Code, Art 339(1), second sentence, requires the security agreement to contain clarifications on possession of the pledged property. In practice the parties will include both requirements in their agreement.

[157] Civil Code, Art 339(2), first sentence and Pledge Law, Art 10(2).

[158] Civil Code, Art 339(2), second sentence and Pledge Law, Art 10(3).

[159] See similarly Pledge Law, Art 5, first sentence, which mentions the possessory pledge first.

[160] Civil Code, Art 341(1).

[161] See Pledge Law, Arts 36–39 for non-possessory pledges on the one hand and ibid Arts 50, 51, 53 for possessory pledges on the other hand and 17.25 below.

the pledgor's expense unless otherwise stipulated by contract)[162] and (b) is entitled to claim the pledged property from third parties who possess the property without having a right to do so.[163] In the case of a pledge of rights, the pledge contract must also refer to the debtor of the pledged right.[164] Where movables are documented in a document of title they will be pledged by a transfer of possession to the document of title.[165] Since there is no registration requirement for the creation of non-registered pledges, some lenders insist that the pledgor affixes equipment plates to valuable assets, thus indicating that the equipment has been pledged.

The pledgor has the right to pledge property if he is the owner or holder of an **14.61** asset[166] or if he has the right of economic management pursuant to Article 295 No 2 of the Civil Code.[167] The right of economic management is a remnant of socialist law and acts as a substitute for ownership if state or municipal unitary enterprises (a special form of company under Russian law) hold property. A state or municipal unitary enterprise is entitled to mortgage immovable property it holds on the basis of economic management rights with the owner's (ie the respective state entity's) consent only. For instance, a unitary enterprise which holds property on the basis of an economic management right, is entitled to pledge the enterprise as a whole, or a part of it being a separate economic unit, only with the owner's consent.[168] Lease rights and other rights may be pledged with the consent of the owner or the person holding the property on the basis of an economic management right, if the law or the contract prohibit selling the property without such person's consent.[169] Other types of property may be pledged without such consent unless stipulated otherwise by law.

A pledge secures an underlying secured obligation to the extent that the debt **14.62** exists at its maturity.[170] For future debts the pledge is created at the time of the pledge contract.[171]

The parties may be limited in their ability to create a pledge for three reasons: **14.63** the creation of a pledge is excluded by agreement, the secured debt cannot be secured, or the pledged property cannot be pledged. A subsequent pledge may be prohibited by a negative pledge clause in prior pledge contracts.[172] The negative pledge clause in a prior pledge contract under Russian law not only creates an obligation not to create a subsequent pledge but excludes the

---

[162] Pledge Law, Art 38.   [163] Civil Code, Art 347 (1).
[164] Pledge Law, Art 55, first sentence.   [165] ibid Art 5, second sentence.
[166] Civil Code, Arts 334(1) ('to whom the property belongs'), 335(2), (3), Pledge Law, Art 19(1).
[167] Civil Code, Art 335(2), Pledge Law, Art 19(1).   [168] Pledge Law, Art 19(2).
[169] Civil Code, Art 335(3), second sentence.   [170] ibid Art 337, Pledge Law, Art 4(4).
[171] Civil Code, Art 341(1).   [172] ibid Art 342(2).

parties' power to create a pledge. Certainly not only pledge contracts can contain negative pledge clauses, they can also be included in other contracts (for example loan agreements). However, it seems that such clauses do not have the same proprietary effects as negative pledge clauses in a pledge contract. The only remedy which the lender may use to protect his rights if a negative pledge clause contained only in a loan agreement is breached by the borrower is to ask the borrower to make early repayment of the loan and to pay default interest agreed under the loan agreement. As far as the secured debt is concerned, the law contains no limitations (provided, of course, that the secured debt is legally valid and binding). Concerning the pledged property, Article 6(1) of the Pledge Law clarifies that assets which are transferable can be subject to a pledge, ie assets which cannot be sold (separately) cannot be the subject of a pledge.[173] Personal rights can also not be pledged.[174] Furthermore, Article 336(2) of the Civil Code excludes property against which enforcement is not possible from pledged property; there are also provisions which exempt property from enforcement and therefore render it impractical to create a pledge in such property.[175]

14.64 It should be noted that the pledge of a debt or other right does not require giving notice to the debtor.[176] There is, hence, no publicity requirement for a pledge of rights.

(b) Mortgage

14.65 For the creation of a registered pledge (mortgage or hypothec), either in real estate or in the assets of an enterprise, in principle the same creation requirements apply as for a non-registered pledge. However, a building can only be mortgaged if the underlying land, or a part of it which serves the building (or lease right to such land plot or portion of it) is mortgaged.[177] Hence, the mortgage of a building is only permitted if the underlying land plot or a part of it (or the lease right to such land plot or a part) owned by the mortgagor is mortgaged as well.[178] It should be noted that the mortgage of a land plot results in an automatic mortgage of the buildings or buildings under construction located on it and owned by the mortgagor unless provided otherwise by the agreement.[179] If a land plot is mortgaged on which there are buildings owned by a third party and

---

[173] Civil Code, Art 336(1) stipulates that property which is 'excluded from circulation' cannot be the subject of a pledge. Pledge Law, Art 6 seems to capture the legal requirement of transferability more clearly than the respective provision of the Civil Code.

[174] See explicitly Civil Code, Art 336(1) and Pledge Law, Art 4(2), second sentence.

[175] The list of property owned by individuals and exempted from enforcement is contained in Civil Procedure Code, Art 446.

[176] See Pledge Law, Arts 54–58.

[177] Civil Code, Arts 340(3), Law on Mortgage, Art 69(2).   [178] Civil Code Art 340(3).

[179] ibid Art 340(4).

the mortgage on the land is enforced, the purchaser assumes the mortgagor's rights and obligations against the third party upon public sale at auction.[180]

The mortgage agreement must also refer to the value of the mortgaged real **14.66** estate or the assets of the enterprise,[181] which is based on the parties' estimates. The value of land plots to be mortgaged must be established by an independent appraiser.[182] The mortgage agreement must further identify the ownership right of the mortgagor.[183]

The Civil Code was amended by Federal Law No 213-FZ of 30 December **14.67** 2004. This reform removed the mandatory requirement for notarization of mortgage agreements. Prior to this amendment, the notary fees for such mandatory notarization were 1.5 per cent of the charged property's value; therefore, the creation of mortgages was uneconomical and thus severely affected.[184] Albeit mandatory notarization has been abolished, voluntary notarization remains available and is in practice often advisable to facilitate the registration of the mortgageholder's rights with the Federal Registration Service. Where the parties have opted for voluntary notarization, registration is facilitated, as either party may apply for registration of the mortgage, whereas without notarization a joint application is currently needed.

The parties have to register a mortgage on real estate or assets of an enterprise.[185] **14.68** For this the mortgage agreement must be registered with the Federal Registration Service ('*federalinaja shlushba registrazii*').[186] This is done by registration of the mortgage in the register of rights in real estate (called the 'Unified Register of Rights to and Transactions with Immovable Property').[187] The rights of a mortgageholder arising out of both the secured debt and the mortgage securing such a debt[188] can be certified by a mortgage certificate, which is a negotiable instrument under Russian law.[189] The mortgage certificate shall be issued by the mortgagor—and if the debtor of the secured debt is a third person, by such third person—and certified and delivered to the mortgageholder by the Federal Registration Service.[190] The mortgage certificate is a registered transferable instrument. The content of a mortgage certificate is regulated by law.[191]

The other requirements for the creation of a registered pledge are the same as the **14.69** requirements for the creation of a non-registered pledge. However, an enterprise

---

[180] Civil Code, Art 340(5).   [181] Law on Mortgage, Art 9(1).
[182] ibid Arts 9(3), 67(2).   [183] ibid Art 9(2).
[184] In practice the parties, in particular in complex financings, tried to minimize the amount of the secured debt in order to minimize the notarial fees payable.
[185] Civil Code, Art 339(3), Pledge Law, Arts 11, 43(2). For registration of mortgages see also Federal Law of the Russian Federation No 122-FZ of 21 July 1997.
[186] Law on Mortgage, Art 10(1), (2).   [187] ibid Art 11(1).
[188] Not for a mortgage in the assets of an enterprise, ibid Art 13(4) No 1.
[189] ibid Art 13.   [190] ibid Art 13(5).   [191] ibid Art 14.

mortgage must be approved by the owner of the property (in most cases the company) or its authorized representative (which, for particularly important transactions, may be the general shareholders' meeting).[192] The mortgage of an enterprise as a whole applies to all assets owned or held by the enterprise, comprising, *inter alia*, claims and other rights (including those which arise only after the time of mortgage creation, unless otherwise provided by the law or the agreement).[193] An enterprise mortgage can be created in present and future property and will, in fact, almost always include future property. The enterprise mortgage can only secure certain types of debt, ie debts whose total amount is not less than half of the value of the enterprise and which are due one year or later from the date of formation of the mortgage agreement. If an enterprise mortgage secures a debt due earlier than one year from the signing of the mortgage agreement, the mortgageholder is not entitled to enforce against the mortgaged enterprise prior to the date on which the one-year period elapsed.[194] It is possible to create enterprise mortgages in present and future debts.

(c) Retention of ownership

14.70 A retention of ownership in movable and immovable things has the following creation requirements:[195]

(1) an agreement about the transfer of ownership in a movable thing;
(2) that the transfer agreement is made under the condition precedent of the payment of the purchase price for the asset (thus linking the security arrangement with a secured debt);
(3) that possession of the asset is transferred to the acquirer;
(4) that the transferor is the owner of the asset.

The existence of the secured debt is not a requirement for the creation of the retention of ownership, hence it is also possible to secure future receivables under retention of ownership arrangements. Consequently, only defences against the retention of ownership and not against the receivables secured by the retention of ownership can be raised against the retention of ownership. There is no registration requirement for contractual retention of ownership arrangements.

(d) Security assignment

14.71 The security assignment of receivables requires[196] an agreement on a security assignment between the parties. The assignor must be the holder of the transferred receivable. It should be noted that the issue of whether or not future

---

[192] Law on Mortgage, Art 70(1). [193] Civil Code, Art 340(2).
[194] Law on Mortgage, Art 71(1), (2). [195] Civil Code, Art 491.
[196] ibid Arts 382ff.

194

rights under already existing contracts can be assigned is still disputed under Russian law. The debtor is entitled to raise against the assignee the defences against the security assignment that the debtor was entitled to raise against the assignor. The debt secured by an assignment must not necessarily be valid and enforceable; however, Russian courts introduced a number of additional validity requirements for an assignment with respect to assigned receivables:

- the receivable to be assigned must become due and payable before the date of assignment;
- the assigned receivable must not be disputed by the debtor or a third party; and
- there must not be an undischarged counterclaim against the assigned receivable.

The security assignment must not be registered or otherwise made public (for **14.72** example by giving notice to the debtor of the assigned receivable), although the assignor and/or the assignee should notify the debtor of the assignment; otherwise the debtor is entitled to perform the secured debt in favour of the assignor (in which case the risks associated with the failure to notify the debtor shall be borne by the assignee).

7. Slovak law

The charge under Slovak law is modelled on the basis of the charge introduced **14.73** by the EBRD Model Law. Hence, the creation of a charge under Slovak law is very similar to the creation requirements found under the EBRD Model Law. In order to create a charge the following requirements have to be met:

(1) a charge agreement is agreed between the parties;[197]
(2) the agreement must be made in writing;
(3) the charge must be publicized by registration or transfer of possession;
(4) the chargor must have the right to give a charge;
(5) the charge must secure a claim;
(6) there are no defences against (a) the charge or (b) the secured claim.

The charge agreement must identify the parties,[198] the secured claim (as to its **14.74** amount or the maximum principal amount), and the charged assets.[199] The law makes it clear that both secured claim and the charged assets must be sufficiently identified in the charge agreement.[200] In addition, it should contain

---

[197] A Rozehnal, *Credits Secured by Charges* (*Úvěry zajištěné zastavním právem*) (Prague, 1997) 58.
[198] The parties are not explicitly mentioned in Civil Code, §151b but their identification is evidently needed for a valid agreement pursuant to the general principles of Slovak law. See also Allen & Overy and EBRD, *Guide for Taking Charges in the Slovak Republic* (Bratislava, 2003) 13. Civil Code, §151e(1).
[199] Civil Code, §151b.   [200] ibid §151b(2)–(4).

the contractual terms agreed between the chargeholder and the chargor regarding the charge,[201] for example the law provides that the charge shall cease when the secured claim ceases to exist.[202] The parties who will want to keep a charge in existence even if an individual claim terminates will determine in the charge agreement that (a) the claim secured is the 'general indebtedness of the chargor' even if at some point in time no specific claim exists, and they may determine in addition, in order to avoid any doubt, that (b) the charge shall not cease if at some point in time an individual claim does not exist. Hence, if the secured claim is defined widely (for example all sums advanced under a credit facility or on overdraft), the secured claim does not cease to exist merely because the facility or overdraft is temporarily unused.

14.75 In principle the charge agreement must be in writing but it does not have to be notarized.[203] However, an exception applies to possessory charges.[204] If such a possessory charge should be translated into a registered charge, a written confirmation of the agreement between chargor and chargeholder is required.[205] Another exception is applicable in the event that real estate is charged, since the land register requires the signature of the chargor to be notarized for the purposes of charge registration.

14.76 An agreement prohibiting the creation of a charge does not prevent the creation of a charge.[206] It is only binding between the parties to the agreement and the creation of a charge in contravention of such an agreement may create liabilities between the parties to the agreement prohibiting the creation.

14.77 In principle the charge must be registered at the electronic Notarial Central Registry of Charges held by the local notaries and administered on a country-wide basis by the Slovak Chamber of Notaries.[207] However, the charges registry does not include registered charges for real estate. Real estate charges must be registered in the land register—the 'cadastre of real estate'.[208] Other specific types of assets must also be registered in the registers which already existed at the time of the reform of the Slovak Civil Code in 2002 (ie the trademark register, the patent register, and the commercial register).[209] Registration in the special registers replaces the registration at the charges registry.[210] No registration is required for possessory charges which are recognized under Slovak law but it is

---

[201] Allen & Overy and EBRD (n 198 above) 14.
[202] Civil Code, §151md(1) a.   [203] ibid §151b(1), first sentence.
[204] ibid §151b(1), second sentence.   [205] ibid §151e(5).   [206] ibid §151d(6).
[207] ibid §151e(1).   [208] ibid §151e(2).   [209] ibid §151e(3).
[210] ibid §151e(4); this refers to the register at the Intellectual Property Office for charges over trademarks, patents, utility designs, and semiconductor topography; the register at the Securities Centre and the Central Depository for charges of book entry securities; the Commercial Registry for charges over participation interest; and the Ships or Aircraft Registries for charges over ships or aircraft. See Allen & Overy and EBRD (n 198 above) 15.

necessary to secure priority for the charge.[211] Possessory charges are created by transfer of possession either to the chargeholder or a third person for deposit.

The creation of a charge clearly requires the chargor's right to create a charge, ie his ownership of the charged asset, although the Civil Code does not specify this requirement in the provisions on charges. It should be noted that the registration of a charge which was created by a non-owner of an asset does not cure this defect. There is no good faith acquisition by third parties under Slovak law with respect to charges.[212] Although in principle a charged asset is required, it is also possible to create a charge in future property.[213] In such a case the charge is created at the time of acquisition of ownership of the charged asset.[214] **14.78**

Lastly, a secured claim is required for the creation of a charge.[215] However, Slovak law explicitly allows the securing of future claims.[216] **14.79**

Clearly, under Slovak law the chargor can raise the defences against the charge (for example that he was incapable of entering into the charge agreement) as well as any defences against the secured debt (for example that the claim has already been satisfied and therefore terminated).[217] However, pursuant to §151j(2) of the Civil Code, the chargor may not raise the objection that the secured claim has expired under a statute of limitations, provided that the secured claim is not duly and timely paid.[218] **14.80**

Slovak secured transactions law has not introduced the concept of an unpaid vendor's charge which was developed in the EBRD Model Law.[219] It has kept the concept of the retention of ownership in movable things as a way of securing sales credit. The creation requirements for a retention of ownership in movable assets are as follows: **14.81**

(1) an agreement about the transfer of ownership in a movable thing;

(2) that the agreement is made under the condition precedent of the payment of the purchase price for the asset (thus linking the security arrangement with a secured debt); and

(3) that the transferor is the true owner of the asset.[220]

---

[211] Civil Code, §151e(5).

[212] Allen & Overy and EBRD (n 198 above) 15–16, 18–19.

[213] Civil Code, §151d(4).   [214] ibid §151f(2), (3).

[215] ibid §§151a, 151c.   [216] ibid §151c(2).

[217] Even if the chargor is different from the person of the debtor of the secured debt. Slovak law contains no explicit provision clarifying this. However, it follows from the dependence of the charge on the secured debt.

[218] The same concept is expressed in German Civil Code, §216(1), in particular for land mortgages and pledges.

[219] See 7.43, 7.57–7.61 above.

[220] Good faith acquisition is possible should the transferor not be the owner of the asset.

There is no registration requirement for a retention of ownership under Slovak law. There should not be defences against the retention agreement (defences against the secured debt are not relevant for the retention of ownership).

14.82 Non-public security transfers of ownership and security assignments of receivables are recognized under Slovak law.[221] However, they seem to be in decline in practice due to the attractive legislative regime for charges.

C. Comparative Remarks and Evaluation

1. Analytical principles

14.83 Bulgaria and Romania adopted a two-step approach to the creation of security rights, whereas the other central and eastern European reference systems use a one-step approach. It could be seen that the central and eastern European reference systems recognize retention of ownership arrangements and often—mostly as a way of dealing with ineffective legislative secured transactions regimes—security transfers.

14.84 In general, little consideration is given to defences against security rights. They are, however, explicitly referred to in Article 14 of the Model Law and also in some central and eastern European reference systems (in particular those of Bulgarian, Hungarian, Polish, and Russian law).

2. Normative evaluation

14.85 Pursuant to Principle 2 of the Core Principles for a Secured Transactions Law: 'The law should enable the quick, cheap and simple creation of a proprietary security right without depriving the person giving the security of the use of his assets.' The key issue in designing a creation regime is to provide the parties with means of establishing a security right which are attractive, rather than deterring them from using security. In particular, if the creation of security rights is coupled with publicity requirements such as registration, it must be ensured that publicity is seen as a benefit and not as a burden (either in terms of its costs or the time needed to perform registration).

14.86 It is clear that neither the possessory security right nor the security which requires giving notice to a debtor for its creation are suitable in modern financing contexts. The use of secured property by the person giving security is of fundamental importance in modern business contexts. Similarly, the notifica-

---

[221] Civil Code, §§553, 554.

tion of an often large number of debtors of secured receivables is frequently not possible in practice.

No major preference can be given to either the one-step approach or the two-step approach for the creation of security rights. The different approaches are often closely tied to the understanding of property rights under a national law. However, a security right which is effective also against third parties (and not just between the parties) provides more protection than a security right which is (as yet) only effective between the parties. The contrary view is that an attached security right provides at least minimal protection (against other attached creditors). **14.87**

15

TRANSFER OF SECURITY

A. Analytical Framework

Security rights may not continue to be held between the initial parties to the **15.01** security agreement but may be transferred to new securityholders. National secured transactions laws therefore have to deal with the requirements of a transfer of security, which may be dependent on, or independent of, the secured debt.

B. Eastern European Secured Transactions Laws

1. Bulgarian law

Both pledge and mortgage under the Law on Obligations and Contracts[1] are **15.02** transferred automatically by operation of law if the secured debt is transferred. A debt secured by a mortgage is transferred validly only if the transfer agreement is made in writing with notarized signatures and recorded with the recording office at the respective regional court.[2]

There is no provision on the transfer of registered pledges in the Law on **15.03**

---

[1] Law on Obligations and Contracts, s 150(1).
[2] ibid s 171. The real estate register has not yet been implemented in Bulgaria.

Registered Pledges. However, since the registered pledge is also a right ancillary to the secured debt, the provisions of the Law on Obligations and Contracts apply by way of analogy. The registration of the pledge can be the basis of a good faith acquisition of the pledge from a pledgeholder who in fact has not validly acquired the pledge. This is despite the fact that there is no requirement for professional involvement (for example by a notary public) in the drafting of the pledge agreement[3] and no checking of the pledge agreement by the pledges register.[4] The registration can thus be the basis for an acquisition of a registered pledge which has not been created validly.

2. Czech law

15.04 Under section 524(2) of the Civil Code liens are transferred automatically if the secured debt is assigned pursuant to sections 524ff of the Civil Code. The transfer of registered liens (like the registered lien on movable things) does not have to be registered to be valid. This appears to apply even where a registered lien in real estate is concerned, since there is no provision similar to section 157(1) of the Civil Code which requires the real estate lien's registration for its initial creation (but not for its transfer). It should also be noted that Czech law only provides for a lien in real estate which is registered in the Land Register. Unlike German law, Czech law does not recognize a lien which is documented by a certificate and does not allow the transfer of the lien simply by transferring the certificate without any registration.[5] Not to introduce a way of facilitated transfer of real estate liens seems logical if the transfer of a real estate lien does not require registration in any case. There is no good faith acquisition of a lien which was not created validly in the first place. Retentions of ownership and security transfers are independent from a transfer of the secured claim. Ownership of an asset must be transferred if it is to secure the receivable upon its transfer to a new party.

3. Hungarian law

15.05 The ancillary registered or possessory charge is transferred automatically by operation of law if the secured claim is transferred.[6] If the transferor was in fact not the true chargeholder of the charge and where the charge is registered the purchaser will acquire the charge if he (a) acts in good faith with respect to the charge and (b) acquires for value ('counter-performance').[7] However, the

---

[3] The only form requirement is that the pledge agreement must be made in writing; Law on Registered Pledges, Art 2.

[4] ibid Art 30(1).

[5] TO Schorling, *Das Recht der Kreditsicherheiten in der Tschechischen Republik* (Berlin, 2000) 40.

[6] Civil Code, s 251(4).   [7] Law Decree No 11/1960, s 47(2).

independent charge, like the German non-ancillary land mortgage, must be transferred, since it does not directly secure a claim.[8] A retention of ownership is independent from a transfer of the secured claim. Ownership must be transferred separately from the secured claim.

4. Polish law

The Civil Code pledge is transferred, as a strictly ancillary right, by simply **15.06** transferring the secured debt.[9]

For the registered pledge the Law provides that both secured claim and regis- **15.07** tered pledge must be assigned.[10] Since the Law has a limited personal scope, ie only the secured claims of qualified persons can be secured,[11] Article 17(1) of the Law on Registered Pledges and the Pledge Registry confirms that the pledge and the secured claim can be transferred only to qualified persons. The registration constitutes public knowledge and can be the basis for a good faith acquisition of a pledge which in fact did not exist by a third party.[12] However, a good faith acquisition is not possible if the registration was not made in accordance with the application and pledgor or pledgeholder immediately requested the appropriate correction of the registry.[13]

As far as mortgages in real estate are concerned, the mortgage is transferred **15.08** automatically with the transfer of the secured debt.[14] Neither the mortgage nor the secured debt can be transferred separately. However, pursuant to Article 107, first sentence, of the Law on Land Registry and Mortgages this does not apply to maximum amount mortgages ('deposit mortgages'). The maximum amount mortgage on real estate must be transferred by agreement and this transfer must be registered in the real estate register.[15] A mortgage cannot be transferred independently from the secured claim and vice versa.[16] Interestingly, the registration of the mortgage in the land register allows third parties not only to assume that the mortgage has been created validly but also that the secured debt validly exists.[17] However, this presumption does not apply to maximum amount mortgages[18] or personal debts ('*wierzytelność osobista*').

The retention of ownership is independent from any transfer of the secured **15.09** debt. Ownership must be transferred separately from the secured debt.

---

[8] Civil Code, s 269(3).   [9] Civil Code, Art 323, §1.
[10] Law on Registered Pledges and the Pledge Registry, Art 17(1).   [11] ibid Art 1.
[12] ibid Art 38.   [13] ibid Art 38(2).
[14] Law on Land Registry and Mortgages, Art 79.   [15] ibid Art 107, second sentence.
[16] ibid Art 79.
[17] ibid Arts 71, 80 (if the secured debt does not exist, the mortgage can still be enforced; however, a claim may not be made under the secured debt on this basis).
[18] ibid Art 105.

5. Romanian law

15.10 The security right is an ancillary right which is in principle transferred automatically by operation of law if the secured debt is assigned. Pursuant to Article 43 of the Law Concerning Certain Measures for the Acceleration of the Economic Process the security right can also be transferred by itself. However, notwithstanding the language used in Article 43, a separate transfer of the security right is possible only in limited cases. One situation in which the security right can be transferred independently from the secured debt pursuant to Article 43 is where several creditors hold security rights in the same asset and a security right with a lower priority relative to other security rights is assigned.

15.11 The transfer must be registered in the security register. However, the registration is not a requirement for the transfer's validity. The security register does not support any good faith acquisition of security rights which do in fact not validly exist. Article 29(2) of the Law Concerning Certain Measures for the Acceleration of the Economic Process confirms that the registration in itself cannot override defects of an attached security right.

15.12 Real estate mortgages are transferred automatically with the transfer of the secured debt. However, in order to make the transfer effective towards third parties, it must be registered in the land register.

6. Russian law

15.13 The non-registered pledge under Russian law is strictly ancillary.[19] It is transferred automatically by operation of law with a transfer of the secured debt.[20]

15.14 The Law on Mortgage provides that the simple registered mortgage (ie a mortgage for which a mortgage certificate has not been issued) is transferred by agreeing on the transfer of the rights under the mortgage agreement and registering the transfer with the Federal Registration Service in the real estate register (called the 'Unified Register of Rights to and Transactions with Immovable Property'.[21] If the mortgaged property is transferred to a third party, the secured debt follows the mortgaged property, unless otherwise established in an individual case.[22] The secured debt will be transferred in the form in which the debt has been created.

15.15 However, in 2004 an alternative simplified procedure was introduced for the transfer of registered mortgages, which allows the transfer to be effective without

---

[19] See Pledge Act, Art 4(4), first sentence.   [20] ibid Art 20, second sentence.
[21] Law on Mortgage, Art 47(2).   [22] ibid Art 47(2).

entering it in the real estate register. When entering into a mortgage, the mortgageholder can obtain a mortgage certificate, issued by the mortgagor and certified by the Federal Registration Service. Once certified, this certificate enables the mortgageholder, and any transferee in turn, to transfer its mortgage without further reference to the Federal Registration Service. In addition, the transfer of a mortgage for which a mortgage certificate has been issued requires a transfer agreement which must be made in writing.[23] At any point, a transferee can apply to the Federal Registration Service to have its right entered in the real estate register. Such a registration must then be completed within one day of application. This simplified procedure is intended to facilitate, in particular, securitizations of receivables secured by mortgages in the form of mortgage-backed securities.

Interestingly, the transfer of a mortgage for which a mortgage certificate has been issued automatically results in a transfer of the secured debt.[24] The transfer must be mentioned in a transfer notice placed on the mortgage certificate, indicating the name of the transferor, the reason for transfer, and the signature of the actual mortgageholder, as well as the previous holder of the mortgage certificate if the mortgage has been transferred more than once.[25] The Law on Mortgage does not state clearly that possession of the mortgage certificate must be transferred to the new mortgageholder; however, pursuant to Article 48(3) of the Law on Mortgage, the holder of the mortgage certificate is presumed to be the true holder of the mortgage. In addition, the transfer can be registered in the real estate register,[26] although this is not a requirement for the transfer becoming effective.[27] **15.16**

Retentions of ownership and security transfers are independent of a transfer of the secured claim. Retained or security ownership in an asset must itself be transferred if it is to secure the secured debt upon its transfer to a new party. This would, however, have to be coordinated with the purchaser under a retention of ownership arrangement and with the transferor under a security transfer, since the arrangement typically assumes that the assets were ultimately transferred to the purchaser or the transferor upon satisfaction of the secured debt. **15.17**

7. Slovak law

Under Slovak law, since the charge is an ancillary right it is simply transferred by transferring the secured claim. The charge follows automatically by operation of **15.18**

---

[23] Law on Mortgage, Art 48(1).   [24] ibid Art 48(1).   [25] ibid Art 48(1).
[26] ibid Art 16(1). For details of the registration procedure, see further ibid Art 20(4).
[27] ibid Art 48(1) simply requires an agreement in writing and the respective transfer notice.

law.[28] The secured debt can be transferred in the same way as any other debt. However, there is a requirement for the transfer of a charge to be registered in the charge register and in a special register (if for a creation of the charge an entry in a special registry is required by law) unless the name of a person authorized to act on behalf of the chargeholder is shown in the register and the same person is authorized by the transferee.[29] If the transfer of the charge is not registered, the charge remains valid against third parties but the chargeholder may have difficulties in proving his right to enforce. If the charge was not validly created in the first place, the purchaser cannot acquire if even he acted in good faith with respect to the existence of the charge. As already stated in the context of the initial creation of the charge, there is no good faith acquisition with respect to charges under Slovak law.

15.19 If the chargeholder transfers the secured debt without the charge, the debt becomes unsecured and the charge terminates since it cannot exist independently from the debt.[30]

C. Comparative Remarks and Evaluation

1. Analytical principles

15.20 Both the ancillary and the non-ancillary model can be found in the central and eastern European reference systems. Under the ancillary model, the transfer of the secured debt automatically leads to a transfer of the security right. The non-ancillary model provides for independent transfers of the security right and the secured debt.

2. Normative evaluation

15.21 The ancillary model is mainly a transactional simplification for the parties involved. The security right follows automatically with the transfer of the secured debt, in most cases provided that this transfer has been registered or a certificate, which has been issued for the security right, has been handed over.

---

[28] Civil Code, §151c(3), first sentence.

[29] This is not explicitly stated in Civil Code, §151c(3) but follows from §151g(2); it is further supported by §151h(5) pursuant to which the chargor and the purchaser of the collateral shall register a change in the owner of the collateral and §151ma(7), second sentence, which expresses the registration requirement for a change in the person of the owner of the collateral. See also Allen & Overy and EBRD, *Guide for Taking Charges in the Slovak Republic* (Bratislava, 2003) 23.

[30] See Civil Code, §151a ('secure a claim'). There is no explicit provision in §151md which deals with termination events of the charge generally. However, the general concept of §151md(1) a pursuant to which the charge terminates when the secured claim ceases to exist can be applied by way of analogy. This opinion seems to be shared by the commentary provided by Allen & Overy and EBRD (n 29 above) 26.

However, the unlimited ancillary model seems to restrict the parties' freedom unnecessarily. The parties should in principle be given the freedom to provide that the secured debt can be transferred without the security right.

Transfers of security rights can be complicated in cases where equal ranking **15.22** security rights are given to a number of securityholders, such as a pool of lending banks or the holders of bonds (where the securityholders may not even be resident in the jurisdiction of the borrower). The concept of a charge manager (under Articles 3.2 and 16 of the Model Law), a pledge administrator (as adopted under Polish law),[31] or a person who can act against third parties as if he is the chargeholder (as adopted under Slovak law)[32] can overcome practical difficulties in these situations.

---

[31] See 13.04.   [32] 13.08.

16

PUBLICITY OF SECURITY

A. Analytical Framework

Security rights are widely held to require publicity to avoid the impression of **16.01** 'false wealth'. Publicizing a security right will ensure that unsecured creditors are aware that assets are allocated to a particular creditor.[1] The most important issue is to determine the method of publicity, be it registration, taking of possession, or giving of notice to a party.

---

[1] PR Wood, *Maps of World Financial Law* (5th edn, London, 2005) 92.

16.02 One of the main means of publicity is registration or filing. Although the terms 'registration' and 'filing' are often used interchangeably, it is more accurate to make a distinction: registration (sometimes also referred to as 'notice filing') is the lodgement of particulars relating to the security, and filing is the lodgement of the security instrument itself or a copy of it.[2] Also a distinction should be made with respect to the terms 'register', 'registry', and 'registrar': the term 'register' is used to refer to the physical file or database that contains the registered information; 'registry' refers to the institution which fulfils the registration function; and 'registrar' refers to the person responsible for operating the registry.[3]

B. Eastern European Secured Transactions Laws

1. Bulgarian law

(a) Recording of mortgages

16.03 Both mortgages of real property and registered pledges must be publicized. For its creation, a mortgage must be recorded with the recording office at the respective regional court.[4] The records are paper-based and contain notarial deeds. Searching has to be done against the names of the parties and is cumbersome in practice. The Law on Cadastre and Property Register provides a land register in electronic form; however, this has not yet been implemented. Once registration has been implemented in practice it will be valid for a period of ten years, but it will be possible to renew the registration prior to its expiry.[5] Any deregistration will require the consent of the pledgeholder.[6]

(b) Registration of pledges

16.04 Bulgaria introduced an electronic pledge register almost at the same time as Hungary. The Law on Registered Pledges entered into force on 1 April 1997. The registry is designed as a central registry, operating as an independent public agency and administered by the Ministry of Justice.[7] Its head office is located in Sofia and there are six local offices throughout Bulgaria. The register is an electronic database, but no remote access is yet possible: all entries must be made in the head office in Sofia. The details are regulated in Articles 22 to 31 of the Law on Registered Pledges and supplementary regulations.[8] The registry is public and, interestingly, persons may obtain confirmations[9] not only of registered but also of non-registered circumstances.

---

[2] R Goode, *Commercial Law* (3rd edn, London, 2004) 649–50.
[3] The same use of terminology is proposed by EBRD, *Publicity of Security Rights, Guiding Principles for the Development of a Charges Registry* (London, 2004) 4 n 10.
[4] Law on Obligations and Contracts, s 166(1).   [5] ibid s 172(1).   [6] ibid s 179.
[7] Law on Registered Pledges, Arts 1(2), 22(1).   [8] See ibid Art 23.   [9] ibid Art 24.

Any 'interested party' may request registration.[10] However, the registration will   **16.05**
only be effected if the person giving the security consents to it either by signing
the registration form in person in front of the registrar[11] or by adding its signature on the form, confirmed by a notary.[12] The registration request can be
submitted to the registry's head office or to one of the local offices, in which case
the request is then forwarded to the head office which will perform the
registration.

The registration form must contain details of the parties, charged assets,   **16.06**
and secured debt (including amount). The following documents have to be
produced:

- annexes, in case the space provided on the forms is not sufficient (there is
  often a schedule describing the secured assets);
- a certificate from the Commercial Registry confirming the status and current
  activity of the chargor as a merchant and including its identification number
  (or a certificate by the office for national statistics including the identification
  number if the chargor is an individual); and
- a certificate from the tax authorities confirming that the chargor has no
  outstanding tax liabilities.

The registration is made immediately upon application and can be refused only   **16.07**
in two cases: if the application does not have the required content or the
registration fee has not been paid.[13] A refusal can be appealed under the rules of
administrative procedure.[14] The registration is valid for a period of five years but
can be renewed prior to expiry.[15]

The content of the registration is quite comprehensive since it records not   **16.08**
only information about the parties—ie the debtor, a third party pledgor, and the
pledgeholder (or the persons providing and receiving a security right under an
arrangement considered similar to a pledge), the secured debt, the secured
property, the duration of the pledge (which in principle is limited to a term of
five years), and its other terms but also the following information:[16]

- certain changes in the secured debt, namely its assignment, subordination,
  novation (or other substitution of the debtor);
- acquisition of rights in the secured property;
- renewal of the registration;
- the termination of enforcement proceedings;

---

[10] ibid Art 27(1), first sentence.   [11] ibid Art 27(1), second sentence.
[12] ibid Art 27(2).   [13] ibid Art 28(1).
[14] ibid Art 29. The reference to administrative procedure rules is unique to Bulgarian law.
Typically the applicable rules are civil procedure or similar rules.
[15] ibid Art 30(2).   [16] ibid Art 26.

- a request for appointment of an enterprise manager and details of an appointed enterprise manager; and
- the commencement and termination of insolvency proceedings.

16.09 The registry clerk generates a unique registration number for each request—a bar code sticker is pasted onto a special box on the form. The form is then scanned and an image file of the form is created in the system and is automatically associated with the generated filing number. Then a special menu opens which enables the operator to key in the data concerning the identity of the pledgeholder and pledgor. All annexed documents are also scanned and attached electronically to the file.

16.10 Searches can be made against the name and ID number of the pledgor. A request for a search can be sent to the registrar by post, fax, or even by telephone, but usually the individual wishing to make the search will go to the registry's offices in person. Three types of search reports may be obtained:

(1) The basic search report provides only a list of pledges (and security arrangements treated like a pledge) existing against the given pledgor, with very basic information (for example the name of the pledgeholder).

(2) A more thorough report provides information about the pledgor, pledgeholder, secured debt, and a full description of the secured assets.

(3) A comprehensive search result produces all information, including the scanned initial and subsequent registration.

16.11 The registration can be the basis of a good faith acquisition of the pledge from a pledgeholder who, in fact, has not validly acquired the pledge. This is despite the fact that there is no requirement for professional involvement (for example by a notary public) in the drafting of the pledge agreement[17] and no checking of the pledge agreement by the pledges register.[18]

(c) Transfer of possession

16.12 The possessory pledge under the Law on Obligations and Contracts requires a transfer of possession to the pledgeholder for its creation.[19] However, particularly in commercial contexts, the transfer of possession is an impracticable means of creating security and, hence, the registered pledge in movable things has quickly gained the dominant position in Bulgarian secured transactions law.

---

[17] The only form requirement is that the pledge agreement must be made in writing; Law on Registered Pledges, Art 2 or, if the assets of an enterprise or shares are pledged, the signatures under the pledge agreement must be notarized, ibid Arts 21(1), 19(1).

[18] ibid Art 30(1).   [19] Law on Obligations and Contracts, Art 156(1).

(d) Notice

The traditional means of providing publicity for the existence of pledges in **16.13** receivables is to provide notice of the pledge to the receivables' debtor. This is indeed the creation requirement for the pledge of non-registered receivables.[20] However, the Law on Registered Pledges has done away with this creation requirement and relies on registration as the decisive perfection requirement.

2. Czech law

(a) Registration of liens on real estate

Liens on real estate must be registered in the cadastre (real estate register).[21] **16.14** Liens on real estate not yet listed in the real estate register must, however, be registered in the collateral register. A lien registered in the real estate register shall be deleted immediately (ie on the same day) upon the lien's termination.[22]

(b) Registration of liens in the collateral register

Non-possessory liens ('liens in movable assets that were not handed over to the **16.15** chargeholder or to a third person') and the lien on assets of an enterprise or other collective assets ('collection of things or aggregate thing') must be registered in the collateral register,[23] a fully computerized database maintained by the Chamber of Notaries of the Czech Republic.[24] It started operating in February 2002 as a non-public register.

The entry in the collateral register must be done by the notary who has previ- **16.16** ously drawn up the notarized deed required for the establishment of such a lien.[25] The following data is recorded:

- description of the lien;
- amount and description of the secured debt;
- identity of the party giving the lien;
- identity of the lienholder;
- date of the lien; and
- date and time of entry in the Register.

Any searching of the register requires a request to a notary, showing a justified **16.17** interest or submitting the written consent of the owner of the movable asset. A copy (including all information relating to a registered lien) or an extract (showing only the present data) from the collateral register, or a certificate

---

[20] ibid Art 162.   [21] Civil Code, s 157(1).   [22] ibid s 171(1).
[23] In addition, liens on real estate not yet listed in the real estate register must be registered in the collateral register.
[24] Civil Code, s 158(1).   [25] ibid s 158(2).

confirming that a given asset has not been taken as security, will then be produced for each search.

16.18 The lien registered in the collateral register shall be deleted upon the lienholder's request or if the termination has been proven to the notary's satisfaction.[26]

(c) Registration of liens on rights other than receivables

16.19 Often liens on rights other than receivables must be registered in special registers, such as the lien on trademarks which, pursuant to section 17 of the Trademark Law, requires registration in the trademark register.

(d) Transfer of possession

16.20 The transfer of possession either to the person taking the security right[27] or to a third party[28] is in principle required for liens in movable things. However, in practice the parties will, in most cases, opt for the non-possessory lien registered in the collateral register.

(e) Secret security rights

16.21 Czech law is not characterized by a strict reliance on the publicity principle but recognizes important exceptions. The retention of ownership in movable things, the security transfer of ownership in movable things, and the security assignment of receivables and other rights are all created without giving publicity either by a form of registration or another means of publicity.

3. Hungarian law

(a) Registration at the charges registry

16.22 Registration at the charges registry[29] is regulated in sections 261 to 263 of the Civil Code and sections 47 and 47A of Law Decree No 11/1960. In addition, a decree of the Ministry of Justice was passed[30] and the rules of civil procedure apply.[31] Hungary introduced a computerized[32] charges registry for the registration of non-possessory charges in movable things and floating charges (*zálogjogi nyilvántartás*, ZONY), which is maintained by the Hungarian National Chamber of Public Notaries[33] and has been in operation since May 1997. The register consists of a single centralized database, which can be accessed by any member

---

[26] Civil Code, s 171(2).   [27] ibid s 157(2).   [28] ibid s 157(3).
[29] See J Simpson, J-H Röver, and J Bates, *Feasibility Study for a Computerised Registration System for Charges in Hungary* (London, 1996).
[30] Law Decree No 11/2001; see Law Decree No 11/1960, s 47A(6).
[31] ibid s 47A(5).   [32] ibid s 47(3).
[33] Civil Code, s 262(2) and Law Decree No 11/1960, s 47(1), first sentence, (2).

of the public at any of 200 notaries' offices across the country. Entries can be made by any notary, although the initial registration of a charge will probably be made by the notary who draws up the notarial deed of charge. The register is open for public inspection.[34] Entries in the charges register 'authenticate' the charge agreement between the parties and can, therefore, be the basis for good faith acquisitions of charges.[35]

16.23 The application is simply made by submitting the charge agreement to any notary in Hungary.[36] The notary may reject the application only if the charge agreement takes the form of a private document and if the agreement is 'obviously invalid'.[37] Thus the notary will not, for example, check whether the secured claim exists but will concentrate on obvious deficiencies, in particular that the charge agreement for a registered charge is made in the form of a public notary's instrument.[38] The application will typically be made by the chargor. The right to apply vests also with the notary if he has drawn up a public notary instrument and is, therefore, in a position to take appropriate steps.[39] If a person other than the chargor (for example the chargeholder) makes an application for deletion of the charge to the register, the deletion will be made but the notary has to notify the chargor.[40] Where the deletion of a charge has been made, the chargor can apply for a new registration of the charge within thirty days from the receipt of the notification, and this new registration will have the same priority as the initial registration.[41]

16.24 The application is decided upon by an order of the notary;[42] this is a technical issue to bring the registration procedure into line with general civil procedure, of which the registration procedure is regarded under Hungarian law as part and parcel. The registration is transmitted electronically to the central database held with the Hungarian National Chamber of Public Notaries and the notary issues a certificate confirming the registration made.[43]

16.25 Registrations must contain the amount and the nature of the secured claim (the latter can be described by reference to the charge agreement).[44] Article 47(5) of Law Decree No 11/1960 further specifies the content of the registration and Article 47(6) specifies the need for an adequate description. The law describes precisely what information must be registered:[45]

- the personal details of the parties (chargor and debtor if different from the chargor, and chargeholder);

---

[34] ibid s 47(1), second sentence.   [35] ibid s 47(2).
[36] ibid s 47(4).   [37] ibid s 47a(2).   [38] See Civil Code, s 262(2).
[39] Decree No 11/1960, s 47A(1), fourth sentence.   [40] ibid s 47A(3).
[41] ibid s 47A(3).   [42] ibid s 47A(4).   [43] ibid s 47A(1).
[44] Civil Code, s 262(3).   [45] Law Decree No 11/1960, s 47(5).

- a description of the charged assets;
- the basis of the secured claim (for example a loan agreement or supply agreement), the currency, due date, amount and/or its maximum amount;
- a description of the charge agreement, the person who has drafted it, the date, and the name of the notary effecting the registration;
- the type of charge; and
- the day and time at which the charge was registered, which is entered automatically by the system.

16.26 Registration and searching are virtually instantaneous. Anybody may have access to all information included in the register by searching under the name of the chargor and may take notes or obtain a printout.

16.27 At present the fee for registration is HUF5,000 (approximately €19), the fee for search is HUF1,000 (approximately €4). The notary's fee for notarization varies according to the transaction value. For example, if the credit secured is an amount higher than HUF5,000,000 (approximately €19,000) but not higher than HUF10,000,000 (approximately €38,000), the notary is entitled to charge a fee of HUF56,700 (approximately €214) plus 0.5 per cent of the amount of the credit exceeding HUF5,000,000. Thus the notarization of a charge agreement securing a credit of HUF10,000,000 (approximately €38,000) will cost HUF81,700 (approximately €308).[46] This is considered expensive in comparison to costs in other countries. The registration procedure is also considered to be cumbersome and slow.[47] The pending reform of the Hungarian secured transaction law is expected to lower registration and notarization costs and also to improve the working of the charges register.

(b) Registration at the real property registry

16.28 Charges in real property are registered in a real property register.[48] The owner of real estate may notify the real property registry that he intends to charge the land with a registered pledge.[49] This will allow the registration of a charge in real estate with its priority set at the time of notification.[50]

(c) Transfer of possession

16.29 The way to publicize the possessory pledge is to transfer possession of the charged asset to the chargeholder or a third person.[51]

---

[46] Ministry of Justice and Law Enforcement, *Discussion Paper on the charges register for the International Seminar on the Law of Proprietary Security Rights in the Proposal for a new Hungarian Civil Code* (Budapest, 2006) para 2.

[47] ibid.   [48] Civil Code, s 262(1), second sentence.

[49] ibid s 262(4), first sentence. Similar to the concept of a pre-notification ('*Vormerkung*') under German law, German Civil Code, §§883–888.

[50] Civil Code, s 262(4), second sentence.   [51] ibid s 265(1), first and second sentences.

4. Polish law

(a) Registration

Pledge agreements for registered pledges are registered pursuant to the Law on **16.30** Registered Pledges at the pledge registry. The pledge register is a centralized electronic database set up by the Ministry of Justice[52] and administered by the regional commercial courts.[53] Registration is made at a regional commercial court, and the information is then sent electronically to Warsaw for entry in the central register. The register is open to public inspection.[54] The registration procedure is regulated mainly in Articles 36 to 44 of the Law on Registered Pledges and the Pledge Registry. In addition, there are a number of decrees issued by the Ministry of Justice, the Ministry of Finance, and the Ministry of Transport dealing with registration details.[55] Furthermore, the court-led registration procedure is subject to the provisions of the Civil Procedure Code dealing with non-adversarial proceedings.[56]

Registrations are made at the registry closest to the debtor's residence (for **16.31** natural persons) or head office (for companies).[57] Any changes in the debtor's residence or main office will not change the competent register once an initial registration has been made.[58] An application for registration is made by either the pledgor or the pledgeholder[59] and must be made within one month from the signing of the pledge agreement.[60] The application must be by a notice in writing to which the pledge agreement is attached[61] and must comply with the prescribed format of the entry form.[62] The content of the entry in the register is defined in Article 40 of the Law on Registered Pledges and the Pledge Registry. The completion of the application form is compulsory and applications made otherwise would be rejected. The information that must be included is:

- identification of the pledgor;
- identification of the pledgeholder;
- identification of the debtor;

---

[52] Law on Registered Pledges and the Pledge Registry, Art 42(1).   [53] ibid Art 36(2).
[54] ibid Art 37.
[55] See the references in ibid Arts 12(2) ('notice of pledge on vehicle registration document'), 39(4) ('format of registration form'), and 43 ('details of pledge registry').
[56] ibid Art 44.
[57] Pursuant to Civil Code, Art 41 the seat of a company is, unless it is provided by law or the company's corporate documents, the place where the board of directors is based. Hence, a company may have only one seat.
[58] Law on Registered Pledges and the Pledge Registry, Art 36(3).
[59] ibid Art 3(3). An application made after this period is rejected for registration.
[60] ibid Art 3(3).   [61] ibid Art 39(1).
[62] ibid Art 39(2). Form RZ-1 can be downloaded from the Ministry of Justice's website <http://www.cors.gov.pl>.

- a description of the subject matter—the name of the asset which is the object of the pledge must be provided according to the Pledge Description Standards Catalogue[63] and the relevant item number;
- details concerning the pledge—the amount of the claim must be indicated (in figures and words) and, if the mortgage secures future or conditional claims, the secured claim's maximum limit;[64] and
- the conditions for enforcement as provided in the pledge agreement.

16.32 Detailed guidelines regarding the length of the application document and the number of types of signs included (symbols, capital letters, etc) are contained in a decree of the Ministry of Justice.[65] The application can be submitted either directly or by post. There are as yet no means to deliver the application electronically.

16.33 The registration procedure is administered by the court represented by judges, and they may refuse registration if the application form is not correctly filled in or the registration fee is not paid.[66] If there are formal mistakes in the application, the court will set a seven-day period for correction of the mistakes in the application. Should the mistakes not be corrected within the time period set by the court, the application will be rejected.[67] The court may also examine the application more generally and, surprisingly for a simple registration procedure, may decide to hold a hearing.[68] If the court decides that the application should be registered it will issue a court decision accordingly.[69]

16.34 The registration constitutes public knowledge and can be the basis for a good faith acquisition of a non-existent pledge by a third party.[70] However, a good faith acquisition is not possible if the registration was not made in accordance with the application and pledgor or pledgeholder requested immediately the respective correction of the registry.[71]

16.35 The termination of a pledge, in particular because the pledgeholder transfers the secured claim to an entity not entitled to secure a claim by a registered pledge, must be noted in the pledge register. The pledgeholder shall immediately file with the court an application to delete the pledge from the register.[72] If the pledgeholder fails to make an immediate motion, he is liable to the pledgor

---

[63] This is provided in the Decree of the Ministry of Justice dated 15 October 1997.

[64] The wording of Law on Registered Pledges and the Pledge Registry, Art 40 refers incorrectly to 'the maximum limit of the pledgor's liability'. It should be noted that under proprietary security the pledgor has no liability. Only the secured property is liable.

[65] Decree of the Ministry of Justice dated 15 October 1997.

[66] Law on Registered Pledges and the Pledge Registry, Art 39(3).

[67] ibid Art 39(3).   [68] ibid Art 41(1).   [69] ibid Art 41(2), first sentence.

[70] ibid Art 38.   [71] ibid Art 38(2).   [72] ibid Art 17(3).

for damages resulting from non-performance of this statutory obligation.[73] At the same time a pledge may be deleted and then terminate.[74]

(b) Special types of publicity

There are also pledges created by tax offices against a debtor. However, they **16.36** are not registered in the pledge register but in a separate Central Register of Treasury Pledges. Since an earlier tax pledge would have priority against a later-registered contractual pledge, pledgeholders are well advised to make a separate inquiry into the Central Register of Treasury Pledges.

Mortgages in real estate are registered in the real estate register for their creation.[75] **16.37** The registration creates the presumption that the mortgage as well as the secured debt exist.[76]

Special rules apply to movable assets taken as security which become part of real **16.38** estate and consequently fall under the real estate regime. The respective mortgage has to be registered not in the pledges register but in the land register.[77] Pursuant to Article 9(2) of the Law on Registered Pledges and the Pledge Registry the pledgeholder may request from the real property's owner creation of a mortgage securing the amount of the asset which became part of the real property. The registration process is complex and thus—in response to the pledgeholder's application—the court places a notice announcing the 'commencement of court proceedings' concerning mortgage registration in the land register prior to making the actual registration.[78]

Where registered motor vehicles are pledged, the pledge is 'noted' in the vehicle **16.39** registration document.[79] This notation is not a constitutive part of the creation process of the registered pledge. There are no legal consequences if the pledge is not noted in the vehicle registration document. Third parties have to refer to the pledge registry to confirm the existence of the pledge as part of the legal due diligence. Therefore, the vehicle registration document cannot support good faith acquisition of a pledge or a vehicle free from a pledge.

(c) Transfer of possession

The Civil Code pledge is created by transfer of possession to the creditor or a **16.40** third party as agreed between the parties of the pledge agreement.[80] The Law on

---

[73] ibid Art 17(3).

[74] ibid Art 18(2). Art 19 lists those with the right to apply for the deletion of a pledge.

[75] Law on Land Registry and Mortgages, Art 67(1).

[76] ibid Arts 71, 80. The presumption that the secured debt exists applies only with respect to claims arising from the mortgage. The presumption cannot be used to make claims under the secured debt itself.

[77] Law on Registered Pledges and the Pledge Registry, Art 9(3).   [78] ibid Art 9(3).

[79] ibid Art 12.   [80] Civil Code, Art 307, §1.

Registered Pledges and the Pledge Registry confirms that, with registered pledges, possession of pledged assets can be left with the debtor or alternatively a third party agreed between the parties to the pledge agreement and if the third party agrees to this.[81] Interestingly, the Law deems it necessary to state that an entry in the pledge register transfers 'constructive' possession of the pledged asset to the creditor.[82]

(d) Notice

16.41   For Civil Code pledges in rights, the debtor of the encumbered right must be notified of the pledge for its creation. This notice must be given in writing.[83] Pursuant to Article 329 §1 of the Civil Code pledge contracts shall be made in writing with a certified date (a procedure in which a notary public or public authorities register the date of a document's creation).

5. Romanian law

(a) Registration

16.42   **Romanian security register for movable assets**   Under Romanian law publicity requirements lead to the perfection of a security right in movables which has already been attached by entering into a security contract. The Romanian security register is a single, electronic register (called 'the Archive').[84] It is a register administered by the Ministry of Justice. The Archive is operated by the 'Corps of Operators', which is a legal entity representing all operators. Each operator is licensed by the Ministry of Justice for three years (on a renewable basis). In principle, anybody can apply for a licence to operate as long as he fulfils a number of criteria, and competes with other operators. All operators (and their agents) can perform registration via the Archive's website with protected access. Currently, seven operators and about 400 agents offer their services throughout the country. They include the Chamber of Commerce, Banca Comerciala Romana (BCR) (who only act as operator on their own credit operations as lender), the Chamber of Notaries, and the Lawyers' Association. The Archive is publicly accessible for inspection purposes.[85] It can be searched by anyone for free via the internet at <http://www.mj.romarhiva.ro>, against the name of the chargor or the securityholder, or the identity of the charged assets. Searches can also be made at the operator's offices; the operator may charge a fee.

---

[81] Law on Registered Pledges and the Pledge Registry, Art 2(2).

[82] ibid Art 2(3), second sentence.

[83] Civil Code, Art 329, §1, first sentence. There is an exception from this requirement if documents certifying the right are transferred or endorsed, ibid Art 329, §2.

[84] Government Decree No 89/2000 on some Measures Related to the Operator's Authorisation and Execution of Filing with the Electronic Archive, Art 2(1).

[85] Law Concerning Certain Measures for the Acceleration of the Economic Process, Art 54.

Registrations are made on the basis of a security right notice,[86] for which there   **16.43**
are special forms[87] and which must contain the following information:[88]

- chargor's name, domicile, residence, or chosen domicile;
- securityholder's name, domicile, residence, or chosen domicile;
- a description of secured assets;
- if the secured debt is conditional, a time limit for the expiry of the registration; and
- optionally, the maximum value of the secured debt.

Information in the security right notice form prevails with respect to third   **16.44**
parties if there are inconsistencies with the security agreement (for example a
differently described secured asset).[89] Registrations are made against the chargor's
name or, in the case of vehicles, against the asset (and their respective serial
number).[90]

The chargor or the securityholder (as well as their respective representatives) can   **16.45**
request registration.[91] Where movable goods are transferred under a consign-
ment contract, the right to file rests with the consignee.[92] The notice form has to
be signed by the person requesting registration and the operator should in
principle only check the identity of the applicant and verify his or her authority.
However, due to the multiplicity of operators, practice varies and, for example,
some operators require a signed copy of the security agreement.

The information to be registered is limited to the identification of the person   **16.46**
giving security (and the debtor of the secured debt if different), identification of
the person taking security, and a description of secured assets. The operator will
type all data and submit the information to the Archive's database. Once the
entry has been submitted to the Archive and successfully received, the operator
will issue two registration certificates, one for the person giving security and
one for the person taking security. The other party must be informed about
the filing by the registering party[93] and to this effect has to receive a copy of the
security right notice from the registering party within twenty-four hours of the

---

[86] ibid Arts 29(1), 56(1), first sentence.   [87] ibid Art 55(1).
[88] ibid Art 59. For the content of a security right notice with respect to security rights in
movables attached to land, see Art 35(1) (it must contain the description of the secured asset, the
address of the land, and details of the registration with the real property registry).
[89] ibid Art 59(2).   [90] ibid Art 49(4).
[91] It should be noted that certain provisions of the Law Concerning Certain Measures for the
Acceleration of the Economic Process suggest that only the securityholder can file an application.
This seems to follow in particular from Art 58 ('notice of copy to be sent by creditor'). See also
ibid Art 56(1), (2) ('intention to create a security right'), and Art 61(1) ('securityholders shall
request . . . to make a respective entry').
[92] ibid Art 31, first sentence.   [93] ibid Art 58.

registration.[94] In practice, this notification is sent by fax and receipt is confirmed by the other party. However, this requirement is not necessary for the perfection of the security right.

16.47 There are a number of provisions which are designed to prevent administrative obstacles to the proper functioning of the register. The register does not control the legality or correctness of the information presented,[95] no other documents than the security right notice have to be presented to the register,[96] and there is no requirement to certify signatures on the filing for an intention to create a security right.[97]

16.48 Pre-registration (intention to register) is possible and the entry will be held for up to two months: if the registrant registers the charge within this time, registration will be deemed to be at the pre-registration date.

16.49 Due to the implementation of the notice filing concept on a streamlined administrative basis, it is no wonder that the security register does not support any good faith acquisition of security rights. Article 29(2) of the Law Concerning Certain Measures for the Acceleration of the Economic Process confirms that the registration in itself cannot override defects of an attached security right.

16.50 The registration is valid for five years from the date of registration but can be renewed.[98] If the registered security right terminates the secured creditor must, within forty days of the termination, send a termination notice to the register.[99] A securityholder who fails to meet this obligation is liable for direct or indirect damages caused to the debtor of the secured debt. The amount of damages payable is a minimum of the equivalent in Lei of €500.[100]

16.51 **Registration of mortgages**　A real estate mortgage is valid between the parties to the mortgage agreement without any registration. However, the registration of the mortgage in the land register is necessary in order to make the mortgage effective against third parties. Either party to the mortgage agreement may file for registration with the land register.[101] However, in practice, the application will be made by the notary public who certified the mortgage agreement.

16.52 **Registrations in special asset registers**　A security right over book-entry securities (such as shares or bonds) is deemed to be made public at the time of the

---

[94] At the address which was mentioned in the security right notice; see Law Concerning Certain Measures for the Acceleration of the Economic Process, Art 60(1), second sentence, unless a party was properly informed about a change of address; ibid Art 60(2).

[95] ibid Art 49(2).　　[96] ibid Art 50.　　[97] ibid Art 56(1), second sentence.

[98] ibid Art 44. The filing of an intention to create a security right expires after a two-month period, ibid Art 56(2).

[99] ibid Arts 27(3), 61.　　[100] ibid Art 61(1).

[101] Law No 7/1996 on the Cadastre and Real Estate Publicity, Art 47(6).

respective entries. Registration with the security register is not necessary for perfection of security rights over these securities.[102] Where a security right is created over ships or aircraft, it has to be registered in the specific registers against the name of the person granting the security rights, ie the owner of the secured asset.[103]

(b) *Transfer of possession*

Transfer of possession to the securityholder is of only subordinate importance **16.53** under Romanian law for security in movable things. Although Article 9(3) of the Law Concerning Certain Measures for the Acceleration of the Economic Process provides that the security right can be created 'with or without dispossession of the person granting the security right', it is from Article 30 of the above Law that one can see clearly how limited the role of a transfer of possession is for the perfection of a security right. Save for cases where the secured asset (being a movable thing) is of minor value (not more than the equivalent in Lei of €300), the security right is created over (physical) money, incorporated securities (such as shares or bonds), documents of title to goods, cheques, or promissory notes, the security right must be registered. The transfer must achieve publicity, ie be transparent to third parties.[104]

(c) *Notice*

Notice to the debtor of the right taken as security is required neither for the **16.54** attachment nor the perfection of security rights in receivables and other rights.

6. Russian law

(a) *Registration*

The following types of security require registration: **16.55**

• The registered pledge (called a 'mortgage' or 'hypothec') on real estate[105] is publicized by registration of the mortgage agreement with the Federal Registration Service ('*federalinaja shlushba registrazii*', an administrative state registration body) in the real estate register (called the 'Unified Register of Rights to and Transactions with Immovable Property')[106] maintained by the region where the mortgaged asset is located.[107]

• The registered pledge of the assets of an enterprise (also referred to as a

---

[102] Law Concerning Certain Measures for the Acceleration of the Economic Process, Art 30(1).
[103] ibid Art 30(1).   [104] ibid Art 30(2).
[105] For mortgages on land, see Law on Mortgage, Art 11(1) (this mortgage is also referred to in Civil Code, Art 334(2) Pledge Law, Art 41) for mortgages on buildings, see Civil Code, Art 334(2) and Pledge Law, Art 43.
[106] See Law on Mortgage, Art 11(1).   [107] Civil Code, Art 43(2).

'mortgage' or 'hypothec')[108] is registered with the Federal Registration Service and entered in the real estate register maintained by the region where the mortgaged enterprise is located.[109]

- Other property subject to state registration in special asset registries.[110] Thus, pledges over certain types of vehicles, for example agricultural vehicles, must be registered in the respective register. Pledges over cars, however, seem to be exempt from registration.[111] Pledges of shares in joint stock companies have to be recorded in the shareholder register held by the company (for companies with more than fifty shareholders, or for companies with fewer than fifty shareholders which prefer to transfer the maintenance of their shareholders' register to an independent registrar). Details of the shares in a limited liability company must be provided in its charter (in per cent and absolute rouble terms), which is registered by the state in the Uniform State Register for Legal Entities.

16.56 In the past, registries for pledges over movables were envisaged on a regional basis, for example in the decree of the Moscow Council No 788 covering the 'creation of a general registration system for pledge contracts at the territory of Moscow' of 20 September 1994. However, these registries are not operating.

16.57 Registration is typically a requirement for the creation of a mortgage in real property.[112] The security right is created at the time of registration of the mortgage.[113] The registers use modern computer technology. If the parties have opted for voluntary notarization of a mortgage agreement, registration is facilitated as either party may apply for registration of the mortgage at the Federal Registration Service,[114] whereas without notarization a joint application is needed. For the registration of a mortgage, the applying party must provide the mortgage agreement, the attachments to it (including a special transfer and acceptance act regarding the mortgaged property) and confirmation of the payment of the registration fees.[115] Fees payable for registration are specified in Federal Law No 226-FZ of 31 December 1995.[116] If a mortgage certificate has been issued for the mortgage, the applicant must also produce the mortgage certificate and any

---

[108] Civil Code, Art 334(2), Pledge Law, Art 43.

[109] Law on Mortgage, Art 11(1), Civil Code, Art 43(2).

[110] Pledge Law, Art 11, eg means of transport (aircraft, sea, and river vessels, rolling stock) (ibid Art 40).

[111] See special decision of the Supreme Arbitration Court of 7 April 1998 (No 3081/97).

[112] For mortgages, see Law on Mortgage, Art 11(2), (3).

[113] ibid Art 20(7). This provision is to be found in the context of procedural provisions on mortgage registration; however, it also is a provision of substantive law since it deals with the creation of mortgages.

[114] See ibid Art 20(1).   [115] ibid Art 20(1).   [116] Pledge Law, Art 15.

attachments.[117] A mortgage must be registered within one month from the application date.[118]

Registration is effected by the Federal Registration Service in two ways: (a) it is **16.58** done by making a note on the original mortgage agreement[119] and putting a copy of the mortgage agreement into the archive;[120] and (b) in addition, an entry of the mortgage itself is made in the register, which contains details of the first mortgageholder, the mortgaged asset, and the amount of the secured debt.[121] The registrar will make the registration not simply on the basis of the application and the documents provided, but will enter into a review of substantive law issues. He or she will check, *inter alia*, whether or not the mortgage agreement, mortgage certificate and attached documents comply with the law[122] and will refuse registration if the mortgaged property is subject to court proceedings.[123] Upon registration the mortgagor and the mortgageholder will receive a registration certificate and, upon request, extracts from the register.[124]

The registers are open to public inspection.[125] However, the state registries do **16.59** not 'authenticate' the information registered and consequently the registration does not cure any defect in the validity of the mortgage or pledge.[126] A third party, even if acting in good faith, may not rely on the facts registered but should verify them. However, a third party can rely on the absence of information in the register. A mortgage cannot be created without registration. Therefore, if no mortgage is shown in the register a third party can assume that no mortgage exists. The parties concerned can challenge the refusal of the registrar to register a mortgage or an unlawful registration in a competent court.[127] The registrar is liable for damages caused by a violation of the registration procedure, for example a registration made after mandatory deadlines have expired; a failure to register a mortgage; an unlawful refusal to register a mortgage or to correct registration errors; or a request for the provision of documents which are not referred to by law.[128]

Once the secured debt has been satisfied, the mortgageholder shall issue to the **16.60** mortgagor a certificate of satisfaction.[129] This certificate should be submitted to the registrar who should make a respective entry in the register.[130]

---

[117] Law on Mortgage, Art 20(3).   [118] ibid Art 20(5).   [119] ibid Art 22(2).
[120] ibid Art 22(4).   [121] ibid Art 22(1).   [122] ibid Art 21(2).
[123] ibid Art 21(4).
[124] Pledge Law, Art 14. Register extracts can also be received by interested parties pursuant to Art 14.
[125] For mortgages, see Law on Mortgage, Art 26.
[126] eg different from the German real estate register; see German Civil Code, §892(1).
[127] Pledge Law, Art 13.
[128] ibid Art 16. For mortgages, see also Law on Mortgage, Art 28.
[129] Pledge Law, Art 17(1).   [130] ibid Art 17(2).

16.61   In other cases than those mentioned, non-possessory security over movable property does not require centralized state registration.

(b) Privately held records

16.62   In many cases Russian law does not rely on public registers but rather on privately held records. A typical example is the shareholders' register maintained by joint stock companies. Article 18(1) of the Pledge Law adds another 'private register'. Pursuant to Article 18(1) of the Pledge Law the pledgor has to keep records on the pledge and to open a private record (a register book) not later than ten days after the creation of the pledge. The pledge book must contain data on the pledged asset and the secured debt. Interested parties can ask for access to the privately held information.[131] The pledgor must register a partial or complete satisfaction of the secured debt in the register book.[132] Although a purely private register, the pledgor is liable in damages if his records are insufficient (ie incomplete or wrong) and a third party who has relied on the records, suffered a loss due to reliance on the register book.[133]

16.63   In theory, the pledge book maintained by the pledgor constitutes the main method of publicity for non-possessory security over movable property. Based on Article 18 of the Pledge Law it is sometimes held that pledgors which are companies or sole entrepreneurs must maintain pledge books which list the pledges and mortgages provided by them. However, this requirement should be regarded as having been modified by the provision of Article 357(3) of the Civil Code, which was enacted later than the Pledge Law and requires a mandatory pledge book only if the pledged assets are goods in circulation. It should also be noted that in practice such entries do not appear to be made, particularly since an entry in the pledge book is not a prerequisite for the validity of the pledge.

(c) Mortgage certificate

16.64   Article 13 of the Law on Mortgage allows the parties to create a mortgage certificate. Initial registration is necessary for the creation of a mortgage for which a certificate was issued.[134] A mortgage certificate facilitates the transfer of mortgages since the transfers can be made without a registration.[135]

---

[131] Pledge Law, Art 18(1).   [132] ibid Art 17.   [133] ibid Art 18(2).

[134] Law on Mortgage, Art 13(5).

[135] Pursuant to ibid Art 16(1) any lawful holder of a mortgage certificate is entitled to request the Federal Registration Service to register the holder as the mortgageholder.

(d) *Transfer of possession*

Transfer of possession of movable things is not considered as a means of pub- **16.65**
licity under Russian law. Possession is in principle not required for the creation
of a pledge under Russian law. However, Russian law allows both possessory and
non-possessory pledges. Article 338(1) of the Civil Code provides that as a rule
('unless otherwise stipulated')[136] the pledgor shall hold possession of the pledged
property. Where movables are documented in a document of title, they will be
pledged by a transfer of possession of the document of title.[137]

(e) *Notice*

The creation of non-registered pledges in receivables and other rights, as well as **16.66**
the security assignment of receivables, do not require that notice should be given
to the debtor of the pledged or assigned right for their creation. The risk that
the debtor performs under the secured debt by satisfying the assignor because
the debtor was unaware of the assignment is borne by the assignee.

7. Slovak law

(a) *Registration*

Slovak law has introduced a registered charge and therefore puts emphasis on **16.67**
registration as the main means of publicity. Publicity through registration is a
creation requirement for all charges except possessory charges. Registration takes
place at the new charges register operated by the Slovak Chamber of Notaries[138]
against the name of the debtor except for the following registered assets, where
registration is conducted at the specified asset-based register:[139]

- charges over immovable assets—at land registries and cadastral offices;[140]
- charges over trademarks, patents, utility designs, and semiconductor topography—at the Intellectual Property Office;[141]
- charges over book entry securities (in particular shares)—at the Central
  Depository (which has now replaced the Securities Centre);

---

[136] See similarly Pledge Law, Art 5, first sentence, which mentions first the possessory pledge.
[137] ibid Art 5, second sentence.
[138] See Act of the National Council of the Slovak Republic No 323/1992 on Notaries and
Notaries' Activities ('the Notary Code') as amended by Acts 232/1995, 397/2000, and 561/2001,
and Law adopted on 19 August 2002.
[139] Allen & Overy and EBRD, *Guide for Taking Charges in the Slovak Republic* (Bratislava,
2003) 14.
[140] Civil Code, §151e(2), (4) and Act No 162/1995 on the Cadastre of Real Estate and on
Entries of Ownership and other Rights to Real Estate.
[141] Civil Code, §151e(3), Act No 55/1997 on Trademarks, as amended by Act No 577/2001,
and Act No 435/2001 on Patents. S Sedlička, 'Charges over Trademarks' ('*Zástavní právo k
ochranné známce*') (1996) 9 *Právní rádce* 48.

- charges over participation interests in limited liability companies (SROs)—at the Commercial Registry of the relevant district court; and
- charges over ships or aircraft—at the respective Ships or Aircraft Registries.

16.68 **Central Register of Charges** The Notarial Central Register of Charges is maintained in electronic form. It consists of a single centralized database which can be inspected by any member of the public via the internet[142] or at any notary's office.

16.69 An application for registration of a charge may be made at any notary's office regardless of the residence or registered office of the chargor. Registration is made by means of a computerized registration application, completed by the notary. Once the registration application form is completed with the requisite information (see 16.72 below) the applicant signs a printed version of this form. Application for registration is made by the debtor or his authorized representative (or by the creditor where the charge is not created by contract).[143]

16.70 The registration application is then transmitted electronically to the central registry. Once the registration is completed (it should normally take not more than a few minutes), the applicant will receive a printed version of the confirmation of the registration, along with an ID number for the transaction.

16.71 The notary need only check the identity of the person filing the application for registration (and, where appropriate, his authority to act) and that the required information for registration has been provided. Due diligence on the charged assets, the secured debt, and any other matters must be performed by the parties. The notary only makes limited checks. The Notarial Central Registry of Charges does not 'authenticate' the information registered. Consequently, any defect in the validity of the charge cannot be made good by registration.[144] A third party, even when acting in good faith, may not rely on the reality of the facts registered but should verify them for himself. However, a third party can rely on the *absence* of information in the register. A registered charge cannot be created without registration. Therefore, if no charge is shown in the register, a third party can assume that no registered charge exists and thus only a possessory charge may be in existence. A special case arises on a charge of a receivable where an extract from the register is adequate proof of creation of the charge for the purpose of notifying the sub-debtor.

16.72 The information which has to be registered concerns the identity of the parties, the charged assets, the secured debt, and limited additional information. As far as the identity of the parties is concerned, the registration must include personal

---

[142] <http://www.notar.sk/register.aspx>.   [143] Civil Code, §151g(1).
[144] eg different from the German land register; see German Civil Code, §892(1).

details of the chargor and the chargeholder. Where the chargor is a different person from the debtor, details of the debtor also have to be registered. If another person is authorized to act on behalf of the chargeholder his or her details may be registered in the place of the chargeholder's, but this must be stated. As far as the 'charged assets' are concerned, a description must be included in such a way that it is possible to identify things, rights, or assets encumbered by the charge at any time throughout its duration. If the charge is created over all or part of an enterprise this must be specifically indicated. Because of the (deliberately!) limited space available in the register, the description may have to be shorter than in the charge agreement or can possibly cross-refer to the relevant provision of the charge agreement for a fuller description. As far as the 'secured claim' is concerned, a description of the claim—including its due date, if determined, and its value or, if not determined on creation, its maximum principal value—is required. Because of the limited space available in the register, the description may have to be shorter than in the charge agreement.

Subsequent to the initial registration, any change concerning the initial information registered (for example the identity of the chargor if the assets are transferred) must be registered, as must the commencement of enforcement of the charge and its termination.[145] Any agreed change in the order of priority between chargeholders, and the period for which the charge has been created, may also be registered. In order to facilitate advance preparation for registration, the templates of the application forms can be downloaded from the website of the Chamber of Notaries.[146] **16.73**

Registrations at special asset registers   As mentioned above, under Slovak law **16.74** some assets are registered in specific asset-based registries, and a charge over them will need to be registered in the respective registry, and not the charges register. For existing immovable property, the charge must always be registered in the local land registry. The land registries are organized by region and the registrations are made by the district land registries in the area in which the relevant immovable property is located. Historically, this process may have taken up to several months. However, recently the situation has improved and charge registration may now be made within two to three weeks (depending on the location of the property to be charged—delays occur mainly in the urban areas). As from 1 January 2002, accelerated registration can be obtained against payment of a higher fee.

---

[145] For termination, see Civil Code, §151md(2), (3). Sometimes the term 'deletion' is used in translation. 'Termination' seems to be the preferable term, since the charge is not actually deleted from the register.

[146] <http://www.notar.sk/register.aspx>.

16.75 In the case of book entry securities which are represented by data entries in the Slovak Securities Centre (the central securities registrar), the charge is over specific existing securities rather than an account. The parties need always to comply with the system's charge rules—usually involving instruction given to the Slovak Securities Centre to register the charge in respect of the specific securities standing to the credit of the chargor's account with the Slovak Securities Centre. Nevertheless, under the recently amended Securities Act, a new system for the registration of security rights over securities was introduced when the first Central Depository (that replaced the Slovak Securities Centre) was granted a licence. Following this, all the security rights over any securities, irrespective of their form (ie physical or book-entry), need to be registered with the Central Depository's register in order to be created.

(b) Transfer of possession

16.76 For possessory charges,[147] the assets have to be handed over to the chargeholder or a third party,[148] and dispossession is treated as adequate publicity, although registration may still be preferable. Transfer of possession is a prerequisite for the creation of the charge. The transfer can be made to the chargeholder or a third person for deposit. If the charge is not registered it automatically terminates if the charged asset is returned to the chargor. The chargeholder is obliged to return the charged asset to the chargor if the charge terminates for any other reason. A possessory charge can at any time be registered in the charges register.[149]

C. Comparative Remarks and Evaluation

1. Analytical principles

16.77 Whereas many security rights are built on the publicity principle and require some form of publicity, there are also a great number of secret security rights (particularly where ownership-based security is used in a legal system). Secret security rights are often found where a legislative secured transactions system is seen not to be working properly in practice.

16.78 Registration or filing are seen more and more as the publicity of choice for security rights. The world of registration or filing has been transformed with the advent of computer technology. Whereas the arguments against registration sounded convincing in view of the contrived reality of paper-based filing or registration systems, an easily available (in terms of registration and publicity for third parties) and low cost computer-based registration system is now feasible.

---

[147] Civil Code, §151b(1), second sentence.   [148] ibid §151e(5), first sentence.
[149] ibid §151e(5), second sentence.

The secured transactions laws of Hungary (the pioneering country in this field) and Slovakia have clearly demonstrated this. Computer-based systems in parts of the United States and Germany's land register demonstrate similar experiences.

There are different models in central and eastern Europe for the operation of **16.79** security registries for movables (ie movable things and rights): (a) Hungary, the Czech Republic, Slovakia, and Slovenia have appointed by law the Chamber of Notaries for the operation of the charges register; (b) in Romania, the number of licences is unlimited as long as the conditions for operating the register are met—currently there are six operators in Romania; (c) in Bulgaria and Albania, the registry was created with one of the ministries, as a separate but dependant entity; and (d) in Poland the register is operated by the commercial courts. The registration of Polish pledges relies on a judicial system, which is in marked contrast to the system of mere 'notice' registration used in most of the other reference systems in central and eastern Europe.[150] The practical effect in Poland is significant; registration in Poland requires a court decision and takes on average two weeks.[151]

Registration can simply be a requirement for the creation of a security right. A **16.80** person searching the respective register who finds an entry for a security right will then know whether or not this creation requirement has been met. A totally different issue is whether a person can acquire in good faith a security right which has been registered although in fact it should not have been (for example because the person giving a security right was incapable of doing so). The Polish law, for example, understands the pledge register as a source of verified and guaranteed information.

2. Normative evaluation

Publicity in the context of secured transactions law serves to avoid an impression **16.81** of 'false wealth', ie that unsecured creditors can get the impression no security rights have been created.[152] Publicity must be seen as an important component of a secured transactions law, since the risk-reducing function of security can only be performed if potential securityholders can obtain accurate information about prior security rights.

The European Bank for Reconstruction and Development has put forward nine **16.82**

---

[150] Only Lithuania has also introduced the judicial review of information provided to the pledge register.

[151] EBRD, *The Impact of the Legal Framework on the Secured Credit Market in Poland* (London, 2005) 5.

[152] PR Wood, *Maps of World Financial Law* (5th edn, London, 2005) 92.

'guiding principles for the publicity of security rights', which can serve as a starting point for building an effective registration or filing system:[153]

- A regime for secured credit should provide for effective publicity of charges.
- As a result of publicity it should be possible to find out what charges are claimed over a person's assets and their chronological order of ranking.
- Publicity is best achieved by registration, most often against the person granting the charge.
- Failure to publicize a charge makes it ineffective against third parties.
- The system for giving publicity and for accessing the publicized information should be simple.
- The system for giving publicity and for accessing the publicized information should be fast and inexpensive.
- The register should be accessible for all persons and all registered information should be public.
- The method of recording, storing and accessing information should protect against error, abuse and fraud.
- The registry should be operated and managed transparently as a public service.

16.83 Whereas traditionally registers were understood as providing an accurate reflection of the facts registered, it is now being put forward that a security register for movables, at least, is not able to provide authenticity of the registered facts, ie good faith reliance on the registered information is not protected. A register for movables is seen as a tool for establishing priority between competing security-holders and it provides a warning about existing security rights to potential creditors. Where registration is introduced it is also a creation requirement for the security right (hence, if a security is not registered it cannot exist or at least not perfected). However, the registration of a security right cannot be taken as showing that a security right legally exists. This would require a detailed checking process by the registrar, which would, however, limit the usefulness of the register in practice. The rationale that a register is a source of verified and guaranteed information is a misconception, since pledge registers should simply serve to publicize data as provided by the parties. The position of the pledge register is thus different from that of a land or companies register, which indeed has to establish a reliable record of the rights that exist in the land or the companies that have been created.[154]

16.84 As far as registration of mortgages in real estate is concerned, it is inherent in the function of a land register that third parties can rely on its contents. When a mortgage is registered this is more than just a notice by the parties that they have entered into a mortgage: it represents confirmation that a mortgage exists.[155]

---

[153] See also EBRD, *Publicity of Security Rights, Guiding Principles for the Development of a Charges Registry* (London, 2004) and EBRD, *Publicity of Security Rights. Setting Standards for Charges Registries* (London, 2005).
[154] See similarly EBRD (n 151 above) 9.   [155] See also EBRD (n 151 above) 13.

17

RIGHTS AND OBLIGATIONS OF THE PERSON GIVING SECURITY AND THE PERSON TAKING SECURITY *INTER SE* PRIOR TO ENFORCEMENT

A. Analytical Framework

Rights and obligations of a person are rights created by agreement or provided **17.01** by operation of law which are *in personam* rights, ie rights which have effect only between the parties to the security agreement.

B. Eastern European Secured Transactions Laws

1. Bulgarian law

Bulgarian law offers a number of rules on the personal rights and obligations of **17.02** the secured parties which are, however, by no means comprehensive nor can they claim to be in any way systematic. The parties are well advised to deal with their rights and obligations contractually.

If secured property of a non-registered pledge is destroyed or damaged, the **17.03** pledgeholder can claim only preferential satisfaction from any insurance or compensation payments;[1] even this (preferential) claim is lost if the pledge-holder is informed about a payment and does not object within a three-month period.[2] Furthermore, under a pledge of movable things the pledgeholder has the right to retain the pledged property until he or she is fully satisfied but does not have the right to use the pledged chattel.[3] If the pledged property is in danger of destruction the pledged asset may be sold and the proceeds of sale deposited in a bank.[4] In the context of a pledge of claims the pledgor must transfer to the pledgeholder any documents which prove the pledge claims.[5] The pledgeholder is obliged to 'carry out any acts to preserve the claim'.[6]

17.04 Special rules on rights and obligations between the parties exist for mortgages. Section 177 of the Law on Obligations and Contracts provides, for example, that the mortgageholder receives compensation for necessary expenditures incurred on the mortgaged property, as well as for useful expenses which increased the value of the mortgaged property. At the same time the mortgagor is liable for any damage to the mortgaged property caused by his gross negligence.[7]

17.05 The Law on Registered Pledges has a separate chapter on rights and obligations of the parties (Articles 8 and 9).[8] Pursuant to Article 8(1) the pledgor can keep possession of the pledged property (ie the pledge under the Law on Registered Pledges is in principle non-possessory). The pledgor who keeps possession of the pledged property can use it (in accordance with its intended use) and dispose of the pledged property in the ordinary course of business.[9] Pursuant to Article 9 the pledgor has, *inter alia*, the following obligations:

- to insure the pledged property;
- to inform the pledgeholder of a number of possible events with implications for the value of the pledged property, including any damage to the pledged property;
- to inform the pledgeholder of any changes which may result in a transfer of ownership to, or the creation of rights by, third parties in the pledged property;
- to inform third parties of the existence of the pledgeholder's rights; and

---

[1] Law on Obligations and Contracts, Art 154, first sentence.
[2] ibid Art 154, second sentence.   [3] ibid Art 157.
[4] ibid Art 158. The proceeds of sale replace the initial pledged property.
[5] ibid Art 163.   [6] ibid Art 164.   [7] ibid Art 177.
[8] Law on Registered Pledges, Art 10 which is included in the chapter on rights and obligations of the parties, deals with issues of secured property, whereas Art 11, another provision of the same chapter, deals rather with enforcement issues.
[9] ibid Art 8(2).

- similar to the obligation under section 158 of the Law on Obligations and Contracts, the pledgor must sell the pledged property if it is in danger of destruction and the proceeds of sale must be deposited in a bank (the proceeds of sale replace the initial pledged property by operation of law and themselves become pledged property).

2. Czech law

Czech law, which offers a rather abbreviated version of codified security law anyway, mainly relies on the parties to deal with the rights and obligations and the agreements made between them. The only statutory provisions on rights and obligations with respect to a lien are Articles 162 and 163 of the Civil Code.[10] Where the lien in movable things is a possessory right, the lienholder is provided a right to hold the asset during the term of the lien in Article 162(1), first sentence, of the Civil Code. In return he or she must observe proper care whilst holding the asset and receives from the person granting the lien reimbursement for any expenditure on the secured asset that may arise.[11] However, the lienholder is entitled to use the secured asset only with the consent of the person granting the lien.[12] He bears liability for any loss, destruction of, or damage to, the secured asset.[13] Conveniently, the lienholder under a possessory lien (as well as a person taking any other form of lien) has the right to ask for additional assets as security if the value of the secured assets deteriorates to an extent that the secured claim is secured 'insufficiently'.[14] The provision seems incomplete because it does not specify the time period within which additional security has to be created for the benefit of the lienholder. The same provision also provides the strict consequence that the part of the receivable which has become unsecured becomes immediately due[15] and the respective lien enforceable. This is surprising, since the lienholder may have taken security in the full knowledge that the person granting the lien cannot offer any additional assets as security.   **17.06**

There are no provisions on the parties' rights and obligations for retentions of ownership or security transfers in the Civil Code. Rights and obligations must be agreed contractually.   **17.07**

---

[10] Civil Code, s 164 is part of the chapter 'rights and duties under a lien'. It deals, however, not with the rights and obligations between the parties but with the rights against third parties and is therefore referred to in ch 18 below.

[11] ibid Art 162(1), second and third sentences.   [12] ibid Art 162(2).

[13] ibid Art 162(3).   [14] ibid Art 163(2), first sentence.

[15] ibid Art 163(2), second sentence.

3. Hungarian law

17.08 Hungarian law is almost as silent on rights and obligations under a charge as Czech law. It relies mainly on the parties dealing with those rights and obligations in their agreements. The few statutory rules which can be found under Hungarian law are allocated to the different types of charges. Among them is section 261(1) and (2) of the Civil Code which covers registered charges. The chargor can keep possession of the charged asset, and can also continue to use it but must maintain the asset. Where the charged asset's condition deteriorates, the chargeholder can claim restoration of the charged asset and, if the chargeholder's demand is not satisfied, he or she may immediately request satisfaction from the secured claim.

17.09 Section 265(3) to (5) of the Civil Code contains rules for possessory charges. The chargeholder who takes possession of the secured asset shall maintain it and must return it to the chargor upon termination of the charge. The chargeholder may not use the charged asset but can collect natural fruits and income, primarily to cover necessary expenses on the charged asset. If the charged asset is in danger of deteriorating the chargor can claim to have it returned but has to offer other appropriate security.

17.10 Rights and obligations with respect to floating charges can be found in section 266(4) and (5) of the Civil Code. If there is a devaluation of the charged assets the chargeholder can immediately ask for satisfaction from the assets. The chargor is under an obligation to notify the chargeholder of the devaluation. The value which is regarded as substantial in terms of triggering the notification obligation can be, and in practice should be, defined in an agreement between the parties to the security agreement. In such an agreement the parties can also agree that the chargeholder 'can supervise the management of the chargor's business'. In addition, the rules of registered charges apply also to floating charges.[16]

17.11 Where the charge is created in rights and receivables, section 267(3) of the Civil Code provides that the chargor may terminate or change the charged asset only with the chargeholder's consent. However, dispositions over a bank account remain possible unless the parties have provided differently.

17.12 There are no provisions on the parties' rights and obligations for retentions of ownership in the Civil Code. Rights and obligations must be agreed contractually.

---

[16] Civil Code, ss 266(6), 265(3)–(5).

4. Polish law

The provisions on rights and obligations of the parties to the security agreement **17.13** are only rudimentary. Article 318 of the Civil Code (a provision on pledges in movable things) provides that the pledgeholder holding possession of the pledged property must keep it in good condition and must return it after termination of the pledge to the pledgor. The pledgeholder's expenses in respect of the pledged property shall be reimbursed by the pledgor.[17] If the pledged property in the possession of the pledgeholder is in danger of being lost or damaged, the pledgor can demand that it is placed in court deposit or returned to him (against providing other security or sale of the asset, neither being an immediately attractive option).[18]

With respect to a pledge of rights the pledgeholder can take all legitimate **17.14** measures to preserve the encumbered right.[19] Article 333 of the Civil Code provides that both pledgor and pledgeholder can receive jointly the proceeds of a pledged receivable. Pledgor and pledgeholder can demand that the proceeds are placed in a court deposit.[20]

Registered pledges terminate if a movable asset encumbered by a registered **17.15** pledge becomes part of an immovable asset.[21] Consequently, the pledgeholder can demand that the real estate is encumbered with a mortgage securing a secured debt of equivalent value.[22] Pursuant to Article 11 of the Law on Registered Pledges and the Pledge Registry the pledgor can use the pledged property 'in accordance with its socio-economic purpose', shall maintain the pledged property in proper condition, and allow the pledgeholder to inspect the pledged property at a time proposed by the pledgeholder.

If actions undertaken by the mortgagor and for which the mortgagor is respon- **17.16** sible reduce the value of property encumbered by a mortgage, the mortgage-holder can demand the termination of such actions, the restoration of the mortgaged property to its initial state, or other security rights sufficient to cover the secured debt.[23] If the requested action is not taken within a time period set by the mortgageholder, the mortgageholder can immediately enforce the mortgage.[24] It is surprising to see that Polish law requires the mortgagor to be

---

[17] Civil Code, Art 320.
[18] ibid Article 321(1). If the secured asset is returned to the pledgor and sold, the pledge will continue in the proceeds of sale which have to be placed in a court deposit, Art 321(2).
[19] ibid Art 330.
[20] ibid Arts 333–334. Art 333 does not provide, like Art 321(2), that the pledge continues in the proceeds of sale.
[21] Law on Registered Pledges and the Pledge Registry, Art 9(1).   [22] ibid Art 9(2).
[23] Law on Land Registry and Mortgages, Art 92, first sentence.
[24] ibid Art 92, second sentence.

'responsible for his actions', ie he must know about an action or his lack of knowledge must be grossly negligent. This puts a burden of proof on the mortgageholder for the mortgagor's responsibility which he should not have to bear if all he does is to preserve the value of his security.

17.17 If actions by the mortgagor threaten to diminish the value of the mortgaged property (without a need for the mortgagor to be responsible for the actions) the mortgageholder can ask for these actions to be terminated.[25]

17.18 There are no provisions on a person's rights and obligations for retentions of ownership in Polish law. Rights and obligations must be agreed contractually.

5. Romanian law

17.19 Rights and obligations between the parties to the security agreement will mainly be established by contract.[26] Reasonable expenses on the secured property (for example insurance costs) incurred by the securityholder are borne by the person giving security.[27] If the person giving security is in possession of the secured property (which will usually be the case) and the property is destroyed or damaged due to the negligence of the person giving security, the securityholder can claim damages in an amount of at least the equivalent in Lei of €500.[28] The chargor can use and dispose of the secured property and its products (including the creation of additional security rights).[29] If the secured property comprises all of the chargor's assets or all of his assets of a certain type, she can request a statement from the securityholder about the current amount of the secured debt.[30] The person giving security must provide the securityholder, together with his request, with the value of the secured debt and an estimated value of the secured property. The securityholder must reply to the chargor's request within thirty days. If he fails to do so, the value of the secured debt estimated by the debtor shall become the actual value of the secured debt.[31]

17.20 The securityholder has the right to inspect the secured property.[32] If the secured property is not properly maintained and payment of the secured debt is thus in danger, the securityholder can proceed with enforcement[33] even if the secured debt is not yet due and payable. A securityholder in possession of the secured property must return the property immediately after the chargor has satisfied

---

[25] Law on Land Registry and Mortgages, Art 91.
[26] See Law Concerning Certain Measures for the Acceleration of the Economic Process, Art 42.
[27] ibid Art 10(2), third sentence.   [28] ibid Art 41.   [29] ibid Art 21(1).
[30] ibid Art 26(1).   [31] ibid Art 26(2).   [32] ibid Art 11(2).   [33] ibid Art 11(2).

the secured debt.[34] Failure to do so will lead to a claim in damages with a minimum amount of the equivalent in Lei of €200.[35]

The possessor of the secured property (which will in most cases be the chargor) **17.21** has to maintain the secured property and may have to keep accounts about the secured property and its products.[36]

Pursuant to the Civil Code the mortgagor is entitled to use, enjoy, or dispose **17.22** of mortgaged real estate. Therefore, the mortgagor is entitled to keep fruits and income of the real estate. Other rights and obligations between the parties will be established by agreement.

6. Russian law

Russian law provides for the rights and obligations of the parties to a pledge or **17.23** mortgage agreement in various laws dealing with secured transactions. Since the laws overlap, there is no coherent legislation of rights and obligations. Therefore parties themselves are advised to specify their rights and obligations in special agreements. The starting point for the provisions on rights and obligations are Articles 342(3) and 343 to 347 of the Civil Code. The pledgor is obliged to inform subsequent pledgeholders about prior pledges; pursuant to Article 342(3) of the Civil Code[37] he is liable in damages if this obligation is violated. Depending on who is in possession of the pledged asset, either the pledgor or the pledgeholder shall insure and maintain the pledged asset (in any case at the pledgor's expense unless otherwise agreed), maintain the pledged asset, and inform the other party of any deterioration of the pledged asset.[38] The person not in the possession of the pledged asset is entitled to check the condition of that asset and, if the pledgeholder holds possession, the pledgor can claim termination of the pledge if the pledged asset is in danger of loss or damage.[39] In addition, the pledgeholder is liable for damages arising out of the loss of or damage to a pledged asset which he keeps in his possession.[40] Unless otherwise provided by contract or resulting from the substance of the pledge, the pledgor can use the pledged asset and keep fruits and income from it.[41] Disposal of the

---

[34] ibid Article 27(4) provides this for attached security rights. Art 40 repeats this rule for perfected security rights and extends it to the securityholder's representative in possession of the secured property.

[35] ibid Art 27(5). Surprisingly, Art 40 does not provide for a minimum amount in damages. The amount in Art 27(5) can, however, be applied by way of analogy.

[36] ibid Art 42.   [37] Pledge Law, Art 22(2) contains the same claim in damages.

[38] Civil Code, Art 343(1).

[39] ibid Art 343(2) and (3). See also Pledge Law, Art 36 for the pledgor's right of inspection of the pledged asset and Art 38 for the pledgor's obligation to insure and maintain the asset.

[40] Civil Code, Art 344(2).

[41] ibid Art 346(1). See also Pledge Law, Art 37 for the pledgor's right to use the pledged asset.

pledged asset is possible with the pledgeholder's consent,[42] unless otherwise provided by contract, by law, or resulting from the substance of the pledge. If, however, the pledgeholder holds the pledged asset, he is entitled to use it to the extent provided in the contract and must report regularly on the use to the pledgor.[43]

17.24 Article 9 of the Pledge Law confirms that the pledged asset has to be insured against loss and damage. However, it refers to law or the pledge agreement when stipulating this duty, hence Article 343(1) of the Civil Code remains the relevant provision with respect to the parties' obligation to insure the pledged asset. In addition, Article 38 of the Pledge Law provides that the pledgor has to insure the pledged asset if she retains possession of it. A pledged asset may be substituted by another asset with the pledgeholder's consent.[44] Article 39 of the Pledge Law contains a far-reaching acceleration clause: if the pledgor breaches his obligations (including that to insure and maintain the pledged asset) the pledgeholder is entitled to enforce the pledge immediately.

17.25 Articles 49(2) and 50 to 53 of the Pledge Law provide for special rights and obligations in the context of possessory pledges which are beyond the scope of this study. However, Articles 56 to 58 of the Pledge Law are important since they provide the rights and obligations in the context of a pledge of rights. Essentially Article 56 stipulates that the pledgor is prohibited from taking any actions which may result in the termination of a pledged right or a decrease in its value.

17.26 The Law on Mortgage provides in Articles 1(3) and 29(1) that the mortgagor keeps the right to use the mortgaged real estate. He is also entitled to keep the fruits and income from the real estate unless otherwise provided in the mortgage agreement.[45] When she enters into the mortgage agreement, the mortgagor has to inform the mortgageholder in writing about any existing third party rights in the real estate.[46] Unless otherwise provided in the mortgage agreement, the mortgagor must maintain the pledged property and bears the respective costs.[47] The obligation to insure the mortgaged property is primarily determined by the parties by written agreement.[48] In the absence of an agreement, the mortgagor has to insure the mortgaged property against loss and damage at his own expense.[49] Other rights and obligations are contained in Articles 32 to 36, 40, 44, and 72(2) of the Mortgage Law. It should be noted that the mortgaged property can be leased to third parties even in the absence of the

---

[42] Civil Code, Art 346(2). Pledge Law, Art 37 takes a similar approach: the pledgor may dispose of the pledged asset but only subject to a simultaneous transfer of the secured debt to the transferee.
[43] Civil Code, Art 346(3).   [44] Pledge Law, Art 8; confirmed in Civil Code, Art 345(1).
[45] Law on Mortgage, Art 29(2).   [46] ibid Art 12.   [47] ibid Art 30.
[48] ibid Art 31(1).   [49] ibid Art 31(2).

mortgageholder's consent if this possibility is not excluded in the mortgage agreement.[50] In practice the parties should include provisions on the mortgagor's right to use the mortgaged property in the mortgage agreement.

There are no detailed provisions on rights and obligations of the parties to a retention of ownership or security assignment in Russian law. Consequently, such rights and obligations must be agreed contractually. **17.27**

7. Slovak law

Slovak law, like the security laws of most other central and eastern European states, has some provision on rights and obligations between the parties without being in any way comprehensive in this area. The law implicitly relies on the parties to agree on their rights and obligations in a contractual manner. **17.28**

(a) Rights and obligations of the chargor

When the chargor remains in possession of the charged asset (which will be the rule, since Slovak law relies mainly on the non-possessory, registered charge)[51] he is entitled to make normal use of it in a usual manner, but must refrain from doing anything capable of being detrimental to the value of the collateral, except for ordinary wear and tear.[52] This right of use probably extends to consumption of the assets where that would be normal use. The parties may make their own agreement as to the use of the assets. **17.29**

The chargor is responsible for maintaining the charged assets in good condition.[53] The law does not put the chargor under any obligation to insure the charged assets,[54] but this will often be required contractually. **17.30**

If the chargor sells the secured asset to a third party, both the chargor and the purchaser must register the change in chargor and are liable in damages if this registration is not made.[55] **17.31**

(b) Rights and obligations of the chargeholder

Where the chargeholder is in possession of the charged asset he must take due care of the asset and protect it from damage, loss, and destruction but receives reimbursement of any reasonable expenses incurred on the charged asset.[56] He may use the charged asset only with the consent of the chargor.[57] **17.32**

The chargeholder faces a number of obligations in enforcement proceedings. In **17.33**

---

[50] ibid Art 40.
[51] M Benedik, 'Remarks on the Charge Law' ('*Niekol'ko poznámok k inštitútu záložného páva*') (2001) 3 *Bulletin slovenskej advokácie* 31.
[52] Civil Code, §151i(1).   [53] ibid §151mc(1).   [54] ibid §151mc(1).
[55] ibid §151h(5).   [56] ibid §151i(2), (3).   [57] ibid §151i(2).

particular she has to notify the chargor and the debtor of the commencement of enforcement proceedings and must also register the event in the charges register.[58] If several charges have been created in the same asset the chargeholder must notify all prior chargeholders of the commencement of enforcement.[59] A prior chargeholder with a secured claim which is due can himself commence enforcement proceedings and demand satisfaction of the secured claim.[60] If the additional enforcement proceeding is commenced within thirty days from the day of delivery of enforcement notices to prior chargeholders, the chargeholder who initially started enforcement proceedings cannot continue with enforcement of his charge.[61]

17.34 After termination of the charge the chargeholder is under an obligation to register the termination.[62] Where the charged asset has been delivered to the chargeholder, he has to return the asset without undue delay after the charge has terminated.[63] A breach of this obligation may make him liable for damages pursuant to §151g(4) of the Civil Code.

C. Comparative Remarks and Evaluation

1. Analytical principles

17.35 Whereas in most issues of security law there are only few options which national laws exercise, the legal relationship between the person giving security and the person taking security displays a wide variety of national solutions which will not be subjected to further differentiation in this study.

2. Normative evaluation

17.36 It is beneficial if a secured transactions law introduces *in personam* rights related to security rights. However, the parties should maintain the freedom to determine their relationship by agreement to keep the secured transactions law flexible.

---

[58] Civil Code, §151l(1).   [59] ibid §151ma(1).   [60] ibid §151ma(8).
[61] ibid §151ma(9).   [62] ibid §151md(3).   [63] ibid §151md(4).

18

EFFECTS ON THIRD PARTIES

A. Analytical Framework

Since security rights have proprietary effect they affect third parties. This may be **18.01**
apparent in three ways:

(1) since there may be several securityholders in an asset it has to be determined whose right takes priority;
(2) secured property may be sold and the issue is whether or not the security right will terminate with such a sale;
(3) there may be rights against third parties which affect the secured property.

B. Eastern European Secured Transactions Laws

1. Bulgarian law

(a) Priorities

18.02 For both pledges and mortgages under the Law on Obligations and Contracts,[1] as well as for registered pledges under the Law on Registered Pledges,[2] several security rights will rank in the order in which the pledges or mortgages were created. If the security right is registered, the time of registration determines its ranking.[3] The ranking will determine in which order various security rights will be satisfied from the proceeds of sale of the pledged property.[4]

18.03 There are a number of situations which merit special attention.

- As far as registered pledges are concerned, an exception from the *prior tempore* rule exists for purchase money security rights which were perfected after a registered pledge[5] but nevertheless rank prior to the earlier registered pledge. A purchase money security right is a pledge in a specific asset securing the purchase price of the pledged property. The prior right may be a registered or a non-registered pledge.

- In addition, a retention of ownership which was perfected after a registered pledge will also be 'prior' to an earlier registered pledge.[6] Since under Bulgarian law the retention of ownership by a merchant (or another person referred to in Article 2 of the Law on Commerce) requires the same registration as a registered pledge, the priority rule on retention of ownership simply confirms the principle that pledges securing purchase money debts will receive priority.

- Registered and non-registered pledges in movable things, receivables, and other rights do not conflict with each other, since the Law on Registered Pledges creates an exclusive security regime for pledges where the pledgor is a merchant or another qualified person.[7]

18.04 The simple priority rules of Bulgarian law are somewhat upset by so-called privileges, a legal order for the satisfaction of claims provided in section 136 of the Law on Obligations and Contracts.[8] Importantly, tax claims of the

---

[1] Law on Obligations and Contracts, Art 53.   [2] Law on Registered Pledges, Art 14.
[3] See Law on Obligations and Contracts, Art 169 for mortgages and Law on Registered Pledges, Art 14 for registered pledges.
[4] This is explicitly stated for mortgages in Law on Obligations and Contracts, Art 175, second sentence.
[5] Law on Registered Pledges, Art 15(1).   [6] ibid Art 15(2).
[7] ibid Art 3(1).
[8] ibid Art 16(1) refers to Law on Obligations and Contracts, Art 136. The provision is therefore also applicable to registered pledges.

Bulgarian state are to be satisfied in priority to pledges and mortgages[9] and thus weaken significantly the economic usefulness of security rights under Bulgarian law.

If several pledges exist in the same asset, a subordination agreement may be **18.05** formed under which a pledge with a lower priority takes precedence in its satisfaction from proceeds of sale of the secured asset over a pledge with a higher priority.[10] This agreement is, however, contractual in nature only and has effect only between the parties to such an agreement.

(b) Sale of pledged property

Under the Law on Obligations and Contracts the property will remain **18.06** encumbered by the pledge or mortgage if the pledged property is sold. However, pursuant to Article 155 of the Law on Obligations and Contracts the purchaser of the pledged property assumes the rights of the pledgeholder or mortgageholder upon payment of the secured debt. This is confirmed in Article 178 of the Law on Obligations and Contracts for mortgages.[11] The acquirer of the mortgaged property can satisfy the mortgagor and, pursuant to Article 178, the mortgage is then transferred to him by operation of law.

Under the Law on Registered Pledges the pledgor has a right to sell the pledged **18.07** property in the ordinary course of business[12] and thus the pledge terminates if (a) the pledged property is transferred in the ordinary course of the pledgor's (who is in principle a merchant) business and (b) the acquired rights are 'incompatible with the security rights'.[13] This means that the pledge will continue if a sale is outside the pledgor's ordinary course of business.[14] Consequently, the purchaser acquires the right in the pledged property subject to the pledge.[15] However, pursuant to Article 13(2) of the Law on Registered Pledges he is obliged to inform the pledgeholder about the rights he has acquired—which may prove difficult in practice!

---

[9] See Law on Obligations and Contracts, Art 136 No 2.

[10] In a subordination agreement the parties can also agree between themselves the priority of their claims in an insolvency and the liquidation of a company. On the basis of the subordination agreement, the parties will have claims against each other. The agreement is, however, not binding on the insolvency administrator or the liquidator.

[11] Strangely, Law on Obligations and Contracts, Art 178 does not refer to the 'debtor', thereby suggesting that the purchaser has only preferential rights as against third persons. This is not a satisfactory situation since the purchaser, after payment of the secured debt, must in particular have a right of recourse against the debtor.

[12] Law on Registered Pledges, Art 8(2).

[13] ibid Art 7; the latter will be the case if the purchaser acquires ownership in the pledged property.

[14] This principle is confirmed in ibid Art 13(1).   [15] ibid Art 13(1).

(c) Other rights against third parties

18.08 Pursuant to section 134 of the Law on Obligations and Contracts the creditor may exercise the debtor's property rights (but only if the debtor does not act and this threatens the creditor's satisfaction). With a pledge of movable things comes the creditor's right to reclaim possession of the asset from a third party.[16] The creditor may ask a court to declare certain acts of the debtor invalid if it was the debtor's wilful intent to threaten the creditor's satisfaction.[17]

2. Czech law

(a) Priorities

18.09 The priority between different liens is determined by the time of their creation. The time of creation of registered liens is determined by their registration. This follows for real estate liens from section 157(1) of the Civil Code, which provides that a real estate lien is 'created upon its registration'. There is no such clear rule in the Civil Code for the priorities between different liens on movable things.[18] However, registered liens on movable things must also rank according to the time of their registration. If several liens exist in the same asset, a subordination agreement may be formed under which a lien with a lower priority takes precedence in its satisfaction from proceeds of sale of the secured asset over a lien with a higher priority.[19] The agreement is, however, contractual in nature only and has effect only between the parties to such agreement.[20]

18.10 The issue of priorities cannot occur between different security transfers of ownership in movable things or the security transfer of rights. The person who receives ownership of an asset first, will be the owner of the asset without any competing owners. He may only lose this position upon good faith acquisition of ownership by another person—this is, however, limited under Czech law since it requires the transfer of possession in the secured asset to the purchaser. In principle there cannot be a conflict between several retentions of ownership if the seller of an asset sells it several times and retains ownership several times. However, a conflict arises between several retentions of ownership if an asset is made from several components which are each subject to a retention of ownership.

---

[16] Law on Obligations and Contracts, Art 157; see also Art 134.
[17] ibid Art 135.   [18] Civil Code, s 160(2) in particular leaves this issue open.
[19] Subordination may not only extend to the satisfaction from the sale of a secured asset but also to the satisfaction in insolvency and the liquidation of a company.
[20] In particular, the agreement is not binding on the insolvency administrator or the liquidator.

(b) Sale of pledged property

Secured property may in principle not be acquired free from a lien. This is **18.11**
clarified by section 164(1) of the Civil Code which provides that a lien is effective
against any subsequent owner or holder of the secured asset. It is irrelevant
whether or not the purchaser of the secured asset acts in good faith with respect
to the lien.

If a person who has received ownership in an asset under a security transfer of **18.12**
ownership transfers the asset to a third person, such person will acquire ownership in the asset. The person giving security will only have contractual rights
against the person who received security and transferred the asset.

An asset subject to a retention of ownership can be transferred by the person **18.13**
who still owes the purchase price to a third party. The third party may acquire
ownership in the asset pursuant to section 446 of the Commercial Code provided, however, that the sale is a commercial sale, possession of the movable
asset is transferred to the purchaser, and that the purchaser acts in good faith
with respect to the existence of the ownership of the transferor.

3. Hungarian law

(a) Priorities

Pursuant to section 256(1), second sentence, of the Civil Code several charges **18.14**
rank according to their time of creation. In addition, section 266(3) of the Civil
Code states that the priority of a floating charge is in principle determined by
the date of its registration. However, prior charges on assets joining the pool of
assets shall have priority over a later enterprise charge.[21] In addition, possessory
charges and charges over rights or receivables shall have priority over an enterprise charge (even if it has been created prior to these former charges) if the
charges were acquired in trade.[22] Surprisingly, a charge registered in a register
other than the charge registry also takes priority.[23] Lastly, the owner of real estate
can lodge a notice at the real property registry to the effect that he intends to
charge the land with a registered pledge.[24] This will permit the registration of a
charge in real estate with the priority of the time of notification.[25]

If several charges exist in the same asset, a subordination agreement may be **18.15**
formed under which a charge with a lower priority takes precedence in its
satisfaction from proceeds of sale of the charged asset over a charge with a higher

---

[21] Civil Code, s 266(3)a.   [22] ibid s 266(3)c.   [23] ibid s 266(3)b.
[24] ibid s 262(4), first sentence. Similar to the concept of a pre-notification ('*Vormerkung*')
under German law, German Civil Code, §§883–888.
[25] Civil Code, s 262(4), second sentence.

priority.[26] The agreement is, however, contractual in nature only and has effect only between the parties to such an agreement.[27]

18.16 In principle there cannot be a conflict between several retentions of ownership if the seller of an asset sells it several times and retains ownership several times. However, a conflict arises between several retentions of ownership if an asset is made up of several components which are each subject to a retention of ownership.

(b) Sale of pledged property

18.17 A transfer of ownership in the charged property or the creation of any other rights does not in principle affect the charge.[28] However, a registered charge[29] terminates upon the sale of a charged asset if the asset is sold in trade or in the ordinary course of the chargor's business and the purchaser acts in good faith with respect to the charge.[30] The registered charge is also terminated if the charged asset is a good of everyday life and is purchased by a buyer in good faith.[31] An acquirer's good faith is assumed unless the other party proves the contrary.[32] Interestingly, a purchaser's bad faith it not assumed simply on the basis of the fact that the charge has been registered properly in the charges register and the purchaser should have looked at the register. As long as the purchaser is (a) acting in good faith and (b) acquires for value ('counter-performance') he acquires ownership in the asset free from the charge.[33]

18.18 A possessory charge can be acquired in good faith from a person who is not the owner of the charged asset provided that the transfer is made 'in the context of trade relationships'.[34]

18.19 An asset subject to a retention of ownership can be transferred by the person who still owes the purchase price to a third party.

4. Polish law

(a) Priorities

18.20 Several registered pledges are ranked according to their time of filing of the application for entry in the pledge registry.[35] Applications filed on the same day

---

[26] Subordination may not only extend to the satisfaction from the sale of a secured asset but also to the satisfaction in insolvency and the liquidation of a company.

[27] In particular, the agreement is not binding on the insolvency administrator or the liquidator.

[28] Civil Code, s 256(1), first sentence.

[29] The provisions on registered charges apply also to floating charges, see Civil Code, s 266(6) and to independent charges, s 269(5).

[30] Law Decree No 11/1960 on Entry into Force and Implementation of Act IV of 1959, s 47(2) and Civil Code, s 262(6), first sentence.

[31] Civil Code, s 262(6), second sentence.   [32] Law Decree No 11/1960, s 47(2).

[33] ibid s 47(2).   [34] Civil Code, s 265(1), second sentence.

[35] Law on Registered Pledges and the Pledge Registry, Arts 15–16.

have the same priority,[36] which is clearly an undesirable rule. There are in principle no priority conflicts between several Civil Code pledges in movable things or pledges in receivables respectively, since the pledge in movable things requires a transfer of possession and a pledge in receivables requires in principle notice to the debtor of the pledged receivable. Hence, the person who is first identified by the necessary act of publicity as the pledgeholder will receive the pledge.

Pursuant to Article 12(1) of the Law on Land Registry and Mortgages the **18.21** priority of limited property rights registered at the land registry (such as mortgages) is set by reference to the day on which a registration becomes effective. Property rights entered on the same day are considered to have the same priority in relation to other property rights.

For retentions of ownership there are no priority issues. The person with whom **18.22** the first agreement was formed prevails. Any subsequent agreement will not create another retention of ownership. Good faith acquisition of a later retention of ownership is not possible under Polish law.

(b) Sale of pledged property

A transfer of ownership in the secured asset by way of sale may terminate a **18.23** registered pledge but only if the purchaser of the secured asset had no actual knowledge of the pledge or could not have knowledge even if it had diligently made the respective enquiries *or* the collateral is sold in the pledgor's ordinary course of business, the purchaser takes the pledged asset for value, and the purchaser is not acting in bad faith (good faith acquisition).[37] However, the pledgor may covenant not to sell or encumber the pledged assets. In such a case a sale or encumbrance will only be valid if the purchaser was acting in good faith.[38]

Under the Civil Code the non-registered pledge does not terminate if the **18.24** pledged asset is sold.[39] It also does not terminate if the pledgeholder acquires ownership of the pledged asset in particular if a third party holds a pledge (or another encumbrance) in the secured asset.[40] Under the Civil Code it is not possible to covenant that the secured asset is not transferred or encumbered.[41]

As far as mortgages are concerned, the Law on Land Registry and Mortgages **18.25** provides that the real estate may be sold and a prohibition on selling the

---

[36] ibid Art 16, third sentence.   [37] ibid Art 13.   [38] ibid Art 14(1), (2).
[39] Civil Code, Art 306, §1 ('regardless of whose property it has become'). Art 325 §2 confirms that the pledge does not terminate if the pledged asset is acquired by the pledgeholder (but only if the secured debt is encumbered with [another] right of a third party).
[40] ibid Art 325, §2. In other words, the pledge terminates if no such right exists.
[41] ibid Art 311.

mortgaged property is invalid.[42] The Law does not state explicitly that the mortgage continues if the mortgaged property is sold; however, since the mortgage is publicized in the real estate register, the third party will acquire the mortgaged property encumbered with a mortgage. A provision rarely used in practice is to be found in Article 90 of the Law on Land Registry and Mortgages: if only part of an immovable asset is sold, the seller and the purchaser may demand from the mortgageholder that he agrees to terminate the mortgage provided that the sold part is relatively unimportant in value terms and the value of the remaining asset is sufficient to provide adequate security to the mortgageholder.

5. Romanian law

(a) Priorities

18.26 The main rule on priorities for security in movables is Article 28 of the Law Concerning Certain Measures for the Acceleration of the Economic Process, pursuant to which perfected security rights rank according to the time of their perfection, ie older rights take priority over more recently established rights.[43] Since the pledge register records the time of registration down to the second,[44] ranking can be determined very precisely. It is of no importance whether subsequent securityholders know about the existence of the perfected security interest; they are presumed to have knowledge of the security right if a registration has been made.[45] The rule in Article 28 is applied in Articles 18(2) and 20(2) for future assets and future debts, respectively. Both the priority of security rights over future assets and the priority of security rights securing future debts are determined by the time of the security right's perfection. Statutory security rights ('privileges'), which typically do not have to be registered for their creation, take priority over a perfected security right only from the time that the privilege meets the same publication requirements, ie it is either registered or the possession of the secured asset is transferred to the privilegeholder.[46]

18.27 There are three main exceptions to the rule.[47] One exception is made in Article 33 of the Law Concerning Certain Measures for the Acceleration of the Economic Process for security rights created for the benefit of a seller of a good

---

[42] Law on Land Registry and Mortgages, Art 72.

[43] The rule is confirmed for security rights in enforcement proceedings by Law Concerning Certain Measures for the Acceleration of the Economic Process, Art 37 as well as by Art 32 of the same Law.

[44] ibid Art 57(2).   [45] ibid Art 29(3).

[46] ibid Art 36(1). Only in the case of the warehouseman's privilege for the payment of warehouse fees it is not sufficient to transfer just possession in the detained goods to the warehouseman. The privilege takes priority only from the time of its registration; Art 36(2).

[47] ibid Art 33 also contains exceptions with respect to agricultural products such as crops and cattle.

or the respective loan creditor. A security right created in the context of a sale of goods takes priority over other prior security rights but only if a security notice has been registered in the security register before the debtor takes possession and if the previously secured creditor has been notified about (a) the sale and (b) the registration.[48] Second, the products initially not covered by the description of the security right in the security register can take the priority of the time of initial registration if the notice form is amended by a (broader) description within fifteen days from obtaining the products[49] and is registered. Third, a security right notice can be filed to make public the mere intention to create a security right.[50] Such a filing will expire after a period of two months from filing.[51] If the security right is created before this time the security right will take its ranking from the date of filing of the intention.[52]

Interestingly, the law does not contain a rule on priorities between attached security rights. **18.28**

Law No 7/1996 on the Cadastre and Real Estate Publicity defines priorities **18.29** between several real estate mortgages. From this it can be seen that several mortgages can be created in the same assets. The priorities will be determined by the time of the mortgages' registration in the land register. However, if more than one mortgage is filed at the same time in the land register, they will be registered with the same ranking. It is up to a court to determine the proper ranking.[53] Prior ranking creditors will recover their secured debt in priority to lower ranking mortgages.

(b) Sale of charged property

A transfer of ownership in an asset which has been encumbered by a security **18.30** right will not terminate an attached security right provided that the purchase price exceeds the equivalent amount in Romanian Lei of €1,000.[54] The same applies for perfected security interests.[55] Article 23(2) of the Law Concerning Certain Measures for the Acceleration of the Economic Process confirms that the security right can be enforced against the secured property and its products

---

[48] The basic concept of this exception derives from the concept of the purchase money security interest under UCC, Art 9.

[49] Law Concerning Certain Measures for the Acceleration of the Economic Process, Art 34.

[50] ibid Art 56(1).   [51] ibid Art 56(2).

[52] ibid Art 56(3). Similar to a reservation of priority ('*Vormerkung*') under German law, German Civil Code, §§883–888.

[53] Law No 7/1996 on the Cadastre and Real Estate Publicity, Art 29(5).

[54] Pursuant to Law Concerning Certain Measures for the Acceleration of the Economic Process, Arts 23(1), 38(1) the security right maintains its existence even if the secured asset has, eg, been sold. However, this does not prevent the chargor from disposing of the secured property, eg by way of sale (ibid Art 21(1)). Art 21(3) confirms that such dispositions are legally valid.

[55] ibid Art 38(1).

even if it has been sold to a third party and that party is now in possession of the secured property. However, as far as a secured asset's products are concerned, an attached security right over products will terminate if a securityholder only seeks enforcement with respect to the products.[56]

18.31 A contractual provision in the security agreement prohibiting the sale of secured property does not affect the validity of the transfer of the secured property.[57] It may, however, lead to claims in damages against the selling debtor. The law confirms the principle that secured property is freely transferable by the debtor in Article 22(2) of the Law Concerning Certain Measures for the Acceleration of the Economic Process, pursuant to which an assignment of accounts receivables cannot be prohibited by a contractual provision.

18.32 Real estate encumbered with a registered mortgage can be acquired by third parties only subject to the mortgage.[58] In practice parties agree to register at the land register a prohibition from selling or creating rights in the secured property for the benefit of the mortgageholder. Such a prohibition, once registered in the land register, prevents future acquisitions of the real estate free from the mortgage. It therefore has proprietary effect.

6. Russian law

(a) Priorities

18.33 Article 22(1) of the Pledge Law confirms that the priority between several non-registered pledges is determined according to the chronological order of their creation. This is confirmed in Article 342(1) of the Civil Code. Article 342(2) allows the prohibition of additional pledges by a respective provision in the pledge contract and such a provision has not only contractual but also proprietary effect. If such a negative pledge provision is agreed, the acquirer of a subsequent pledge cannot acquire the pledge in good faith. The law does not address the possibility of establishing by contract a ranking between several pledges other than that established by the law or of subordinating an earlier pledge to a later one. In order to exclude the existence of prior pledges creditors have to conduct due diligence reviews of the pledgor's legal situation. They will also include provisions in the loan documentation that grant them, *inter alia*, a right to request that the borrower (a) repay a loan early if any undisclosed prior pledges exist or (b) grants additional security rights.

---

[56] Law Concerning Certain Measures for the Acceleration of the Economic Process, Art 23(1). In practice the securityholder will therefore never limit enforcement to the products.
[57] ibid Art 21(3).
[58] Civil Code, Art 1746(3).

The Law on Mortgage allows the creation of subsequent mortgages in real estate **18.34** or enterprises for securing a debt which was created after another mortgage has already been established.[59] Subsequent mortgages are possible only if they are not prohibited by the agreement on the prior ranking mortgage; if the parties to the mortgage agreements on the prior and the subsequent mortgage are the same persons, the prohibition does not apply.[60] If a mortgage is created despite such a prohibition, the mortgageholder under the prior ranking mortgage can have the subsequent mortgage agreement declared invalid by a court decision (this provision does not apply if the parties to a prior and a subsequent mortgage agreement are the same persons).[61] The subsequent mortgage is subject to state registration like any other mortgage.[62] Registration involves a note being made by the registrar of the Federal Registration Service on the subsequent mortgage agreement concerning all prior mortgages, as well as an entry in the real estate register (where entries are made with the prior mortgages noting that a subsequent mortgage has been created).[63] The prior mortgage is satisfied in priority to any subsequent mortgages.[64]

Both for retention of ownership and security assignments of receivables there are **18.35** no priority issues. The person with whom the first agreement was formed prevails. Neither subsequent retention of ownership nor security assignment is provided for by law. Good faith acquisition of a later retention of ownership or security assignment of receivables is not possible under Russian law.

(b) Sale of charged property

If ownership of the pledged property is transferred, the non-registered pledge **18.36** will continue to exist[65] unless a pledge over goods in circulation or processing has been created.[66] If pledged property is transferred without the consent of the pledgeholder, some Russian courts declare such a transfer invalid, whereas other courts rule that the transferee (even if in good faith) receives ownership encumbered by a pledge.

Mortgaged property can only be sold or transferred to a third party in another **18.37** way if the mortgagor agrees or if provided in the mortgage agreement.[67] If a mortgage certificate has been issued, the right to transfer has to be provided explicitly in the certificate and the requirements contained in the certificate must be complied with.[68] If the transfer rules for mortgaged property are not complied with, the mortgageholder can claim to have the transfer declared

---

[59] Law on Mortgage, Arts 43–46.   [60] ibid Art 43(2), (4).   [61] ibid Art 43(3).
[62] ibid Art 45.   [63] ibid Art 45.   [64] ibid Art 46.
[65] Pledge Law, Art 32. The pledgor has an unfettered right to dispose of the pledged asset unless the parties agree otherwise, ibid Art 20, first sentence.
[66] ibid Art 46(2).   [67] Law on Mortgage, Art 37(1).   [68] ibid Art 37(2).

invalid or request the mortgagor to satisfy the secured debt early and enforce the mortgage even if the secured debt is not yet due.[69] If the third party to whom mortgaged property has been transferred in violation of the transfer rules knew or should have known about the mortgage, he may become liable (jointly and severally with the mortgagor) for the secured debt (but limited to the value of the mortgaged property).[70]

(c) Protection against third parties

18.38   Pursuant to Article 347(1) of the Civil Code the pledgeholder who possessed or should have possessed the pledged property is entitled to reclaim the pledged property from third parties and the pledgor who received it without a right to do so. He may also claim that other violations of a right of possession are removed.[71]

7. Slovak law

(a) Priorities

18.39   An asset can be charged several times to different chargeholders to secure different debts.[72] Priority between charges is determined by law according to the chronological order of their registration. The first chargeholder will have first priority.[73] This rule applies equally to the determination of priorities between several registered and possessory charges. However, registered charges have priority over possessory charges.[74] Thus a possessory charge which is not registered will lose priority to a subsequent registered charge.[75] The rule is also applicable to charges created by previous owners. If the charged asset acquired by the chargor was already subject to a charge, the charge created by the previous owners will have priority over any charge created by the chargor.[76]

18.40   In the case of charges over after-acquired (ie future) assets, the charge is not created until the chargor acquires ownership.[77] However, the priority vis-à-vis other charges is from the time of registration.[78]

18.41   The parties may not want to rely on the legal order of priorities but may want to change the priority or agree a subordination. In the case of registered charges,

---

[69] Law on Mortgage, Art 39, first sentence.   [70] ibid Art 39, second sentence.
[71] Civil Code, Art 347(2).
[72] There is an exception: it is not possible to create a charge over securities (eg shares) which have already been charged; Act No 566/2001 on Securities; Allen & Overy and EBRD, *Guide for Taking Charges in the Slovak Republic* (Bratislava, 2003) 9.
[73] Civil Code, §151k; Allen & Overy and EBRD (n 72 above) 21, 24.
[74] Civil Code, §151k.   [75] Allen & Overy and EBRD (n 72 above) 24.
[76] Allen & Overy and EBRD (n 72 above) 25.   [77] Civil Code, §151d(2).
[78] This follows from the general rule in Civil Code, §151k(1); see also Allen & Overy and EBRD (n 72 above) 24.

chargeholders can agree amongst themselves to a different order of priority and have the changed order registered.[79] Under a subordination agreement a charge with a lower priority takes precedence in its satisfaction from proceeds of sale of the secured asset over a charge with a higher priority.[80] Such an agreement is only effective upon registration and has no effect as against a chargeholder who is not party to the agreement if it has a 'negative impact' on the enforcement of his claim.[81] Any chargeholder in the middle is likely to suffer negative impact from any charge that leapfrogs his priority. Any chargeholder who can show negative impact can claim that the priority agreement has no effect on him.

The order of priorities is subject to creditors benefiting from a retention right.   **18.42** Creditors having a legal retention right have a preferential right to the extent of their claim which relates to the asset. This may be relevant, for example, to warehousemen, carriers, forwarders, and repairers vis-à-vis the assets in their possession.[82]

Where a person has retained ownership in an asset but the chargor has neverthe-   **18.43** less provided a charge in the secured asset which was not (yet) owned by him, the chargeholder will in principle not validly acquire this charge and consequently will not be able validly to transfer such a charge. As already discussed, there is no good faith acquisition of charges by third parties under Slovak law. However, a charge may be created over future assets (assets to be acquired) and will only be created on acquisition of ownership by the purchaser, although with priority from the date of registration.

(b) Sale of charged property

A transfer of ownership in the charged property leads, in principle, to a transfer   **18.44** of ownership to the new owner including the encumbrance.[83] Thus, if the owner of the charged asset sells those assets to a third party, then the normal rule is that the acquirer of the charged assets acquires them subject to the charge. A person acquiring the asset can find out about the charge from the registry (or by investigation about the possession of the potentially charged asset) and has to accept that the chargeholder has the right to enforce against the asset, should the secured debt not be paid. The acquirer's right to recover from the original chargor will depend on the terms on which he acquired the asset. However, all

---

[79] Civil Code, §151k(3).

[80] In a subordination agreement the parties can also agree between themselves the priority of their claims in an insolvency and the liquidation of a company. On the basis of the subordination agreement, the parties will have claims against each other. The agreement is, however, not binding on the insolvency administrator or the liquidator.

[81] Civil Code, §151k(3).   [82] Allen & Overy and EBRD (n 72 above) 25.

[83] Civil Code, §151h(1).

rights and obligations concerning enforcement of the charge become effective against the acquirer.

18.45 Upon a change of ownership, the entry for the charge in the charges register must be amended. The chargor and the acquirer are jointly responsible for registering the change in the person of the chargor. Failure to undertake this obligation may result in a claim in damages.[84]

18.46 However, the charge agreement may stipulate that ownership in the charged property can be transferred free from the charge.[85] In addition, if ownership in the charged property is transferred, the charge terminates provided that (a) the chargor transfers in the normal course of business and (b) within its business activities.[86] Lastly, the purchaser acquires free from the charge if he acts in good faith with respect to the non-existence of a charge.[87] However, a good faith acquisition will be difficult if the charge is registered at the charges registry since the purchaser will then have to prove that he acted in good faith.[88] It should be noted that this last exception does not apply where the charge is registered in a specific register.

C. Comparative Remarks and Evaluation

1. Analytical principles

18.47 Central and eastern European reference systems protect the security right upon the sale of the secured property to varying degrees. There are still a number of security rights for which the power to sell secured property free from the security right does not exist (see, for example, Czech law).

2. Normative evaluation

18.48 The sale of secured property is an important issue for commercial practice and the person giving security may need the power to sell secured property free of the security right, thus making constant changes to a pool of secured property. Hence, the power to use and dispose of the charged property is an important feature of a dynamic security right, and has already been highlighted as an important element for a workable secured transactions law.[89]

---

[84] Civil Code, §151h(5).   [85] ibid §151h(1).

[86] ibid §151md(1)f. Confusingly §151h(3) states that the charge is 'not effective against the purchaser of the charged property'. The termination of the charge pursuant to §151md(1)f seems to be the overriding legal consequence.

[87] ibid §151h(3), first sentence.   [88] ibid §151h(3), second sentence.

[89] See 12.55 above.

19

ENFORCEMENT OF SECURITY

A. Analytical Framework

19.01 Enforcement is the ultimate stage of the security right; the mere prospect of an enforcement of the security right may in itself affect the debtor's actions as well as the actions of the person giving security. The security right may be enforced simply by the securityholder against the person giving security. However, other creditors may enforce against the securityholder as well, in which case the securityholder will find himself in competition, with the race going to the swiftest which is avoided under the insolvency regime.[1] Outside an insolvency situation the following issues have to be considered:

- the enforceability of the security right;
- the methods of enforcement and commencement of enforcement proceedings;
- the distribution of realization proceeds;
- the protection of the person giving security during enforcement proceedings; and
- the protection of the securityholder against enforcement by third parties.

19.02 Although secured transactions law is predominantly regarded as a part of the substantive law of a country since it creates rights *in rem*, an understanding of the related procedural rules is necessary for a comprehensive study of secured transactions law.

B. Eastern European Secured Transactions Laws

1. Bulgarian law

(a) Enforceability of the security

19.03 The pledge and mortgage under the Law on Obligations and Contracts,[2] as well as the registered pledge under the Law on Registered Pledges,[3] are enforceable once the debtor has failed to satisfy the secured debt which was due and payable. Article 11 of the Law on Registered Pledges adds that a registered pledge may also be enforced if an obligation under the pledge agreement has not been met, even if the secured debt itself is not yet due and payable.

(b) Methods of enforcement and commencement of enforcement proceedings

19.04 Security rights under the Law on Obligations and Contracts are enforced in a court-led procedure pursuant to the rules of the Civil Procedure Code. The enforcement requires a writ of execution, which is typically issued by a court

---

[1] See ch 20 below.   [2] Law on Obligations and Contracts, Art 134.
[3] Law on Registered Pledges, Art 32(1).

and is in principle followed by a public sale of the secured asset.[4] To obtain the writ of execution the pledgeholder must, apart from demonstrating that a pledge was created, produce to the court any written contract from which the secured debt or, if the pledge is over claims, the claim taken as security arises if such a written contract existed in the first place.[5] Although the parties may not agree on simply transferring ownership in the secured asset to the pledgeholder prior to the enforceability of the pledge,[6] this can be done by a separate agreement between the parties following the pledge becoming enforceable.

For registered charges pursuant to the Law on Registered Pledges there are various methods of enforcement: **19.05**

- sale of the pledged asset in whatever form;[7]
- specific provisions dealing with special types of secured assets;[8]
- enforcement of pledges on the assets of an enterprise.[9]

The commencement of enforcement proceedings must be registered in the pledge register.[10] In addition, the pledgor must be notified about the commencement of enforcement proceedings in writing.[11]   **19.06**

The pledgeholder is entitled to take possession of the secured assets,[12] take measures to preserve the pledged property,[13] and to sell it.[14] Should the debtor cooperate with the pledgeholder there will be no problem in taking possession or taking other measures. However, where the pledgor refuses to cooperate with respect to providing possession to secured assets or allowing preservation measures, the pledgeholder cannot take self-help measures but has to apply to an executive judge for assistance.[15]   **19.07**

A sale of the secured property is possible only two weeks after registration of the commencement of enforcement measures in the pledge register.[16] There are no instructions in the Law as to how the sale must be conducted save that the pledgeholder shall carry out the sale 'with the care of a good merchant'.[17] Hence, the sale can be by public auction or by way of private sale.   **19.08**

---

[4] See Law on Obligations and Contracts, Art 175 for mortgages.

[5] See ibid Arts 160 (secured debt is monetary obligation) and 165 (secured asset is claim). See also Art 173(3) which provides that in order to obtain a writ of execution for enforcement of a mortgage, the mortgageholder must produce an excerpt from the land register showing the registration of the mortgage to the court.

[6] ibid Art 152. Similar to the prohibition of an automatic transfer clause ('*Verfallklausel*') under German pledge law (German Civil Code, §1229).

[7] Law on Registered Pledges, Art 37.   [8] ibid Arts 44, 44a, and 45.   [9] ibid Art 46.
[10] ibid Art 32(3).   [11] ibid Art 33(1).   [12] ibid Art 34 No 1.
[13] ibid Arts 32(4), 34 No 3.   [14] ibid Arts 32(4), 37.
[15] ibid Art 35(1) and Civil Procedure Code, Art 414.
[16] Law on Registered Pledges, Art 37(1).   [17] ibid Art 37(3).

19.09 There are special provisions on special types of secured assets. Securities or negotiable instruments can be sold in the manner 'appropriate' to the particular type of secured asset,[18] which will often result in the asset being sold on an exchange.[19] Account receivables may be sold[20] (either as a single claim or as a pool of claims) or, in the case of a monetary claim, simply collected. Where the secured asset is an account receivable the pledgeholder will often notify the account debtor,[21] even if he sells the account receivable to a third party. Lastly, shares can be enforced not only by selling the shares to a third party under Article 37(1) of the Law on Registered Pledges but also by dissolving the company and receiving the respective proportion of the liquidation proceeds.[22]

19.10 A pledge on the assets of an enterprise can be enforced either by enforcing against individual assets of the enterprise or by selling the enterprise as a whole.[23] In order to realize the sale of the whole enterprise the pledgeholder can appoint an enterprise manager[24] to manage the business in the place of its previous directors.[25] This goes beyond the concept of a floating lien under Article 9 of the UCC and comes close to the traditional concept of a floating charge under English law and also the concept of an enterprise charge under the EBRD Model Law.

19.11 The pledgor may challenge the enforcement measures in particular on the basis that (a) the security right has not been created validly or terminated or (b) the secured debt has not been created validly or terminated.[26]

19.12 The enforcement provisions of the Law on Registered Pledges are relatively open. It therefore seems advisable for the parties to deal more specifically with the rights and duties arising in an enforcement situation in the pledge agreement.

(c) Distribution of realization proceeds

19.13 For the distribution of proceeds, privileges established by operation of law must be taken into account.[27] The proceeds from a sale of secured assets are deposited with a depositary who is appointed by the pledgeholder.[28] He collects all the claims against the pledged property, clarifies any objections against claims, and

---

[18] Law on Registered Pledges, Art 44(1).　　[19] ibid Art 44(2).　　[20] ibid Art 44a(1).
[21] ibid Art 34 No 2 confirms his right to do so.　　[22] ibid Art 45(1).
[23] ibid Art 46(1).　　[24] Similar to a charge manager under the EBRD Model Law.
[25] Law on Registered Pledges, Arts 48–51.
[26] ibid Art 36(1) and Civil Procedure Code, Arts 250–255.
[27] See Law on Obligations and Contracts, Arts 133, 136 and Law on Registered Pledges, Art 16(1).
[28] Law on Registered Pledges, Arts 38–39. Similar to a proceeds depositary under the EBRD Model Law.

then distributes the proceeds.[29] In effect, the depositary's role is similar to the role of an insolvency administrator in that he tries to satisfy several claims in an objective procedure. Disputes among several creditors will be settled in court proceedings.[30]

2. Czech law

(a) Enforceability of the security

The lien becomes enforceable once the secured claim is not paid in a timely manner.[31] The Civil Code clarifies that the lien is enforceable also if the secured claim is paid only partially at the due time or if appurtenances of the secured claim (in particular interest payments) were not made in time or in the full amount due.[32] **19.14**

There are no provisions on the enforcement of security transfers and retentions of ownership. The parties will have to determine contractually that the security arrangements become enforceable once the secured claim has not been satisfied in the agreed manner. **19.15**

(b) Methods of enforcement and commencement of enforcement proceedings

Enforcement of liens is governed by sections 165 to 169 of the Civil Code, the Civil Procedure Code, and the Law on Public Auctions. Enforcement is rightly regarded as critical for the practical effect of a security right and the parties cannot, therefore, agree that the 'lien creditor may not demand satisfaction from the sale of the secured asset after the secured claim has become due'.[33] There are four principal ways of enforcing a lien: **19.16**

• by way of court proceedings (which eventually means judicial sale); or
• by public auction;[34] or
• in a way agreed between the parties;[35] or
• by making use of a special regime for enforcing a lien which encumbers a receivable.[36]

A judicial sale of real estate or movable things requires that there is an executory act. This will typically require a court judgment on the creditor's right to enforce his lien. Alternatively, an executory notarial act[37] or a payment order[38] **19.17**

---

[29] For the latter see Law on Registered Pledges, Art 41(1).   [30] ibid Art 42.
[31] Civil Code, s 165(1), first sentence.   [32] ibid s 165(1), second sentence.
[33] ibid s 169.   [34] ibid s 165a(1) and Commercial Code, s 299(2), first alternative.
[35] ibid s 299(2), second alternative. Although pursuant to Civil Code, s 169 the parties cannot agree that the 'lien creditor may claim satisfaction from the sale of the secured asset in a manner other than that stipulated by law', the option provided by Commercial Code, s 299(2), second alternative, practically renders the Civil Code provision meaningless.
[36] Civil Code, s 167.   [37] Civil Procedure Code, s 274.   [38] ibid s 172(1).

can serve as executory acts under Czech law. A payment order is a specific type of judicial order which is granted by a judge where a payment claim is based on the claimant's submission to the court. Once an executory act is obtained, the enforcement procedure in a narrow sense can begin. A lien on real estate is enforced pursuant to section 258(1) of the Civil Code in connection with sections 335ff of the Civil Procedure Code. The court will set a time for the judicial sale of the secured property[39] (at least thirty days before the date of the judicial sale).[40] The owner of the secured asset may challenge the sale and may raise an objection that (a) the lien agreement is invalid or (b) that there are defences against the secured debt.[41] Such a challenge may prevent the sale from going forward. Parties interested in acquiring the property will have to make a deposit of 50 per cent of the estimated value of the property (either in cash or by cheque).[42] The property is sold to the highest bidder.

19.18 A lien on movable things is enforced pursuant to section 258(1) of the Civil Code in connection with sections 323ff of the Civil Procedure Code. Enforcement is pursued by the person entitled under the executory act.[43] The debtor is informed of the enforcement only at the time of enforcement, thus enhancing the probability of its success. The auctioning of the secured asset itself is done by a court bailiff.[44] The minimum offer for the auction is two-thirds of the secured asset's estimated value. An acquirer of the secured asset becomes owner at the time of payment.[45]

19.19 Public auctions of real estate or movable assets pursuant to section 299(2), first alternative, of the Commercial Code[46] follow the procedure laid out in the Law on Public Auctions. Prior to the enactment of the Law on Public Auctions there was a law dealing with the public sale of movable things which has now been superseded by the new law.[47] Although prior to the enactment of the new law, public sales of real estate were also possible pursuant to section 299(2), first alternative, of the Commercial Code, there was no indication as to how such public auctions should be conducted.[48] This legal gap for real estate has now

---

[39] Civil Procedure Code, s 335(1).   [40] ibid s 336b(1).
[41] Civil Code, s 166(1). The time limits set in s 166(2) and (3) for a challenge of a public sale do not apply to a judicial sale.
[42] Civil Procedure Code, s 336d.   [43] ibid s 323(1).   [44] ibid s 328b(3).
[45] ibid s 329(3).
[46] The Commercial Code applies not only to merchants in their entrepreneurial activities (Commercial Code, s 261(1)) but also to so-called 'absolute business transactions', including loan agreements and security rights securing obligations arising from loan agreements (s 261(3)d, (4)). Hence, Commercial Code, Art 299 finds general application and is not limited to merchants in their entrepreneurial activities.
[47] Law No 174/1950.
[48] See TO Schorling, *Das Recht der Kreditsicherheiten in der Tschechischen Republik* (Berlin, 2000) 146, 151.

been filled by the Law on Public Auctions. The Law on Public Auctions deals with the enforcement of liens as well as public auctions at the request of the sold property's owner or other persons. A public auction does not require an executory act.[49] The procedure is initiated at the request of the person taking security.[50] The auction is held by a 'licenced person'. The auctioneer must value the secured asset, in the case of movable things, prior to any sale. Real estate must be valued by an expert.[51] After the valuation has been made, the auctioneer must notify the owner of the secured asset, the creditors, the debtor and other persons holding proprietary rights in the secured asset about the public sale.[52] The owner of the secured asset may challenge the sale within one month from receiving the notification and may claim that (a) the lien agreement is invalid or (b) that there are defences against the secured debt.[53] Such a challenge may prevent the sale going forward. The challenge period of one month provided in section 166(1) of the Civil Code results in a minimum period during which the asset cannot be sold.

The auctioneer opens the auction by setting an initial bidding price which is at least 50 per cent of the secured asset's value. The person buying the asset in the public auction becomes the owner of the assets at the time of payment but with effect as at the time of acceptance of a bid.[54]   **19.20**

The parties can agree on a way to enforce a lien over real estate of movable things pursuant to section 299(2), second alternative, of the Commercial Code. However, the parties cannot agree to an automatic transfer of ownership of the secured property to the person taking security upon the event of enforceability.[55] The parties will typically agree a procedure of selling the secured property by the person holding the lien. There is some disagreement under Czech law as to how the sale of secured property by the person holding the lien is effected legally, and in particular whether the seller is acting as a legal or contractual representative of the owner of the secured property. There are also practical difficulties for the buyer of real estate with regard to being registered in the land register, if the previous owner does not agree to this.[56]   **19.21**

---

[49] ibid 154. However, if the enforcement is challenged pursuant to Law on Public Auctions, s 7(3) a court decision may still be required. Note the difference from German law: the enforcement of a possessory pledge in movable things does not necessarily need an executory act under German law. The German pledge is a 'sales pledge'.

[50] Law on Public Auctions, s 2(2).   [51] ibid s 5(1).   [52] ibid s 6.

[53] ibid s 7(3). See also Civil Code, s 166(1)–(3) which also deals with a challenge against a public auction.

[54] Law on Public Auctions, s 11(2).

[55] Civil Code, s 169. Similar to the prohibition of an automatic transfer clause ('*Verfallklausel*') under German pledge law (German Civil Code, §1229).

[56] See comprehensively Schorling (n 48 above) 147–9.

19.22 In practice, both judicial sales and public auctions are still regarded as risky undertakings fraught with legal obstacles.[57] Typically, the parties will agree on a way to enforce the lien pursuant to section 299(2), second alternative, of the Commercial Code. However, creditors faced with enforcement proceedings will try to avoid legal issues by making an out-of-court settlement with the debtors.

19.23 It should be noted that although Czech law provides for a lien in the assets of an enterprise or other collective assets, it does not provide the additional remedy of an 'enterprise administrator'. The enterprise lien is thus merely a way of describing the secured assets in simple terms.

19.24 Under a retention of ownership arrangement the person retaining ownership will ask the purchaser of the secured asset to return possession to him. Where a security transfer has been agreed, the parties will have to agree how the security transfer can be enforced. In most cases the parties will agree that the secured asset should be sold.

(c) Distribution of realization proceeds

19.25 Where real estate is sold by judicial sale, a hearing will be held by the court concerning the distribution of proceeds.[58] Pursuant to section 337 of the Civil Procedure Code there is a distribution ranking of claims which the court will implement. Enforcement costs will be satisfied first,[59] then claims secured by real estate liens covering mortgage backed securities (MBS),[60] third, tax claims covered by a prior tax lien,[61] and fourth, (unsecured) claims of the enforcing creditor but also claims secured by liens (in particular real estate liens) and claims secured by a prohibition on the sale of the secured property.[62] The claim secured by a real estate lien will typically fall into the fourth distribution class. It seems from the wording of section 337 of the Civil Procedure Code that tax liens have priority over real estate liens. However, in practice section 337(1)b of the Civil Procedure Code seems not to have any real scope, since tax liens pursuant to section 72 of the Tax Administration Law will have priority only in accordance with the time of their creation and will, therefore, have to be satisfied together with real estate liens in class four of the distribution order.[63] Also, it seems strange that unsecured claims of the enforcing creditor are mentioned in section 337(1)d of the Civil Procedure Code alongside claims secured by a real estate lien. Section 337(1)d must be interpreted in such a way that, in any event, claims secured by a real estate lien take priority in distribution to other

---

[57] See Schorling (n 48 above) 137, 149. Schorling's opinion on public auctions is still based on the situation prior to the enactment of the Law on Public Auctions in 2000. However, the situation has not changed significantly since the new Law was enacted.
[58] Civil Procedure Code, s 336n.   [59] ibid s 337(1)a.   [60] ibid s 337(1)b.
[61] ibid s 337(1)c.   [62] ibid s 337(1)d.   [63] Schorling (n 48 above) 142–3.

(unsecured) claims, otherwise real estate liens would not be able to have their full effect and there would also be a clear conflict with section 165(2) of the Civil Code, which provides that real estate liens shall be satisfied according to the time of their creation.[64] Hence, within section 337(1)d of the Civil Procedure Code claims secured by a real estate lien will be satisfied prior to unsecured claims (even if they are held by the enforcing creditor). The law is unclear as to whether the priority of secured claims extends also to secured claims which are not yet due. However, the provision must clearly be extended to secured claims which are not yet due, since any other solution would render liens ineffective.[65]

Sales proceeds from a judicial sale of movable things pursuant to section 258(1) **19.26** of the Civil Code in connection with sections 323ff of the Civil Procedure Code will simply be distributed if only one claim exists against the debtor of the secured debt.[66] However, if there are several claims, in principle the time of the enforcement request will decide which claim will be satisfied first.[67] However, claims secured by a lien will have priority over unsecured claims.[68]

The sale proceeds are distributed in a similar way to those of a judicial sale if a **19.27** public auction is held pursuant to section 299(2), first alternative, of the Commercial Code in connection with the Law on Public Auctions. The auctioneer will hold a distribution meeting and invite creditors, the owner of the secured asset, the debtor, and other persons holding proprietary rights in the secured asset.[69] From the proceeds of sale enforcement costs will be satisfied first, then liens, third tax claims which have become due during the last three years prior to the auction, and fourth all other notified claims. The distribution rankings are thus significantly different from those applying in judicial sales, and put liens clearly ahead of other claims.

3. Hungarian law

(a) Enforceability of the charge

A charge under Hungarian law becomes enforceable once the debtor fails to **19.28** perform the secured claim.[70] In addition, where the condition of an asset subject to a registered charge deteriorates, the chargeholder can claim restoration of the charged asset and, if the chargeholder's demand is not satisfied, he may immediately demand satisfaction from the secured claim. Similarly, if the charged asset

---

[64] Similarly ibid 143.   [65] Similarly ibid 157.   [66] Civil Procedure Code, s 331(1).
[67] ibid s 332(1).   [68] ibid s 371(1).   [69] Law on Public Auctions, s 15.
[70] Civil Code, s 251(1). The law refers to the 'chargor' but clearly means the 'debtor' where debtor and chargor are different persons.

of a possessory charge is in danger of deteriorating, the chargor can claim to have it returned but has to offer other appropriate security.

(b) Methods of enforcement and commencement of enforcement proceedings

19.29   There are various enforcement methods under Hungarian law:

- court proceedings which require a court decision;[71]
- agreement between the parties;[72] and
- enforcement of a floating (enterprise) charge.[73]

19.30   Where the charge is enforced on the basis of an agreement between the parties, the agreement must be made in writing and determine the lowest sale price or the method of its calculation, a final date for the realization of the charged asset, and other possible terms.[74] The chargeholder may sell the charged asset himself only if it is a credit institution (in particular a bank) or if the charged asset has an officially registered market price (such as listed securities).[75] Otherwise the chargeholder must either commission a third party to sell the charged asset[76] or proceed within the framework of judicial enforcement.[77] An even simpler way for the chargeholder to receive satisfaction from the charged asset is if the parties agree on a transfer of ownership in the charged asset to the chargeholder. However, such an agreement can only be made *after* the charge becomes enforceable.[78]

19.31   Prior to enforcement, pursuant to an agreement between the parties, the chargor must be notified of the intention to sell the charged asset.[79] A violation of this rule does not affect the transfer of ownership to a third party; however, the enforcing chargeholder becomes liable for damages of the chargor. The Civil Code provides explicitly for a right to sell the charged asset in section 258(1). The person selling the charged asset, be it the chargeholder himself or a third party, will act in the name of the chargor (ie will represent him in entering into the sales contract) and will be entitled to transfer ownership of the charged asset. Thus a person acquiring the charged asset does not need any good faith protection in acquiring the asset.

19.32   A floating (enterprise) charge will, in most cases, be enforced on the basis of an

---

[71] Civil Code, s 255(1).
[72] ibid s 257 and additional regulation Government Decree No 12/2003 on the Sale of Charged Property through Non-judicial Enforcement pursuant to Civil Code s 258(4).
[73] Civil Code s 266(2).   [74] ibid s 257(1).   [75] ibid s 257(2).
[76] ibid s 257(3).
[77] That this is the case is confirmed by the reference to judicial enforcement in ibid, s 257(2).
[78] ibid s 255(2). Similar to the prohibition of an automatic transfer clause ('*Verfallklausel*') under German pledge law (German Civil Code, §1229).
[79] Civil Code, s 258(2).

agreement between the parties. In particular, the parties can agree that the chargeholder 'can supervise the management of the chargor's business'.[80] In addition, the rules of registered charges apply also to floating charges.[81] However, section 266(2) of the Civil Code provides in addition that the enforcement can result (a) in the transfer of the enterprise as a whole or (b) the sale of the enterprise's individual assets. For the latter option, the floating charge must be transformed into a registered charge covering the individual assets.[82] The chargeholder can realize the second option by delivering a written notice to the chargor. It was initially planned to enact subordinate legislation providing detailed rules on the enforcement of enterprise charges. However, the provision on enforcement by the sale of the enterprise as a whole was never supplemented with such detailed legislation and therefore remained a mere theoretical possibility. It cannot be used in practice, and it is therefore currently planned to abolish the enterprise charge as a sub-type of the charge.

Where rights are subject to a charge, any enforcement of the charge requires that **19.33** the debtor of the encumbered right is notified about the charge (this is not a creation requirement for the charge and must, therefore, be done at the enforcement stage at the latest).[83]

Under a retention of ownership arrangement the person retaining ownership **19.34** will ask the purchaser of the secured asset to return possession to him.

(c) Distribution of realization proceeds

Proceeds from the sale of a charged asset will be used to cover the costs of **19.35** the secured claim, and satisfy the secured claim in full as well as any related claims ('incidental claims' such as interest payments).[84] Any surplus will then be transferred to the chargor.

4. Polish law

(a) Enforceability of the pledge

Although not explicitly provided by law, pledges and mortgages become **19.36** enforceable if a due debt is not performed in accordance with the agreement between the parties. Under a retention of ownership the parties will provide in their agreement when the security becomes enforceable. Typically they will also rely on the event that the secured debt is not satisfied.

---

[80] This demonstrates that the floating charge of Hungarian law is not a mere means of describing the secured asset but encompasses special remedies.
[81] Civil Code, ss 266(6), 265(3)–(5).   [82] Similar to 'crystallization' under English law.
[83] Civil Code, s 267(2).   [84] ibid s 258(3).

(b) Methods of enforcement and commencement of enforcement proceedings

19.37 **Enforcement regimes** There are different enforcement regimes. The Civil Code pledge and the mortgage in real estate are enforced under court execution procedures pursuant to the Civil Procedure Code,[85] whereas there are special enforcement proceedings in the Law on Registered Pledges and the Pledge Registry for registered pledges.[86] The Law on Registered Pledges and the Pledge Registry distinguishes between:

(1) judicial enforcement procedures;[87]

(2) the seizing of the secured assets within the non-judicial enforcement procedure which may be stipulated in the pledge agreement if:

    (a) there is a pledge on publicly traded securities and the Securities and Exchange Commission has agreed to and has defined the conditions for such a seizure,

    (b) the secured asset is a commonly traded commodity,

    (c) the secured asset consists of movable things, receivables, or rights the value of which has been defined precisely in the pledge agreement;

(3) the public sale of the secured asset (if permitted under the pledge agreement) either by a notary public or a court enforcement officer (ie a court bailiff);[88] and

(4) appointment of a receiver over the enterprise if the pledge agreement for a registered pledge covering the assets of an enterprise allows the pledgeholder to satisfy the secured claim from the profits made by an enterprise.[89]

19.38 Further to point (4), the identity of the receiver will be specified in the pledge agreement. The receiver must act in accordance with the bank's submission to the court for an executory title, the provisions of the Civil Procedure Code on compulsory administration of real property, or pursuant to the provisions of the pledge agreement.[90] An enterprise may be leased in order to satisfy claims secured by the registered pledge from rent receipts, if the pledge agreement so provides. The pledge agreement may stipulate that the pledgeholder must consent to the leasing contract. Clearly, the parties will make additional specific

---

[85] Civil Code, Art 312 for Civil Code pledges and Law on Land Registry and Mortgages, Art 75 for real estate mortgages.

[86] Law on Registered Pledges and the Pledge Registry, Arts 20–35, 47–48.

[87] ibid Art 21.

[88] ibid Art 24. Art 24(2) provides that a decree shall be issued by the Minister of Justice. This decree has so far not been issued. Hence, Polish law is currently lacking viable out-of-court realization procedures for registered pledges.

[89] ibid Art 27. Art 25 (providing the requirement of servicing an enforcement notice) does not refer to Art 27 and it therefore seems that the enforcement notice is not a requirement for an enterprise pledge.

[90] ibid Art 33.

provisions in the pledge agreement to gain some benefit from an enterprise pledge. It should be noted, however, that without an agreement between the parties, it is unclear how the pledgeholder could ensure control of the enterprise pending realization.[91] The satisfaction of the secured claim from the profits of an enterprise shall be registered at the pledge registry.

Parties can agree that the ownership in secured property passes to the pledge-holder in the event that the secured debt is not satisfied.[92] The transfer of ownership shall occur at the time when the secured claim becomes due and after the pledgeholder has submitted a declaration that the transfer is valid. However, for Civil Code pledges this will only be possible if the pledged asset has a specified price fixed by an order of a competent state authority.[93] The secured asset shall become owned by the pledgeholder in the appropriate proportion and at the respective price on the day when the secured claim becomes due. For registered pledges this possibility is limited to certain classes of property, namely publicly traded securities (provided, however, that the Securities and Exchange Commission has approved this and defined the conditions for such transfer of ownership), commonly traded commodities as well as movables and receivables, or other rights with a value clearly defined in the pledge agreement.[94] **19.39**

Enforcement proceedings for registered pledges Enforcement proceedings for registered pledges are commenced by a written enforcement notice to be sent by the pledgeholder to the pledgor.[95] This gives the pledgor the opportunity either to satisfy the claim or to file a motion in court against the secured claim, in particular to the effect that it does not exist or that it is not due.[96] Strangely the motion can only be directed against the secured claim; it should, however, also be possible to bring a motion against the registered pledge. After a seven-day period from the date on which the pledgor receives the notice, the pledgeholder can continue enforcement proceedings. **19.40**

It is not sufficient simply to send an enforcement notice. As in other civil law jurisdictions, civil enforcement procedures require a special executory title either in the form of a court order,[97] a bank executory title (or bank writ or **19.41**

---

[91] EBRD, *The Impact of the Legal Framework on the Secured Credit Market in Poland* (London, 2005) 19.

[92] Similar to the prohibition of an automatic transfer clause ('*Verfallklausel*') under German pledge law (German Civil Code, §1229).

[93] Civil Code, Art 313.

[94] Law on Registered Pledges and the Pledge Registry, Art 22. Art 23 sets out how the value of securities shall be determined.

[95] ibid Art 25(1).   [96] ibid Art 25(2).

[97] ibid Art 29 refers to the Code of Civil Procedure.

attachment),[98] an executory notarial act,[99] a settlement involving a mediator, or a court settlement. The court order has to be provided by the court within three days from the filing of the application.[100] The court order will contain a deadline for commencement of further proceedings which shall be one week after the issuance of the court order at the earliest and two weeks from that date at the latest.[101] An executory notarial act in itself will not be sufficient; enforcement can only be pursued if a court issues an additional execution order.[102] As at the stage of the enforcement notice the pledgor can, at the stage of an executory title, file a motion against the secured claim, in particular stating that it does not exist or that it is not due.[103] Again the motion can only be directed against the secured claim; it should, however, also be possible to bring a motion against the registered pledge.

19.42 **Enforcement of Civil Code pledges** The Civil Code pledge may be enforced only through court proceedings. It should be noted that the enforcement proceedings vary depending on the subject of the pledge. The enforcement procedure with respect to the pledge is as follows:

(1) A pledgeholder wishing to enforce the Civil Code pledge must first obtain an executory title (ie a court judgment, an arbitration award, etc). Subsequently, the pledgeholder must obtain confirmation from the court by way of an enforcement clause that the executory title can be enforced. The executory title together with the enforcement clause is known as an enforcement title. The pledgeholder must then present the enforcement title to the court bailiff.

(2) The pledgeholder must obtain the enforcement title described above (if the title is granted in the form of a court judgment or arbitration award, the timing depends on the length of court or arbitration proceedings which is difficult to predict, whereas if the title is in the form of a notarial act containing the pledgor's submission to execution, the title is held by the pledgeholder; the court should grant the enforcement clause within a maximum three days).

(3) The pledgeholder must request the court bailiff ('*komornik*') to start enforcement proceedings against the encumbered assets pursuant to Article 796 of the Civil Procedure Code.

(4) The court bailiff then seizes the pledged assets, which results in a situation

---

[98] Law on Registered Pledges and the Pledge Registry, Art 30 and Banking Law, Art 53, §1.
[99] Code of Civil Procedure, Art 47. Similar to an enforceable instrument ('*vollstreckbare Urkunde*') under German civil procedural law; see German Civil Procedure Code, §794(1) No 5.
[100] Law on Registered Pledges and the Pledge Registry, Art 31(2).   [101] ibid Art 32(1).
[102] ibid Art 32(2).   [103] ibid Art 35.

where the pledgor can neither dispose of the seized assets nor exercise any rights thereunder (for example under seized shares).

(5) If, after the seizure of the pledged assets (or shares), the due execution of the pledgor's rights so requires, the supervising court shall, at the request of the pledgeholder or the pledgor, appoint an administrator or order the sale of the assets (which is not to be performed before the expiry of seven days from the seizure). In case of a pledge of shares, if their sale is, pursuant to the company's charter, conditional upon the company's consent, the company may appoint the buyer of the seized shares, who will buy the shares at the price determined by the supervising court on the basis of a valuation made at the request of the company. If the company fails to make a request for valuation within the prescribed time or the appointed buyer fails to pay the determined price to the bailiff, the sale of the seized shares will be executed as described below.

(6) If the assets are sold during either the first or second public auction (which may be required by the pledgeholder within two weeks from the date of notification by the bailiff), the sale takes the form of an adjudication ('*przybicie*') of the supervising court. This decision may be appealed against.

(7) If the second sale was not performed, the pledgeholder may, within two weeks from the notification by the bailiff, take over the assets for a price not lower than the initial auction price.

Enforcement of mortgages   The enforcement of a claim secured by a mortgage **19.43** involves a compulsory sale of the encumbered property, which is to be carried out by means of a public tender by a court bailiff or a private sale agreement approved by a committee of creditors in the case of the property of an insolvent person.

The mortgage is enforceable only through court proceedings. In order to start **19.44** the enforcement of a mortgage, an 'enforcement order' is required. An enforcement order is issued by a court within three working days from the date on which the claimant presents the 'enforcement title'. Such an enforcement title may be a court order, arbitration award, bank documents, or a voluntary submission to enforcement (a notarial deed pursuant to Article 777 of the Civil Procedure Code). A voluntary submission to enforcement may shorten the period for the enforcement of a claim, or even eliminate the need for a court hearing. A debtor can voluntarily submit to the execution of debts on given dates. If the debtor then defaults, the creditor may go directly to the court to request enforcement of the debt. The statement by the debtor must be made in notarial form, but it may be done in the same notarial deed as the statement on the establishment of the mortgage. If the lender is a bank acting in accordance with Polish banking law, the voluntary submission to enforcement may also be made in written form in accordance with the provisions of the banking law.

19.45 Once a request to start enforcement proceedings is filed with a court bailiff, the court bailiff shall seize the real property encumbered with the mortgage and request the mortgagor to pay the secured claims within two weeks. If no payments are made within this period, the mortgageholder needs to file a request with the bailiff to prepare a description and valuation of the real property.[104]

19.46 Once the description and valuation are final (ie one may no longer file a complaint against them), the court bailiff shall set the date of the public auction at which the seized property is to be sold. During the first public auction, the real property cannot be sold for a price lower than three-quarters of the valuation of the real property.[105] If the real property is not sold during the first public auction, the bailiff—acting at the request of the mortgageholder—shall set a date for a second public auction during which real property cannot be sold for less than two-thirds of the valuation.[106] If real property is sold during the first or the second auction, the supervising judge shall adjudicate the real property to the highest bidder. Adjudication ('*przybicie*') takes the form of a court decision which can be appealed against.[107] Once a decision on adjudication becomes final, the court will issue another decision confirming acquisition of the real property by the highest bidder ('*przysadzenie*').[108]

19.47 If the real property is not sold in the course of the second public auction, the mortgageholder shall have the right to acquire the title to the real property in exchange for not less than two-thirds of its valuation.

19.48 The proceeds from the sale of such property are then paid to the claimants according to the priority of their claims as specified below.

19.49 The sale of an encumbered property (irrespective of whether the debtor was solvent or insolvent) has no impact on the tenants of such property provided that (a) their leases were for a fixed period, (b) they were created by a lease with a 'certified date', and (c) the tenant has gone into possession. The property would therefore be sold with the benefit of all its rental income. Due diligence is required when accepting a mortgage of leased properties to ensure that they could be sold with the benefit of their leases if necessary.

(c) Distribution of realization proceeds of mortgages

19.50 In the case of enforcement against a solvent debtor, the claims of the creditor secured by a mortgage would be paid after the costs of enforcement, labour law claims (if any are enforced at the time), taxes, and fees for perpetual usufruct (together with penalties for delays and enforcement costs if applicable).

---

[104] Civil Procedure Code, Art 942. [105] ibid Art 965. [106] ibid Art 983.
[107] ibid Art 987. [108] ibid Art 998.

In the case of enforcement against an insolvent debtor, the claims of the creditor **19.51** secured by a mortgage would be paid after (a) the costs of the bankruptcy proceedings (including remuneration of the receiver), (b) debts incurred by the receiver while administering the bankrupt's estate, (c) debts resulting from the actions of the court supervisor of the insolvent entity (applicable only if the bankrupt went through a settlement procedure before insolvency and such procedure ended or was redeemed three months before the announcement of the insolvency), and (d) tax, other public levies, and social security contributions due for the year preceding the date of declaration of bankruptcy.

(d) Distribution of realization proceeds of registered pledges

The proceeds of sale from a secured asset are not only used to satisfy the **19.52** enforcement costs and the claims secured by a registered pledge. Article 20(1) of the Law on Registered Pledges and the Pledge Registry provides that the order of distribution (priorities) is (1) enforcement costs, (2) alimony claims (of the pledgor's creditors), (3) workers' claims (against the pledgor) for a period of up to three months, (4) claims in damages by third parties (against the pledgor) for causing injury or unfitness for work, (5) costs of a last illness of the pledgor, and (6) standard funeral costs (of the pledgor). In addition, the proceeds may have to satisfy a prior statutory tax lien.[109] The tax lien must be registered in a special registry but not in the general pledge registry. A payment to the pledgeholder from realization proceeds cannot simply be made but the pledgeholder must apply to the court to order payment to him[110]

Article 28 of the Law on Registered Pledges and the Pledge Registry is peculiar **19.53** to Polish law. It provides that where the pledgeholder is a foreign bank its secured claim may be satisfied in foreign currency if this is provided by the security agreement. However, beyond stating this fact and allocating the satisfaction to specially admitted Polish banks, the provision does not provide any further guidance.

5. Romanian law

(a) Enforceability

The security right in movables or a mortgage become enforceable when the **19.54** chargor fails to fulfil the secured obligation.[111] It should be noted that in principle clauses in the security agreement (or contracts related to it)[112] under which

---

[109] Law on Registered Pledges and the Pledge Registry, Art 20(2).   [110] ibid Article 34.
[111] Law Concerning Certain Measures for the Acceleration of the Economic Process, Arts 11(1), 62(1), 63(1).
[112] This extension of ibid Art 22(1) is necessary to prevent this provision from being circumvented in practice by simply placing such an immediate payment clause in a separate agreement.

the secured debt can be accelerated (and thus becomes immediately due and payable), in the event that the chargor grants additional security rights, are null and void (unless such an acceleration is in response to the secured property being in danger of being impaired or the payment of being impaired).[113] Both an attached and a perfected security right can become enforceable. It suffices that the security right has properly attached only if there are no third parties with additional security rights. The securityholder may also proceed with enforcement of the security right if the secured property is not properly maintained and payment of the secured debt is thus in danger[114] even if the secured debt is not yet due and payable.

(b) Methods of enforcement and commencement of enforcement proceedings

19.55 There are two enforcement procedures provided under Romanian law for security in movables:[115]

- the procedure provided under the Law Concerning Certain Measures for the Acceleration of the Economic Process; and
- the enforcement procedure provided under the Civil Procedure Code.

19.56 For enforcement of an attached security right against the person giving security there is no need to obtain a separate executory title to be issued by a court or to put the security agreement in a notarial form; the security agreement itself serves as executory title.[116]

19.57 Once the security right has become enforceable the securityholder has three options. He is entitled to take possession of the secured property, to retain it, or to sell it.[117] He may also exercise his rights over the secured property against a third party holding the property.[118]

19.58 The right to take possession requires that the security agreement contains the following clause, written in capital letters in at least 12 point size: 'IN CASE OF NON-PERFORMANCE, THE CREDITOR MAY USE ITS OWN MEANS IN TAKING POSSESSION OF THE SECURED PROPERTY'.[119] The right of taking possession can be exercised only by 'peaceful means',[120] ie with the consent of the person holding possession. The securityholder cannot receive assistance—at this stage—from public officials, such as a police officer or a court bailiff.[121] The right to possession cannot be exercised by the securityholder employing self-help against the chargor's will. In order to enforce the right to possession, the securityholder has to involve an enforcement officer (possibly

---

[113] Law Concerning Certain Measures for the Acceleration of the Economic Process, Art 22(1).
[114] ibid Art 11(2).   [115] ibid Art 62(1).   [116] ibid Art 17.
[117] ibid Art 11(1).   [118] ibid Art 23(2).   [119] ibid Art 63(4).
[120] ibid Art 63(1), second sentence, (2).   [121] ibid Art 63(3), first sentence.

with the support of police officers)[122] to take possession of the secured property (but does not have to go to court or have an executory title to obtain execution).[123] In order to use this route the securityholder must make an application to the court bailiff[124] to which the official shall respond within forty-eight hours by taking possession and delivering it to the securityholder.[125] The securityholder also has the right to claim the transfer of possession against third parties once the security right has become enforceable and, where the person holding possession is itself a securityholder with respect to the secured property, the claiming securityholder has a higher ranking security right.[126]

The right to sell secured property is always attached to the security right and needs no special mention in the security agreement. The securityholder may sell secured property even if it is in the possession of the chargor.[127] The person giving security may at any time during the enforcement prevent further enforcement proceedings by simply paying the secured debt and the 'reasonable' costs of the enforcement proceedings.[128] The method of selling the secured property can be agreed between the parties[129] or, in the absence of such an agreement, shall follow the procedure laid out in Articles 69(2) to 79 of the Law Concerning Certain Measures for the Acceleration of the Economic Process. If the securityholder sells under the procedure provided in the Law, he is under a duty to sell in a reasonable, commercial manner.[130] **19.59**

The procedure laid out in the Law provides the following. Prior to any sale the chargor shall be notified by the securityholder at least five days before a sale.[131] The sale shall be implemented by the securityholder within a reasonable period of time.[132] **19.60**

A person acquiring from the securityholder (acting as the representative of the person granting security) acquires ownership free from the security right, but **19.61**

---

[122] ibid Art 63(2), third sentence.   [123] ibid Art 67.   [124] ibid Art. 67(2).

[125] ibid Art 68(1).   [126] ibid Art 64(1).

[127] ibid Art 65. Article 77(1) confirms that the parties may also agree that the sale of the secured property can take place without taking possession. Although the purchaser will acquire ownership free of the security right pursuant to Article 71 the chargor has the right to retain possession as a lessee if this is agreed between chargor and securityholder (ibid Art 77(2)).

[128] ibid Art 66, first sentence.

[129] ibid Art 69(1). This includes an agreement that the securityholder shall acquire ownership in the secured property if the person giving security fails to satisfy the secured obligation (ibid Art 73). However, the securityholder may not transfer the property to himself if he has invited third parties to participate in the sale unless the securityholder and the person giving security otherwise agree (ibid Art 73).

[130] ibid Art 69(2), (3). A court may relieve the securityholder of this duty without the Law providing any guidance as to when the court may grant such leave.

[131] ibid Art 71(1), (2). The securityholder can sell prior to this if the secured property is perishable (ibid Art 71(4)).

[132] ibid Art 72.

apparently only if the enforcement procedure (agreed between the parties or provided in Articles 69(2) to 79 of the Law Concerning Certain Measures for the Acceleration of the Economic Process) has been adhered to.[133] This seems to apply even to security rights which rank ahead of the enforcing securityholder's security right.[134] The securityholder may seek satisfaction under the secured debt for any amounts of the secured debt which have not been paid from the proceeds of the sale of the secured property.[135]

19.62 Where amounts are deposited in a bank account, the securityholder has to take additional steps. Amounts can be transferred to a bank account either because they are proceeds from the sale of secured property by the debtor (so-called 'products' under Romanian law)[136] or the secured property itself represents an account receivable with a bank. In such cases the securityholder has to notify the bank.[137] Upon receiving such an enforcement notice the bank shall verify in particular the security right and its priority and freeze the bank account, ie not make payments from the account.[138] In addition, the bank shall make the requested payment, if justified, to the securityholder.[139] Where a security right other than the enforced security right has a higher priority, the bank must first satisfy such higher ranking security right before it satisfies the demand of the enforcing securityholder.[140] The chargor has to be informed about the enforcement by the bank and the account is immediately 'unfrozen' (ie payment can be made again) once the demands of the securityholder have been satisfied.[141]

19.63 The law provides for a number of other special procedures for security rights in documents of title,[142] in accounts receivables (which are not against bank accounts),[143] and in payment claims.[144]

19.64 The enforcement of real estate mortgages follows the rules of the Civil Procedure Code. There are two main procedures under Romanian law through which mortgaged real estate can be sold: public auction or direct sale.[145]

19.65 For the commencement of enforcement proceedings, the creditor must apply to a court for an executory judgment pursuant to the Civil Procedure Code. A public auction is organized and conducted by a judicial executor who drafts a protocol identifying the mortgaged assets and orders the debtor to pay the

---

[133] See Law Concerning Certain Measures for the Acceleration of the Economic Process, Art 71 ('subject to nullity').

[134] See the explicit reference to higher ranking security rights in ibid Art 73 (which applies to a purchase of the secured asset by the securityholder itself). A similar reference is missing from ibid Art 70(1).

[135] ibid Art 74.   [136] See ibid Art 12.   [137] ibid Art 80(1), (2).

[138] ibid Art 81(1), (2). The bank may only make payments to the securityholder, if justified.

[139] ibid Art 82(1).   [140] ibid Art 82(2).   [141] ibid Art 82(4).

[142] ibid Art 83.   [143] ibid Art 84.   [144] ibid Art 85.

[145] Civil Procedure Code, Art 494.

secured debt. This order is registered with the land register, the function of which is to prevent fraudulent disposals of the secured asset by the debtor.

19.66 Should the debtor not pay the secured debt within fifteen days from receipt of the payment order, the judicial executor shall hold a public auction.[146] At the time of announcing the auction, the judicial executor will define the opening bidding price or ask a real estate expert for an independent valuation of the mortgaged property. If the enforcement is initiated against several mortgaged assets securing the same secured debt, several auctions shall be conducted, one for each asset.[147] A bidder must provide a deposit of 10 per cent of the opening bidding price prior to participating in an auction.

19.67 Pursuant to Article 507(2) of the Civil Procedure Code the debtor and any persons affiliated with him are prevented from bidding in the auction. If the mortgaged asset is acquired by the mortgageholder the purchase price may not be lower than 75 per cent of the opening bidding price.[148] The winning bidder must pay the purchase price within thirty days or a new public auction must be organized.[149] Ownership of the purchased asset passes to the winning bidder free and clear from any encumbrances, claims, or security rights of any kind if the 'auction protocol' is signed by the purchaser and the judicial executor. The auction protocol serves as a sale and purchase agreement and the transfer of ownership shall be registered with the land register.[150]

(c) Protection of chargor during enforcement proceedings

19.68 Pursuant to the Civil Procedure Code the debtor can challenge the enforcement proceedings in court but only within an extremely short time period, namely within five days from the receipt of the enforcement notice pursuant to Article 71(1) of the Law Concerning Certain Measures for the Acceleration of the Economic Process.[151] The debtor may either raise (a) defences against the security right under substantive law (for example that it has not attached, not been properly perfected, or that the secured debt has been satisfied)[152] or (b) procedural defences (for example that the time periods for an enforcement procedure provided under the above-mentioned Law have not been complied with). The court must decide on the challenge within three days from receiving the application and an appeal can be brought against this decision within a further three days. The appeal shall not, however, suspend the enforcement proceedings.[153]

19.69 If the securityholder breaches Article 69(2) or (3) of the Law Concerning Certain Measures for the Acceleration of the Economic Process (dealing with

---

[146] ibid Art 500. [147] ibid Art 508(1). [148] ibid Art 510(2).
[149] ibid Art 512(1). [150] ibid Art 516. [151] ibid Art 75(1).
[152] See for payment ibid Art 75(3). [153] ibid Art 75(2).

the sales procedure) a court may rule that the secured property can be sold in another 'commercially appropriate way'.[154] The person giving security can claim significant damages if the securityholder breaches the procedural provision in Articles 69(2)[155] to 85 of the Law. If either the taking of possession in the secured property or the sale of secured property is made in breach of any procedural provisions, the person giving security has a claim in damages in an amount of 30 per cent of the amount of the secured debt.[156] Where the secured property is sold in breach of procedural provisions, the claim in damages may alternatively be calculated as the difference between the secured property's market price and its actual sale price.[157]

19.70 As far as real estate mortgages are concerned, the mortgagor can raise in enforcement proceedings the defence of subsidiarity, meaning that if (a) mortgagor and debtor are different persons and (b) the mortgageholder holds a mortgage also over the debtor's assets which is enforceable, the latter mortgage shall be enforced primarily.[158]

(d) Protection of the securityholder against enforcement by third parties

19.71 The securityholder has the right to pursue the secured asset with every third person who holds possession to it. Thus, a person holding possession to the secured asset has a duty to hand over the secured property at the securityholder's request. If there are several securityholders, the highest ranking securityholder shall receive the property. In addition to this, no general creditor may, during enforcement proceedings pursued by a higher ranking securityholder, request to take possession of secured property.[159]

19.72 Third parties can enforce their rights against the secured property at any time prior to the start of enforcement proceedings by the secured creditor. The security right does not prevent the enforcement of rights by third parties.[160]

(e) Distribution of realization proceeds

19.73 Article 78 of the Law Concerning Certain Measures for the Acceleration of the Economic Process provides in which order sales proceeds shall be distributed

---

[154] Civil Procedure Code, Art 516.
[155] It is unclear to what extent the claims in damages apply also to an agreement on the method of selling secured property pursuant to Law Concerning Certain Measures for the Acceleration of the Economic Process, Art 69(1). Presumably the parties can agree their own remedy regime.
[156] ibid Arts 87, 88(1).
[157] ibid Art 88(1); and with reference to how the market value of the secured property shall be determined, ibid Art 89.
[158] Civil Procedure Code, Art 492(2).
[159] Law Concerning Certain Measures for the Acceleration of the Economic Process, Art 64(2).
[160] ibid Art 21(2).

among securityholders and creditors. The order is (1) expenses, (2) first priority security rights, even if such rights have not become due and payable, (3) lower ranking security rights in the order of their priority, even if such rights have not become due and payable, and (4) lastly, proceeds to the person giving security. Where the chargor is not the owner of the secured property and the securityholder is aware of this, the securityholder shall distribute the surplus to the owner.[161] Article 76 of the Law is not coordinated with the distribution order in Article 78 but, in the *author's* opinion, the distribution should be made after distributions (1) to (3) pursuant to Article 76. In addition, the security-holder and the person giving security are unable to change the distribution order.[162] This is a mandatory public policy provision; therefore securityholders cannot change priorities by agreement. However, among themselves they can enter into subordination agreements (in which they can agree distribution priorities contractually).

Articles 562 to 571 of the Civil Procedure Code provide for the distribution **19.74** order of sales proceeds among creditors with respect to mortgages. Proceeds from the sale of property encumbered by a real estate mortgage are distributed to the mortgageholder, after deduction of the costs for enforcement and sale of the mortgaged property; any balance is distributed to the mortgagor. If there are several mortgageholders, distributions are made pursuant to Article 563(1) of the Civil Procedure Code, namely in the order of the mortgages' priority ranking.

6. Russian law

(a) Enforceability of the pledge or mortgage

A non-registered pledge becomes enforceable in principle if the secured debt is **19.75** not satisfied when due.[163] At any time until the sale of the pledged property, the pledgor has the right to terminate the enforceability of the pledge by satisfying the secured debt.[164] This right cannot be opted out of by contract.[165]

A mortgage becomes enforceable if the secured debt is not satisfied when due **19.76** unless otherwise provided in the mortgage agreement.[166] For secured debts, which have to be performed in periodical instalments, the mortgage becomes enforceable if the debtor makes late performance of instalments more than three times within twelve months, unless the mortgage agreement provides other-wise.[167] This applies even if the delay is insignificant. One would have expected that in itself a simple (ie repeated) failure to pay would be sufficient to make the mortgage enforceable.

---

[161] ibid Art 76.   [162] ibid Arts 78(4) and 79.   [163] Pledge Law, Art 24.
[164] ibid Art 31(1), (2).   [165] ibid Art 31(3).   [166] Law on Mortgage, Art 50(1).
[167] ibid Art 50.

19.77 Where several mortgages have been created over the same property for the benefit of several mortgageholders,[168] a prior mortgage can be enforced even if the secured debt is not yet due.[169] If the prior mortgage is, however, not enforced and the subsequent mortgageholder enforcing the mortgage sells the mortgaged property to a third party, the property remains mortgaged by the prior mortgage.[170] If the transfer rules for mortgaged property are not complied with, the mortgageholder can claim satisfaction of the secured debt and enforcement of the mortgage even if the secured debt is not yet due.[171]

19.78 Under a retention of ownership or a security assignment of receivables the parties will provide in their agreement when the security become enforceable. Typically, the triggering event for the right to enforce these types of security will be the failure of the debtor to discharge the secured debt.

(b) Methods of enforcement and commencement of enforcement proceedings

19.79 Both non-registered and registered pledges (both in movable and immovable property) are enforced in two stages: (a) confirmation of the enforceability of the pledge in principle by a court judgment, and (b) sale of the pledged property. It should be noted that in principle the pledged property cannot simply be transferred to the pledgeholder upon the debtor's default but must be sold at an auction. The pledgeholder may become owner of the pledged property only if a number of auctions failed to sell the pledged property.

19.80 **Non-registered pledges** Pledged property can, once the non-registered pledge becomes enforceable, be sold in two different procedures under Russian law:[172]

(1) court procedure in accordance with the Arbitrazh Procedure Code and/or the Civil Procedure Code; and
(2) procedure provided in the pledge contract (to the extent permitted by law).

19.81 Non-registered pledges (which are created in assets other than immovable property) are enforced as follows. In principle, enforcement shall be made on the basis of a court judgment (either by a so-called court of common jurisdiction or a so-called *arbitrazh* court, a special commercial court in the Russian legal system), unless court proceedings are excluded in the contract between the pledgeholder and the pledgor.[173] A pledge can also be enforced in accordance with the procedure established by the pledge contract unless the law stipulates otherwise.[174] However, in the following cases the pledge may be enforced on the basis of a court judgment only:[175]

---

[168] Law on Mortgage, Art 46(5).   [169] ibid Art 46(2), first sentence.
[170] ibid Art 46(2), second sentence.   [171] ibid Art 39, first sentence.
[172] Pledge Law, Art 28(2).   [173] Civil Code, Art 349(2).   [174] ibid Art 349(2).
[175] ibid Art 349(3).

- where the enforcement of the pledge is subject to the consent by a third party;
- where the pledged property has a substantial historical or other cultural value; and
- where the pledgor's location cannot be identified.

On the basis of a court judgment on enforcement of the pledge, the court shall **19.82** issue a writ of execution. Although Article 28(1) of the Pledge Law allows a notary's executory note as a substitute for court writs of execution, it is impossible in practice to obtain such an executory note from a Russian notary public, since this provision of the Pledge Law has been replaced by the Civil Code which does not provide for this.

The pledged property (both immovable and movable) subject to enforcement **19.83** shall be sold at a public auction in accordance with the procedure established by Russian civil or *arbitrazh* procedure law, unless the law provides otherwise.[176]

Mortgages   The enforcement of a mortgage requires a respective judgment[177] **19.84** or an agreement on out-of-court enforcement between the parties entered into after the mortgage has become enforceable, which must comply with the content requirements provided by law[178] and which has been certified by a public notary.[179] It is obvious that in many cases the mortgagor will not be willing to enter into such an agreement because this would potentially speed up the enforcement procedure and thus lead to an earlier termination of his ownership of the immovable property. Furthermore, the parties are prohibited from agreeing on out-of-court enforcement in the following situations (in these events the mortgage may only be enforced using the court procedure):

- where the mortgage is subject to a consent by a third party;
- where the mortgaged property is an enterprise as a whole;
- where the mortgaged property is an agricultural land plot;
- where the mortgaged property has a substantial historical or other cultural value; or
- where the immovable property is jointly owned by several owners and one of the owners does not grant his consent to an out-of-court enforcement.

If the court procedure is the chosen method of enforcement, the mortgage- **19.85** holder must sue the mortgagor for enforcement of the mortgage in a court. The enforcement can be rejected by the court if the non-satisfaction of the secured debt is considered to be 'extremely minor'.[180] The enforcement can also be

---

[176] ibid Art 350(1).   [177] Law on Mortgage, Arts 51, 52.   [178] ibid Art 55(4).
[179] ibid Art 55(1). For limitations see ibid Art 55(2). Note that a court can invalidate the agreement if it violates the rights of a party, Art 55(5).
[180] ibid Art 54(1).

delayed by the court for up to one year (!) simply because the mortgagor is a natural person,[181] unless this delay would result in a substantial deterioration of the mortgageholder's financial condition.[182] The enforcement judgment given by the court must give details of not only the payable amount and the mortgaged property but also the sale procedure, the initial offering price, and protective measures.[183]

19.86 Mortgaged assets are typically sold in public auction[184] unless the parties have agreed on an out-of-court enforcement (to the extent that an out-of-court enforcement may be agreed upon)[185] or a private auction (to the extent that a private auction may be agreed upon).[186] A public auction must be announced at the latest thirty days, but not earlier than sixty days, prior to the auction date.[187] Participants in a public auction must make a deposit of a maximum of 5 per cent of the initial offer price.[188] The asset goes to the bidder offering the highest purchase price.[189] The highest bidder and the auctioneer (who stands in for the mortgagor) sign the auction minutes to confirm the sale. The actual sale and purchase agreement is then entered into between the auctioneer and the successful bidder, not later than five days after full payment of the purchase price.[190]

19.87 A private auction is conducted by a specialized auctioning organization.[191] The privately-held auction must be public like a court auction.[192] As in a court auction, the sale and purchase agreement is entered into by the auctioneer and the successful bidder not later than five days from full payment of the purchase price.[193] The procedure of enforcement and sale of immovable property is cumbersome and not suitable to encourage financial institutions, in particular, to use Russian law mortgages.

19.88 Enterprises subject to an enterprise hypothec can only be sold pursuant to a court judgment.[194] They shall be sold at auction as a whole.[195] The transfer of ownership in the assets of the enterprise must be registered with the Federal Registration Service.[196] It should be noted that the enterprise mortgage under Russian law does not provide the remedy of appointing a receiver or manager over the enterprise.

19.89 **Retention of ownership and security assignments**   Under a retention of ownership arrangement the person retaining ownership will ask the purchaser

---

[181] Law on Mortgage, Art 54(3).   [182] ibid Art 54(4).   [183] ibid Art 54(2).
[184] ibid Art 56(1).   [185] ibid Art 55(1).
[186] ibid Arts 56(2), 59. The requirements and limitations are the same as for out-of-court enforcement, ibid Arts 56(2), second and third sentences, 55(1), (2).
[187] ibid Art 57(3).   [188] ibid Art 57(4), second sentence.   [189] ibid Art 57(6).
[190] ibid Art 57(8).   [191] ibid Art 59(1).   [192] ibid Art 59(2).
[193] ibid Art 59(3).   [194] ibid Art 73(1).   [195] Pledge Law, Art 44(4).
[196] Law on Mortgage, Art 73(2).

of the secured asset to return possession of the secured asset to him. Where a security assignment of receivables has been agreed, the parties will have to agree how the security assignment can be enforced. In most cases the parties will agree that the assigned receivable has to be satisfied directly to the transferee.

(c) Distribution of realization proceeds

Distribution proceeds are paid in priority to the holder of the non-registered pledge up to the amount of the secured debt. Where the proceeds are not sufficient to satisfy the pledgeholder's secured debt he can seek satisfaction from the debtor's other assets under the secured debt. The law clarifies the point that in respect of the pledgor's assets, other than the secured assets, the pledgeholder has no preferential claims.[197] Any surplus from the sale of the pledged property has to be returned to the pledgor.[198]

19.90

Proceeds from the sale of mortgaged property are distributed to the mortgageholders, after deduction of the costs of enforcement and the sale of mortgaged property, the mortgageholders having notified the auctioning body of their secured debts. Remaining amounts are distributed to the mortgagor's other creditors and, lastly to the mortgagor.[199]

19.91

7. Slovak law

(a) Enforceability of the charge

If the claim secured by the charge is not duly (ie in the required amount and manner) and timely paid, the chargeholder may initiate enforcement of the charge.[200] The trigger for enforcement is failure to pay and other failures by the debtor or chargor; for example failure to maintain the charged assets or the violation of a financial covenant under the loan agreement (such as a certain relationship between a company's equity and debt) will not automatically give a right to enforce. However, it is usual to provide contractually for the creditor to be able to claim immediate payment if certain 'events of default' occur which extend well beyond the mere non-payment of a payment obligation.[201] In that way the chargeholder can choose to 'accelerate' the debt (ie to declare it due and payable) if the chargor is in breach and can then commence enforcement if there is a failure to pay the debt that has become due.[202]

19.92

---

[197] Civil Code, Art 29.   [198] ibid Art 30.   [199] Law on Mortgage, Art 61.

[200] Civil Code, §151j(1).

[201] See eg J-H Röver, 'Projektfinanzierung', in UR Siebel (ed), *Handbuch Projekte und Projektfinanzierung* (Munich, 2001) 217–22.

[202] Allen & Overy and EBRD, *Guide for Taking Charges in the Slovak Republic* (Bratislava, 2003) 27.

(b) Methods of enforcement and commencement of enforcement proceedings

19.93 The chargeholder can choose between different methods of realization:[203]

(1) the method defined by the parties under the charge agreement, which will often be a private sale to a third party or the transfer of ownership in the charged asset to the chargeholder (the latter agreement is only possible after the secured claim has become due[204] and thus the charge becomes enforceable pursuant to §151j(1) of the Civil Code—it seems also that an agreement on a transfer of ownership in the charged asset to the chargeholder is rare in practice and it can only be defined in the charge agreement subject to later agreement);

(2) a public auction under the Law on Voluntary Public Auctions which was introduced at the same time as the new Slovak provisions on charges;[205]

(3) a distinct way of receiving satisfaction of the secured claim exists for charges over claims for money by receiving direct payments from the sub-debtor;

(4) similarly the chargeholder may have a distinct way of receiving satisfaction where the charged property extends to insurance claims;

(5) although Slovak law provides for enterprise charges and enforcement of these charges is envisaged,[206] the law does not include any special provisions concerning realization of a charge over an enterprise; however, the legislator seems to have been open to agreements between the chargor and the chargeholder on the method of enforcement of an enterprise charge.[207]

19.94 It is noteworthy that Slovak law puts strong emphasis on alternative methods of enforcement. This is driven by the experience that court procedures are often lengthy. The Slovak legislator expects that public auction and private sale should dramatically shorten the time needed for enforcement since the process will be within the control of the chargeholder.[208] Although there are no public statistics to prove this, practical experience since enactment of the new provisions on charges seems to support this expectation.

19.95 In order to commence enforcement of the charge, the chargeholder has to notify the chargor (and the debtor, if different from the chargor) in writing about such commencement, specifying the method of realization. In addition, the

---

[203] Civil Code, §151j(1).

[204] ibid §151j(3). Similar to the prohibition of an automatic transfer clause ('*Verfallklausel*') under German pledge law (German Civil Code, §1229).

[205] Act No 527/2002 on Voluntary Auctions and supplementing Act No 323/1992 on Notaries and Notaries' Activities.

[206] Civil Code, §151j(5).

[207] Allen & Overy and EBRD (n 202 above) 30 (practice note). A model for respective provisions may be found in the EBRD Model Law on Secured Transactions.

[208] Allen & Overy and EBRD (n 202 above) 28.

commencement of enforcement shall be registered if the charge is registered in the charges register.[209]

Prior to realization by public auction or by the enforcement method defined in the charge agreement (mostly private sale) a period of thirty days—after (a) the notice of commencement of enforcement is given to the chargor (and the debtor, if different from the chargor), or (b) if later, the date of registration of the commencement of enforcement of the charge in the charges register (for a registered charge)—has to elapse.[210] However, the chargor may agree to a shorter period than thirty days *after*[211] the commencement notice has been given.[212]   **19.96**

The chargor is obliged to hand over to the chargeholder the charged assets and any documents necessary for taking over, transfer, and enjoyment of the charged assets, and further to cooperate as provided in the charge agreement.[213] The same duty is imposed on a third party in possession of the charged assets or of any such documents. The chargor is liable for any damages arising from his breach of these obligations.[214] However, it should be noted that in order to enforce the right to possession, the chargeholder would have to go to court or have an executory title such as a notarial deed, to obtain execution.[215] The right to possession cannot be exercised by the chargeholder's self-help against the chargor's will.   **19.97**

The parties may provide in the charge agreement for the method of sale on enforcement. The chargeholder acts in the name of the chargor for purposes of the sale.[216] Hence, the chargeholder acts as the representative of the chargor for the purposes of forming the sales agreement. Consequently, the purchaser will acquire from the chargor (and receive ownership from him).[217] The chargeholder is also under a duty to inform the chargor about the process of enforcement, and in particular about facts that may have a negative impact on the price achieved at sale.[218] The chargeholder must act with due care so that the charged asset is sold for a price for which it or a similar asset is normally traded under comparable circumstances at the time and place of sale.[219] Subject to that, the method of sale can be as agreed between the parties in the charge agreement. Any agreement made before the secured claim becomes due which allows the   **19.98**

---

[209] Civil Code, §151l. Where there are several chargeholders, the enforcing chargeholder shall notify all chargeholders who have priority to the enforcing chargeholder, ibid §151ma(1).

[210] ibid §151m(1). Where there are several chargeholders, the thirty-day period runs from the date of delivery of the notification to all chargeholders, ibid §151ma(2).

[211] Hence, no *prior* agreement between the parties is possible.

[212] Civil Code, §151m(2).   [213] ibid §151m(4).   [214] ibid §420.

[215] Allen & Overy and EBRD (n 202 above) 29.   [216] Civil Code, §151m(6).

[217] Under Slovak law it is unclear whether the purchaser can acquire the asset in good faith if the chargor was not the owner of the secured asset.

[218] ibid §151m(7).   [219] ibid §151m(8).

chargeholder to acquire the charged assets as satisfaction for his claim, is null and void.[220] After the secured claim has become due such agreement is permitted.[221] During enforcement proceedings governed by the charge agreement the chargeholder may decide that it wants to change the manner of enforcement of the charge and sell the collateral at auction or claim satisfaction in enforcement proceedings led by executors. The private executors are licenced to conduct auctions; they have replaced court bailiffs, who were previously responsible for enforcing security rights under Slovak law. The chargeholder must notify the chargor of such a change.[222]

19.99 The new Law on Voluntary Public Auctions, which came into force in January 2003, provides a framework for the rapid and efficient sale of the charged assets at auction. The chargeholder acts in the name of the chargor for purposes of the sale (ie as the chargor's representative)[223] and is under a duty to inform the chargor about the process of enforcement, and in particular about facts that may have a negative impact on the price obtained at sale.[224]

19.100 The secured creditor may apply for enforcement by an assigned executor once judgment has been obtained or on the basis of an enforceable notarial deed. The submission is made to the executor under the Execution Act. The executor organizes the sale of the charged assets by auction and the proceeds are paid to the enforcing chargeholder after deduction of costs. The procedure tends to take a long time, even where an enforceable notarial deed is used.

19.101 In principle, the method of realization for claims of the chargor against a sub-debtor is the same as for any other asset, and the claims can be sold by auction, private sale, or enforcement by an assigned executor.[225] In practice this may often be unsatisfactory, particularly where the claims are close to maturity. Alternatively the chargeholder may wait for the claims to be paid by the sub-debtor without taking any enforcement procedures. If the sub-debtor has been notified of the charge, he is obliged to pay to the chargeholder and the chargeholder is entitled to satisfy his claim out of the money so received. Any surplus must be returned to the chargor.[226]

19.102 Where the charged property extends to insurance claims the chargeholder may wait for the claims to be paid by the insurer without taking any enforcement procedures. If the insurer has been notified of the charge he is obliged to pay to

---

[220] ibid §151j(3). Similar to the prohibition of an automatic transfer clause ('*Verfallklausel*') under German pledge law (German Civil Code, §1229).
[221] Allen & Overy and EBRD (n 202 above) 30.   [222] Civil Code, §151m(3).
[223] ibid §151m(6).   [224] ibid §151m(7).   [225] ibid §151mb(5).
[226] ibid §151mb(3), (4); Allen & Overy and EBRD (n 202 above) 30.

the chargeholder and the chargeholder is entitled to satisfy his claim out of the money so received. Any surplus must be returned to the chargor.[227]

The purchaser of the charged asset in enforcement procedures is protected even **19.103** if he acquires by way of private sale or public auction. The chargeholder acts in the name of the chargor for purposes of the sale of the collateral (ie as the chargor's representative)[228] and the purchaser will acquire free from the charge.[229] A purchaser of the assets on enforcement does not have to concern himself with the validity of enforcement procedures. It is adequate for him or her to check that the commencement of enforcement is registered (where relevant).[230] The position is less clear where no valid charge was created in the first place: in such a situation the purchaser will have contracted with the chargeholder who is not able to sell the supposedly charged property without the consent of the chargor. In these situations the most likely outcome is that the purchaser will not acquire ownership in the supposedly charged asset. Note that this situation is different from the situation in which the chargor is not the owner or holder of the charged asset, in this case the purchaser can obtain ownership under the good faith provisions of the Civil Code.

The costs of the different enforcement procedures[231] will, in practice in most **19.104** cases, lead to an enforcement by private sale or public auction. Enforcement by the executor involves in addition to the parties' own costs (such as the fees of professional advisers) and any taxes payable on the transfer of the charged assets, court fees, the fees of the executing court officer under the Civil Procedure Code (2 per cent of the enforced claim, with a maximum of SKK100,000), or the fees of the executor under the Execution Act (20 per cent of the enforced claim, with a maximum of SKK1 million). A public auction will involve, in addition to the parties' own costs, the fees and costs of the public auctioneer. A private sale will involve the parties' own costs and any costs incurred for realizing the private sale (such as advertising costs).

---

[227] Civil Code, §151mc(4).   [228] ibid §151m(6).

[229] ibid §151l(2), second sentence. Where there are several chargeholders, the purchaser will acquire the charged asset free of the charges of all other chargeholders if the chargeholder with first priority pursues enforcement, ibid §151ma(3), first sentence. However, if the chargeholder with first priority does not pursue enforcement, the purchaser will acquire ownership subject to the charges of the other chargeholders who have priority to the enforcing chargeholder, §151ma(5). Chargeholders who rank lower in the priority order will lose their charge (§§151ma(5), 151ma(3)) but are entitled to receive any remaining surplus of the realization proceeds. In the situation of §151ma(5), Civil Code, §151ma(7) places the difficult obligation on the enforcing chargeholder to inform the purchaser of the fact of acquisition subject to charges. §151ma(7) also requires the enforcing chargeholder and the purchaser to register the change in the person of the chargor in the charges register.

[230] Allen & Overy and EBRD (n 202 above) 31.   [231] ibid 29.

(c) Protection of charged assets during enforcement proceedings

19.105 The person in possession of the secured assets during enforcement must refrain from doing anything which might be detrimental to the value of the charged assets, except for normal wear and tear.[232] The chargor is not allowed to transfer the collateral without the consent of the chargeholder.[233] However, a person who acquires the charged assets from the chargor in the normal course of business within the scope of the business activities of the chargor will acquire ownership which is free from the charge unless he knew, or ought to have known (ie did not act in good faith), of the commencement of enforcement.[234]

19.106 An unsecured creditor whose claim against the debtor is supported by either an enforceable judicial decision or an enforceable notarial deed may resort to a forced enforcement procedure against the debtor's assets in order to recover his debt. However, he may only obtain execution against the charged assets if the chargeholder consents.[235] Thus, a chargeholder cannot find that he has involuntarily lost his prior right in the charged assets to an unsecured creditor.

(d) Distribution of realization proceeds

19.107 In the case of private sale and public auction the chargeholder must prepare a written account of the sale for the chargor, giving all details of costs and the distribution of proceeds. The chargeholder must account for expenses incurred relating to enforcement of the charge.[236] Pursuant to §151l(3) of the Civil Code the chargeholder is entitled to receive reimbursement of such expenses.

19.108 If proceeds of sale of the collateral exceed the secured claim, the chargeholder shall hand over the surplus to the chargor without undue delay after deduction of reasonable expenses incurred in relation to the enforcement.[237] Where other chargeholders have a claim on the proceeds of sale, the surplus is deposited with a notary.

---

[232] Civil Code, §151m(5).   [233] ibid §151l(2), first sentence.

[234] ibid §151l(2), second sentence. The wording does not clearly distinguish between the acquisition of ownership in the charged asset and the acquisition free from the encumbrance. However, the chargor is not limited by the charge to transfer *in rem* ownership in the charged asset. §151l(2), second sentence, therefore, clarifies only that the purchaser acquires the ownership free from the charge.

[235] ibid §151h(6); Allen & Overy and EBRD (n 202 above) 25.   [236] ibid §151m(9).

[237] ibid §151m(10). Where there are several chargeholders the surplus will first be distributed among chargeholders before any remaining surplus will be distributed to the chargor, ibid §151ma(3), second sentence, and (4). Any surplus must be deposited by the enforcing charge-holder with a notary, §151ma(5).

C. Comparative Remarks and Evaluation

1. Analytical principles

Although the majority of security rights will never reach the enforcement stage, **19.109** particular attention has to be paid as to what happens on enforcement, as the entire value of the security rights depends upon it. In normal commercial practice, the parties should want enforcement to be fair, quick, and efficient. In view of the risk-reducing function of security, the aim must be to maximize the securityholder's recovery. In this context it should be remembered that the security right not only has a positive function but also a negative one. It is not unusual for it to be used for protection against the enforcement actions of third parties.[238] It can be added that the mere prospect of an enforcement of the security right may in itself affect the debtor's actions as well as the actions of the person giving security.

A particular issue of enforcement is to what extent the enforcement system relies **19.110** on courts during the enforcement process. Most reference systems in central and eastern Europe now allow out-of-court sales for pledges in movable things. The only exceptions are Poland and Estonia. Enforcement systems, for example in Hungary and the Slovak Republic, have largely disbanded the requirement for court involvement. The only requirement for the secured creditor upon default is to notify the commencement of proceedings to the debtor and to publicize it in the pledge register.

2. Normative evaluation[239]

Out-of-court enforcement procedures seem generally more suited to maximize **19.111** the securityholder's recovery and thereby realize the risk-reducing function of security.

A critical feature for a workable enforcement system is the extent to which the **19.112** debtor can obstruct enforcement proceedings at every step of the process. Procedural review rights and long periods prior to the commencement of enforcement proceedings can significantly reduce the value of security.

---

[238] See 2.14 above.
[239] For a study on the efficiency of enforcement of security rights in central and eastern Europe, see EBRD, *Legal Indicator Survey 2003*; also printed in EBRD, *The Impact of the Legal Framework on the Secured Credit Market in Poland* (London, 2005) Appendix B.

20

SECURITY IN INSOLVENCY

A. Analytical Framework

Security rights face their ultimate test in the insolvency of the person giving **20.01** security (who may be different from the debtor of the secured debt). Although insolvency law is typically a separate area of law from secured transactions law, the following issues must be considered:[1]

(1) the nature of the remedies available to the securityholder (in particular whether the securityholder has the right of separation of secured assets from the insolvency estate, or the right of preferential payment out of the secured asset's proceeds of sale);

(2) the right of the insolvency administrator to postpone or modify such remedies in the interest of general creditors;

(3) priority rules, especially priorities granted to privileged claims such as unpaid wages, taxes, costs of the insolvency administrator, debts incurred by the insolvency administrator;

(4) the right of the insolvency administrator to avoid fraudulent or gratuitous transactions or transactions in the period leading up to insolvency.

The following comments will only provide general introductions to the insolv- **20.02** ency laws of the eastern European reference countries as far as security rights in

---

[1] See also E-M Kieninger (ed), *Security Rights in Movable Property in European Private Law* (Cambridge, 2004) 667.

insolvency are concerned. Insolvency law as such is outside the scope of this study.

B. Eastern European Secured Transactions Laws

1. Bulgarian law

20.03 An insolvency of the pledgor does not suspend the enforcement proceedings already started with respect to an asset encumbered by a registered pledge. In addition, if insolvency proceedings are opened but the enforcement of the registered pledge has not yet begun, the insolvency administrator has to surrender pledged assets to the pledgeholder for enforcement outside insolvency proceedings.[2] In principle, the registered pledge provides a right for separate enforcement to the pledgeholder[3] which confirms the nature of the registered pledge as a property right. The non-registered pledge and the mortgage, however, give only the right to preferential satisfaction. Retention of ownership and security transfers provide a right of separate satisfaction. The respective assets can be separated from the insolvency estate and sold separately from the insolvency proceedings.

2. Czech law

20.04 Security rights can fall into one of two categories under Czech insolvency law. Either (1) the securityholder can claim the secured asset from the insolvency administrator and enforce his security right independently from insolvency proceedings,[4] or (2) the insolvency administrator can enforce the security right and the securityholder has a right to preferential satisfaction from the sales proceeds.[5] Retention of ownership clauses fall into the first category whereas liens, security transfer of ownership, and security assignments of receivables and other rights fall into the second category. Should the insolvency estate not be sufficient to satisfy all claims against the debtor, security rights from the second category will receive only up to 70 per cent of the sales proceeds from the sale of the secured asset.[6] This clearly limits the effectiveness of liens and security transfers under Czech law.[7]

---

[2] Law on Registered Pledges, Art 43.
[3] Similar to the separation of assets (‘*Aussonderung*’) under German insolvency law which does, however, not extend to limited security rights under German law.
[4] Insolvency Act, s 19(2).   [5] ibid s 28(1).   [6] ibid s 28(4).
[7] Also critical, TO Schorling, *Das Recht der Kreditsicherheiten in der Tschechischen Republik* (Berlin, 2000), 168–9.

3. Hungarian law

In insolvency proceedings the holder of a charge is in principle not entitled **20.05**
to sell the charged assets him or herself. Rather, the trustee in insolvency is
entitled to sell charged assets.[8] The chargeholder may not exercise his rights of
enforcement during insolvency proceedings[9] but he is satisfied from sales
proceeds.[10]

The insolvent person's debts shall be satisfied from its assets that are subject to **20.06**
insolvency proceedings in the following order:

(1) insolvency expenses;
(2) claims secured by a charge created prior to the time that insolvency proceedings were opened up to the value of the charged property and taking into
account the amounts already paid; if there is more than one charge on the
charged property the charges shall be satisfied in the order provided in
section 256(1) of the Civil Code; and
(3) unsecured claims.

Under Hungarian insolvency rules, the chargeholder is entitled to preferred **20.07**
satisfaction in insolvency proceedings, but the current rule of the Insolvency Act
grants a separate satisfaction of the secured claim only up to 50 per cent of the
proceeds of the sale of the charged asset, the other 50 per cent is withheld for the
satisfaction of administrative costs and certain privileged claims. This changed
from 1 January 2006, when the 2006 amendment of the Insolvency Act entered
into force and the chargeholder is granted preferential satisfaction of its claims
after the deduction of the insolvency administrator's fees and the costs of
preservation and sale of the charged asset. The limitation of the preferred
satisfaction to the 50 per cent of the proceeds of the sale of the charged asset
no longer applies.

However, assets under a retention of ownership agreement do not become part **20.08**
of the insolvency estate and, therefore, the secured asset can be claimed by the
chargeholder from the insolvency administrator, enabling him to enforce his
security right independently from insolvency proceedings.

Security transfers of ownership and security assignments are recognized under **20.09**
Hungarian law but are rather unattractive. The Hungarian Supreme Court
decided that claims assigned by way of security are part of the insolvency estate
of the debtor and the assignee is not entitled to collect the claims assigned by
way of security after the commencement of insolvency proceedings. It was
argued that the assignee is to be treated as an unsecured creditor since the

---

[8] Law Decree No 11/1960, s 48(4).   [9] ibid s 48(1).   [10] ibid s 48(2).

Insolvency Act recognizes only a chargeholder as a secured creditor. The security transfer of ownership was re-characterized as a charge by the Supreme Court and is therefore subject to the respective form requirements.

4. Polish law

20.10   In insolvency proceedings secured property of a Civil Code or registered pledge is to be sold at public auction or by private sale if a judge consents.[11] The proceeds of sale will be used first to meet the costs of the sale and then for the satisfaction of the secured claim. Any remaining proceeds will go to the insolvency estate.

20.11   As far as mortgages are concerned, real estate is to be sold in a public auction or by private sale if the council of creditors consents (Article 320 of the Law on Insolvency and Restructuring (LIR)). For the obligations which are to be satisfied first see Articles 345 and 346 of the LIR:

> [Article 345] 1. Unless a special provision stipulates otherwise, liabilities secured by a mortgage, pledge, registered pledge, fiscal pledge, mortgage of ships, or rights as well as personal rights and claims encumbering immovable property . . . shall be satisfied out of the proceeds of the sale of the encumbered asset, diminished by costs related to the sale. 2. Obligations referred to in para. 1 shall be satisfied in the order of their priority. 3. Interest included in the security referred to in para. 1 and costs of proceedings in an amount of not more than one tenth of the principal obligation shall be satisfied together with the principal obligation.
>
> [Article 346] In the case of sale of immovable property, a right to perpetual usufruct, cooperative right to a housing unit or sea ship entered in the register of ships, which is encumbered by a mortgage, mortgage of ships or rights as well as personal rights and claims . . . the obligations satisfied before satisfaction of obligations thus secured shall be obligation from child support and alimony as well as wages of the bankrupt's employees working on the sold immovable property or sea ship for the last three months before the day of their sale, but only up to the amount of three times the minimum wage, as well as pensions due for causing an illness, incapacity to work, invalidity or death.

20.12   According to Article 70 of the LIR parts of assets not belonging to assets of the bankrupt (in particular assets under a retention of ownership clause) shall be excluded from the bankruptcy estate. When the bankrupt has sold assets subject to exclusion, the performance provided for the sold assets shall be issued to the person to whom these assets had belonged, if the performance is separated in the bankruptcy estate (Article 71(1) of the LIR). According to Article 72

---

[11] Law on Insolvency and Restructuring (LIR), Arts 320, 325, 326.

the owner of the assets may demand their release or a counter-performance with reimbursement of expenses for maintaining these assets or for obtaining counter-performance, borne by the bankrupt or out of the bankruptcy estate.

5. Romanian law

In principle, the secured property will be sold by the insolvency administrator **20.13** in insolvency proceedings as provided by Law No 85/2006 on Insolvency Proceedings (the 'Insolvency Act'). However, if the securityholder has started steps to enforce his security right in movables, he may continue enforcement even during an intervening insolvency. The securityholder may even claim a transfer of possession of secured movables from the insolvency administrator.[12] Furthermore, pursuant to Article 39 of the Insolvency Act the person holding a security right in movables or a mortgage shall file an application with an insolvency court to order the immediate appraisal and sale of the secured asset. However, this is will be approved only if the following requirements are met:

(1) the secured property is of minor importance for successfully completing a reorganization of a company;
(2) the secured property is part of a functional unit and the value of the remaining assets will not be impaired by the secured asset's sale; or
(3) satisfaction from the secured asset is jeopardized because:
   (a) the value of the secured asset can decrease due to a real danger of constant deterioration,
   (b) the value of a lower ranking security right or mortgage can decrease because of an increase in the principal amount, the amount of accrued interest, or the amount of penalty payments secured by a higher ranking security right, or
   (c) of a lack of the secured asset's insurance against loss or deterioration.

However, in case (3) the insolvency judge may reject the creditor's application if **20.14** the insolvency administrator or the debtor proposes to taken certain measures providing comfort to the securityholder or the mortgageholder such as:

• periodical payments to the securityholder or mortgageholder covering the value decrease of the secured property or the value of a debt secured by a security right or mortgage with a lower ranking;
• periodical payments to the securityholder or mortgageholder; or
• the creation of additional proprietary or personal security.

The Insolvency Act specifies the order in which proceeds from the sale of **20.15** secured property shall be distributed among the creditors holding security rights

---

[12] Law Concerning Certain Measures for the Acceleration of the Economic Process, Art 86(2).

in movables or mortgages.[13] These are used, first, to pay expenses incurred in connection with the sale of the secured assets (and include expenses for the management and protection of such assets) and second, the debts secured by security rights in movables and mortgages (including the principal amount, any increases in the principal amount, interest and penalty payments, and incurred expenses (such as financing fees). Any surplus from a sale of secured property must be transferred by the securityholder to the insolvency estate of the person who has provided the security right.[14]

20.16 Security rights in movables created after the opening of insolvency proceedings are null and void.[15] The same applies to real estate mortgages.

6. Russian law

20.17 Another Achilles' heel of Russian secured transactions law is the treatment of non-registered and registered pledges in an insolvency of the pledgor. If the pledgor is a company, the pledged assets become part of the bankrupt's estate and are sold by the insolvency administrator. Pledges are satisfied from the proceeds of sale—once the costs of the insolvency have been satisfied—in third priority, after (a) the claims in damages for an individual's death or injury and (b) employee's claims arising under an employment contract with the pledgor.[16] If a bank becomes insolvent, a pledgeholder's claims under a pledge are also preceded by depositors' claims if the depositors are natural persons. This treatment of pledges seriously undermines the attractiveness of pledges and mortgages under Russian law. Assets secured under a retention of ownership or a security assignment remain outside the bankrupt's estate in an insolvency of the person giving security.

7. Slovak law

20.18 Where the chargor is declared insolvent, the right of sale of the chargor's estate (including the charged assets) is exclusively vested in the insolvency administrator.[17] Hence, the chargeholder can demand separate satisfaction from the charged asset in case of the chargor's insolvency, but he cannot himself enforce the charge during the insolvency proceedings. The chargeholder will cease to have the right to enforce the charge. Any enforcement proceedings underway when an insolvency declaration is made would automatically be discontinued. Under the previous version of the Bankruptcy Code, the

---

[13] Insolvency Act, Art 121.
[14] Law Concerning Certain Measures for the Acceleration of the Economic Process, Art 86(3).
[15] ibid Art 86(4).   [16] Civil Code, Art 64(1).
[17] Hence, the chargeholder can demand separate satisfaction from the charged asset in an insolvency of the chargor but he cannot himself enforce the charge in an insolvency situation.

chargeholder was entitled to receive the proceeds of realization of the charged assets subject to the administrator's right to retain up to 30 per cent (!) of the proceeds to cover the costs of the insolvency.[18] This provision has now been abolished with the new version of the Bankruptcy Code (Act No 7/2005) which came into force on 1 January 2006.

However, if the charge was created less than two months immediately preceding **20.19** the filing of a petition for the insolvency declaration, then the rights of the chargeholder to separate satisfaction from the charged assets cease to exist and the creditor will rank along with other unsecured creditors. Pending reform of the Slovak Bankruptcy Code it is unclear whether the relevant date for future assets is the date of charge registration or the date of acquisition of the assets by the chargor.[19]

As a general rule, no charge can be acquired over the debtor's assets during **20.20** insolvency proceedings, except for charges over future assets that were created and registered on behalf of the chargeholder prior to the insolvency declaration. This exception does not apply to charges over (future) proceeds from the sale of the chargor's assets during the insolvency proceedings.

Where an insolvent company's business is sold as a going concern, there is a risk **20.21** that the chargeholder may receive less than the real value of the charged asset because of the rules applicable to pro-rating the price between the assets of the business. This applies in particular to collateral which is more readily realizable, such as accounts receivable.[20]

The retention of ownership is not explicitly recognized as a security right by **20.22** the Bankruptcy Code enabling separate satisfaction from the secured assets. However, pursuant to the Slovak legal rules on the retention of ownership, the ownership of the movable assets does not pass to the purchaser before payment of the entire purchase price. Thus, the separation of the movable things from the debtor's assets during insolvency proceedings must be considered.

C. Comparative Remarks and Evaluation

Since the discussion of security rights in the insolvency of the person giving **20.23** security has been rather cursory, no discussion of comparative aspects will be included here. However, it should be mentioned that there are limits to the preferential treatment of the secured creditor in insolvency which do not render

---

[18] Allen & Overy and EBRD (eds), *Guide for Taking Charges in the Slovak Republic* (Bratislava 2003) 25, 30.
[19] ibid 14.   [20] ibid 25.

the security impractical per se. In particular, there are three limitations which have to be considered:

(1) Even if the secured creditor can satisfy its secured claims in a preferential way in the insolvency of the person providing security, he may not be the first one to be satisfied out of the insolvency estate. The costs of the insolvency procedure and the claims of a company's employees (for a certain limited period even after the insolvency has been opened) typically and justly rank prior to the secured claims of the secured creditors.

(2) A limitation of the secured creditor's security right may arise where the security has been received in a dubious way. This is mainly the case if the security was obtained only shortly before the insolvency was opened and also if security was granted without the person receiving security providing some real value in exchange. In such situations the security is vulnerable to avoidance by the insolvency administrator.

(3) In the insolvency of a company it must be the primary goal to ensure the survival of the company as a going concern by restructuring (either the company itself or the company's liabilities) or by selling it in its entirety. The secured creditors can easily defeat the attempt to achieve survival of an insolvent company by enforcing its security over assets which are essential for the operation of the company (such as machinery or real estate). For 'essential' assets of an insolvent company (what is essential must be defined by the insolvency administrator), the enforcement of security interests must be subject to a stay period. In effect, secured creditors may not, for a certain period of time, be able to seek satisfaction for the assets taken as security if those assets are essential for running an enterprise, unless the insolvency administrator allows the enforcement of the security rights.

21

TERMINATION OF SECURITY

A. Analytical Framework

Security rights create security only for a limited period of time. Their relation- **21.01**
ships to the secured debt and the secured property, which are typically close, are
reflected in the termination events of security rights.

B. Eastern European Secured Transactions Laws

1. Bulgarian law

The Law on Obligations and Contracts only provides the following cases of **21.02**
a termination of the pledge and mortgage:

- a pledge in movable things terminates if the pledged asset is returned to the
  pledgor;[1]
- if the registration of a mortgage (which is valid for ten years from the time of
  registration) expires, the registration may be renewed;[2]

---

[1] Law on Obligations and Contracts, Art 159 expresses this in a complicated way. According to
this provision the creditor 'shall be entitled to preferential satisfaction . . . only if he has not
returned the pledged asset to the debtor'.
[2] ibid Art 172.

- a mortgage expires if the mortgage property is sold publicly;[3] however, if prior to a public sale the mortgaged property was purchased by a third party and the property is then sold at a public auction, the mortgage also expires but other property rights will continue to exist.[4]

21.03 The Law on Registered Pledges is similarly silent on the events of termination of the registered pledge:

- The pledge terminates if the pledged property is transferred in the ordinary course of the pledgor's (who is in principle a merchant) business and the acquired rights are 'incompatible with the security rights'.[5] This means that the pledge will continue if a sale is outside the pledgor's ordinary course of business.
- The registration of the pledge is valid for a period of five years but can be renewed prior to its expiry.[6]

2. Czech law

21.04 A lien terminates:[7]

- if the secured claim terminates—this may occur if the secured claim is satisfied[8] or if the creditor waives the secured claim in writing pursuant to section 574 of the Civil Code; however, the lien is not affected if the secured claim is statute barred;[9]
- with the secured asset ceasing to exist;
- if the lien is waived by the lienholder in a written unilateral act;
- if a time limit of the lien has expired;
- if the secured asset has been exchanged by a deposit in an amount equal to the market value of the secured asset, however, the method for determining the secured assets value is controversial;[10]
- if the person giving the lien and the person taking the lien so agree;
- other cases provided by law—including the case where a lien has been created

---

[3] Law on Obligations and Contracts, Art 175.

[4] ibid Art 176. See also ibid Art 178 for the situation where a third party purchases the mortgaged property from the mortgagor.

[5] Law on Registered Pledges, Art 7; the latter will be the case if the purchaser acquires ownership in the pledged property.

[6] ibid Art 30(2).   [7] Civil Code, s 170(1).

[8] Pursuant to Civil Code, s 559(1) if the Civil Code is applied to the secured claim, or under Commercial Code, ss 324 *et seq* if the Commercial Code is applied to the secured claim.

[9] Civil Code, s 170(2); this is similar to German Civil Code, §216(1).

[10] See TO Schorling, *Das Recht der Kreditsicherheiten in der Tschechischen Republik* (Berlin, 2000) 57–8, whose remarks are related to the respective provision in effect prior to the Civil Code revision becoming effective from 2002 (ie Civil Code, s 151g).

two months or less before the debtor's insolvency[11] and the situation of a judicial sale of the secured real estate, which terminates the lien.[12]

A special provision exists for a lien on a right to claim transfer of possession to an asset. If the asset is delivered to the creditor, the lien on the right will terminate. However, as a substitute, the asset will now be encumbered automatically by operation of law by a lien.[13]   **21.05**

The security transfer of ownership in movable things terminates once ownership is re-transferred to the person giving security. This can occur on the basis of a condition subsequent (payment of the secured debt) or by way of a contractual retransfer of ownership.[14]   **21.06**

The retention of ownership in movable things terminates upon payment of the sales price or if ownership is acquired from the purchaser in good faith pursuant to section 446 of the Commercial Code. In the latter case the sale must be a commercial sale, possession to the movable asset must be transferred, and the purchaser must act in good faith with respect to the existence of the ownership of the transferor.[15] This is an exception to the general rule that good faith acquisition in movable things is not possible under Czech law.[16]   **21.07**

3. Hungarian law

A charge terminates in the following situations: **21.08**

- if the secured claim is satisfied from the charged asset, and debtor and chargor are different persons (the secured claim will be transferred by operation of law to the chargor to the extent that the secured claim was satisfied);[17]
- if the secured claim terminates or is transferred without transfer of the charged (unless the charge is maintained to secure a recourse claim);[18]
- if the secured claim becomes statute barred;[19]
- if the chargeholder acquires ownership of the charged asset;[20]
- if the charged asset is destroyed;[21]
- a possessory charge, if the charged asset is returned by the chargeholder to its owner (ie the chargor)[22] or the chargeholder loses possession to the charged asset without recovering it within one year.[23]

---

[11] See Insolvency Act, ss 14(1)f, 28(1); Schorling (n 10 above) 60 rightly pointed out that this provision seems to be too rigid in the sense that it does not take into account whether or not the debtor's creditors have actually suffered a disadvantage. Hence, the restructuring of loans to debtors in a critical economic phase is almost impossible to provide.

[12] Civil Procedure Code, s 337(1)d.   [13] Civil Code, s 167(2).

[14] Schorling (n 10 above) 88, 159.   [15] ibid 88.   [16] ibid 103.

[17] Civil Code, s 259(1).   [18] ibid s 259(3).   [19] ibid s 264(1).

[20] ibid s 259(4).   [21] ibid s 260(1).   [22] ibid s 265(6), first sentence.

[23] ibid s 265(6), second sentence.

21.09 A retention of ownership in movable things terminates upon payment of the sale price (ie if the condition precedent is realized) or if the asset is destroyed.

4. Polish law

21.10 Termination of a registered pledge will occur if a movable thing which has been taken as security becomes a component part of an immovable.[24] The pledge will also terminate if the pledged asset is sold pursuant to Article 13 of the Law on Registered Pledges and the Pledge Registry. The registered pledge also terminates if the secured claim terminates.[25] Apparently the termination of the pledge occurs automatically and any deregistration in the pledge register is merely of a declaratory nature. However, the parties must strike the pledge from the register once it terminates.[26] In addition, the registered pledge terminates if it is deregistered from the pledge register at the motion of the pledgeholder.[27] The law does not provide particular cases in which the pledgeholder shall deregister the pledge; in any event such deregistration will have constitutive effect. The Law on Registered Pledges and the Pledge Registry does not contain a provision on the termination of the pledge following the destruction of secured property but this must be a case in which the security right terminates by its very nature. However, Article 10 of the Law on Registered Pledges and the Pledge Registry stipulates that 'unless otherwise specified in the pledge agreement the collateral shall include any compensation obtained by the pledgor for the loss, destruction, damage, or devaluation of the collateral'.

21.11 A Civil Code pledge terminates if possession of the pledged asset is returned to the pledgor.[28] It also terminates if the secured debt is transferred without the pledge.[29] However, a Civil Code pledge does not terminate if the pledged asset is acquired by the pledgeholder, in particular if the pledged asset is also encumbered with the right of a third party and there is, thus, a reason for the pledge to continue;[30] in the opposite situation where there is no such right of a third party the pledge will terminate.[31]

21.12 The Law on Land Registry and Mortgages provides in detail for the various cases of termination of mortgages in real estate:

- termination of the secured debt[32]—however, if the personal debtor (who is different from the mortgagor) satisfies the mortgageholder, the mortgage is

---

[24] Law on Registered Pledges and the Pledge Registry, Art 9(1). In such a case the pledgeholder has the right to demand the creation of a mortgage over the real estate, Law on Registered Pledges and the Pledge Registry, Art 9(2).

[25] ibid Art 18(1).   [26] ibid Art 19.   [27] ibid Art 18(2).

[28] Civil Code, Art 325, §1.   [29] ibid Art 323, §1, second sentence.

[30] ibid Art 325, §2.   [31] ibid Art 325, §2 (indirectly).

[32] Law on Land Registry and Mortgages, Arts 84, 94.

transferred to him automatically by operation of law to the extent that it can secure a claim to receive satisfaction from the mortgagor;[33]

- deregistration of the mortgage from the land register without valid legal reason provided that ten years have expired;[34]
- release by the mortgageholder,[35]
- provision of a deposit with a court in the amount of the secured debt by the mortgagor without the right to receive the deposit back, provided that the secured debt has become due and the mortgageholder does not accept the satisfaction of the secured debt.[36]

The termination of the mortgage must be documented in the land register (but **21.13** is in most cases not essential for the termination to become effective) and there is an obligation on the parties to undertake the necessary actions, for example to apply for deregistration at the land registry.[37]

As far as retentions of ownership are concerned, there are two main situations in **21.14** which they terminate: (1) if the sales price is paid (and, hence, the condition precedent for the transfer of ownership in the secured asset fulfilled), and (2) if the secured asset is destroyed.

5. Romanian law

A security right in movables (no matter whether it is attached or perfected) **21.15** terminates in the following situations:

- satisfaction of the secured debt (unless the parties have agreed to cover also future debts);[38]
- release by the chargor;[39]
- the issue of a court order;[40]
- expiration of the security right notice after five years, unless the notice is renewed;[41]
- the Law Concerning Certain Measures for the Acceleration of the Economic Process does not contain a provision on the destruction of secured property but this must be a case in which the security right terminates by its very nature.

The security right does *not* terminate if the secured property is incorporated in **21.16** a new asset[42] or if it becomes accessory to real estate.[43] A termination of the

---

[33] ibid Art 97.   [34] ibid Art 95.   [35] ibid Art 96.   [36] ibid Art 99(1).
[37] ibid Art 100.
[38] Law Concerning Certain Measures for the Acceleration of the Economic Process, Art 27(1).
[39] ibid Art 27(2).   [40] ibid Art 27(2).   [41] ibid Art 44.
[42] ibid Art 24(1), second alternative ('an asset which incorporates the value of the secured property').
[43] ibid Art 24(2).

security right pursuant to Article 27(1) or (2) of the above-mentioned Law must be registered within forty days of the termination event.[44] An attached security right in movables will terminate over a secured asset's products if a securityholder only seeks enforcement with respect to the products.[45]

21.17 The following termination events are provided for real estate mortgages:

- the termination of the secured debt;
- the release of the mortgage by the mortgageholder;[46]
- the termination of the mortgage agreement;
- the termination of the mortgagor's ownership in the mortgaged real estate (*inter alia* if a third party acquires ownership by holding 'adverse' possession to the real estate,[47] so-called '*usucapio*');
- the destruction of the mortgage real estate, the mortgage over the destroyed asset ceases but the mortgage will be satisfied from the compensation paid under an insurance policy;
- expropriation of the real estate in the public interest; the mortgage will however, be satisfied from the compensation paid.

The termination of a real estate mortgage must be registered with the land register. In cases where the secured debt has been satisfied, the mortgageholder must issue a notarized declaration to the mortgagor.[48]

6. Russian law

21.18 Under Russian law a pledge terminates in the following situations:[49]

- if the secured debt ceases—however, if the debt is satisfied only partially the pledge will continue to exist (although only securing the remaining debt amount)[50] and in addition, where the secured debt is satisfied by a third person (ie not the debtor) the person satisfying the debt shall acquire both the secured debt (by way of legal assignment) and the pledge (again by operation of law);[51]
- if the pledged property is destroyed;
- if the right which has been pledged expires;
- if the pledgeholder acquires ownership of the pledged asset;

---

[44] Law Concerning Certain Measures for the Acceleration of the Economic Process, Art 27(3), first sentence.
[45] ibid Art 23(1). In practice the securityholder will therefore never limit enforcement to the products.
[46] Civil Code, Art 1800(1) No 3.   [47] ibid Art 1800(1) No 4 and (2).
[48] Law No 7/1996 on the Cadastre and Real Estate Publicity, Art 29(5).
[49] Pledge Law, Art 34.   [50] ibid Art 25.   [51] ibid Art 27.

- in other cases provided by law;[52]
- the parties may also agree to waive the rights under the pledge or to terminate the pledge.[53] In particular, the parties may terminate the pledge contract by novation (for example transforming the pledge relationship into a true sale and purchase) or the pledgor may transfer the ownership of the pledged property to the pledgeholder as token payment (or 'earnest money', in Russian '*ostupnoye*').

The Law on Mortgage provides almost no termination events for the mortgage. **21.19** One event mentioned is that the mortgage shall terminate upon the sale of the mortgaged property at public auction.[54] Since the mortgage is related to the secured debt the mortgage will terminate if the secured debt terminates.[55]

The contractual retention of ownership in movable things terminates upon **21.20** payment of the sale price. The purchaser cannot acquire ownership in the secured asset in good faith and hence this is not an event of termination for a retention of ownership arrangement. A security assignment of receivables terminates once the secured debt is satisfied.

7. Slovak law

Slovak law deals comprehensively with the termination events of security rights. **21.21** A charge under Slovak law terminates in the following situations:

- when the secured claim ceases to exist;[56]
- if the chargeholder transfers the secured debt without the charge, the debt becomes unsecured and the charge terminates since it cannot exist independently from the debt.[57]
- if the charged property ceases to exist[58]—if a charge covers several assets it will cease only if all assets cease to exist, if the charged assets are destroyed but

---

[52] Note that under the Civil Code the list of reasons for termination of a pledge is exhaustive despite the wording 'in other cases provided by law'.

[53] This is obvious. However, it is also indicated in Pledge Law, Art 25 ('unless otherwise provided for by the contract').

[54] Law on Mortgage, Art 58(2).

[55] For termination of the mortgage, see also Law on Mortgage, Art 42. If property has been mortgaged which was not owned by the mortgagor and he has to return the property to the rightful owner, the mortgage (which should not have been created in the first place) will terminate.

[56] Civil Code, §151md(1)a.

[57] See ibid §151a ('secure a claim'). There is no explicit provision in §151md which deals with termination events of the charge generally. However, the general concept of §151md(1)a pursuant to which the charge terminates when the secured claim ceases to exist, can be applied by way of analogy. This opinion seems to be shared by the commentary in Allen & Overy and EBRD (eds), *Guide for Taking Charges in the Slovak Republic* (Bratislava, 2003) 26.

[58] Civil Code, §151md(1)b.

were insured the charge will continue and cover any claim for insurance[59] (the charged assets will also cease to exist (and with them the charge), if they are merged with or incorporated into other assets and thus cease to be identifiable or separate, for example this is the case when raw materials are used in a manufacturing process and become merged with or incorporated into new goods;[60]

- if the chargeholder gives up the charge;[61]
- if a time period for which the charge has been established lapses[62]—however, in principle (and in practice!) the registration does not have to be renewed after a certain period of time;[63]
- upon return of a movable charged asset to the chargor if the charge has been created by way of transfer of possession, ie is a possessory charge;[64]
- if the chargor transfers ownership in the collateral and the charge agreement provides that the chargor may transfer the collateral or part thereof free of the charge;[65]
- another reason specifically provided in the charge agreement;[66]
- if the chargor and the chargeholder agree to terminate the charge; and
- if the chargeholder waives his right to the charge.[67]

21.22 It should be noted that the continuing registration of an already terminated charge is not able to create any rights for third parties. There is no good faith acquisition of a charge on the basis of a registration in the charges register.

21.23 Most of the above-mentioned termination grounds apply *mutatis mutandis* to the retention of ownership.

C. Comparative Remarks and Evaluation

1. Analytical principles

21.24 Typically national laws are not systematic when it comes to defining termination events of security rights. Termination of ancillary security rights is mainly a consequence of the close relationship between the security right and (a) the secured debt and (b) the secured property.

---

[59] Civil Code, §151mc(3); Allen & Overy and EBRD (n 57 above) 11–12, 26. However, the chargor is under no obligation to insure the charged property, §151mc(1)—hence, 'charged property' in §151md(1)b must not be the asset initially taken as security.
[60] Allen & Overy and EBRD (n 57 above) 26.   [61] Civil Code, §151md(1)c.
[62] ibid §151md(1)d.   [63] Allen & Overy and EBRD (n 57 above) 23.
[64] Civil Code, §151md(1)f.   [65] ibid §151md(1)g.   [66] ibid §151md(1)h.
[67] Allen & Overy and EBRD (n 57 above) 26.

2. Normative evaluation

Termination is far from being a mere technical issue of secured transactions law. **21.25**
Without the ability to create flexible security rights with respect to the secured
debt and the secured property, a secured transactions law is unworkable in
commercial practice.[68] Hence, termination events must be drafted in a way that
reflects the need for flexible security rights.

---

[68] See 11.48 and 12.62 above.

22

CONCLUSION

A. The International Interest in Secured Transactions [1]

22.01 If contract law was the favourite subject of comparative lawyers from the 1950s, security law has joined the ranks of the favourite subjects of studies and international reform efforts since the early 1990s. This was supported by two factors: first, the fundamental importance of security in lending transactions and thus for the economy at large; second, the difficulty of creating effective security due to (a) outdated national laws and (b) the fact that national limitations on the scope of security interests in cross-border situations demanded action at both national and international level. There are three main approaches demonstrating the international interest in secured transactions: (1) international treaties, (2) regulations and directives of the European Union, and (3) proposals for national laws deriving from various sources.

1. International treaties

22.02 The first group of international treaties relates to transport law. The conventions in the area of transport law provide for the mutual recognition of national security interests. To a large extent they also define the minimum content of

---

[1] For an overview of the various efforts to reform secured transactions law by way of international or supranational instruments, see Röver, *Prinzipien* 27–42 and HL Buxbaum, 'Unification of the law governing secured transactions: progress and prospects for reform' (2003) 8 *Uniform Law Review/Revue de droit uniforme* 321.

recognition. The conventions on security interests in ships are a case in point.[2] They regulate contractual and statutory security interests in ships and have largely unified the rules in this area. They provide, in particular, for the recognition of national, contractual security interests in the convention's Member States[3] as far as they are registered; the security interests' creation requirements are left to the applicable national law. In addition, the conventions provide statutory security rights which secure special types of debt.[4] The conventions stipulate that for statutory security interests with a wider scope established by national law,[5] and for enforcement issues,[6] national law continues to be applicable. Hence, the conventions contain some rules of substantive law on the content of the recognition (in particular the priority of security rights in ships and their termination) as well as conflict rules for determining the applicable law. Where the conventions do not provide a rule of substantive law or conflict of laws, a solution has to be found with the assistance of conflict rules of national law.

22.03 There are further conventions for aircraft[7] and transport assets.[8] The Geneva Convention on the International Recognition of Rights in Aircraft regulates, in particular, the recognition of contractual interests *in rem* which are registered,

---

[2] International Convention for the Unification of Certain Rules Relating to Maritime Liens and Mortgages, Brussels 10 April 1926 ('Brussels Convention 1926'); International Convention for the Unification of Certain Rules Relating to Maritime Liens and Mortgages, Brussels 17 May 1967 ('Brussels Convention 1967'); Convention on the Registration of Inland Navigation Vessels, Geneva 25 January 1965 and Protocol No 1 Concerning Rights *in Rem* in Inland Navigation Vessels and Protocol No 2 Concerning Attachment and Forced Sale of Inland Navigation Vessels ('Protocol No 1 and Protocol No. 2'); International Convention on Maritime Liens and Mortgages, Geneva 6 May 1993 ('Geneva Convention 1993', not yet in force), which will replace the Brussels conventions of 1926 and 1967.

[3] See Brussels Convention 1926, Art 1; Brussels Convention 1967 Art 1; Protocol No 1, Arts 5, 8; Geneva Convention 1993, Art 1.

[4] See Brussels Convention 1926 Art 2; Brussels Convention 1967, Art 4(1); Protocol No 1, Art 11; Geneva Convention 1993, Art 4(1).

[5] Brussels Convention 1926, Art 3(2); Brussels Convention 1967, Art 6(1); Protocol No 1 Arts 12–13; Geneva Convention 1993, Arts 6, 7.

[6] Brussels Convention 1926, Art 16; Brussels Convention 1967, Art 2; Protocol No 1 Arts 10, 18c; Protocol No 2, Arts 4, sentence 2, and 13; Geneva Convention 1993, Art 2.

[7] Convention on the International Recognition of Rights in Aircraft, Geneva 19 June 1948; this convention is related to the Convention on International Civil Aviation, Chicago 7 December 1944, dealing with registration issues of aircraft; see also the Convention for the Unification of Certain Rules Relating to the Precautionary Arrest of Aircraft, Rome 1933, which, however, has not not been ratified by a single Member State of the Geneva Convention; these conventions will eventually be replaced by the UNIDROIT Convention on International Interests in Mobile Equipment and the Protocol Thereto on Matters Specific to Aircraft Equipment (see 22.04 below).

[8] International Convention Concerning the Carriage of Goods by Rail (CIM) of 1961, Art 56; International Convention Concerning the Carriage of Passengers and Luggage by Rail (CIV) of 1961, Art 56(3). These rules provide that rolling stock and transport equipment can in principle only be attached in enforcement proceedings in the state which owns the assets.

including security interests,[9] and the content of recognition. It underlines again that the enforcement procedure is governed by national law.[10]

The UNIDROIT Convention on International Interests in Mobile Equipment **22.04** and the Protocol Thereto on Matters Specific to Aircraft Equipment[11] is a modern attempt to reform the, now dated, framework of transport conventions. Prior to this convention UNIDROIT had already approached the subject of secured transactions with two instruments, namely the Convention on International Financial Leasing (Ottawa, 28 May 1988)[12] and the Convention on International Factoring (Ottawa, 28 May 1988).

The United Nations (UNCITRAL) Convention on the Assignment of Receiva- **22.05** bles in International Trade[13] and the Hague Convention on the Law Applicable to Certain Rights in Respect of Securities held with an Intermediary must also be mentioned in this context.[14] Whereas the former is concerned with the assignment of receivables, the latter deals with securities (both debt and equity instruments). Both conventions are currently in the process of collecting potential signatories and it is too early to tell how important they will become in practice.

2. Regulations and directives of the European Union[15]

To date, the European Union has only launched a few initiatives in the area of **22.06** the Member States' property law.[16] In force is Directive 2002/47/EC of the

---

[9] Convention on the International Recognition of Rights in Aircraft, Geneva 19 June 1948, Art I(1).

[10] ibid Art VII(1).

[11] R Goode, *Convention on International Interests in Mobile Equipment and Protocol Thereto on Matters Specific to Aircraft Equipment. Official Commentary* (Rome, 2002). In an earlier draft of the Convention, see J-H Röver, 'Preparation of a Unidroit Convention on security interests in mobile equipment' (Summer 1994) *Law in Transition* 15–16.

[12] C Dageförde, *Internationales Finanzierungsleasing* (Munich 1992).

[13] The text can be found at <http://www.uncitral.org>. For an analysis of the convention, see SV Bazinas, 'Der Beitrag von UNCITRAL zur Vereinheitlichung der Rechtsvorschriften über Forderungsabtretungen: Das Übereinkommen der Vereinten Nationen über Abtretungen von Forderungen im internationalen Handel' (2002) ZEuP 782; SV Bazinas, 'Key Policy Issues of the United Nations Convention on the Assignment of Receivables in International Trade' (2003) 11 Tulane JICL 275; E-M Kieninger and E Schütte, 'Neue Chancen für internationale Finanzierungsgeschäfte: Die UN-Abtretungskonvention' (2003) ZIP 2181. In an earlier draft of the Convention, see J-H Röver, 'Unification work by UNCITRAL on assignment of claims' (Winter/Spring 1994) *Law in Transition* 28.

[14] F Reuschle, 'Haager Übereinkommen über die auf bestimmte Rechte in Bezug auf Intermediär-verwahrte Wertpapiere anzuwendende Rechtsordnung' (2003) IPRax 495.

[15] For more detail, see E-M Kieninger (ed), *Security Rights in Movable Property in European Private Law* (Cambridge, 2004) 22–4.

[16] Initiatives in the area of national property law are not excluded by Art 295 EC, which provides that the EC 'Treaty shall in no way prejudice the rules in Member States governing the

---

European Parliament and of the Council of 6 June 2002 on Financial Collateral Arrangements,[17] which the Member States had to implement by 27 December 2003. Financial collateral arrangements are ownership transfers (for example repurchase or so-called 'repo' arrangements) or limited security rights (for example pledges) in financial assets (such as shares and debt instruments). These arrangements are based on the security rights to be found under national laws.

22.07 Initially there were plans to deal with retention of title arrangements under the Late Payment Directive.[18] However, the current Article 4(1) of this Directive refers to national conflict of laws rules only[19] and adds no provisions of substantive law.

22.08 For some time now the European Commission has also been looking into proposals with respect to mortgage credits.[20] One potential approach is the introduction of a European mortgage with identical, or at least similar, rules throughout the Member States of the European Union.[21]

3. Proposals for national laws

22.09 Many academics have held Article 9 of the Uniform Commercial Code (UCC) to be a model for the reform of their own or foreign national legislation. The Code has certainly influenced academic writing a great deal. In central and eastern Europe, however, so far only Albania,[22] Kosovo,[23] Montenegro,[24] and to

---

system of property ownership' since this provision's scope is limited to ownership issues (in particular expropriation) and does not extend to property rights as such; see M Schweitzer in E Grabitz and M Hilf (eds), *Das Recht der Europäischen Union* (Munich, looseleaf) vol III, Art 295 EC n 3.

[17] KM Löber, 'Der Entwurf einer Richtlinie für Finanzsicherheiten' (2001) BKR 118; KM Löber, 'Die EG-Richtlinie über Finanzsicherheiten' (2002) BKR 601.

[18] [2000] OJ L200/35.   [19] Kieninger (n 15 above) 23–4.

[20] Green Paper: *Mortgage Credit in the EU* COM(2005) 327 final.

[21] OM Stöcker, *Die 'Eurohypothek'.* (Berlin, 1992).

[22] Law on Securing Charges (adopted in October 1999), Art 2 provides: 'This Law governs any transaction, whatever its form and however it is denominated, that creates, whether by transfer of ownership, by possession such as in the case of a pledge or otherwise, a securing charge in movable things, intangible property, or rights of their owner.'

[23] Regulation 2001/5 (adopted on 7 February 2001), Art 1(3), which provides that 'the present regulation applies to all transactions, regardless of form, intended to create a pledge'. It excludes mainly mortgages in real estate from the scope of the regulation.

[24] Law on Secured Transactions (adopted on 19 July 2002), Art 1(3) has the same wording as the respective provision of the security regulation of Kosovo. Mortgages in real estate are also excluded.

a certain extent Bulgaria[25] and Romania[26] have introduced security rights in movables which are modelled closely on Article 9.[27]

The EBRD contributed to the discussion of the reform of national secured **22.10** transactions laws in 1994 with the publication of the Model Law on Secured Transactions. Later the EBRD added Core Principles for a Secured Transactions Law (1997) and in 2004 Guiding Principles for the Development of a Charges Registry.

The idea of producing a model law on secured transactions had already been **22.11** pursued in the 1970s and early 1980s by UNCITRAL (although its effort was limited to movable property). The most significant result at the time was a comparative report produced by Ulrich Drobnig.[28] This study was ground-breaking in that for the first time it attempted to provide an overview of the security laws of the world with a special focus on Europe, the Americas, and Australia.[29] The project of producing a model law was, however, halted because the differences between various security regimes around the world were deemed to be too great to draft a model law which would bridge differences, in particular between common and civil law jurisdictions. UNCITRAL recently revived its efforts in the area of secured transactions and has taken an approach similar to that of the EBRD by drafting a Legislative Guide on Secured Transactions.[30] This has to be seen in combination with the UNCITRAL Legislative Guide on Insolvency Law[31] as far as the situation of security interests in insolvency is concerned. At some stage UNIDROIT also contemplated the preparation of a model law on secured transactions[32] but abandoned this plan.[33]

---

[25] Security devices, such as retention of ownership in movable things, leasing, security assignments of receivables, and security transfers of ownership created by a merchant or another qualified person, are perfected only if they are registered in the pledges register. However, they keep their distinct legal nature. For more detail, see 9.14 above.

[26] As under Bulgarian law, security devices are not re-qualified as security rights. See 9.19 above.

[27] For the importance of UCC, Art 9 in other parts of the world, see 6.20–6.21 above.

[28] Legal principles governing security interests (document A/CN.9/131 and annex) (1977) *VIII UNCITRAL Yearbook* 171–221. See also UNCITRAL, Note by the Secretariat on article 9 of the Uniform Commercial Code of the United States of America (document A/CN.9/132) ibid 222–31.

[29] For an overview of Asian laws, see DE Allan, ME Hiscock, and D Roebuck (eds), *Law and Development Finance in Asia* 11 vols (St Lucia, New York 1973–1980).

[30] The guide is still in draft form; its text is to be found at <http://www.uncitral.org>.

[31] This guide was adopted on 25 June 2004; its text is also to be found at <http://www.uncitral.org>.

[32] UNIDROIT, 1993, Study LXXII-Doc 7, para 15; UNIDROIT, 1993, Report on the 72nd Session of the Governing Council (International Aspects of security interests in mobile equipment); UNIDROIT, 1994, Study LXXII-Doc 12, para 8; J Simpson and J-H Röver, 'Comments on the UNIDROIT project for drawing up a check list of the issues to be addressed in a possible future model law in the general field of secured transactions', UNIDROIT, 1994, Study LXXIIA-Doc 3.

[33] See, however, the Organization of American States' (OAS) Model Inter-American Law on Secured Transactions which was adopted in 2002; for the text, see <http://www.oas.org/DIL/CIDIP-VI-securedtransactions_Eng>.

22.12 On the academic side, the 'Common Core of European Private Law' (or 'Trento') project has set out to establish the 'common core' of European laws. The project is based on Rudolf Schlesinger's factual approach[34] and is searching for the common ground for the future construction of a European *ius commune*. However, the part of the project which is dedicated to secured transactions[35] has not only pointed out limitations in the factual approach in the context of secured transactions law[36] but has not even assumed the presence of a common core. It remains, in its own words, an 'agnostic legal cartography'.[37] Also noteworthy are the drafts prepared by the Study Group on a European Civil Code, a network of academics from EU Member States preparing a codified set of principles of European law for the law of obligations and core aspects of the law of property.[38] The Study Group has already published draft articles on 'proprietary security rights in movable assets'.

4. The pattern of international efforts

22.13 Even this brief overview demonstrates the increased interest in secured transactions in recent years. A competition of international proposals seems to have developed, with Article 9 of the UCC still being one of the major models for the legal reform of secured transactions laws in the world. It is to be expected that in future even more models will come to the market.

22.14 It cannot be assumed that national secured transactions laws will converge soon. Security law remains deeply rooted in national property law. Harmonization efforts remain, therefore, limited to very specific security interests. General proposals are presented as guides and models (such as the EBRD Model Law on Secured Transactions) with the exception of Article 9 of the UCC. However, the interesting issue is whether an international consensus with respect to secured transactions is emerging from the international efforts. It seems, indeed, that on a general level such a consensus is developing which is also reflected in the development of central and eastern European secured transactions laws.[39]

22.15 A *functional* approach as found under Article 9 of the UCC, although often promoted, seems not to be the preferred route. Although the UNICTRAL Draft Legislative Guide on Secured Transactions recommends this approach[40] and the UNIDROIT Convention on International Interests in Mobile Equipment has adopted a functional approach towards interests[41] in mobile equipment covered

---

[34] See 4.31 above.   [35] Kieninger (n 15 above).   [36] ibid 27–8.
[37] ibid 28, 29.   [38] <http://www.sgecc.net>.
[39] See also Kieninger (n 15 above) 647–55, 658–63.
[40] UNCITRAL Legislative Guide on Secured Transactions, III.A.4.
[41] Note the terminology: the convention refers to 'interests' instead of 'security interests'.

by the convention (in particular aircraft),[42] it seems to remain an approach limited to a few jurisdictions or conventions. This does not necessarily coincide with a loss of economic efficacy in secured transactions law as some commentators believe. The requirements of publicity and the rules for priorities, enforcement, and insolvency cannot be implemented efficiently *only* under the reign of the functional approach.[43]

The renunciation of the functional approach coincides with the dichotomy   **22.16** of limited security interests and retention of title arrangements and other ownership-based devices. In particular, reservation of title now has such importance in the sale of goods that it is difficult to imagine economic life without it. The money purchase security interest under Article 9 of the UCC (which allows a party to perfect a security interest without filing notice, provided filing is eventually effected within a grace period of twenty days)[44] and the unpaid vendor's charge of the EBRD Model Law (which was not implemented in any of the central and eastern European countries) seem to remain as isolated examples. However, whether the retention of title must be registered to be perfected or to become effective is an issue which continues to arise in arguments for both solutions.

Another consensus seems to have developed with respect to party autonomy in   **22.17** the area of secured transactions. Security interests must be flexible as far as the secured debt and the secured property are concerned. Although property law is typically strictly regulated, general opinion now seems to favour the idea of allowing parties to remain flexible with respect to their arrangements regarding secured debt and secured property. As far as secured property is concerned, it should be possible to extend security interests to proceeds of sale and products by the parties' agreement. A further point is that the parties should be free in arranging the transfer of security. Security may often follow the transfer of the secured debt. However, the parties should remain free to agree otherwise.

Hand in hand with the decline of the requirement to transfer possession in   **22.18** order to create or perfect security in movable things, goes the rise of registration or filing as the appropriate means for publicizing security. Modern computer technology has made it possible to establish cheap and simple-to-administer computerized registration systems which have, however, been implemented only in a few places (for example Bulgaria, Hungary, and Slovakia, three central and eastern European reform countries). The difference in approach between notice filing (where reference to the security agreement is advisable) or registration

---

[42] Convention on International Interests in Mobile Equipment, Art 1(2).
[43] Röver, *Prinzipien* 177–8; see also 10.24–10.30 above.
[44] UCC, §9-317(e); see also the 'super-priority' of purchase money security interests over previously registered security interests provided in UCC, §9-324.

(which typically provides a summary of the most important elements of the security agreement) seems not to be material. Notification of the debtor of rights is—like possession in the area of movable things—on the decline.

22.19 Opinion seems to be divided on security in the assets of an enterprise. Although it is recognized as a useful tool in several countries (for example England, France, Hungary, and the Russian Federation)[45] it is rejected in other countries (such as the United States and Germany).[46] The property which can be subject to an enterprise security varies greatly from country to country. Certainly the tools of the administrator under English law and the enterprise administrator under the Model Law[47] remain isolated phenomena.

22.20 Furthermore, the security interest is predominantly seen as an ancillary interest to the secured debt. This results, in particular, in an automatic transfer of security where the secured debt is concerned (although the parties should remain free to provide otherwise). To a certain degree this may come into conflict with the registration requirement for the creation of security; however, this conflict can be avoided where the transfer of security is valid only if it has been registered. The automatic transfer does not take place where security is granted in the form of retention of title.

22.21 As far as priorities between several security interests are concerned, the consensus on registration means that the precise time of creation is the dominant priority rule.

22.22 Nowadays enforcement of security is no longer considered to be solely the domain of courts. Certainly the positive experience of common law countries (in particular the United States and England) with self-help mechanisms has opened the way for alternative methods of enforcement. There is now widespread support for enforcing security on the basis of the parties' agreement as long as the parties have not agreed a forfeiture clause (*pactum commissarium*) pursuant to which title in the secured property is transferred automatically to the securityholder if the person providing security defaults on the secured debt.

22.23 Lastly, the recognition of security and the effective protection of security in insolvency proceedings are widely supported. However, what limitations security interests should have in the debtor's insolvency is not yet clear. It seems that with this crucial question the emerging consensus on security currently ends.

---

[45] For an account of recent legislative developments in European countries, see Kieninger (n 15 above) 650–1.

[46] Note that Kieninger (n 15 above) 651 qualifies general security transfers of ownership and general security assignments as forms of enterprise charges. This is, however, debatable since these security rights cover only one type of property.

[47] Model Law on Secured Transactions, Art 25.

B. Security in Central and Eastern Europe

In reviewing several central and eastern European secured transactions laws, **22.24** the following examples of approaches to reform of this area of law were identified:

- A number of countries, for example Albania, Kosovo, and Montenegro, and to a limited extent Bulgaria and Romania, were strongly influenced by Article 9 of the UCC.
- The EBRD Model Law on Secured Transactions was influential, in particular, in Hungary, Moldova, and the Slovak Republic.
- The Russian Pledge Act has influenced a number of CIS countries.
- There were a number of countries which advanced national solutions, ie the Czech Republic, Poland, and the Baltic countries.

On the basis of this study it is possible to approach the question of whether a **22.25** consensus is emerging between central and eastern European laws and whether this consensus is similar to the international consensus formulated above. Broadly speaking, although one can identify four different strands of secured transactions law reform, the influence of Article 9 of the UCC and the EBRD Model Law in central and eastern Europe (either directly or indirectly), which both form part of the developing international consensus, largely assisted in the laws being reformed along the lines of the international consensus.

First, it should be mentioned that many of the central and eastern European **22.26** countries have reformed their secured transactions laws by introducing new laws which do *not* form part of their Civil Codes, the traditional place for secured transactions provisions in continental European countries.

The functional approach adopted by Article 9 of the UCC has been imple- **22.27** mented only by a few laws directly influenced by that Article.

The dichotomy between limited security rights and retention of ownership or **22.28** other ownership devices has become a characteristic of many central and eastern European secured transactions laws. In this respect it is interesting to note that, for example, Polish law has developed in a way similar to German law. Whereas the registered pledge in movables seems to be in decline, security transfers of ownership and security assignments of receivables seem to be on the rise in Polish practice.

Party autonomy in the form of flexibility concerning secured debt and secured **22.29** property has largely been welcomed by the central and eastern European secured transactions laws, although few laws express this as clearly as Slovak law. It was found that most laws introduced flexible security rights but the implementation of these concepts in practice seems to be in need of further work. There is, however, no clear trend in laws allowing secured property to extend to proceeds of sale or products by way of the parties' agreement.

22.30 The concept of a security right in the assets of an enterprise has been implemented to varying degrees, in particular as far as the property covered by such a security right is concerned. However, none of the central and eastern European countries has introduced a concept like the administrator under English law or the enterprise administrator under the EBRD Model Law.

22.31 Only a few countries still resist registration as a general means of publicity for security rights. Those central and eastern European countries (in particular Bulgaria, Hungary, and Slovakia) which have introduced workable computerized security registries (built on the advances of registration technology) have made a lasting contribution to the understanding of security practice.

22.32 Since most central and eastern European countries provide a security right as a right ancillary to the secured debt (with the notable exception of Hungarian law, which introduced an 'independent charge'), the transfer of the secured debt leads also to an automatic transfer of security.

22.33 Priorities are determined mostly in accordance with the time of the security right's creation. Defining priorities is greatly facilitated by the introduction of registries. Central and eastern European laws have often introduced out-of-court enforcement mechanisms and are fully united as far as the prohibition of the forfeiture clause (*pactum commissarium*) is concerned.

22.34 Insolvency law is the ultimate test of the efficacy of rights, and in particular of security rights. Although central and eastern European laws recognize in principle security rights in the insolvency of the person giving security, a consensus on the limitations of this recognition has not yet emerged.

22.35 Although a general consensus seems to be emerging from the reforms of central and eastern European laws, a major conclusion must still be that a reform of secured transactions law in central and eastern Europe cannot start from a simple, one-fits-all solution. Each country evidently needs a tailor-made solution which is suited in particular to its property law. Thus, the EBRD's approach of providing a model law as a drafting guideline in 1994, as well as its assistance in the form of 'guiding principles' which combine economically desirable approaches and legal issues, and practical reform projects tackling individual issues (in particular the establishment and improvement of registration systems) seems to be well suited to the special challenges of the reform of secured transactions law in the region.

22.36 Even though legal approaches may vary in different countries, there are overriding economic goals for secured transactions law which are sometimes obscured in individual systems. Legal reforms are sometimes focused on typical legal issues (for example fitting good faith acquisition into the national law) instead of identifying the economic basis for the new provisions. This can result in laws which are satisfactory from a purely technical point of view but which fail in practice. The Polish law on registered pledges in movables is a case in point.

Fifteen years after the commencement of the legal reform process in central and **22.37** eastern European secured transactions laws a diverse pattern of national laws has developed. It is a picture of successfully reformed countries, largely unreformed countries, and unsuccessfully reformed countries still struggling with the issue of security. Several countries have already announced that they will now open the next round of reform efforts (in particular Hungary). Despite the difficulties in drafting adequate secured transactions laws and implementing them properly, central and eastern European countries should be given credit for the enormous advances which they have achieved in a relatively short period of time. It is to be hoped that the reforms will continue with a clear focus on the economic rationale of secured transactions: to reduce the creditor's risk of extending credit.

Appendices*

* The information contained in the appendices may not be reproduced or transmitted in any form without the written permission of the EBRD.

APPENDIX 1

Text of the Model Law on Secured Transactions prepared by the European Bank for Reconstruction and Development (1994) [1]

TABLE OF CONTENTS

---

[1] See also <www.ebrd.com/country/sector/law/st.htm>.

PART 1
GENERAL PROVISIONS

Article 1
Nature of a Charge

1.1 Things and rights may be encumbered by the owner with a security right (called a charge) in order to grant security for a debt.
1.2 This law does not prevent a security right arising
   1.2.1 by operation of law or by judicial or administrative act; or
   1.2.2 pursuant to *[specific exceptions to be determined separately for each jurisdiction]*.

Article 2
Person Giving a Charge

Any person may grant a charge over his things and rights except that a natural person may grant a charge only as part of his business activity and only over things and rights used for that activity at the time of creation of the charge pursuant to Article 6.7. The person granting the charge is called the chargor.

Article 3
Person Receiving a Charge

3.1 A charge may be granted to any person or persons to whom the debt or any of the debts being secured is owed. The person receiving the charge or to whom it is transferred is called the chargeholder.
3.2 The chargeholder may appoint another person (called a charge manager) to act in his place in relation to a charge pursuant to Article 16.

Article 4
Secured Debt

4.1 A charge may secure one or more debts (called a secured debt).
4.2 For the charge to be valid the secured debt must be capable of expression in money terms whether in national or foreign currency or monetary units of account or any combination of these. A charge securing an obligation which is not yet translated into a money obligation is not enforceable until this translation occurs.
4.3 A secured debt may be
   4.3.1 owed by any person or persons who need not be the chargor;
   4.3.2 identified specifically or generally;
   4.3.3 governed by national or foreign law;
   4.3.4 conditional or future.

4.4 A debt which is created after the date of the charging instrument will be included in the secured debt if that debt is identified in the charging instrument.

4.5 The amount of the debt secured by a charge is limited to the maximum shown on the registration statement pursuant to Article 8.4.3 or, in the case of a possessory charge, in the charging instrument pursuant to Article 7.3.3 plus any additional amounts included pursuant to Article 4.6.

4.6 The following additional amounts are included in the secured debt unless otherwise agreed between the chargor and the chargeholder

   4.6.1 interest on the secured debt to the extent contractually payable from the time at which the charge is created or deemed to be created pursuant to Article 6.7 or 6.8 until the date of payment; and

   4.6.2 interest on the secured debt payable by operation of law; and

   4.6.3 reasonable costs properly incurred by the chargeholder in preserving and maintaining the charged property and in enforcing the charge; and

   4.6.4 damages for any breach of the contract under which the secured debt arises up to twenty per cent.

      4.6.4.1 of the maximum amount of the secured debt included in the registration statement pursuant to Article 8.4.3 or the charging instrument pursuant to Article 7.3.3; or

      4.6.4.2 in the case of an unpaid vendor's charge, of the unpaid part of the purchase price referred to in Article 9.2.1.

Article 5
Charged Property

5.1 A charge may encumber one or more things or rights (called charged property).

5.2 Charged property may comprise anything capable of being owned, in the public sector or in the private sector, whether rights or movable or immovable things, and including debts due from the chargeholder to the chargor. The charged property includes any thing or right which, at the time of creation of the charge or subsequently, is attached or related to the charged property and which on a transfer of ownership of the charged property as described in the charging instrument would be included with the charged property by operation of law.

5.3 Things or rights which are not capable in law of being transferred separately cannot be charged separately.

5.4 A charge is valid notwithstanding any agreement entered into by the chargor not to charge things or rights except

   5.4.1 where the charged property is a contractual obligation which is not a debt for money; or

   5.4.2 as provided under Article 12.6.

      An agreement that a contractual right which is not a debt for money is not transferable is deemed unless otherwise provided to be an agreement that the right cannot be charged.

5.5 Charged property may be identified specifically (in which case the charge is a specific charge) or generally (in which case the charge is a class charge).

5.6 Where a class charge covers

   5.6.1 all the things and rights used in an enterprise which is capable of operating as a going concern; or

   5.6.2 such part of the things and rights of an enterprise as needs to be transferred to enable an acquirer to continue the enterprise as a going concern;

   the charge may be registered as an enterprise charge pursuant to Article 8.4.5.

5.7 Charged property may be situated within or outside the jurisdiction.

5.8 A charge may be expressed to cover things and rights not owned by the chargor at the time at which the charge is deemed to be created pursuant to Article 6.8.

5.9 A charge extends to things and rights which become owned by the chargor after the charge is deemed to be created pursuant to Article 6.8 if they are identified in the charging instrument.

5.10 The charged property automatically extends to any rights of the chargor under any insurance policy which covers loss or reduction in value of the charged property.

PART 2
CREATION OF A CHARGE

Article 6
General Rules for the Creation of a Charge

6.1 A charge may be only
    6.1.1 a registered charge; or
    6.1.2 an unpaid vendor's charge; or
    6.1.3 a possessory charge.

6.2 A registered charge is created by
    6.2.1 the chargor and the chargeholder entering into a charging instrument pursuant to Article 7; and
    6.2.2 registration of the charge pursuant to Article 8.

6.3 An unpaid vendor's charge is created pursuant to Article 9.1.

6.4 A possessory charge is created by
    6.4.1 the chargor and the chargeholder entering into a charging instrument pursuant to Article 7; and
    6.4.2 possession of the charged property being given pursuant to Article 10.1.

6.5 A charge is created only if
    6.5.1 the chargor as referred to in Article 2 is the owner of the charged property; and
    6.5.2 the chargor has the power to grant the charge at the time the charge is created or deemed to be created pursuant to Article 6.7 or 6.8; and
    6.5.3 the charge secures a debt as referred to in Article 4.2.

6.6 An enterprise charge may only be created by a [*company*].

6.7 The time at which a charge over things or rights owned by the chargor is created is
    6.7.1 in the case of a registered charge, the time of registration of the charge pursuant to Article 34.4 unless the charge was initially created as an unpaid vendor's charge or a possessory charge in which case it is the time of initial creation in accordance with Article 6.7.2 or 6.7.3;
    6.7.2 in the case of an unpaid vendor's charge, the time at which title to the charged property is transferred to the purchaser pursuant to Article 9.1;
    6.7.3 in the case of a possessory charge, the later of possession of the charged property being given pursuant to Article 10.1 and the date of signature of the charging instrument by or on behalf of the chargor.

6.8 Where a registered charge is granted over things or rights not yet owned by the chargor the charge is deemed to have been created at the time provided under Article 6.7.1.

6.9 An unpaid vendor's charge or a possessory charge is converted into a registered charge upon registration in accordance with Article 8.2.

6.10 A chargor and a chargeholder may agree to add to the debt secured by a charge, to increase the maximum amount of the secured debt pursuant to Article 4.5, to add to the charged property or to convert a charge as described in Article 5.6 into an enterprise charge. Such addition, increase or conversion is treated as the creation of a new charge and is accordingly subject to all the provisions of this law.

Article 7
Charging Instrument

7.1 The chargor and the chargeholder must enter into an agreement (called a charging instrument) except in the case of an unpaid vendor's charge. One charging instrument may relate to one or more charges.

7.2 The charging instrument may be in the form set out in schedule 1.

7.3 In order to be valid the charging instrument must be in writing and include

    7.3.1 identification of the chargor, the person owing the secured debt (if not the chargor) and the chargeholder; and

    7.3.2 specific or general identification of the secured debt; and

    7.3.3 in the case of a possessory charge, the maximum amount of the secured debt expressed in national or foreign currency or monetary units of account or any combination of these; and

    7.3.4 specific or general identification of the charged property; and

    7.3.5 signatures by or on behalf of

        7.3.5.1 the chargor; and

        7.3.5.2 the chargeholder; and

    7.3.6 the date of the charging instrument being the date of signature by or on behalf of the chargor.

7.4 A charge is not valid unless the charging instrument contains a statement that the purpose of the document is to create a charge or such purpose is implied from the instrument.

7.5 The charging instrument may include such other matters as the parties agree and may, subject to Article 6.10, subsequently be amended by the parties. In order for an amendment to be of effect against third parties it must be registered pursuant to Article 33.1.1.

7.6 If a charging instrument is signed by a person acting on behalf of the chargor the charge is valid only if that person is independent of the chargeholder.

Article 8
Registered Charge

8.1 In order to obtain registration of a registered charge as referred to in Article 6.2 a registration statement must be presented at the charges' registry not later than 30 days after the date of the charging instrument as defined in Article 7.3.6. If a registration statement is not presented by that date the charge is not created.

8.2 In order to convert an unpaid vendor's charge or a possessory charge into a registered charge a registration statement must be presented at the charges' registry during the time provided in Article 9.3 or Article 10.2.

8.3 The registration statement may be in the form set out in schedule 2.

8.4 In order for a registered charge to be valid the registration statement must include

    8.4.1 identification of the chargor, the person owing the secured debt (if not the chargor), the chargeholder and the charge manager (if appointed); and

    8.4.2 specific or general identification of the secured debt; and

    8.4.3 the maximum amount of the secured debt expressed in national or foreign currency or monetary units of account or any combination of these; and

    8.4.4 specific or general identification of the charged property; and

    8.4.5 in the case of an enterprise charge, a statement that the charge is an enterprise charge; and

    8.4.6 signature by or on behalf of

        8.4.6.1 the chargor and the charge manager (if appointed); or

        8.4.6.2 in the case of a registration statement pursuant to Article 8.2, the chargeholder; and

8.4.7 the date of the charging instrument except where an unpaid vendor's charge is converted into a registered charge; and

8.4.8 any additional information required pursuant to Article 8.5 or 8.6.

8.5 Where an unpaid vendor's charge is being converted into a registered charge the registration statement must in addition to the information required under Article 8.4 include

    8.5.1 a statement that the unpaid vendor's charge is being converted into a registered charge; and

    8.5.2 the date on which title to the charged property was transferred to the chargeholder as referred to in Article 9.1; and

    8.5.3 the date and identification of the written agreement referred to in Article 9.1.

8.6 Where a possessory charge is being converted into a registered charge the registration statement must in addition to the information required under Article 8.4 include

    8.6.1 a statement that the possessory charge is being converted into a registered charge; and

    8.6.2 the date on which possession of the charged property was given pursuant to Article 10.1 if given after the date of the charging instrument.

8.7 Where there is more than one chargor a separate registration statement must be presented for each chargor.

8.8 If a registration statement is signed by a person acting on behalf of the chargor the charge is valid only if that person is independent of the chargeholder.

8.9 The time of registration is as provided in Article 34.4.

Article 9
Unpaid Vendor's Charge

9.1 Where at or before the time of transfer of title by way of sale of a movable thing there is written agreement between the vendor and the purchaser that the vendor retains title or obtains a security right in the thing until payment of the purchase price

    9.1.1 title to the thing is not retained by the vendor but is transferred to the purchaser as if such agreement does not exist; and

    9.1.2 the vendor simultaneously receives a charge over the thing unless the parties otherwise agree without any requirement for a charging instrument or registration.

9.2 A charge created pursuant to Article 9.1 only secures

    9.2.1 any part of the purchase price of the charged property that remains unpaid at the time the charge is created; and

    9.2.2 additional amounts included pursuant to Article 4.6.

9.3 At any time within six months of the date on which an unpaid vendor's charge is created it may be converted into a registered charge by registration in accordance with Article 8.2.

9.4 An unpaid vendor's charge terminates

    9.4.1 six months after the date on which it was created unless an enforcement notice has been delivered pursuant to Article 22.2 in respect of the charge or any other charge over the same charged property; or

    9.4.2 in the other events provided under Article 32.

Article 10
Possessory Charge

10.1 Where the charged property is capable of transfer by delivery the chargeholder or a person nominated by the chargeholder or a person holding on terms agreed between the chargeholder and the chargor may before or after the date of the charging instrument be given possession of the charged property by the chargor in which case registration pursuant to Article 8 is not required.

10.2 At any time while possession as referred to in Article 10.1 continues a possessory charge may be converted into a registered charge by registration in accordance with Article 8.2.

Additional Registration

11.1 Where additional registration of a charge is required pursuant to this Article 11 a charge created pursuant to Article 6 cannot be enforced until such registration has been made.

11.2 [*Add specific requirements for additional registration to be determined separately for each jurisdiction.*]

Article 12
Charge of a Debt

12.1 Where the charged property is a debt for money the person owing the charged debt may satisfy it in a manner agreed with the chargor unless the chargeholder notifies that person pursuant to Article 12.2.

12.2 The chargeholder may at any time notify the person owing the charged debt that the charge exists. In that event

    12.2.1 the charged debt can be satisfied only by payment to the chargeholder or to such person as the chargeholder nominates unless the chargeholder otherwise agrees; and

    12.2.2 the chargeholder may directly pursue the person owing the charged debt for that debt.

12.3 For a notice given pursuant to Article 12.2 to be valid it must

    12.3.1 be in writing; and

    12.3.2 identify the chargor; and

    12.3.3 describe the charged debt either specifically or generally in a manner which enables the person owing the charged debt to identify it; and

    12.3.4 include clear instructions as to the person to whom the charged debt is to be paid.

12.4 The instructions given pursuant to Article 12.3.4 may be amended by a subsequent notice in accordance with Article 12.3.

12.5 Upon a charged debt being satisfied the charge terminates pursuant to Article 32.1.3.

12.6 Where the charged property is a secured debt the charge over the secured debt extends to the charge given in respect of that debt unless otherwise provided in the charging instrument for either charge. Where the charged property is described as the charge given in respect of a secured debt it is deemed to include that debt.

Article 13
Charge of a Contractual Obligation other than a Debt

Where the charged property is a contractual obligation which is not a debt for money the person owing the contractual obligation may satisfy it in the manner agreed with the chargor unless

13.1 the person owing the contractual obligation has received notice from the chargeholder pursuant to Article 23.3; and

13.2 the chargeholder exercises the chargor's rights pursuant to Article 23.3.3.

Article 14
Rights and Defences

14.1 A chargeholder may only claim rights arising out of a charge if the charge has been created pursuant to Article 6 and has not been terminated pursuant to Article 32.

14.2 A chargeholder may only claim rights arising out of a charge in relation to a debt if the charge extends to that debt.

14.3 A chargeholder may only claim rights arising out of a charge in relation to charged property if the charge extends to that property.

14.4 A charge is valid and enforceable only to the extent that the secured debt is valid and enforceable.

14.5 In any proceedings brought by the chargeholder claiming rights arising out of the charge

    14.5.1 the chargeholder must prove that the charge has been created; and

    14.5.2 the chargor or other party must prove that the charge has terminated or that any defences which he claims apply.

14.6 A chargor, any other chargeholder with a charge over the same charged property or any other party claiming rights in the charged property who disputes the creation or validity of the charge or claims that a charge has been terminated may apply to the court for a declaration that the charge is not created, is invalid or has been terminated.

Article 15
Rights and Obligations of Chargor and Chargeholder

15.1 The chargor and the chargeholder are free to determine the rights and obligations of each of them except as otherwise provided by law.

15.2 The chargor is under an obligation not to deal in the charged property except under a licence pursuant to Article 19 or Article 20 and is liable to the chargeholder for any loss suffered as a result of breach of this obligation.

15.3 The chargor has, except in the case of a possessory charge and unless otherwise agreed, the right

    15.3.1 to make use of or apply the charged property including to combine the charged property with any other thing or right, to apply the charged property in any manufacturing process and, where the charged property has been acquired for consumption, to consume the charged property; and

    15.3.2 to receive any fruits arising out of the charged property.

    Rights arising pursuant to this Article 15.3 terminate upon an enforcement notice being delivered pursuant to Article 22.2.

15.4 The chargor and the chargeholder have unless they otherwise agree the following further rights and obligations

    15.4.1 except in the case of a possessory charge, the chargor must preserve and maintain the charged property subject to his right to use it pursuant to Article 15.3.1. Where possession of the charged property is passed to a third party the chargor remains under an obligation to ensure that the charged property is preserved and maintained; and

    15.4.2 in the case of a possessory charge, the chargeholder must preserve and maintain the charged property; and

    15.4.3 the party not in possession of the charged property has a right to inspect; and

    15.4.4 the chargor must insure the charged property against such risks as are habitually insured against by a prudent person owning similar things or rights.

Article 16
Charge Manager

16.1 The chargeholder may at any time appoint a charge manager for a registered charge either in the charging instrument or in a separate document.

16.2 The charge manager may be a chargeholder or a third party. Where a charge is granted to more than one chargeholder the appointment of the charge manager and any termination of that appointment must in order to be valid be made by or on behalf of all the chargeholders.

16.3 The powers and obligations of the charge manager are as provided in this Article 16 and any agreement relating to those powers and obligations is of effect only between the parties to that agreement.

16.4 Immediately upon a charge manager being registered pursuant to Article 8.4.1 or 33.1.2

    16.4.1 the charge manager becomes entitled to exercise in the place of the chargeholder all the rights of the chargeholder arising under the charge including but not limited to the right to take enforcement proceedings pursuant to Articles 22 to 25 but excluding any right to transfer the secured debt;

    16.4.2 the chargeholder ceases to be entitled to exercise such rights while the charge manager is appointed;

    16.4.3 the charge manager becomes liable to perform all the obligations of the chargeholder to third parties arising out of the charge notwithstanding the continuing liability of the chargeholder.

16.5 When a person is registered as a charge manager pursuant to Article 8.4.1 or 33.1.2, any act of that person as charge manager is binding on the chargeholder even if the appointment of the charge manager is invalid except where the person claiming against the chargeholder has actual knowledge at the time of the act of the invalidity of the appointment.

16.6 The appointment of a charge manager can be terminated by the chargeholder or the charge manager at any time subject to any agreement between them. The termination becomes effective against a third party at the time when he has actual knowledge of the termination or, if he does not have such knowledge, at the time when the termination is registered pursuant to Article 33.1.3.

16.7 Upon any transfer by a chargeholder of the secured debt extending to the charge the powers and obligations of a charge manager pursuant to this Article 16 continue and the charge manager acts in the place of the new chargeholder.

Part 3
Involvement of Third Parties

Article 17
Priorities between Chargeholders

17.1 A chargor may grant more than one charge over the same right or thing.

17.2 The priority between different charges over the same charged property is determined in accordance with the time at which they were created or deemed to be created pursuant to Articles 6.7 or 6.8 except as otherwise provided in this Article 17. Where title to a thing or right is acquired subject to a charge that charge will have priority over any charge granted by the acquirer.

17.3 An unpaid vendor's charge takes priority over any other charge granted by the purchaser over the thing transferred.

17.4 A possessory charge over negotiable instruments or negotiable documents takes priority over any prior charge.

17.5 The priority of a charge over a thing or right to which additional registration under Article 11 applies is determined by the later of the time of its creation or deemed creation pursuant to Articles 6.7 or 6.8 and the time at which such additional registration is made.

17.6 A security right arising by operation of law for money due for services in relation to a thing or right held takes priority over any prior charge.

17.7 [*Specific exceptions to be determined separately for each jurisdiction to cover charges under other laws*].

17.8 The priority of a charge may be changed at any time by written agreement between chargeholders or between the chargor and a chargeholder. An agreement to change the priority of a charge is valid only upon written consent being obtained from

    17.8.1 the chargeholder of any other charge which would cease to have priority over that charge as a result of the change; and

    17.8.2 the chargeholder of any other charge which as a result of the change

17.8.2.1 would cease to have the same priority as that charge; and

17.8.2.2 would not acquire priority over that charge.

Article 18
Transfer of a Secured Debt

18.1 A transfer of a secured debt by the chargeholder extends to the charge given in respect of that debt unless otherwise provided in the charging instrument or agreed between the parties to the transfer. An agreement which provides for the transfer of a charge is deemed to be a transfer of the debt secured by that charge. The charge terminates pursuant to Article 32.1.9 if the secured debt is transferred without the charge.

18.2 In the case of a transfer of a debt secured by a possessory charge, the transfer extends to the charge only if at the time of the transfer

18.2.1 the transferor passes possession of the charged property to the new chargeholder or a person nominated by the new chargeholder; or

18.2.2 the transferor agrees to hold the charged property on behalf of the new chargeholder.

18.3 Where a secured debt which extends to a registered charge has been transferred the charge is not enforceable unless

18.3.1 the transfer is registered pursuant to Article 33.1.4; or

18.3.2 a charge manager is registered in respect of the charge pursuant to Article 8.4.1 or 33.1.2.

18.4 The chargor may claim any defences which he has against the transferor also against the new chargeholder.

18.5 A transfer of a secured debt which extends to the charge automatically extends also to all rights of the chargeholder under the charging instrument unless otherwise provided in the charging instrument or agreed between the parties to the transfer.

18.6 Where only part of a secured debt and a charge is transferred the new chargeholder becomes entitled to the charge and any transferred rights under the charging instrument jointly with the transferring chargeholder up to the amount of the secured debt transferred.

18.7 A transfer of a secured debt by operation of law extends to the charge given in respect of that debt.

Article 19
Legal Licence to Transfer Charged Property

19.1 The chargor has a licence to transfer title to the charged property by way of sale free from the charge in the terms set out in this Article 19 except in the case of a possessory charge.

19.2 The chargor may transfer title to items of his charged trading stock by way of sale in the ordinary course of his trading activity.

19.3 The chargor may transfer title to other charged property by way of sale in the ordinary course of his business provided that the thing or right transferred is of a kind that is habitually transferred by him in the ordinary course of his business.

19.4 In the case of an enterprise charge the chargor may transfer title by way of sale in any charged property in respect of which applicable additional registration as provided in Article 11 has not been made.

19.5 The licence to transfer title by way of sale pursuant to this Article 19 is suspended automatically

19.5.1 upon possession of the charged property being given pursuant to Article 10.1 until the time when such possession ceases; or

19.5.2 upon an enforcement notice in respect of the charge being delivered pursuant to Article 22.2 until enforcement proceedings may no longer be continued pursuant to Article 22.4.

19.6 Any agreement between the chargor and the chargeholder restricting or terminating the licence pursuant to this Article 19 is of effect only between the parties.

Article 20
Contractual Licence to Deal in Charged Property

20.1 The chargeholder may, except in the case of a possessory charge, grant the chargor a contractual licence to transfer title to the charged property free from the charge in addition to the licence granted pursuant to Article 19.

20.2 In any contractual licence granted pursuant to Article 20.1 the charged property may be identified specifically or generally and the licence may be granted on such terms as the chargor and chargeholder may agree.

20.3 The grant of a contractual licence pursuant to Article 20.1 may be included in the charging instrument and in that event a person dealing with the chargor acquires charged property free from the charge pursuant to Article 21.2.3 without being under an obligation to make further enquiries.

20.4 A contractual licence granted pursuant to Article 20.1 is suspended automatically in the events as provided in Article 19.5 and may subject to Article 20.3 be terminated at any time by the chargeholder or in accordance with its terms.

Article 21
Third Party Acquiring Charged Property

21.1 Any person acquiring title to charged property will acquire subject to the charge except as provided in Article 21.2.

21.2 If a person acquires title to charged property he acquires it free from the charge

    21.2.1 where the chargor transfers title to the charged property by way of sale under the licence granted pursuant to Article 19; or

    21.2.2 while the licence granted pursuant to Article 19 is suspended where the transfer of title by the chargor by way of sale if made prior to suspension would have been under the licence and where either

        21.2.2.1 the purchaser does not have actual knowledge at the time of the transfer of the existence of the charge; or

        21.2.2.2 the purchaser believes in good faith at the time of the transfer that the licence exists; or

    21.2.3 where the chargor transfers title to the charged property under a contractual licence granted pursuant to Article 20.1; or

    21.2.4 while a contractual licence granted pursuant to Article 20.1 is suspended or after it is terminated where the transfer of title by the chargor if made prior to suspension or termination would have been under the licence and where the acquirer believes in good faith at the time of the transfer that the licence exists. Except where a contractual licence is contained in the charging instrument the acquirer is under an obligation to enquire of the chargeholder; or

    21.2.5 where the price paid for the charged property is less than [*amount*] and where the purchaser believes in good faith at the time of the transfer that no charge exists; or

    21.2.6 where the charged property is

        21.2.6.1 a negotiable instrument or negotiable document; or

        21.2.6.2 a share or debt instrument or a contract quoted on a recognised exchange or habitually traded in a recognised market; or

    21.2.7 where the charge is to an unpaid vendor pursuant to Article 9 unless

        21.2.7.1 a purpose of the chargor is to terminate the unpaid vendor's charge; and

        21.2.7.2 the acquirer has actual knowledge at the time of the transfer of that purpose or circumstances exist which should make him aware of that purpose.

21.3 For the purposes of Articles 21.2.2.2 and 21.2.4 a purchaser or an acquirer believes in good faith that a licence exists if

    21.3.1 he does not have actual knowledge of the termination of the licence; and

    21.3.2 there do not exist circumstances which should make him aware of the termination of the licence.

21.4 For the purposes of Article 21.2.5 a purchaser believes in good faith that no charge exists if

    21.4.1 he does not have actual knowledge of the existence of the charge; and

    21.4.2 there do not exist circumstances which should make him aware of the existence of the charge.

21.5 For the purposes of Articles 21.2.2, 21.2.4 and 21.2.5 the purchaser or acquirer is not under an obligation to search the charges' register unless the particular circumstances are abnormal and such as to make a search of the charges' register prudent.

21.6 Where a person acquires title to charged property subject to a registered charge the chargeholder may at any time register the charge against the name of such person pursuant to Article 33.1.5.

PART 4
ENFORCEMENT AND TERMINATION

Article 22
General Rules on Enforcement

22.1 A charge becomes immediately enforceable if there is a failure to pay the secured debt and it remains immediately enforceable until

    22.1.1 the chargeholder agrees that the charge is no longer immediately enforceable; or

    22.1.2 the secured debt is satisfied in full or otherwise ceases to exist; or

    22.1.3 the charge terminates for any other reason.

22.2 The chargeholder of a charge which has become immediately enforceable may commence enforcement proceedings by delivering an enforcement notice to the chargor containing the information set out in Article 22.7.

22.3 When a chargeholder has delivered an enforcement notice pursuant to Article 22.2 he has the right to take protective measures pursuant to Article 23 and to realise the charge pursuant to Article 24 or, in the case of an enterprise charge, to have the charge enforced pursuant to Article 25.

22.4 Enforcement proceedings cannot be continued if

    22.4.1 a supplementary registration statement in respect of the enforcement notice delivered pursuant to Article 22.2 has not been presented at the charges' registry pursuant to Article 33.1.6 within seven days of delivery to the chargor; or

    22.4.2 the enforcement notice is declared invalid by the court; or

    22.4.3 the charge ceases to be immediately enforceable in accordance with Article 22.1.

22.5 In the event of the chargeholder failing to register the enforcement notice as required by Article 22.4.1 the chargeholder is liable to the chargor, any other chargeholder with a charge over the same property and any other party claiming rights in the charged property for any loss suffered by any of them as a result of the protective measures. This does not apply where the charge ceases to be immediately enforceable in accordance with Article 22.1 within seven days of delivery of the enforcement notice to the chargor and where the protective measures were taken while the charge was immediately enforceable.

22.6 The chargeholder may at any time request deregistration of the enforcement notice pursuant to Article 33.1.11 and is under an obligation to do so in the events referred to in Article 22.4.2 and 22.4.3.

22.7 An enforcement notice delivered pursuant to Article 22.2 must in order to be valid be in writing and

22.7.1 identify the charge in respect of which enforcement proceedings are being commenced

    22.7.1.1 in the case of a registered charge, by reference to the charges' register and the date of registration; or

    22.7.1.2 in the case of an unpaid vendor's charge or a possessory charge, by reference to the information required to register such a charge pursuant to Articles 8.4 to 8.6; and

22.7.2 identify the debt in respect of which enforcement proceedings are being commenced which may be the secured debt or any part of that debt; and

22.7.3 contain a statement that the charge has become immediately enforceable; and

22.7.4 where the chargeholder elects for a charged enterprise to be transferred as a going concern pursuant to Article 25.3 state that such election is being made and identify the person appointed as enterprise administrator; and

22.7.5 be signed by or on behalf of the chargeholder and, where Article 22.7.4 applies, the enterprise administrator; and

22.7.6 in the case of an enterprise charge, be signed by or on behalf of the chargeholder of any prior ranking enterprise charge.

Article 23
Measures for Protection of Charged Property

23.1 When an enforcement notice has been delivered pursuant to Article 22.2 the chargeholder has the right to possession of charged property which is in the form of movable things.

23.2 Where taking possession of charged property referred to in Article 23.1 is impracticable or is disputed by a third party in possession of the charged property the chargeholder may take such steps as are necessary to immobilise the charged property, to prevent the chargor or a third party using it and to prevent the chargor transferring title to it.

23.3 Where an enforcement notice has been delivered pursuant to Article 22.2 in respect of charged property which is a contractual obligation other than a debt for money the chargeholder may notify the person owing the charged obligation that it is subject to a charge and that enforcement proceedings have been commenced. Upon such notification

23.3.1 the chargor cannot modify the contractual obligation without the agreement of the chargeholder; and

23.3.2 the chargor cannot take any steps to exercise his rights in respect of the contractual obligation without the agreement of the chargeholder; and

23.3.3 the chargeholder may exercise the chargor's rights in respect of the contractual obligation but in such case the chargeholder must comply with any corresponding obligation owed by the chargor.

23.4 Where an enforcement notice has been delivered pursuant to Article 22.2 the chargeholder may take reasonable steps

23.4.1 to preserve, maintain and insure the charged property; and

23.4.2 with a view to increasing the sale price or reducing the sale costs including enhancing the charged property or renting it on commercially prudent terms to a third party.

23.5 Upon application by the chargeholder the court may make an order for other appropriate measures to protect the charged property after the enforcement notice has been registered as required by Article 22.4.1.

23.6 The chargeholder at any time may take protective measures as agreed with the chargor.

23.7 If in order to obtain possession as referred to in Article 23.1 or to take other steps as provided in Article 23.2 the chargeholder does not have the right to enter upon the site where the charged property is situated or where any such rights are refused to the chargeholder he may appoint a [*bailiff*] for such purpose. The [*bailiff*] may on the chargeholder's behalf take the protective measures to which the chargeholder is entitled provided

23.7.1 he is satisfied that the charge is registered or, in the case of an unpaid vendor's charge or a possessory charge, the enforcement notice is registered; and

23.7.2 he receives from the chargeholder a copy of the enforcement notice delivered pursuant to Article 22.2.

Article 24

Measures for Realisation of Charged Property

24.1 When at least 60 days have elapsed since delivery of an enforcement notice pursuant to Article 22.2 the chargeholder has the right to transfer title to the charged property by way of sale in order to have the proceeds of sale applied towards satisfaction of the secured debt.

24.2 Any agreement entered into prior to delivery of an enforcement notice pursuant to Article 22.2 which provides for the transfer of title to charged property by way of sale by or to the chargeholder after delivery of the enforcement notice is invalid.

24.3 The chargeholder must

24.3.1 endeavour to realise a fair price for the charged property; and

24.3.2 advise the purchaser that he is transferring title to charged property in the capacity of chargeholder and that the proceeds of sale must be paid directly to a proceeds depositary appointed pursuant to Article 27.1.

24.4 The chargeholder may subject to the obligation under Article 24.3.1 transfer title to the charged property by way of sale in such manner as he considers appropriate which may include transfer by private agreement on the open market or at public or private auction. The chargeholder may appoint a person to act on his behalf for the transfer or for any matter connected with it.

24.5 A chargeholder is treated as having fulfilled his obligation under Article 24.3.1 if he can demonstrate that

24.5.1 in the case of charged property of a kind for which there is a recognised market, he acted in the manner of a prudent person operating in that market; or

24.5.2 in all other cases, he took such steps to realise a fair price as could be expected in the circumstances of a prudent person.

Article 25

Enterprise Charge Administration

25.1 An enterprise charge may be enforced pursuant to Articles 23 and 24 or pursuant to this Article 25.

25.2 Any agreement entered into prior to delivery of an enforcement notice pursuant to Article 22.2 which provides for the transfer of title to the charged enterprise by way of sale by or to the chargeholder after delivery of the enforcement notice is invalid.

25.3 A chargeholder of an enterprise charge who delivers an enforcement notice pursuant to Article 22.2 may elect for the enterprise to be transferred as a going concern pursuant to this Article 25 and in that case the enforcement notice must comply with the requirements of Articles 22.7.4, 22.7.5 and 22.7.6.

25.4 A chargeholder may only make an election under Article 25.3 if he believes that the enterprise is capable of being transferred as a going concern.

25.5 When an election is made pursuant to Article 25.3

25.5.1 the chargeholder must appoint a person (called an enterprise administrator) who has the powers and obligations set out in this Article 25; and

25.5.2 the chargeholder may not, except as provided under Article 25.20, exercise any rights pursuant to Articles 23 and 24 unless the election is rescinded.

25.6 In order for the appointment of the enterprise administrator to be valid

25.6.1 he must be a [*qualified accountant or lawyer*]; and

25.6.2 he must not be a chargeholder or the charge manager; and

25.6.3 a statement of his appointment must be presented at the [*registry where the chargor is registered*] within seven days of delivery of the enforcement notice pursuant to Article 22.2.

25.7 Where an election is made pursuant to Article 25.3

25.7.1 the powers of the persons authorised by law or by the chargor's constitution to administer the enterprise and to deal in the charged property cease upon delivery of the enforcement notice; and

25.7.2 such powers are immediately vested in the enterprise administrator.

25.8 Each of the persons whose powers cease pursuant to Article 25.7.1 is under an obligation to give all necessary information and assistance to the enterprise administrator to enable him to manage the enterprise and to carry out his functions and may in addition be given such powers in relation to the enterprise as may be agreed with the enterprise administrator.

25.9 Each of the persons whose powers cease pursuant to Article 25.7.1 is liable for any loss suffered by the chargor or any third party as a result of any exercise by that person of any of his former powers after he has actual knowledge that his powers have ceased.

25.10 The enterprise administrator must

25.10.1 fulfil all those obligations that are provided by law for the persons whose powers are vested in him pursuant to Article 25.7.2 (but not including the obligation under Article 15.2); and

25.10.2 continue the enterprise as a going concern; and

25.10.3 advise the chargeholder promptly if he believes that the enterprise is not capable of being transferred as a going concern; and

25.10.4 endeavour to transfer the enterprise as a going concern and to realise a fair price; and

25.10.5 advise the purchaser that he is transferring title to charged property in the capacity of enterprise administrator and that the proceeds of sale must be paid directly to a proceeds depositary appointed pursuant to Article 27.1.

25.11 The appointment of an enterprise administrator terminates upon

25.11.1 his death; or

25.11.2 his becoming incapable of performing his obligations; or

25.11.3 his resignation; or

25.11.4 his being removed by the chargeholder; or

25.11.5 his being removed by the court; or

25.11.6 the transfer of the enterprise by way of sale; or

25.11.7 the administration of the enterprise ceasing pursuant to Article 25.22 or 25.23.

25.12 When the appointment of an enterprise administrator is terminated pursuant to Articles 25.11.1 to 25.11.5 a new enterprise administrator must be appointed

25.12.1 in the case of Articles 25.11.1, 25.11.2 or 25.11.3, by the chargeholder within seven days of the occurrence of the death, incapacity or resignation;

25.12.2 in the case of Article 25.11.4, by the chargeholder at the time of the removal of the previous enterprise administrator;

25.12.3 in the case of Article 25.11.5, by the court at the time of his removal and in such case the court may, if appropriate, appoint a new enterprise administrator nominated by the chargeholder.

25.13 If the chargeholder fails to appoint a new enterprise administrator

25.13.1 within seven days as provided in Article 25.12.1 the court may appoint a new enterprise administrator or rescind the election to have the enterprise transferred as a going concern pursuant to Article 25.3;

    25.13.2 at the time of the removal by him of the previous enterprise administrator as referred to in Article 25.11.4 the removal is not valid.

25.14 The appointment of a new enterprise administrator after the seven days as provided in Article 25.12.1 is valid but the chargeholder is liable to the chargor, any other chargeholder with a charge over the same charged property and any other party claiming rights in the charged property for any loss suffered by reason of any delay in the appointment caused by the chargeholder.

25.15 The chargeholder is under an obligation to present at the charges' registry pursuant to Article 33.1.7 or 33.1.8 and at [*the registry where the chargor is registered*] a request for registration of any termination of the appointment of an enterprise administrator or any appointment of a new enterprise administrator within seven days of the termination or appointment.

25.16 Within 60 days of delivery of an enforcement notice pursuant to Article 22.2 the enterprise administrator may renounce any contract to which the chargor is party and which imposes continuing obligations on the chargor.

25.17 Where a contract imposes continuing obligations on the chargor the other party may serve a notice on the enterprise administrator at any time within the 60 day period requiring the enterprise administrator to state whether or not he will be exercising his right under Article 25.16. Until the enterprise administrator replies to that notice the obligation of the other party to perform is suspended.

25.18 When at least 60 days have elapsed since delivery of an enforcement notice pursuant to Article 22.2 the enterprise administrator has the right to transfer the enterprise by way of sale in order to have the proceeds of sale applied towards satisfaction of the secured debt.

25.19 The enterprise administrator may subject to the obligation under Article 25.10.4 transfer the enterprise as a going concern by way of sale in such a manner as he considers appropriate which may include transfer by private agreement, on the open market or at public or private auction. The enterprise administrator may appoint a person to act on his behalf for the transfer or for any matter connected with it.

25.20 If the enterprise administrator determines that any part of the charged property can be transferred separately from the enterprise without preventing the transfer of the enterprise as a going concern he may agree with the chargeholder that such property is transferred by the chargeholder pursuant to Article 24.

25.21 An enterprise administrator is treated as having fulfilled his obligation under Article 25.10.4 if he can demonstrate that he took such steps as could be expected in the circumstances of a prudent person transferring an enterprise of that nature.

25.22 The election to have the enterprise transferred as a going concern pursuant to Article 25.3 must be rescinded by the chargeholder if he determines that the enterprise is no longer capable of being transferred as a going concern.

25.23 The election to have the enterprise transferred as a going concern pursuant to Article 25.3 may be rescinded

    25.23.1 by the chargeholder if he determines that to do so is in the interests of other creditors of the chargor; or

    25.23.2 by the court pursuant to Article 25.13.1 or 29.

25.24 In the event of the election being rescinded pursuant to Article 25.22 or 25.23 the charge may be enforced pursuant to Articles 23 and 24.

Article 26
Purchaser from Chargeholder or Enterprise Administrator

26.1 If a person acquires title to charged property from the chargeholder pursuant to Article 24 or from the enterprise administrator pursuant to Article 25 he acquires it free from any charge if

26.1.1 the enforcement notice and, in the case of a transfer pursuant to Article 25, the enterprise administrator remain registered on the charges' register until at least the third day (excluding weekends and public holidays) before the date of the transfer and no interim order remains registered pursuant to Article 33.1.9 at such time; and

26.1.2 the sale price is paid to a proceeds depositary appointed by the chargeholder pursuant to Article 27.

26.2 A purchaser will not acquire title free from any charge if he has actual knowledge at the time of the purchase that

26.2.1 the charge being enforced is not created, invalid or unenforceable; or

26.2.2 the charge has ceased to be immediately enforceable in accordance with Article 22.1; or

26.2.3 the enforcement notice has been declared invalid by a court; or

26.2.4 an order made by the court pursuant to Article 29.3 is still outstanding; or

26.2.5 in the case of transfer of an enterprise pursuant to Article 25, the election made pursuant to Article 25.3 has been rescinded.

26.3 The purchaser has no obligation to enquire as to the creation, validity and enforceability of the charge or as to the powers of the enterprise administrator registered on the charges' register.

Article 27
Proceeds Depositary

27.1 Prior to the day on which any proceeds of sale under Articles 24 or 25 become payable the chargeholder must appoint a person to receive the proceeds of sale (called a proceeds depositary). Such appointment may be made at any time after delivery of an enforcement notice pursuant to Article 22.2.

27.2 In order for the appointment of the proceeds depositary to be valid

27.2.1 he must be a [qualified accountant or recognised bank]; and

27.2.2 he cannot be the chargor, a chargeholder, the charge manager or the enterprise administrator.

27.3 The chargeholder or the enterprise administrator must cause the proceeds of sale to be paid to the proceeds depositary.

27.4 The proceeds depositary must place all amounts received by him on deposit on commercial terms with a prime bank in a segregated account.

27.5 Promptly after his appointment the proceeds depositary must establish a list setting out

27.5.1 the persons entitled to the proceeds of sale; and

27.5.2 the amount of the entitlement of each; and

27.5.3 the priority of the entitlement of each.

27.6 In order to establish the list pursuant to Article 27.5 the proceeds depositary

27.6.1 must examine the charges' register; and

27.6.2 must enquire of the chargor and the enterprise administrator; and

27.6.3 where the charged property includes a movable thing which may be subject to an unpaid vendor's charge, must determine the date of acquisition and, if appropriate, enquire of the vendor; and

27.6.4 must take note of any claim directly addressed to him; and

27.6.5 may but is not obliged to make other appropriate enquiries.

27.7 The proceeds depositary may exclude from the list any person who fails to provide information necessary to establish the list referred to in Article 27.5 if

    27.7.1 the proceeds depositary has delivered two notices to that person requesting information as to his entitlement; and

    27.7.2 there are at least 15 days between delivery of the first and of the second notice; and

    27.7.3 both notices state that the information is needed for establishing the list and that any failure to provide the required information may cause loss of entitlement to proceeds of sale held by the proceeds depositary; and

    27.7.4 the required information has not been received within 15 days of delivery of the second notice.

27.8 When the list is established pursuant to Article 27.5 the proceeds depositary must deliver a copy to the chargeholder, the enterprise administrator, the chargor, any chargeholder shown on the charges' register with a charge over the same charged property and any other person who, to the proceeds depositary's actual knowledge, has or claims to have a right in the charged property.

27.9 Any person who claims entitlement to the proceeds of sale and does not agree with the list as established by the proceeds depositary may within 21 days of delivery of the list pursuant to Article 27.8 notify the proceeds depositary of his disagreement. In this case the proceeds depositary must deliver to the persons referred to in Article 27.8 either an amended list or a statement that a disagreement has been notified but that the list remains unchanged.

27.10 Where establishment of a definitive list is delayed for any reason, the proceeds depositary may establish a provisional list making full reserve for any undetermined or disputed amounts.

Article 28
Distribution of Proceeds of Sale

28.1 The proceeds depositary must, subject to any order made by the court pursuant to Article 29, distribute the proceeds of sale promptly upon 30 days elapsing after the latest of

    28.1.1 receipt by the proceeds depositary of the proceeds of sale; or

    28.1.2 delivery of the list pursuant to Article 27.8; or

    28.1.3 delivery of the list or statement pursuant to Article 27.9.

28.2 The proceeds depositary may make an initial distribution of proceeds of sale on the basis of a provisional list established pursuant to Article 27.10.

28.3 The proceeds depositary must distribute the proceeds of sale as follows

    28.3.1 first, in payment of his fees and costs up to [*amount*];

    28.3.2 second, where an election has been made pursuant to Article 25.3, in payment of the liabilities referred to in Article 28.4.1;

    28.3.3 third, where an election has been made pursuant to Article 25.3, in payment of the liabilities referred to in Articles 28.4.2 and 28.4.3;

    28.3.4 fourth, to chargeholders of charges over the charged property transferred in accordance with the priorities of their respective charges;

    28.3.5 fifth, to other persons with rights in the charged property which entitle them to the proceeds of sale; and

    28.3.6 sixth, to the chargor.

28.4 Where an election has been made pursuant to Article 25.3 the following liabilities have priority in any distribution of the proceeds of sale

    28.4.1 reasonable remuneration of the enterprise administrator for continuing the enterprise as a going concern but excluding any remuneration or costs in respect of the transfer of the enterprise and any amounts due to an enterprise administrator by reason of termination of his appointment; and

28.4.2 liabilities incurred by the enterprise administrator in continuing the enterprise as a going concern; and

28.4.3 liabilities becoming due under contracts renounced pursuant to Article 25.16 after delivery of the enforcement notice pursuant to Article 22.2 and prior to renunciation excluding any liability arising by reason of such renunciation.

28.5 Where any amount payable by the proceeds depositary pursuant to this Article 28 is payable in a currency other than the currency held by the proceeds depositary he must purchase the necessary amount of that currency to make the payment.

28.6 The proceeds depositary must continue to hold the amount of the proceeds of sale attributable to any secured debt until it becomes payable.

28.7 The secured debt is satisfied to the extent that the proceeds depositary pays proceeds of sale to a chargeholder.

28.8 Any payment by the proceeds depositary to a non-resident chargeholder is treated for the purpose of currency exchange regulations as a payment of the secured debt by the debtor.

Article 29
Court Remedies on Enforcement

29.1 If at any time after delivery of an enforcement notice pursuant to Article 22.2 a chargor, any other chargeholder with a charge over the same charged property or any other party claiming rights in the charged property disputes the creation, validity or enforceability of the charge or claims termination of the charge he may apply to the court to have the enforcement notice declared invalid. Any application under this Article 29.1 must be treated by the court as urgent business [*state time limit for decision*]. Notwithstanding such application until the enforcement notice is declared invalid and subject to any order made by the court pursuant to Articles 29.3 to 29.5

29.1.1 the chargeholder may continue to take protective measures pursuant to Article 23; and

29.1.2 the chargeholder may continue to realise the charge pursuant to Article 24; and

29.1.3 where an election has been made pursuant to Article 25.3 the enterprise administrator may continue to operate the enterprise as a going concern and to realise the charge pursuant to Article 25.

29.2 If the court declares the enforcement notice invalid the chargor or the party who applied to the court may require the chargeholder to present at the charges' registry a request for deregistration of the enforcement notice pursuant to Article 33.1.11.

29.3 If upon an application being made pursuant to Article 29.1 the court is

29.3.1 unable to give its final decision within 60 days of the enforcement notice being delivered pursuant to Article 22.2; and

29.3.2 satisfied that there are reasonable grounds on which to claim that the charge is not created, invalid, or not enforceable or that it has been terminated; and

29.3.3 satisfied that, after taking into account the interests of all the parties, it is appropriate to make an order pursuant to this Article 29.3;

the court may if so requested by the applicant make an interim order that the charged property may not be transferred pursuant to Article 24 or 25 until the court has rendered its final decision. The applicant is under an obligation to present at the charges' registry pursuant to Article 33.1.9 a request for registration of the interim order within seven days of it being made and pursuant to Article 33.1.12 a request for deregistration of the order within seven days of it being terminated. The applicant is liable to third parties for any loss suffered as a result of breach of this obligation.

29.4 A chargor, any other chargeholder with a charge over the same charged property or any other party claiming rights in the charged property who alleges that the chargeholder, the enterprise administrator or the proceeds depositary has failed to comply with the requirements of Articles 22 to 28 may apply to the court for an order

29.4.1 to declare any measure taken which was not in compliance with the requirements of Articles 22 to 28 invalid subject to Article 26;

29.4.2 requiring the chargeholder, the enterprise administrator or the proceeds depositary to comply with those requirements;

29.4.3 for such other matter as the court considers appropriate.

29.5 A chargor, any other chargeholder with a charge over the same charged property or any other party claiming rights in the charged property who alleges that the chargeholder, the enterprise administrator or the proceeds depositary has taken in relation to enforcement of a charge measures to which he is not entitled may apply to the court for an order

29.5.1 to declare the measures to which the application relates invalid subject to Article 26;

29.5.2 requiring the chargeholder, the enterprise administrator or the proceeds depositary to refrain from taking any further measures to which he is not entitled;

29.5.3 for such other matter as the court considers appropriate.

Article 30
Damages

A chargor, any other chargeholder with a charge over the same charged property or any other party claiming rights in the charged property has an action in damages

30.1 in the case of an enforcement notice declared invalid by the court pursuant to Article 29.1, for any loss suffered by any of them as a result of enforcement; and

30.2 for any loss suffered as a result of any failure by a chargeholder, charge manager, enterprise administrator or proceeds depositary to comply with the requirements of Articles 22 to 28 or as a result of any measure taken by any such person in relation to enforcement of a charge to which he is not entitled.

Article 31
Insolvency Principles

The provisions to be included to cover the event of the insolvency of the chargor have to be drafted jurisdiction by jurisdiction to take into account local insolvency rules. The following basic principles must be respected:

1. The charge remains valid notwithstanding insolvency.
2. Any right to set aside a charge as an act in the period immediately prior to insolvency is in the same terms as for other pre-insolvency acts.
3. Either the charge remains enforceable by the chargeholder separately from insolvency proceedings or the liquidator is under an obligation to transfer the charged property rapidly at a fair price and to satisfy the chargeholder's claim out of the proceeds of sale.
4. The creditors who may rank ahead of the chargeholder in respect of the proceeds of sale are limitatively defined.

Article 32
Termination of a Charge

32.1 A charge terminates if and to the extent that

32.1.1 the chargor and the chargeholder so agree; or

32.1.2 the secured debt is satisfied or otherwise ceases to exist; or

32.1.3 the charged property ceases to exist; or

32.1.4 the charged property is changed or incorporated with another thing or right in such a manner that it ceases to exist in identifiable or separable form; or

32.1.5 the charged property becomes part of another thing or right in such manner that the charged property and the other thing or right are transferable as a single item; or

32.1.6 the charged property becomes owned by the chargeholder; or

32.1.7 in the case of an unpaid vendor's charge, as provided in Article 9.4; or

32.1.8 in the case of a possessory charge pursuant to Article 10, if possession of charged property ceases; or

32.1.9 the secured debt is transferred and the transfer does not extend to the charge; or

32.1.10 a third party acquires title to charged property free from the charge pursuant to Article 21.2; or

32.1.11 a person acquires title to charged property free from any charge pursuant to Article 26.1.

32.2 A charge also terminates if the chargor or another chargeholder with a charge over the same charged property

32.2.1 deposits a sum equal to 130 per cent. of the maximum amount of the secured debt referred to in Article 4.5 or, in the case of an unpaid vendor's charge, of the unpaid part of the purchase price referred to in Article 9.2.1 and in the same currency as the secured debt with a prime bank on terms agreed with the chargeholder or failing agreement on commercial terms then prevailing for similar sums in that currency; and

32.2.2 grants to the chargeholder whose charge is being terminated a registered charge over the sum deposited pursuant to Article 32.2.1 in order to secure the debt previously secured by the charge that is terminated.

32.3 Upon termination of a charge the chargeholder must

32.3.1 in the case of a registered charge, register the termination of the charge pursuant to Article 33.1.10; or

32.3.2 in the case of a possessory charge, return the charged property to the chargor unless otherwise agreed between chargor and chargeholder.

PART 5

REGISTRATION

Article 33

Supplementary Registration Statement

33.1 In order to obtain registration of

33.1.1 an amendment to a charging instrument; or

33.1.2 the subsequent appointment of a charge manager; or

33.1.3 the termination of the appointment of a charge manager; or

33.1.4 the transfer of a secured debt extending to a charge; or

33.1.5 a charge against the name of a person who has acquired title to charged property; or

33.1.6 an enforcement notice; or

33.1.7 the termination of the appointment of an enterprise administrator; or

33.1.8 the appointment of a new enterprise administrator; or

33.1.9 an interim order made under Article 29.3; or

33.1.10 the termination of a registered charge; or

in order to obtain deregistration of

33.1.11 an enforcement notice; or

33.1.12 an interim order made under Article 29.3;

a supplementary registration statement must be presented at the charges' registry.

33.2 A supplementary registration statement presented pursuant to Article 33.1 must

33.2.1 identify the charge by reference to the chargor, the date of registration (in the case of a registered charge) and other information as necessary; and

33.2.2 state the purpose of the supplementary registration statement; and

33.2.3 comply with the requirements of Article 33.3.

33.3 A supplementary registration statement presented pursuant to Article 33.1 must also include

    33.3.1 in the case of an amendment to a charging instrument pursuant to Article 7.5

        33.3.1.1 the date of the charging instrument; and

        33.3.1.2 the date of the amendment; and

        33.3.1.3 signatures by or on behalf of the chargor and the chargeholder; or

    33.3.2 in the case of the subsequent appointment of a charge manager pursuant to Article 16

        33.3.2.1 identification of the charge manager; and

        33.3.2.2 signatures by or on behalf of the chargeholder and the charge manager; or

    33.3.3 in the case of the termination of the appointment of a charge manager pursuant to Article 16

        33.3.3.1 identification of the charge manager; and

        33.3.3.2 signature by or on behalf of the chargeholder or the charge manager; or

    33.3.4 in the case of the transfer of a secured debt extending to a charge pursuant to Article 18.1

        33.3.4.1 identification of the transferor and the new chargeholder; and

        33.3.4.2 signatures by or on behalf of the transferring chargeholder and the new chargeholder; or

    33.3.5 in the case of registration of a charge against the name of a person who has acquired title to charged property as referred to in Article 21.6

        33.3.5.1 identification of the person who has acquired title; and

        33.3.5.2 signature by or on behalf of the chargeholder; or

    33.3.6 in the case of an enforcement notice delivered pursuant to Article 22.2

        33.3.6.1 the date of delivery of the enforcement notice; and

        33.3.6.2 where the enforcement notice relates to an unpaid vendor's charge or a possessory charge the information required to register such a charge pursuant to Articles 8.4 to 8.6; and

        33.3.6.3 where an election has been made pursuant to Article 25.3, a statement that this is the case; and

        33.3.6.4 signature by or on behalf of the chargeholder; or

    33.3.7 in the case of termination of the appointment of an enterprise administrator pursuant to Article 25.11

        33.3.7.1 identification of the enterprise administrator; and

        33.3.7.2 signature by or on behalf of the chargeholder; or

    33.3.8 in the case of appointment of a new enterprise administrator pursuant to Article 25.12

        33.3.8.1 identification of the enterprise administrator; and

        33.3.8.2 signatures by or on behalf of the chargeholder and the enterprise administrator; or

    33.3.9 in the case of an interim order made under Article 29.3

        33.3.9.1 a description of the interim order; and

        33.3.9.2 identification of the person who applied for the order; and

        33.3.9.3 signature by or on behalf of the person who applied for the order; or

    33.3.10 in the case of the termination of a registered charge pursuant to Article 32, signature by or on behalf of the chargeholder; or

    33.3.11 in the case of deregistration of an enforcement notice pursuant to Article 22.6

        33.3.11.1 the date of delivery of the enforcement notice; and

33.3.11.2 signature by or on behalf of the chargeholder; or

33.3.12 in the case of deregistration of an interim order made under Article 29.3

    33.3.12.1 a description of the interim order; and

    33.3.12.2 signature by or on behalf of the person who applied for the order.

33.4 Where there is more than one chargor a separate supplementary registration statement must be presented for each chargor.

Article 34
Registration Procedure

34.1 The registrar may accept a registration statement pursuant to Article 8 or a supplementary registration statement pursuant to Article 33 in such form as he deems fit and can only refuse to register

    34.1.1 if the registration statement or supplementary registration statement does not comply with the requirements of Article 8 or 33; or

    34.1.2 if the required registration fee is not paid.

34.2 Upon acceptance of a registration statement or a supplementary registration statement the registrar must immediately

    34.2.1 mark the time and date of presentation and the stamp of the registration office on the registration statement or supplementary registration statement and, if supplied, on a copy; and

    34.2.2 place the registration statement or supplementary registration statement on the register against the name of the chargor and hand the copy, if supplied, to the presenter.

34.3 If the registrar refuses to accept a registration statement or a supplementary registration statement for one of the reasons in Article 34.1 he must at the same time notify the person presenting the registration statement or supplementary registration statement in writing of the reasons for his refusal and that person may present

    34.3.1 a new registration statement within the 30 day period pursuant to Article 8.1 or, if later, within 15 days of such notification; or

    34.3.2 a new supplementary registration statement within seven days in the cases referred to in Articles 33.1.6 to 33.1.9 or at any time in any other case.

34.4 The time of registration is the time when the registration statement or supplementary registration statement is presented at the charges' registry or, where Article 34.3 applies, the time when the new registration statement or new supplementary registration statement is presented at the charges' registry.

Article 35
Access to the Register

Any person may against payment of the required fee have access to the register and receive a copy of any entry on it.

35.1 The registrar may accept a registration statement pursuant to Article 8 or a supplementary registration statement pursuant to Article 33 in such form as he deems fit and can only refuse to register

    35.1.1 if the registration statement or supplementary registration statement does not comply with the requirements of Article 8 or 33; or

    35.1.2 if the required registration fee is not paid.

35.2 Upon acceptance of a registration statement or a supplementary registration statement the registrar must immediately

35.2.1 mark the time and date of presentation and the stamp of the registration office on the registration statement or supplementary registration statement and, if supplied, on a copy; and

35.2.2 place the registration statement or supplementary registration statement on the register against the name of the chargor and hand the copy, if supplied, to the presenter.

35.3 If the registrar refuses to accept a registration statement or a supplementary registration statement for one of the reasons in Article 34.1 he must at the same time notify the person presenting the registration statement or supplementary registration statement in writing of the reasons for his refusal and that person may present

35.3.1 a new registration statement within the 30 day period pursuant to Article 8.1 or, if later, within 15 days of such notification; or

35.3.2 a new supplementary registration statement within seven days in the cases referred to in Articles 33.1.6 to 33.1.9 or at any time in any other case.

35.4 The time of registration is the time when the registration statement or supplementary registration statement is presented at the charges' registry or, where Article 34.3 applies, the time when the new registration statement or new supplementary registration statement is presented at the charges' registry.

SCHEDULE I

CHARGING INSTRUMENT (ARTICLE 7.2 MLST)

CHARGING INSTRUMENT

1. [*Name of chargor*]
   [*Address of chargor*]
   [*Other identification of chargor as necessary*]

   agrees to grant to

   [*Name of chargeholder*]
   [*Address of chargeholder*]
   [*Other identification of chargeholder as necessary*]

   a charge of the things and rights described below to secure the debt described below.

2. The debt secured by the charge is [*describe secured debt*].
3. [*Include identification of person owing the secured debt if not chargor. For a possessory charge state maximum amount of secured debt*]
4. The things and rights charged are [describe charged property].
5. [*Other matters pursuant to Article 7.5*]

Signature of chargor and date of signature

Signature of chargeholder

SCHEDULE 2

REGISTRATION STATEMENT (ARTICLE 8.3 MLST)

REGISTRATION STATEMENT

1. [*Name, address and other identification as necessary of chargor*]
2. [*Name, address and other identification as necessary of person owing the secured debt (if not the chargor)*]

3. [*Name, address and other identification as necessary of chargeholder*]
4. [*Name address and other identification as necessary of charge manager (if appointed)*]
5. [*Identification of the secured debt*]
6. [*Maximum amount of the secured debt*]
7. [*Identification of the charged property*]
8. [*If appropriate*] The charge is an enterprise charge.
9. [*Date of the charging instrument*] [*Except where an unpaid vendor's charge is being converted into a registered charge*]
10. [*Where an unpaid vendor's charge is being converted into a registered charge*]
    10.1 This registration statement is for the conversion of an unpaid vendor's charge into a registered charge.
    10.2 [*Date on which charged property was transferred to the chargeholder*]
    10.3 [*Date and identification of the written agreement giving rise to the unpaid vendor's charge*]
11. [*Where a possessory charge is being converted into a registered charge*]
    11.1 This registration statement is for the conversion of a possessory charge into a registered charge.
    11.2 [*Date on which possession of the charged property was given*] [*If later than the date of the charging instrument*]

Signature of chargor   Signature of charge manager (if appointed)

[*Or where an unpaid vendor's charge or a possessory charge is being converted into a registered charge Signature of chargeholder*]

Core Principles for a Secured Transactions Law prepared by the European Bank for Reconstruction and Development (1997) [1]

Since the publication of the EBRD Model Law in 1994 there has been a continuing programme of reform of security laws in the Bank's countries of operation. During the country-specific work of the Bank's Legal Transition Team it became evident that the Model Law is an important and helpful instrument for local reformers. However, it also became clear that a more general formulation of the goals and principles of successful reform to foster economic development would be useful. This has led the EBRD to define a set of ten core principles for modern secured transactions legislation. These principles form the basis for assessing a country's secured transactions law and for identifying the need for reform.

The principles have been drawn up on the assumption that the role of a secured transactions law is economic. It is not needed as part of the essential legal infrastructure of a country: its only use is to provide the legal framework which enables a market for secured credit to operate. The principles do not seek to impose any particular solution on a country—there may be many ways of arriving at a particular result—but they do seek to indicate the result that should be achieved. As with any set of general principles of this nature they must be read within the context of the law and practice of any particular country and they do not aim to be absolute; exceptions inevitably have to be made.

1. Security should reduce the risk of giving credit leading to an increased availability of credit on improved terms.

This goes to the basic assumption made by EBRD in all its work on secured transactions law reform.

2. The law should enable the quick, cheap and simple creation of a proprietary security right without depriving the person giving the security of the use of his assets.

In most market economy scenarios depriving the debtor of the use of his assets is self-defeating; non-possessory security which gives a remedy attached to the charged asset is an essential element of a modern secured transactions law. Any delay, cost, or complexity in the creation process reduces the economic efficiency of security.

3. If the secured debt is not paid the holder of security should be able to have the charged assets realised and to have the proceeds applied towards satisfaction of his claim prior to the other creditors.

The exact nature of the proprietary right that arises when security is granted has to be defined in the context of the relevant laws. If it is to be effective it must link to the creditor's claim the remedy of recovering from the assets given as security.

4. Enforcement procedures should enable prompt realisation at market value of the assets given as security.

---

[1] See also <www. ebrd.com/country/sector/law/st.htm>.

A remedy is only as good as the procedures and practice for exercising it allow it to be. If the value received on realization is expected to be only half the market value, then the provider of credit will require more assets to be given as security. If it is expected that enforcement will take two years, then the creditor will give less favourable credit terms to the debtor.

5. The security right should continue to be effective and enforceable after the bankruptcy or insolvency of the person who has given it.

The position against which the creditor most wants protection is the insolvency of the debtor. Any reduction of rights or dilution of priority upon insolvency will reduce the value of security. A limited exception to this principle may be necessary to make it compatible with rules which permit a moratorium at the commencement of insolvency.

6. The costs of taking, maintaining and enforcing security should be low.

A person granting credit will usually ensure that all costs connected with the credit are passed on to the debtor. High costs of security will be reflected in the price for credit and will diminish the efficiency of the credit market.

7. Security should be available (a) over all types of assets (b) to secure all types of debts and (c) between all types of person.

This principle covers a multitude of issues that may arise between the way in which law is applied and the needs of commercial reality. They may appear technical but can be of critical importance when seeking to implement a commercial agreement. With very limited exceptions (eg personal clothing) a person should be able to give security over any of his assets, including assets he may acquire in the future. Similarly a charge should be capable of securing any type of present or future debt or claim that can be expressed in money terms. The charged assets and the secured debt should be capable of general description (eg all machines in a factory, all debts arising under a sales contract). It should also be possible to charge constantly changing 'pools' of assets such as inventory, debts receivable, and stocks of equipment and to secure fluctuating debts, such as the amount due under a bank overdraft facility. Any physical or legal person (whether in the public or private sector) who is permitted by law to transfer property should be able to grant security.

8. There should be an effective means of publicising the existence of security rights.

Where security is possessory, the mere fact that the assets are held by the creditor is enough to alert third parties to the fact that the debtor has charged them. Where security is non-possessory, some other means (normally a public registry or notification system) is needed to ensure that third parties do not acquire charged assets without being made aware of the existence of the charge.

9. The law should establish rules governing competing rights of persons holding security and other persons claiming rights in the assets given as security.

Even when an effective means of publicity is in place there remain some cases for which the law has to provide, for example sales of charged assets in the ordinary course of the owner's business (where the purchaser cannot be expected to inspect a register before purchasing).

10. As far as possible the parties should be able to adapt security to the needs of their particular transaction.

The law is there to facilitate the operation of the secured credit market and to ensure that necessary protections are in place to prevent the debtor, the creditor, or third parties being unfairly prejudiced by secured transactions. It should not be the purpose of the law to create rules and structures for the operation of secured credit which are aimed principally at directing the manner in which parties to secured credit should structure their transactions.

BIBLIOGRAPHY

GENERAL LITERATURE (NOT SPECIFICALLY RELATED TO SECURED TRANSACTIONS)

Akerlof, George A, 'The market for "lemons": qualitative uncertainty and the market mechanism' (1970) 84 QJ Econ 488

Albrecht, Barthold, *Transformation durch Partizipation. Die Bedeutung alternativer Privatisierungsmethoden für den Erfolg der Reformen in Osteuropa* (Frankfurt am Main, 1996)

—— 'Privatization, Coordination and Agency Costs: The Case for Participation in Eastern Europe' (1996) 3 *International Tax and Public Finance* 351

Alexy, Robert, *Theorie der Grundrechte* (Frankfurt am Main, 1986)

Ammelung, Ulrich and Röver, Jan-Hendrik, 'Mezzaninefinanzierungen in der Praxis. Teil 1: Grundlegende wirtschaftliche, rechtliche und steuerliche Aspekte' (2006) *Finanzbetrieb News* 2; 7–8 'Teil 2: Instrumente mit fremdkapitalnahen Gestaltungen' (12 2006) 12 *Finanzbetrieb News* 2

Anderson, James H, Bernstein, David S, and Gray, Cheryl W, *Judicial Systems in Transition Economies. Assessing the Past, Looking to the Future* (Washington, DC, 2005)

Berman, Nathaniel, 'Aftershocks: Exoticization, Normalization, and the Hermeneutic Compulsion' (1997) Utah LR 281

Bernstein, Peter L, *Against the Gods. The Remarkable Story of Risk* (New York, 1996)

Canaris, Claus-Wilhelm, 'Bewegliches System und Vertrauensschutz im rechtsgeschäftlichen Verkehr' in Franz Bydlinski, Heinz Krejci, Bernd Schilcher and Viktor Steininger (eds), *Das Bewegliche System im geltenden und künftigen Recht* (Vienna, 1986) 103

Coase, Ronald H, *The Firm, the Market, and the Law* (Chicago, 1990)

Curran, Vivian Grosswald, 'Cultural Immersion, Difference and Categories in U.S. Comparative Law' (1998) 46 AJCL 43

Dagef, Carsten, *Internationales Finanzierungsleasing. Deutsches Kollisionsrecht und Konvention von Ottawa (1988)* (Munich, 1992)

Dalhuisen, Jan Hendrik, *Dalhuisen on International Commercial, Financial and Trade Law* (Oxford, 2000; 2nd edn, Oxford, 2004)

David, René and Brierley, John EC, *Major Legal Systems in the World Today. An Introduction to the Comparative Study of Law* (3rd edn, London, 1985)

—— and Spinosi, Camille Jauffret, *Les grands systèmes de droit contemporains* (8th edn, Paris, 1982)

Drobnig, Ulrich, 'Methodenfragen der Rechtsvergleichung im Lichte der "International Encyclopedia of Comparative Law"' in Ernst von Caemmerer, Soia Mentschikoff, and Konrad Zweigert (eds), *Ius Privatum Gentium. Festschrift für Max Rheinstein zum 70. Geburtstag am 5. Juli 1969* (Tübingen, 1969) 221

—— 'Vergleichende und kollisionsrechtliche Probleme der Girosammelverwahrung von Wertpapieren im Verhältnis Deutschland-Frankreich' in Herbert Bernstein,

Ulrich Drobnig and Hein Kötz (eds), *Festschrift für Konrad Zweigert zum 70. Geburtstag* (Tübingen, 1981) 73

—— 'Dokumentenloser Effektenverkehr' in Karl Kreuzer (ed), *Abschied vom Wertpapier? Dokumentenlose Wertbewegungen im Effekten-, Gütertransport- und Zahlungsverkehr. Arbeitssitzung der Fachgruppe für vergleichendes Handels- und Wirtschaftsrecht anläßlich der gemeinsamen Tagung der Deutschen und Österreichischen Gesellschaft für Rechtsvergleichung in Innsbruck vom 16.–19.9.1987* (Neuwied, 1988) 11

Eidenmüller, Horst, 'Rights, Systems of Rights, and Unger's System of Rights: Part 1' (1991) 10 *Law and Philosophy* 1; 'Part 2' (1991) 10 *Law and Philosophy* 119

Engisch, Karl, *Die Idee der Konkretisierung in Recht und Rechtswissenschaft unserer Zeit* (Heidelberg, 1968)

Esser, Josef, *Vorverständnis und Methodenwahl in der Rechtsfindung. Rationalitätsgrundlagen richterlicher Entscheidungsfindung* (Frankfurt am Main, 1972)

—— *Grundsatz und Norm in der richterlichen Fortbildung des Privatrechts. Rechtsvergleichende Beiträge zur Rechtsquellen- und Interpretationslehre* (4th edn, Tübingen, 1990)

Eucken, Walter, *Grundsätze der Wirtschaftspolitik* (6th edn, Tübingen, 1990)

Fahrholz, Bernd, *Neue Formen der Unternehmensfinanzierung* (Munich, 1998)

Feuer, Guy and Hervé Cassan, *Droit international du développement* (2nd edn, Paris, 1991)

Fikentscher, Wolfgang, *Methoden des Rechts in vergleichender Darstellung, vol III: Mitteleuropäischer Rechtskreis* (Tübingen, 1976)

—— *Modes of Thought. A Study in the Anthropology of Law and Religion* (Tübingen, 1995)

—— and Heinemann, Andreas, 'Der "Draft International Antitrust Code"—Initiative für ein Weltkartellrecht im Rahmen des GATT' (1994) *Wirtschaft und Wettbewerb* 97

Fleisig, Heywood, 'Economic Functions of Security in a Market Economy' in Joseph Norton and Mads Andenas (eds), *Emerging Financial Markets and Secured Transactions* (London, 1997) 15

Frankenberg, Günter, 'Critical Comparisons: Re-thinking Comparative Law' (1985) 26 Harv. ILJ 411

—— 'Stranger than Paradise: Identity and Politics in Comparative Law' (1997) Utah LR 259

Galbraith, John Kenneth, *Economics in Perspective. A Critical History* (Boston, 1987)

Gerber, David J, 'Constitutionalizing the Economy: German Neo-Liberalism, Competition Law and the New Europe' (1994) 42 AJCL 25

Heilbronner, Robert, *Worldly Philosophers. The Lives, Times and Ideas of the Great Economic Thinkers* (7th edn, London, 1999)

Heinemann, Andreas, *Die Freiburger Schule und ihre geistigen Wurzeln* (Munich, 1989)

Higson, Chris, *Business Finance* (2nd edn, London, 1995)

Hill, Jonathan, 'Comparative Law, Law Reform, and Legal Theory' (1989) OJLS 101

Jensen, Erik G and Heller, Thomas C (eds) *Beyond Common Knowledge. Empirical Approaches to the Rule of Law* (Stanford, 2003)

Kelman, M, *A Guide To Critical Legal Studies* (Cambridge, Mass, 1987)

Kennedy, David, 'New Approaches to Comparative Law: Comparativism and International Governance' (1997) Utah LR 545

Kötz, Hein, 'Rights of Third Parties. Third Party Beneficiaries and Assignment' in Arthur von Mehren (ed.) *International Encyclopedia of Comparative Law, vol VII: Contracts in General* (Tübingen, 1992) ch 13

Larenz, Karl and Canaris, Claus-Wilhelm, *Methodenlehre der Rechtswissenschaft* (3rd edn, Berlin, 1995)

Leenen, Detlef, *Typus und Rechtsfindung* (Berlin, 1971)

Legrand, Pierre, *Fragments on Law-as-Culture* (Deventer, 1999)

—— *Le Droit Comparé* (Paris, 1999)

—— 'Review of "Walter van Gerven et al. (eds.), Torts (Oxford 1998)"' (1999) CLJ 439

Lyotard, François, *La condition postmoderne: Rapport sur le savoir* (Paris, 1979)

Mann, FA, *The Legal Aspects of Money* (4th edn, Oxford, 1982); Proctor, Charles, *Mann on the Legal Aspects of Money* (6th edn, Oxford, 2005)

Mattei, Ugo, *Comparative Law and Economics* (Ann Arbor, Mich, 1997)

Mill, John Stuart, *A system of logic: ratiocinative and inductive, being a connected view of the principles of evidence and the methods of scientific investigation* (1843), also published as *The Logic of the Moral Sciences* (Chicago, 1994)

Newburg, Andre, 'The Nuclear Safety Account' (Autumn 1995) *Law in Transition* 7

—— 'Some Reflections on the Role of Law in the Transition Process' (August 1995) 58 and 59 *International Practitioner's Notebook* 22

North, Douglass C, *Institutions, Institutional Change and Economic Performance* (Cambridge, 1990)

—— and Thomas, Robert Paul, *The Rise of the Western World. A New Economic History* (Cambridge, 1973)

Örücü, Esik, 'Review of "Pierre Legrand, Fragments on Law-as-Culture (1999)" and "Pierre Legrand, Le Droit Comparé (1999)"' (2000) 49 ICLQ 996

Peters, Anne and Schwenke, Heiner, 'Comparative Law Beyond Post-Modernism' (2000) 49 ICLQ 800

Posner, Richard, *Economic Analysis of Law* (5th edn, Boston, 1998)

Rabel, Ernst, 'International Tribunals for Private Matters' (1948) *The Arbitration Journal* 209

—— 'Aufgabe und Notwendigkeit der Rechtsvergleichung' in Ernst Rabel, *Gesammelte Aufsätze*, vol III: *Arbeiten zur Rechtsvergleichung und zur Rechtsvereinheitlichung 1919–1954. Mit einem Verzeichnis der Schriften Ernst Rabels* (Hans G Leser (ed)) (Tübingen, 1967) 1

Ragin, Charles C, *The Comparative Method: Moving Beyond Qualitative and Quantitative Strategies* (Berkeley, Cal, 1989)

—— *Fuzzy-Set Social Science* (Chicago, 2000)

Richter, Rudolf, *Institutionen ökonomisch analysiert. Zur jüngeren Entwicklung auf einem Gebiet der Wirtschaftstheorie* (Tübingen, 1994)

Röver, Jan-Hendrik, *Vergleichende Prinzipien dinglicher Sicherheiten. Eine Studie zur Methode der Rechtsvergleichung* (Munich, 1999) (herein cited as: Röver, *Prinzipien*)

—— 'Projektfinanzierung' in Ulf R Siebel (ed), *Projekte und Projektfinanzierung* (Munich, 2001) 153

Rogers, Catherine, 'Gulliver's Troubled Travels, or the Conundrum of Comparative Law' (1998) 67 GWLR 149

Schlesinger, Rudolf B, 'Research on the General Principles of Law Recognized by Civilized Nations. Outline of a New Project' (1957) 51 AJIL 734

—— 'The Common Core of Legal Systems. An Emerging Subject of Comparative Study' in Kurt H Nadelmann, Arthur T von Mehren, and John N Hazard (eds), *XXth Century Comparative and Conflicts Law. Legal Essays in Honor of Hessel E. Yntema* (Leiden, 1961) 65

Schlesinger, Rudolf B (ed), *Formation of Contracts. A Study of the Common Core of Legal Systems*, 2 vols (Dobbs Ferry, NY, 1968)

—— *Comparative Law. Cases—Texts—Materials* (4th edn, New York, 1980)

—— 'The Past and Future of Comparative Law' (1995) 43 AJCL 477

——, Baade, Hans W, Damaska, Mirjan, and Herzog, Peter E, *Comparative Law. Cases—Texts—Materials* (5th edn, New York, 1988)

Smith, Adam, *Theory of Moral Sentiments* (DD Raphael and AL Macfie (eds)) (Oxford, 1978)

—— *Lectures on Jurisprudence* (RL Meek, DD Raphael and PG Stein (eds)) (Oxford, 1978)

—— *An Inquiry into the Nature and Causes of the Wealth of Nations* (RH Campbell, AS Skinner and WB Todd (eds)), vols I and II (Oxford, 1979)

Stiglitz, Joseph E, *Economics* (New York, 1993)

—— 'Whither Reform? Ten Years of Transition' in B Pleskovic and JE Stiglitz (eds), *Annual World Bank Conference on Economic Development* (Washington, DC, 2000) 27–56 also published in Ha-Joon Chang (ed), *The Rebel Within* (London, 2001) 127

—— and Weiss, Andrew, 'Credit rationing in markets with imperfect information' (1981) 71 *American Economic Review* 393

Unger, Roberto *The Critical Legal Studies Movement* (Cambridge, Mass, 1983)

USAID (ed), *Weighing in on the Scales of Justice: Strategic Approaches for Donor-Supported Rule of Law Programs* (Washington, DC, 1994)

Vorkink, Andrew N, *The World Bank and Legal Technical Assistance. Current Issues* (Washington, DC, 1997)

Waelde, Thomas W and Gunderson, James L, 'Legislative Reforms in Transition Economies: Western Transplants—A Short-cut to Social Market Economy Status' (1994) 43 ICLQ 345

Weber, Max, *Wirtschaft und Gesellschaft. Grundriß der verstehenden Soziologie* (5th edn, Tübingen, 1972)

Wood, Philip R, 'Where Now in World Financial Law?' (1995) *Butterworths Journal of International Banking and Financial Law* 55

—— *Law and Practice of International Finance. Comparative Financial Law* (London, 1995)

—— *Project Finance, Subordinated Debt and State Loans* (London, 1995)

—— *Comparative Law of Security and Guarantees* (London, 1995)

—— *Maps of World Financial Law* (5th edn, London, 2005)

World Bank Legal Department, 'The World Bank and Legal Technical Assistance. Initial Lessons', Policy Research Working Paper 1414 (Washington, DC, 1995)

World Bank, 'World Development Report 2005—A better investment climate for everyone' (Washington, DC, 2005)

Zweigert, Konrad and Kötz, Hein, *An Introduction to Comparative Law* (trans. Tony Weir) (Oxford, 1977); (2nd edn, Oxford, 1987); (3rd edn, Oxford, 1998)

GENERAL LITERATURE ON SECURED TRANSACTIONS LAW

Ali, Paul, *The Law of Secured Finance. An International Survey of Security Interests over Personal Property* (Oxford, 2002)

Allan, David E and Drobnig, Ulrich, 'Secured Credit in Commercial Insolvencies. A Comparative Analysis' (1980) 44 RabelsZ 615

Allan, David E, Hiscock, Mary E, and Roebuck, Derek (eds), *Law and Development Finance in Asia*, 11 vols (St Lucia, New York, 1973–1980); individual volumes are:

Allan, David E, Hiscock, Mary E, and Roebuck, Derek, *Credit and Security. The Legal Problems of Development Financing* (1974);

Gautama (Gouwgioksiong), Sudargo, Allan, David E, Hiscock, Mary E, and Roebuck, Derek, *Credit and Security in Indonesia. The Legal Problems of Development Finance* (1973);

Lian, Koh Khen, Allan, David E, Hiscock, Mary E, and Roebuck, Derek, *Credit and Security in Singapore. The Legal Problems of Development Finance* (1973);

Tanikawa, Hisashi, Allan, David E, Hiscock, Mary E, and Roebuck, Derek, *Credit and Security in Japan. The Legal Problems of Development Finance* (1973);

Kwack, Yoon Chick, Allan, David E, Hiscock, Mary E, and Roebuck, Derek, *Credit and Security in Korea. The Legal Problems of Development Finance* (1973);

Weerasooria, Wickrema, Allan, David E, Hiscock, Mary E, and Roebuck, Derek, *Credit and Security in Ceylon (Sri Lanka). The Legal Problems of Development Finance* (1973);

Jen-kong, Loh, Allan, David E, Hiscock, Mary E, and Roebuck, Derek, *Credit and Security in the Republic of China. The Legal Problems of Development Finance* (1973);

Guzman, Jr, Sixto TJ de, Allan, David E, Hiscock, Mary E, and Roebuck, Derek, *Credit and Security in the Philippines. The Legal Problems of Development Finance* (1973);

Tingsabadh, Chitti, Allan, David E, Hiscock, Mary E, and Roebuck, Derek, *Credit and Security in Thailand. The Legal Problems of Development Finance* (1974);

Allan, David E, Hiscock, Mary E, Masel, Leigh, and Roebuck, Derek, *Credit and Security in Australia. The Legal Problems of Development Finance* (1977);

Singh, (Jagundiv), Allan, David E, Hiscock, Mary E, and Roebuck, Derek, *Credit and Security in West Malaysia. The Legal Problems of Development Finance* (1980)

Bates, Jonathan, Blumenfeld, Lane, Fagelson, David, Fedorov, Vladimir, Labin, Dmitry, Röver, Jan-Hendrik, and Simpson, John (eds), *International Conference on Secured Commercial Lending in the Commonwealth of Independent States. Conference Proceedings* (London, 1995)

Bazinas, Spiros, 'An International Legal Regime for Receivables Financing: UNCITRAL's Contribution' (1998) 8 *Duke Journal of Comparative and International Law* 315

—— 'Der Beitrag von UNCITRAL zur Vereinheitlichung der Rechtsvorschriften über Forderungsabtretungen: Das Übereinkommen der Vereinten Nationen über Abtretungen von Forderungen im internationalen Handel' (2002) ZEuP 782

—— 'Key Policy Issues of the United Nations Convention on the Assignment of Receivables in International Trade' (2003) 11 Tulane JICL 275

Bebchuk, Lucian A and Fried, Jesse M, 'The Uneasy Case for the Priority of Secured Claims in Bankruptcy' (1996) 105 YLJ 857

Bridge, Michael and Stevens, Robert (eds), *Cross-border Security and Insolvency* (Oxford, 2001)

Buxbaum, HL, 'Unification of the law governing secured transactions: progress and prospects for reform' (2003) 8 *Uniform Law Review/ Revue de droit uniforme* 321

Cohen, Neil B, 'Harmonising the Law Governing Secured Credit: the Next Frontier' (1998) *Texas International Law Journal* 173

Cuming, Ronald CC and Wood, Roderick J, *Saskatchewan and Manitoba Personal Property Security Acts Handbook* (Toronto, 1994)

Dahan, Frédérique, 'Secured Transactions Law in Western Economies: Exposing Myths' (Autumn 2000) *Law in Transition* 37, also published in (2001) 16 *Butterworths Journal of International Banking and Financial Law* 60

Dalhuisen, Jan Hendrik, 'Security in Movable and Intangible Property. Finance Sales, Future Interests and Trusts' in AS Hartkamp, MW Hesselink, EH Hondius, CE du Perron and JBM Vranken (eds), *Towards a European Civil Code* (Nijmegen, 1994) 361

—— 'International Aspects of Secured Transactions and Finance Sales Involving Movable and Intangible Property' in D Kokkini-Iatridou and FW Grosheide (eds), *Eenvormig en Vergelijkend Privaatrecht 1994* (Lelystad, 1994) 405

—— *Dalhuisen on International Commercial, Financial and Trade Law* (2nd edn, Oxford, 2004)

Drobnig, Ulrich, *Empfehlen sich gesetzliche Maßnahmen zur Reform der Mobiliarsicherheiten? Gutachten F für den 51. Deutschen Juristentag* (Munich, 1976)

—— 'Legal principles governing security interests (document A/CN.9/131 and annex)' (1977) VIII *UNCITRAL Yearbook* 171

—— 'Security Rights in Cross-border Insolvencies' in Ian F Fletcher (ed), *Cross-border Insolvency: Comparative Dimensions* (London, 1990) 216

—— 'Die Verwertung von Mobiliarsicherheiten in einigen Ländern der Europäischen Union' (1996) 60 *RabelsZ* 40

—— 'A Comparative Introduction to Security Over Movables and Intangibles' in Joseph J Norton and Mads Andenas (eds), *Emerging Financial Markets and Secured Transactions* (London, 1998) 5

—— 'Transfer of Property' in AS Hartkamp, MW Hesselink, EH Hondius, CE du Perron and JBM Vranken (eds), *Towards a European Civil Code* (2nd edn, Nijmegen, 1998) 495

—— 'Security Rights in Movables' in AS Hartkamp, MW Hesselink, EH Hondius, CE du Perron and JBM Vranken (eds), *Towards a European Civil Code* (2nd edn, Nijmegen, 1998) 511

—— 'Mobiliarsicherheiten—Vielfalt oder Einheit? Vergleichender Generalbericht' in Karl F Kreuzer (ed), *Mobiliarsicherheiten—Vielfalt oder Einheit* (Baden-Baden, 1999) 9

Eidenmüller, Horst, 'Vertragliche Vorkehrungen gegen Insolvenzrisiken' in Dieter Hart (ed), *Privatrecht im 'Risikostaat'* (Baden-Baden, 1997) 43

—— 'Internationale Entwicklungen im Recht der Kreditsicherheiten' in Walther Hadding, Klaus J Hopt, and Herbert Schimansky (eds), *Aktuelle Entwicklungen im Recht der Kreditsicherheiten—national und international* (*Bankrechtstag*, 2004) (Berlin, 2005) 117

Garro, Alejandro M, 'Security Interests in Personal Property in Latin America: A Comparison with Article 9 and a Model for Reform' (1987) 9 *Houston Journal of International Law* 157

—— 'The Reform and Harmonization of Personal Property Security Law in Latin America' (1990) 59 *Revista Juridíca Universidad de Puerto Rico*, 1

Goode, Sir Roy, *Convention on International Interests in Mobile Equipment and Protocol Thereto on Matters Specific to Aircraft Equipment. Official Commentary* (Rome, 2002)

——, Kronke, Herbert, McKendrick, Ewan, and Wool, Jeffrey (eds), *Transnational Commercial Law. International Instruments and Commentary* (Oxford, 2004)

Gretton, George L, 'Mixed Systems: Scotland' in Joseph J Norton and Mads Andenas (eds), *Emerging Financial Markets and Secured Transactions* (London, 1998) 279

Guynn, Randall D, Rogers, James Steven, Sono, Kazuaki, and Than, Jürgen, *Modernizing Securities Ownership, Transfer and Pledging Laws. A Discussion Paper on the Need for International Harmonization* (London, 1997)

Kieninger, Eva-Maria, *Mobiliarsicherheiten im Europäischen Binnenmarkt. Zum Einfluß der Warenverkehrsfreiheit auf das nationale und internationale Sachenrecht der Mitgliedstaaten* (Baden-Baden, 1996)

—— (ed), *Security Rights in Movable Property in European Private Law* (Cambridge, 2004)

—— 'Evaluation: A Common Core? Convergence, Subsisting Differences and Possible Ways for Harmonization' in Eva-Maria Kieninger (ed), *Security Rights in Movable Property in European Private Law* (Cambridge, 2004) 647

—— and Schütte, Elisabeth, 'Neue Chancen für internationale Finanzierungsgeschäfte: Die UN-Abtretungskonvention' (2003) ZIP 2181

Kreuzer, Karl F, 'Europäisches Mobiliarsicherungsrecht oder: Von den Grenzen des Internationalen Privatrechts' in *Conflits et harmonisation. Mélanges en l'honneur d'Alfred E. von Overbeck* (Freiburg, Switz, 1990) 613

Löber, Klaus M, 'Der Entwurf einer Richtlinie für Finanzsicherheiten' (2001) BKR 118

—— 'Die EG-Richtlinie über Finanzsicherheiten' (2002) BKR 601

Muent, Holger and Pissarides, Francesca, 'Impact of collateral practice on lending to small and medium sized enterprises' (Autumn 2000) *Law in Transition* 54

Pedrazzini, Massimo and Simpson, John, 'The Legal Framework for Secured Credit: A Suitable Case for Treatment' (1999) *Business Law International* 127

Reuschle, Fabian, 'Haager Übereinkommen über die auf bestimmte Rechte in Bezug auf Intermediär-verwahrte Wertpapiere anzuwendende Rechtsordnung' (2003) IPRax 495

Röver, Jan-Hendrik, 'Preparation of a Unidroit Convention on security interests in mobile equipment' (Summer 1994) *Law in Transition* 15

—— Unification work by UNCITRAL on assignment of claims (Winter/Spring 1994) *Law in Transition* 28

—— *Vergleichende Prinzipien dinglicher Sicherheiten. Eine Studie zur Methode der Rechtsvergleichung* (Munich, 1999) (herein cited as: Röver, *Prinzipien*)

—— *Comparative Principles of security interests: secured debt and charged property* (PhD thesis, King's College London, 2004)

Rott, Thilo, *Vereinheitlichung des Rechts der Mobiliarsicherheiten. Möglichkeiten und Grenzen im Kollisions-, Europa-, Sach- und Vollstreckungsrecht unter Berücksichtigung des US-amerikanischen Systems der Kreditsicherheiten* (Tübingen, 2000)

Simpson, John, 'Ten years of secured transactions reform' (2001) *Butterworths Journal of International Banking and Financial Law* 5

—— and Menze, Joachim, 'Ten years of secured transactions reform' (Autumn 2000) *Law in Transition*, 20, 22–24

—— and Röver, Jan-Hendrik, 'Comments on the UNIDROIT project for drawing up a check list of the issues to be addressed in a possible future model law in the general field of secured transactions', UNIDROIT, 1994, Study LXXIIA-Doc 3

Stöcker, Otmar M, *Die 'Eurohypothek'. Zur Bedeutung eines einheitlichen nicht-akzessorischen Grundpfandrechts für den Aufbau eines 'Europäischen Binnenmarktes für den Hypothekarkredit' mit einer Darstellung der Verwendung der Grundschuld durch die deutsche Hypothekarpraxis sowie des französischen, spanischen und schweizerischen Hypothekenrechts* (Berlin, 1992)

Tajti, Tibor, *Comparative Secured Transactions Law* (Budapest, 2002)

Wood, Philip R, *Comparative Law of Security and Guarantees* (London, 1995)

—— *Title Finance, Derivatives, Securitisations, Set-off and Netting* (London, 1995)

—— *Principles of International Insolvency* (London, 1997)

—— 'World-Wide Security—Classification of Legal Jurisdictions' in Joseph J Norton and Mads Andenas (eds), *Emerging Financial Markets and Secured Transactions* (London, 1998) 39

EBRD MODEL LAW ON SECURED TRANSACTIONS AND CORE PRINCIPLES FOR A MODERN SECURED TRANSACTIONS LAW

Akahane, Takashi, 'The EBRD's Model Law on Secured Transactions: new developments' (Autumn/Winter 1997) *Law in Transition* 12

Albrecht, Barthold, *Transformation durch Partizipation. Die Bedeutung alternativer Privatisierungsmethoden für den Erfolg der Reformen in Osteuropa* (Frankfurt am Main, 1996)

—— 'Privatization, Coordination and Agency Costs: The Case for Participation in Eastern Europe' (1996) 3 *International Tax and Public Finance* 351

Bates, Jonathan, 'EBRD's model law on secured transactions' (4 August 1994) *Project Finance International* 36

—— 'EBRD's Model law on secured transactions and the reform process' (January 1995) *The Moscow Letter* 114

Bókai, Judit and Szeibert, Orsolya Erdôs, 'Die Mobiliarhypothek und deren Register' in Bundesnotarkammer (ed), *Festschrift für Helmut Schippel zum 65. Geburtstag* (Munich, 1996) 843

Dageförde, Carsten, 'Five years of the Secured Transactions Project—a survey' (Spring 1997) *Law in Transition* 12

—— 'Das besitzlose Mobiliarpfandrecht nach dem Modellgesetz für Sicherungsgeschäfte der Europäischen Bank für Wiederaufbau und Entwicklung (EBRD Model Law on Secured Transactions)' (1998) ZEuP 686

Dahan, Frédérique and McCormack, Gerard, 'Secured Transactions in Countries in Transition (The Case of Poland): From Model to Assessment' (1999) *European Business Law Review* 85

—— and McCormack, Gerard, 'International Influences and the Polish Law on Secured Transactions: Harmonisation, Unification or What?' (2002–3) *Uniform Law Review* 713

—— and Simpson, John, 'The European Bank for Reconstruction and Development's Secured Transactions Project: a model law and ten core principles for a modern secured transactions law in countries of Central and Eastern Europe (and elsewhere!)' in Eva-Maria Kieninger (ed), *Security Rights in Movable Property in European Private Law* (Cambridge, 2004) 98

Dowmunt-Iwaszkiewicz, Aniela, Roggeman, Juliette, and Wasserman, Karen, *Un nouveau droit des sûretés pour les pays d'Europe de l'est. La loi-modèle sur les sûretés de la Banque Européenne pour la Reconstruction et le Développement (BERD)* 2 vols (dissertation, Paris I Pantheon-Sorbonne, 1995)

Drobnig, Ulrich, 'First working draft of the Model Law on Security Rights for Eastern Europe' (Autumn 1993) *Law in Transition* 7

EBRD, *Model Law on Secured Transactions. Speeches given at the Presentation of the Model Law during the Third Annual Meeting of the EBRD on 16 April 1994 in St Petersburg* (London, 1994)

EBRD, *Legal Indicator Survey 2003*, also printed in EBRD, *The Impact of the Legal Framework on the Secured Credit Market in Poland* (London, 2005) Appendix B

EBRD, *Publicity of Security Rights. Guiding Principles for the Development of a Charges Registry* (London, 2004)

EBRD *Publicity of Security Rights. Setting Standards for Charges Registries* (London, 2005)

Editorial, 'A Regional Approach to Secured Transactions' (Autumn 1992) *Law in Transition* 3

Editorial, 'Secured Transactions Project' (Winter 1992/93) *Law in Transition* 4

Editorial, 'The EBRD's Secured Transactions Project' (Autumn 1993) *Law in Transition* 6

Editorial, 'A model law with nowhere to go?' (May 1994) *Financial Times Eastern European Business Law* 2

Editorial, 'A model way of doing business' (May/June 1994) *East European Banker* 14

Editorial, 'Presentation of the Model Law on Secured Transactions in St Petersburg' (Summer 1994) *Law in Transition* 12

Fairgrieve, Duncan, 'Reforming Secured Transactions Laws in Central and Eastern Europe' (1998) *European Business Law Review* 245

Gárdos, István and Bánhegyi, Ilona, 'EBRD-zálogjogmodell' (7 March 1993) *Bank & Tözsde* 19

Gavalda, Christian, 'L'assemblée du Conseil des Gouverneurs de la B.E.R.D. Un Modèle de loi uniform sur les sûretés des conventions passées avec les pays de l'est élaboré par l'Office du Conseil Général de la B.E.R.D. Révision de Saint-Pétersbourg des 15 au 19 Avril 1994' (8 June 1994) *Les Petites Affiches* 6

Kieninger, Eva-Maria, *Mobiliarsicherheiten im Europäischen Binnenmarkt. Zum Einfluß der Warenverkehrsfreiheit auf das nationale und internationale Sachenrecht der Mitgliedstaaten* (Baden-Baden, 1996)

Kreuzer, Karl, 'The Model Law on Secured Transactions of the EBRD from a German Point of View' in Joseph J Norton and Mads Andenas (eds), *Emerging Financial Markets and Secured Transactions* (London, 1998) 175

McCormack, Gerard and Dahan, Frédérique, 'The EBRD Model Law on Secured Transactions: Comparison and Convergence' (1998) 3 *Company, Financial and Insolvency Law Review* 65

Mistelis, Loukas, 'The EBRD Model Law on Secured Transactions and Its Impact on Collateral Law Reform in Central and Eastern Europe and the former Soviet Union' (1998) 5 *Parker School Journal of East European Law* 455

Newburg, Andre, 'Some Reflections on the Role of Law in the Transition Process' (1995) 58 and 59 *International Practitioner's Notebook* 22

—— 'Legal Assistance in Eastern Europe: The EBRD's Model Law on Secured Transactions' in Albrecht Weber in cooperation with Ludwig Gramlich, Ulrich Häde, and Franz Zehetner (eds), *Währung und Wirtschaft. Das Geld im Recht. Festschrift für Hugo J. Hahn zum 70. Geburtstag* (Baden-Baden, 1997) 441

Rice, Robert, 'Clearing the way for capital' *Financial Times* 14 June 1994, 20

Rott, Thilo, *Vereinheitlichung des Rechts der Mobiliarsicherheiten. Möglichkeiten und*

Grenzen im Kollisions-, Europa-, Sach- und Vollstreckungsrecht unter Berücksichtigung des US-amerikanischen Systems der Kreditsicherheiten (Tübingen, 2000)

Röver, Jan-Hendrik, 'Security in central and eastern Europe and the EBRD's Model Law on Secured Transactions' (Autumn 1994) *Law in Transition* 10

—— 'The Model Law on Secured Transactions Prepared by the European Bank for Reconstruction and Development for the Countries of Central and Eastern Europe and the Commonwealth of Independent States', paper given at the seminar 'Current Trends in the Modernisation of the Law Governing Personal Property Security' held by UNIDROIT and the International Bar Association on 28 November 1994 in Rome; unpublished

—— 'Das EBWE-Modellgesetz für Sicherungsgeschäfte' in Karl F Kreuzer (ed), *Mobiliarsicherheiten—Vielfalt oder Einheit?* (Baden-Baden, 1998) 125

—— 'An Approach to Legal Reform in Central and Eastern Europe: The European Bank's Model Law on Secured Transactions' (1998/1999) 1 *European Journal of Law Reform*, 119

—— *Vergleichende Prinzipien dinglicher Sicherheiten. Eine Studie zur Methode der Rechtsvergleichung* (Munich, 1999) (herein cited as: Röver, *Prinzipien*)

—— *Comparative Principles of security interests: secured debt and charged property* (PhD thesis, King's College London, 2004)

—— and Simpson, John, *General Principles of a Modern Secured Transactions Law* (London: EBRD, 1997), also published in (1997) III *NAFTA: Law & Business Review of the Americas* 73 and in Joseph J Norton and Mads Andenas (eds), *Emerging Financial Markets and Secured Transactions* (London, 1998) 143

Seif, Ulrike, *Der Bestandsschutz besitzloser Mobiliarsicherheiten im deutschen und englischen Recht* (Tübingen, 1997)

Simpson, John, 'Ten years of secured transactions reform' (2001) *Butterworths Journal of International Banking and Financial Law* 5

—— and Röver, Jan-Hendrik, 'Second working draft of the Model Law' (Autumn 1993) *Law in Transition*, 10

—— and Röver, Jan-Hendrik, 'Model Law on Secured Transactions completed' (Winter/Spring 1994) *Law in Transition*, 1

—— and Röver, Jan-Hendrik, 'Introduction' in EBRD (ed), *Model Law on Secured Transactions* (London, 1994) v–vii, also published as 'An Introduction to the European Bank's Model Law on Secured Transactions' in Joseph J Norton and Mads Andenas (eds), *Emerging Financial Markets and the Role of International Financial Organisations* (London, The Hague, and Boston 1996) 165, also published in Joseph J Norton and Mads Andenas (eds), *Emerging Financial Markets and Secured Transactions* (London, 1998), 439

—— and Röver, Jan-Hendrik, *EBRD Model Law on Secured Transactions. A Response to Comments by John A. Spanogle* (Washington, DC, 1995)

—— and Röver, Jan-Hendrik, 'The EBRD's Secured Transactions Project: a progress report' (Spring 1996) *Law in Transition*, 20

Spanogle, John A, *EBRD Model Law on Secured Transactions* (Washington, DC, 1994)

—— 'A Functional Analysis of the EBRD Model Law on Secured Transactions' (1997) III *NAFTA: Law & Business Review of the Americas* 82, also published in Joseph J Norton and Mads Andenas (eds), *Emerging Financial Markets and Secured Transactions* (London, 1998) 157

Summers, Elizabeth A, 'Recent Secured Transactions Law Reform in the Newly

Independent States and Central and Eastern Europe' (1997) 23 *Review of Central and Eastern European Law* 177

Tajti, Tibor, *Comparative Secured Transactions Law* (Budapest, 2002)

Tveiten, Margit F, 'Generalpant for Øst-Europa. En Modell-lov for nasjonale pantelover' (1995) *Lov og Rett* 188

Ziegel, Jacob S, 'The EBRD Model Law on Secured Transactions—Some Canadian Observations' in Jürgen Basedow, Klaus J Hopt, and Hein Kötz (eds), *Festschrift für Ulrich Drobnig zum siebzigsten Geburtstag* (Tübingen, 1998), 209

ENGLISH SECURED TRANSACTIONS LAW

Bell, Andrew P, *Modern Law of Personal Property in England and Wales* (London, 1989)

Benjamin, Joanna, *Interests in Securities. A Proprietary Law Analysis of the International Securities Markets* (Oxford, 2000)

Bridge, Michael, *Personal Property Law* (2nd edn, London, 1996)

—— 'The English Law of Security: Creditor-friendly but Unreformed' in Eva-Maria Kieninger (ed), *Security Rights in Movable Property in European Private Law* (Cambridge, 2004) 81

Collier, JG, *Conflict of Laws* (3rd edn, Cambridge, 2001)

Dalhuisen, Jan Hendrik, *Dalhuisen on International Commercial, Financial and Trade Law* (2nd edn, Oxford, 2004)

Department of Trade and Industry, *The Registration of Companies' Security Interests (Company Charges). The Economic Impact of the Law Commissions Proposals (Consultation Document)* (London, 2005)

Diamond, Aubrey L, *A Review of Security Interests in Property* (London, 1989)

Dicey, Morris, and Collins on the Conflict of Laws (14th edn, London, 2006)

Drobnig, Ulrich, 'Das trust receipt als Sicherungsmittel im amerikanischen und englischen Recht' (1961) 26 RabelsZ 401

Ferran, Eilís, *Company Law and Corporate Finance* (Oxford, 1999)

Goode, Sir Roy, *Legal Problems of Credit and Security* (2nd edn, London, 1988); (3rd edn, London, 2003)

—— *Proprietary Rights and Insolvency in Sales Transactions* (2nd edn, London, 1989)

—— *Principles of Corporate Insolvency Law* (London, 1990)

—— 'Security Interests in Movables under English Law' in Karl F Kreuzer (ed), *Mobiliarsicherheiten—Vielfalt oder Einheit?* (Baden-Baden, 1998) 43

—— *Commercial Law* (2nd edn, London, 1995); (3nd edn, London, 2004)

—— and Gower, LCB, 'Is Article 9 of the Uniform Commercial Code Exportable? An English Reaction' in Jacob S Ziegel and William F Foster (eds), *Aspects of Comparative Commercial Law: Sales, Consumer Credit, and Secured Transactions* (Montreal, 1969) 298

Gough, William James, *Company Charges* (2nd edn, London, 1996)

Gower, LCB, *Gower's Principles of Modern Company Law* (5th edn, London, 1992)

Guest, Anthony G and Lomnicka, Eva, *An Introduction to the Law of Credit and Security* (London, 1987)

Law Commission, *Registration of Security Interests: Company Charges and Property other than Land* (Law Com No 164, 2002) <http://www.lawcom.gov.uk>

—— *Company Security Interests* (Law Com No 176, 2002) <http://www.lawcom.gov.uk>

Law Commission, *Company Security Interests* (Law Com No. 296, 2005) <http://www.lawcom.gov.uk>

Lord Hailsham of St Marylebone (ed), *Halsbury's Laws of England* (4th edn, reissue, London, 1973ff)

Lawson, FH and Rudden, Bernhard, *The Law of Property* (2nd edn, Oxford, 1982); (3rd edn, Oxford, 2002)

Lipstein, Kurt, 'Introduction: Some Comparisons with English Law' in Rolf Serick (ed), *Securities in Movables in German Law: An Outline* (trans Tony Weir) (Deventer, 1990) 1

McCormack, Gerard, *Reservation of Title* (London, 1990)

—— *Secured Credit Under English and American Law* (Cambridge, 2004)

Morse, GK *et al* (eds), *Palmer's Company Law* (1992, looseleaf)

Pennington, Robert R, *Corporate Insolvency Law* (London, 1991)

—— *Company Law* (7th edn, London, 1995)

Seif, Ulrike, *Der Bestandsschutz besitzloser Mobiliarsicherheiten im deutschen und englischen Recht* (Tübingen, 1997)

Tennekoon, Ravi, *The Law and Regulation of International Finance* (London, 1991)

ter Meulen, Edzard, *Die Floating Charge—ein Sicherungsrecht am Vermögen einer englischen Company. Ein rechtsvergleichender Beitrag zu den Problemen der Sicherungsübertragung* (Frankfurt am Main, 1969)

Triebel, Volker, Hodgson, Stephen, Kellenter, Wolfgang, and Müller, Georg, *Englisches Handel- und Wirtschaftsrecht* (2nd edn, Heidelberg, 1995)

Tyler, ELG, *Fisher & Lightwood's Law of Mortgages* (11th edn, London, 1997)

Wenckstern, Manfred, 'Die englische Floating Charge im deutschen Internationalen Privatrecht' (1992) 56 RabelsZ 624

GERMAN SECURED TRANSACTIONS LAW

Baur, Jürgen F and Stürner, Rolf, *Lehrbuch des Sachenrechts* (17th edn, Munich, 1999)

Becker, Christoph, *Maßvolle Kreditsicherung* (Cologne, 1999)

Becker-Eberhard, Eberhard, *Die Forderungsgebundenheit der Sicherungsrechte* (Bielefeld, 1993)

Blaurock, Uwe, *Aktuelle Probleme des Kreditsicherungsrechts* (3rd edn, Cologne, 1990)

Blomeyer, Karl, *Hypotheken und Grundschulden* (Frankfurt au Main, 1980)

Bülow, Peter, *Recht der Kreditsicherheiten. Sachen und Rechte, Personen. Ein Lehrbuch* (6th edn, Heidelberg, 2003)

Clemente, Clemens, *Recht der Sicherungsgrundschuld* (3rd edn, Cologne, 1999)

Dilcher, Hermann, *Sachenrecht in programmierter Form* (5th edn, Berlin, 1990)

Drobnig, Ulrich, *Empfehlen sich gesetzliche Maßnahmen zur Reform der Mobiliarsicherheiten? Gutachten F für den 51. Deutschen Juristentag* (Munich, 1976)

Eckert, Jörn, *Sachenrecht* (3rd edn, Baden-Baden, 2002)

Eichler, Herrmann, *Institutionen des Sachenrechts*, vol 1: *Allgemeiner Teil* (Berlin, 1954); vol 2/1: *Besonderer Teil. Eigentum und Besitz* (Berlin, 1957); vol 2/2: *Besonderer Teil. Die dinglichen Rechte* (Berlin, 1960)

Fikentscher, Wolfgang and Heinemann, Andreas, *Schuldrecht* (10th edn, Berlin, 2006)

Früh, Andreas, *Bürgerliches Recht* (Heidelberg, 2002)

Gaberdiel, Heinz, *Kreditsicherung durch Grundschulden* (7th edn, Stuttgart, 2004)

Grunewald, Barbara, *Bürgerliches Recht* (6th edn, Munich, 2002)

Hadding, Walther and Schneider, Uwe H (eds), *Gesellschaftsanteile als Kreditsicherheit* (Berlin, 1979)

Hager, Johannes, *Verkehrsschutz durch redlichen Erwerb* (Munich, 1990)

Heck, Philipp, *Grundriß des Sachenrechts* (Tübingen, 1930; reprint Aalen, 1960)

Hellner, Thorwald and Steuer, Stephan (eds), *Bankrecht und Bankpraxis* (BuB), 5 vols (looseleaf, Cologne)

Huber, Ulrich, *Die Sicherungsgrundschuld* (Heidelberg, 1965)

Köndgen, Johannes, *Gewährung und Abwicklung grundpfandrechtlich gesicherter Kredite* (4th edn, Cologne, 2000)

Lwowski, Hans-Jürgen and Gößmann, Wolfgang, *Kreditsicherheiten. Grundzüge für Studium und Praxis* (6th edn, Berlin, 1987)

Medicus, Dieter, *Bürgerliches Recht* (20th edn, Cologne, 2004)

—— 'Die Akzessorietät im Privatrecht' (1971) *Juristische Schulung* 597

—— *Grundwissen zum Bürgerlichen Recht. Ein Basisbuch zu den Anspruchsgrundlagen* (6th edn, Cologne, 2004)

Müller, Klaus, *Sachenrecht* (4th edn, Cologne, 1997)

Neuner, Jörg, *Beck'sches Examinatorium: Sachenrecht* (2nd edn, Munich, 2005)

Nordhues, Hans-Günter, *Globalzession und Prioritätsprinzip* (Munich, 1993)

Palandt, *Bürgerliches Gesetzbuch* (66th edn, Munich, 2007)

Pallas, Maren, *Die Rechtsstellung der Sicherungsgeber bei der Verwertung des Sicherungseigentums* (Cologne, 2003)

Pottschmidt, Günter and Rohr, Ulrich, *Kreditsicherungsrecht. Ein Handbuch für Studium und Praxis* (4th edn, Munich, 2002)

Rauch, Wolfgang and Zimmermann, Steffen, *Grundschuld und Hypothek. Der Realkredit in der Bankenpraxis* (2nd edn, Munich, 1998)

Reeb, Hartmut, *Recht der Kreditfinanzierung* (Munich, 1994)

Reinicke, Dietrich and Tiedtke, Klaus, *Kreditsicherung durch Schuldbeitritt, Bürgschaft, Patronatserklärung, Garantie, Sicherungsübereignung, Sicherungsabtretung, Eigentumsvorbehalt, Pool-Vereinbarungen, Pfandrecht an beweglichen Sachen und Rechten, Hypothek und Grundschuld* (4th edn, Neuwied, 2000)

Rimmelspacher, Bruno, *Kreditsicherungsrecht* (2nd edn, Munich, 1987)

Röver, Jan-Hendrik, *Vergleichende Prinzipien dinglicher Sicherheiten. Eine Studie zur Methode der Rechtsvergleichung* (Munich 1999) (herein cited as: Röver, *Prinzipien*)

—— 'Comparative Principles of security interests: secured debt and charged property' (PhD thesis, King's College London, 2004)

Schaarschmidt, Wilhelm, Engelken, Heiko, Fischer, Reinfrid, and Herbst, Gerhard, *Die Sparkassenkredite* (Stuttgart, 2001)

Schapp, Jan and Schur, Wolfgang, *Sachenrecht* (3rd edn, Munich, 2002)

Schimansky, Herbert, Bunte, Herrmann-Josef, and Lwowski, Hans-Jürgen (eds), *Bankrechts-Handbuch*, 3 vols (2nd edn, Munich, 2001)

Scholz, Hellmut and Lwowski, Hans-Jürgen, *Das Recht der Kreditsicherung* (6th edn, Berlin, 1986)

Schreiber, Klaus, *Sachenrecht* (4th edn, Munich, 2003)

Schwab, Karl Heinz and Prütting, Hanns, *Sachenrecht* (32nd edn, Munich, 2006)

Serick, Rolf, *Eigentumsvorbehalt und Sicherungsübertragung*:

    vol I: *Der einfache Eigentumsvorbehalt* (Heidelberg, 1963);

    vol II: *Die einfache Sicherungsübertragung—Erster Teil* (Heidelberg, 1965);

    vol III: *Die einfache Sicherungsübertragung—Zweiter Teil* (Heidelberg, 1970);

    vol IV: *Verlängerungs- und Erweiterungsformen des Eigentumsvorbehalts und der*

Sicherungsübertragung—Erster Teil: Verlängerungsformen und Kollisionen (Heidelberg, 1976);

vol V: *Verlängerungs- und Erweiterungsformen des Eigentumsvorbehalts und der Sicherungsübertragung—Zweiter Teil: Erweiterungsformen,—Dritter Teil: Sonstiges: Insolvenzrecht (Konkurs)* (Heidelberg, 1982);

vol VI: *Verlängerungs- und Erweiterungsformen des Eigentumsvorbehalts und der Sicherungsübertragung,—Dritter Teil: Sonstiges: Insolvenzrecht (Vergleich); Insolvenzrechtsreform* (Heidelberg, 1986)

—— *Eigentumsvorbehalt und Sicherungsübertragung. Neue Rechtsentwicklungen* (2nd edn, Heidelberg, 1993)

Vieweg, Klaus and Werner, Almuth, *Sachenrecht* (Cologne, 2003)

Weber, Hansjörg, *Kreditsicherheiten. Recht der Sicherungsgeschäfte* (8th edn, Munich, 2006)

Weirich, Hans-Armin, *Grundstücksrecht* (2nd edn, Munich, 1996)

Westermann, Harm Peter, *Sachenrecht* (10th edn, Heidelberg, 2002)

——, Eickmann, Dieter, and Gursky, Karl-Heinz, *Sachenrecht* (7th edn, Heidelberg, 1998)

Westermann, Harry, *Sachenrecht* vol I: *Grundlagen und Recht der beweglichen Sachen* (6th edn, Heidelberg, 1990); vol II: *Immobiliarsachenrecht* (6th edn, Heidelberg, 1988)

Wieling, Hans Josef, *Sachenrecht I*, vol 1: *Sachen, Besitz und Rechte an beweglichen Sachen* (Berlin, 1990)

—— *Sachenrecht* (4th edn, Berlin, 2001)

Wilhelm, Jan, *Sachenrecht* (2nd edn, Berlin, 2002)

Wolf, Manfred, *Sachenrecht* (22nd edn, Munich, 2006)

Wolff, Martin and Raiser, Ludwig, *Sachenrecht* (10th edn, Tübingen, 1957)

US SECURED TRANSACTIONS LAW

Anderson, Ronald A, *Uniform Commercial Code* (Rochester, 1981ff)

——, Fox, Ivan, and Twomey, David P, *Business Law and the Legal Environment* (Cincinnati, Ohio, 1993)

Bailey III, Henry J and Hagedorn, Richard B, *Secured Transactions in a Nutshell* (3rd edn, St Paul, Minn, 1988)

Baird, Douglas G and Jackson, Thomas H, *Cases, Problems, and Materials on Security Interests in Personal Property* (Mineola, NY, 1984)

Clark, Barkley, *The Law of Secured Transactions under the Uniform Commercial Code* (looseleaf, Boston, Mass)

Coogan, Peter F, Hogan, William E, Vagts, Detlev F, and McDonnell, Julian B, *Secured Transactions under the Uniform Commercial Code* (looseleaf, New York)

Dalhuisen, Jan Hendrik, *Dalhuisen on International Commercial, Financial and Trade Law* (2nd edn, Oxford, 2004)

Duncan, RF and Lyons, WH, *The Law and Practice on Secured Transactions: Working with Article 9* (New York, 1989)

Gilmore, Grant, *Security Interests in Personal Property* 2 vols (Boston, Toronto 1965)

Harris, Steven L and Mooney Jr, Charles W, 'How Successful Was the Revision of Article 9? Reflections of the Reporters' (1999) 74 *Chicago-Kent Law Review* 1357

Henson, Ray D, 'Secured Transactions under the Uniform Commercial Code' (2nd edn, St Paul, Minn, 1979)

Honnold, John, Harris, Steven L, and Mooney Jr, Charles W, *Cases, Problems and Materials on Security Interests in Personal Property* (3rd edn, 2000)

McCormack, Gerard, *Secured Credit Under English and American Law* (Cambridge, 2004)

Milger, Karin, *Mobiliarsicherheiten im deutschen und im US-amerikanischen Recht. Eine rechtsvergleichende Untersuchung* (Göttingen, 1982)

Permanent Editorial Board for the Uniform Commercial Code, 'PEB Study Group Uniform Commercial Code Article 9, Report (December 1, 1992)' (Philadelphia, 1992)

Rakob, Julia, *Ausländische Mobiliarsicherungsrechte im Inland* (Heidelberg, 2001)

Riesenfeld, Stefan, 'Introduction: Some Comparisons with American Law' in Rolf Serick (ed), *Securities in Movables in German Law: An Outline* (trans Tony Weir) (Deventer, 1990) 15

UNCITRAL, 'Note by the Secretariat on article 9 of the Uniform Commercial Code of the United States of America' (1997) VIII *UNCITRAL Yearbook* 222

White, James, 'Secured Lending in Market Economies: Law and Practice' in Jonathan Bates, Lane Blumenfeld, David Fagelson, Vladimir Fedorov, Dmitry Labin, Jan-Hendrik Röver, and John Simpson (eds), *International Conference on Secured Commercial Lending in the Commonwealth of Independent States* (London, 1995) 30

White, James J and Summers, Robert S, *Uniform Commercial Code* (3rd edn, St Paul, Minn, 1988); (4th edn, St Paul, Minn, 1995); (5th edn, St Paul, Minn, 2000)

Winship, Peter, 'Selected Security Interests in the United States' in Joseph J Norton and Mads Andenas (eds), *Emerging Financial Markets and Secured Transactions* (London, The Hague, Boston, 1998) 267

CENTRAL AND EASTERN EUROPEAN SECURED TRANSACTIONS LAWS

Regional reports of central and eastern European secured transactions laws

Arner, Douglas, Ramasastry, Anita, and Sanders, Gerard, 'Legal foundations for sound finance' in EBRD, *Transition report 1998: Financial sector in transition* (London, 1998) 105

Breidenbach, Stephan (ed), *Handbuch Wirtschaft und Recht in Osteuropa* (looseleaf, Munich)

——, Campbell, Christian, and EBRD (eds), *Business Transactions in Eastern Europe* (looseleaf, New York)

Dahan, Frédérique, 'Law Reform in Central and Eastern Europe: The Transplantation of Secured Transactions Laws' (2000) 2 *European Journal of Law Reform* 369

—— and Simpson, John, 'Secured Transactions in Central and Eastern Europe: EBRD Assessment' (2004) 36 *Uniform Commercial Code Law Review* 77

——, Kutenićovà, Eliška and Simpson, John, 'Enforcing secured transactions in central and eastern Europe: an empirical study' (2004) *Law in Transition* 4

Drobnig, Ulrich, Hopt, Klaus J., Kötz, Hein, and Mestmäcker, Ernst-Joachim (eds), *Systemtransformation in Mittel- und Osteuropa und ihre Folgen für Banken, Börsen und Kreditsicherheiten* (Tübingen, 1998)

EBRD Regional Survey <http://www.ebrd.com/country/sector/law/st>

Fairgrieve, Duncan, 'Reforming Secured Transactions Laws in Central and Eastern Europe' (1998) *European Business Law Review* 245

Fairgrieve, Duncan, Provision of security in transition countries' (Spring 1998) *Law in Transition* 1

—— and Andenas, Mads, 'Securing progress in collateral law reform: the EBRD's regional survey of secured transactions law' (Autumn 2000) *Law in Transition* 30

Horn, Norbert and Pleyer, Klemens (eds), *Handelsrecht und Recht der Kreditsicherheiten in Osteuropa* (Berlin, 1997)

Summers, Elizabeth A, 'Recent Secured Transactions Law Reform in the Newly Independent States and Central and Eastern Europe' (1997) 23 *Review of Central and Eastern European Law* 177

Timmermans, Wim, 'Survey of Legislation on Secured Transactions in Central and Eastern Europe' (Summer 1994) *International Bar Association Eastern European Forum Newsletter* 10

Bulgaria

Simpson, John and Röver, Jan-Hendrik, *Comments on the Current State and Reform of Bulgarian Collateral Law* (Washington, DC, 1995)

Czech Republic

Daubner, Robert, ' "Sicherungsübereignung" und "verlängerter Eigentumsvorbehalt" in der Tschechischen Republik' (1997) RIW 648

Giese, Ernst, Dušek, Peter, Koubová, Jana, and Dietschová, Lucie, *Securing Claims in the Czech Republic* (*Zajištění závazků v České republice*) (Prague, 1999)

Jähnke, Jana, 'Gutgläubiger Erwerb an beweglichen Sachen nach tschechischem Recht' (1997) WiRO 333

Köhne, Hans Clemens, 'Eigentumsordnung und Immobilienerwerb in der Tschechischen Republik' (1996) 1 *Osteuropa Recht* 48

Piltz, Albrecht and Randak, Monika, 'Czechia' in Winnibald E Moojen and Matthieu P Van Sint Truiden (eds), *Bank Security and Other Credit Enhancement Methods. A Practical Guide on Security Devices Available to Banks in Thirty Countries Throughout the World* (The Hague, 1995) 105

Sauer, Stefan, 'Kreditbesicherung durch Immobilien in Tschechien' (1996) RIW 646

Schorling, Tom Oliver, *Das Recht der Kreditsicherheiten in der Tschechischen Republik* (Berlin, 2000)

—— 'Secured transactions in the Czech Republic—a case of pre-reform' (Autumn 2000) *Law in Transition* 66

Tichý, Luboš, 'Secured Transactions Involving Movables in Czech Law: Selected Issues' in Jürgen Basedow, Klaus J Hopt, and Hein Kötz (eds), *Festschrift für Ulrich Drobnig zum siebzigsten Geburtstag* (Tübingen, 1998) 683

Hungary

Bókai, Judit and Szeibert, Orsolya Erdôs, 'Die Mobiliarhypothek und deren Register' in Bundesnotarkammer (ed), *Festschrift für Helmut Schippel zum 65. Geburtstag* (Munich, 1996) 843

Gárdos, István, 'New Hungarian legislation on security interests: an improvement in the Hungarian secured lending environment' (Summer 1996) *Law in Transition* 1

—— and Bánhegyi, Ilona, 'EBRD-zálogjogmodell' (7 March, 1993) *Bank & Tözsde* 19

Gárdos, Füredi, Mosonyi, Tomori, and EBRD (eds), *Guide for Taking Charges in*

Hungary (Budapest, 2004); see also <http:www.ebrd.com/country/sector/law/st/core/modellaw/guidehungary.pdf>

Harmathy, Attila, 'The Hungarian Experience with the Model Law' in EBRD, *Model Law on Secured Transactions. Speeches given at the Presentation of the Model Law during the Third Annual Meeting of the EBRD on 16 April 1994 in St Petersburg* (London, 1994) 3–4

—— 'The EBRD Model Law and the Hungarian Law' in Joseph J Norton and Mads Andenas (eds), *Emerging Financial Markets and Secured Transactions* (London, 1998) 197

—— 'Das Recht der Mobiliarsicherheiten—Kontinuität und Entwicklung in Ungarn' in Karl F Kreuzer (ed), *Mobiliarsicherheiten. Vielfalt oder Einheit?* (Baden-Baden, 1999) 75

Ministry of Justice and Law Enforcement, *Background Paper for the International Seminar on the Law of Proprietary Security Rights in the Proposal for a new Hungarian Civil Code* (Budapest, 2006)

—— *Discussion Paper on Functional Equivalents to Security for the International Seminar on the Law of Proprietary Security Rights in the Proposal for a new Hungarian Civil Code* (Budapest, 2006)

—— *Discussion Paper on the Charges Register for the International Seminar on the Law of Proprietary Security Rights in the Proposal for a new Hungarian Civil Code* (Budapest, 2006)

Simpson, John, 'New system for the registration of charges in Hungary' (Summer 1996) *Law in Transition* 7

—— and Fairgrieve, Duncan, 'Registration of charges in Hungary' (Autumn 1998) *Law in Transition* 10

——, Röver, Jan-Hendrik, and Bates, Jonathan, *Feasibility Study for a Computerised Registration System for Charges in Hungary* (London, 1996)

Poland

Dahan, Frédérique, 'International Influences and the Polish Law on Secured Transactions: Harmonisation, Unification or What?' (2002–3) VII *Uniform Law Review* 713

—— and McCormack, Gerard, 'Secured Transactions in Countries in Transition (The Case of Poland): From Model to Assessment' (1999) *European Business Law Review* 1

EBRD, *The Impact of the Legal Framework on the Secured Credit Market in Poland* (London, 2005)

Ernst, Ulrich, *Mobiliarsicherheiten in Deutschland und Polen. Sicherungseigentum—Registerpfandrecht—Kollisionsrecht* (Tübingen, 2005)

Liebscher, Marc and Zoll, Fryderyk (eds), *Einführung in das polnische Recht* (Munich, 2005)

Rich, William Arthur, 'Poland's new collateral law' (Summer 1997) *Law in Transition* 1

Romania

Boroi, Gabriel and Boroi, Dana, 'The Security Interests Regulated by Title VI of Law 99/1999' ('*Garanția reală mobiliară reglementată de titlul VI al Legii No. 99/1999*') (2000) 4 *Juridica* 129

Mocanu, Livia, *Security Rights* (*Garanțiile reale mobiliare*) (Bucharest, 2004)

Poenaru, Emil, *Security Rights* (*Garanțiile reale mobiliare*) (Bucharest, 2004)

Rizoiu, Radu, 'Redefining Security Rights' ('*Încercare de (re)definire a garanţiei reale mobiliare*') (2004) 4 *Pandectele române* 150

—— 'Security Interests as Blanket Security' ('*Garanţia reală mobiliară asupra universalităţii de bunuri*') (2005) 2 *Pandectele române* 137

—— 'Introduction to the Objects of Security Rights' ('*Aspecte introductive privind obiectul garanţiei reale mobiliare*') (2006) 1 *Revista română de drept al afacerilor* (Romanian Business Law Review) 9

—— *Security Interests* (*Garanţii reale mobiliare—Legislatie comentata si adnotata*) (Bucharest, 2006)

—— and Dincă, Razvan, 'Security Interests in Receivables' ('*Garanţiile reale mobiliare asupra drepturilor de creanţă*') (2002) 5 *Pandectele române* 108

Simpson, John, Dageförde, Carsten, and Fairgrieve, Duncan, *Reforming the Romanian Laws on Secured Transactions* (London, 1998)

Stoica, Cristiana, and Rizoiu, Radu, 'Theoretical and Practical Considerations on the Legal Regime Applicable to the Security Rights in Commercial Matters ('*Consideraţii teoretice şi practice asupra regimului juridic aplicabil garanţiilor reale mobiliare în materie comercială*') (2000) 1 and 2 *Revista română de drept comercial* (Commercial Law Review) 47

Teves, Iulian, 'Agreement on Security Rights' ('*Contractul de garanţie reală mobiliară*') (2000) 8 *Juridica* 289

Russian Federation

Asset Capital Partners and Nörr Stiefenhofer Lutz (author: Jan-Hendrik Röver), *M & A guide for the Russian oil & gas industry. Legal and tax issues of mergers, divestitures and acquisitions in the Russian oil & gas industry* (Moscow, 2006)

Bates, Jonathan, Blumenfeld, Lane, Fagelson, David, Fedorov, Vladimir, Labin, Dmitry, Röver, Jan-Hendrik, and Simpson, John (eds), *International Conference on Secured Commercial Lending in the Commonwealth of Independent States. Conference Proceedings* (London, 1995)

Beiten Burkhardt, *Bankenrecht in Russland. Beteiligung ausländischer Banken an Kreditverhältnissen* (Moscow, 2006)

Blumenfeld, Lane H, 'Russia's New Civil Code: The Legal Foundation for Russia's Emerging Market Economy' (1996) 30 *The International Lawyer* 477

Boguslawskij, Mark M, 'The Model Law from the Russian Perspective' in EBRD (ed), *Model Law on Secured Transactions. Speeches given at the Presentation of the Model Law during the Third Annual Meeting of the EBRD on Saturday 16 April 1994 in St Petersburg* (London, 1994) 5

Butler, WE, *Soviet Law* (2nd edn, London, 1988)

—— *Russian Law* (2nd edn, Oxford, 2003)

——, Braginskii, MI and Rubanov, AA, 'Towards an All-Union Law on Pledge: The London Draft' (1996) 1 *Sudebnik* 549

Dahan, Frédérique and Dine, Janet, 'Transplantation for transition—discussion on a concept around Russian reform of the law on reorganisation' (2003) 23 *Legal Studies* 284

Danilenko, Gennady M, Burnham, William, and Maggs, Peter B, *Law and Legal System of the Russian Federation* (3rd edn, Huntington, NY, 2004)

Horvat, Miljenco, 'Secured Lending in Russia and the CIS in Practice' in Jonathan Bates, Lane Blumenfeld, David Fagelson, Vladimir Fedorov, Dmitry Labin, Jan-Hendrik Röver and John Simpson (eds), *International Conference on Secured Commercial*

Lending in the Commonwealth of Independent States Conference Proceedings (London and Maryland, 1995) 23 (English version) 116 (Russian version)

Kron, Constantin, 'Taking security over offshore foreign currency accounts of a Russian borrower in Law' (Autumn 2000) *Law in Transition* 61

Makovsky, Alexander, 'The Law of Secured Lending in Russia and the CIS' in Jonathan Bates, Lane Blumenfeld, David Fagelson, Dmitry Labin, Jan-Hendrik Röver, and John Simpson (eds), *International Conference on Secured Commercial Lending in the Commonwealth of Independent States. Conference Proceedings* (London, 1995) 13 (English version) 105 (Russian version)

Markovich, Inez M, 'Real Estate Transactions in Russia: New Land Code Gives Green Light to Foreign Investment' (2001) 8 *Journal of Eastern European Law* 129

Nörr Stiefenhofer Lutz, *Collaterals for Russian Projects and Transactions* (Moscow, 2006)

Rubanov, AA, 'Pledge in the Civil Code of Russia' (1996) 1 *Sudebnik* 515

Simpson, John and Röver, Jan-Hendrik, *Comments on the Draft Federal Act on Mortgage (Pledge of Real Estate) of the Russian Federation* (London, 1996)

Timmermans, Wim A, 'Secured Transactions in Russian Civil Law' in Donald D Barry, George Ginsburgs, William B. Simons, and FJM Feldbrugge (eds), *The Revival of Private Law in Central and Eastern Europe: Essays in Honour of Ferdinand J. M. Feldbrugge* (Leiden, 1996) 339

Waehler, Jan Peter, 'Rußland: Pfandgesetz (Gesetz über Sicherheiten)' (1993) WiRO 342

Zverev, Alexei, 'Security Issues under Russian Law' in Joseph J Norton and Mads Andenas (eds), *Emerging Financial Markets and Secured Transactions* (London, 1998) 293

Slovak Republic

Allen & Overy and EBRD, *Guide for Taking Charges in the Slovak Republic* (Bratislava, 2003); see also <http:www.ebrd.com/country/sector/law/st/core/modellaw/guideslovak.pdf>

Benedik, Marek, 'Remarks on the Charge Law' ('*Niekol'ko poznámok k inštitútu záložného páva*') (2001) 3 *Bulletin slovenskej advokácie* 31

Bičovský, Jaroslav, Fiala, Jozef, and Holub, Milan, *Commentary on the Civil Code* (*Občiansky zákonník–poznámkové vydanie s judikatúrou, I. diel, 6 doplnené vydanie*) (Bratislava, 1998)

Búreš, Jaroslav, and Drápal, Ljubomír, *Pledge Law in Court Practice* (*Zástavní právo v soudní praxi*) (Prague, 1997)

Faldyna, František, Hušek, Ján, and Des, Zdeněk, *Securing and Discharging Debts* (*Zajištění a zánik závazků*) (Prague, 1995)

Fiala, Jozejf, Hurdík, Ján, and Sedláková, Alica, *Pledge Law and Easements* (*Zástavní právo a věcná břemena*) (Brno, 1992)

Giese, Ernst, Dušek, Peter, Koubová, Jana, and Dietschová, Lucie, *Securing Claims in the Czech Republic* (*Zajištění závazků v České republice*) (Prague, 1999)

Rozehnal, Aleš, *Credits Secured by Charges* (*Úvěry zajišténé zástavním právem*) (Prague, 1997)

Sedlička, S, 'Charges over Trademarks' ('*Zástavní právo k ochranné známce*') (1996) 9 *Právní rádce* 48

Števček, Marek, 'Non-Possessory Charges' ('*Nepossesórne záložné právo—de lege ferenda*') (2000) 6 *Bulletin slovenskej advokacie* 51

Svoboda, Jaromír, 'Commentary on the Slovak Civil Code' ('*Občiansky zákonník. Komentár*') (1999) 1–2 EPP 221

INDEX

371